Ethical Issues in Information Systems

Roy Dejoie
Texas A & M University

George Fowler
Texas A & M University

David Paradice
Texas A & M University

bf

boyd & fraser publishing company

Credits:

Publisher: Tom Walker
Acquisitions Editor: James H. Edwards
Production Coordinator: Pat Donegan
Director of Production: Becky Herrington
Cover Design: Ken Russo
Manufacturing Director: Dean Sherman
Typesetting: Graphic Typesetting Service, Inc.
Cover Photo: Tony Stone Worldwide

 © 1991 by boyd & fraser publishing company
A Division of South-Western Publishing Company
Boston, MA 02116

Manufactured in the United States of America

Library of Congress Cataloging-in-Publication Data

Ethical issues in information systems / [edited by] Roy Dejoie, George
    Fowler, David Paradice.
       p.   cm.
    Includes bibliographical references and index.
    ISBN 0-87835-562-6
    1. Computers—Moral and ethical aspects.   I. Dejoie, Roy, 1963-
        II. Fowler, George C., 1953-   III. Paradice, David B.
    QA76.9.M65E83   1991
    174′.90904--dc20
                                     90-23932
                                         CIP

2 3 4 5 6 7 8 9 10 MT 4 3 2 1

Dedication

Dedicated to the memory of my father, Roy M. Dejoie Sr.,
and all the rest of my family.

R. D.

Dedicated to my wife, Tia, my son, Michael,
and all the rest of my family.

G. F.

Dedicated to my wife, Kathy,
and all the rest of my family.

D. P.

Contents

Foreword

According to George Santayana, a fanatic is a person who has lost sight of his goals and redoubled his efforts. This loss of foresight is perhaps the most serious tendency of our information age. We have more available information than any previous generation and, as a result, more potential for learning and improving the human condition, but there is no guarantee. An abundance of information and data may be decidedly useful in improving life, but it can be equally useful in lessening and even threatening our existence. An avalanche of details and facts may only push aside our moral perspectives, cause us to lose sight of our goals, and to become buried in the tumble of routine and self-interest. Such a gray forecast is captured in T. S. Eliot's question, "Where is the wisdom we have lost in knowledge; where is the knowledge we have lost in information?"

If loss of forethought or vision is one of the chief tendencies of our age, retaining our moral vision is one of our major challenges. All human enterprises highlight moral decision making whenever questions of usage and value are raised, and the undertakings of IS punctuate these issues forcefully because of their foundational impact on major questions. What repercussions will IS have on the structure and nature of basic human institutions: family, education, government, business, and law? What are the personal and public responsibilities of those select and well-trained few who gather, organize, and disseminate our information? How is it possible, if at all, to incorporate ethical issues and decision making in our educational process? Are privacy, piracy, accuracy, and accessibility the major inherent issues of IS, or are there more? With the dramatic increase of available information, what restrictions are to be placed on access, and can our present economic system guarantee that all who need the information will have access to it?

No doubt, the technical issues of IS require immense intelligence and creativity. However, if we allow the larger, more fundamental moral issues to rest in a compost of shallow ideas and foggy beliefs, we are likely to find ourselves lost in a maze of information without either clear goals or motives. Tackling major ethical issues in IS directly and intelligently is greatly needed, and the essays in this book are a clear step in that direction.

Herman J. Saatkamp, Jr.
Professor and Department Head of Philosophy
Texas A&M University
August 30, 1990

Preface

E*thical Issues in Information Systems* was compiled to provide a support tool for teaching ethics in an MIS curriculum. Ethical issues are typically covered at the junior or senior level in four-year colleges, in the second year of a two-year program, or at the MBA level. This book could be used as a supplement in a capstone MIS course or in an MIS principles course. In addition, because of the increasing use of computerized information systems in all facets of the workplace, this book would make an excellent supplement to professional ethics courses traditionally taught by faculty in philosophy departments. However used, we recommend that at a minimum students should have been exposed to programming and systems analysis before being confronted with these issues.

Often, ethical issues are only tangential topics wherever they appear. Few MIS faculty feel adequately trained to cover the subject. Consequently, ethical issues are mentioned and perhaps discussed, but rarely studied. We compiled these readings to assist the MIS professor who wants to provide a more structured approach to covering ethical issues in the information systems field.

HOW TO USE THIS BOOK

The book is structured for maximum flexibility and minimal faculty investment. Each chapter attempts to provide basic coverage of an important topic.

Part I comprises two chapters. The first chapter contains general readings on ethics studies. The second chapter also provides general readings, but with a focus on the information systems field. Professors who want a global overview of ethical issues in MIS could cover only these two chapters.

Part II also contains two chapters. This part refines the focus of Chapter 2 to consider specific MIS concepts. The book's third chapter emphasizes privacy and accuracy issues. The fourth chapter stresses property and access issues. If a curriculum contains a required ethics course, a professor could construct a study module around Mason's article from Chapter 2 and selected readings from Chapters 3 and 4.

Part II also includes approximately 20 scenarios that give students an opportunity to explore their ethical beliefs. These scenarios present ethical dilemmas and require students to decide whether an action described in the scenario is unacceptable, questionable, or acceptable. We have found that these scenarios provide an excellent mechanism for initiating class discussions of ethical issues in MIS. For some cases we have data on how students have responded to these dilemmas. If you administer these scenarios, we would like to add your data to our database. You are welcome to obtain updated information regarding this data.

Part III contains one chapter that highlights questions involving ethical issues and artificial intelligence. We believe the expanding role of expert systems and other artificial intelligence technologies dictates including these papers.

In addition to the readings in each chapter, we included articles from the *CPSR Newsletter*. This provides students with current socially oriented readings, giving additional viewpoints on important ethical issues.

ACKNOWLEDGMENTS

We would like to thank all the authors who contributed to this book and all the publishers for their willingness to give us permission to include their articles in this collection of readings.

Special mention must be made of those who helped us with this effort. Connie Clore, Mary Ellen Brennan, and Anne Dejoie provided much-needed assistance converting these readings into computer-based documents. We are very grateful for their efforts. At boyd & fraser, Jim Edwards and Tom Walker coordinated our efforts, and Donna Villanucci and Pat Donegan helped us shape the text into its final format. We also appreciate their assistance.

And finally, a very heartfelt and special thanks to Dr. Herman Saatkamp, professor and chairman of the Department of Philosophy at Texas A&M University. We are very grateful to and appreciative of Dr. Saatkamp for the foreword to this book. His contribution was the element that truly underscored the importance of this endeavor.

We believe this book is a unique supplement, and we have attempted to incorporate readings that will be both interesting and instructive. We hope you agree with us after using this book. However, if you know of other readings that you feel could be included, please bring them to our attention.

Roy Dejoie
George Fowler
David Paradice

PART I

Ethical Issues in Business and Information Systems

HISTORICAL PERSPECTIVE

Over the course of human development, several institutions have evolved for guiding human behavior, for example religion to attain ideals and law evolved to standardize acceptable behavior. Fundamental to these institutions is a philosophy of correct behavior, a code that directs our decisions.

A distinction needs to be made between the terms "moral" and "ethical." *Moral* refers to conformity with generally accepted standards of goodness or rightness in conduct or character. *Ethical* refers to conformity with an elaborated, ideal code of moral principles, such as those often found in the codes of professional organizations (Harris, 1986).

Ethical Philosophies

There are four generally accepted theories for resolving moral and ethical conflicts: egoism, natural law, utilitarianism, and respect for persons. These theories reflect several basic themes. Egoism stipulates that what is best for a given individual is right. Natural law refers to the belief that moral laws apply to humans by virtue of their nature as rational beings. Natural law stresses the idea that humans have an obligation (1) to promote their own health and life, (2) to propagate, (3) to pursue knowledge of the world and God, and (4) to pursue close relationships with other human beings and to submit to the legitimate authority of the state. Utilitarianism deals with the belief that those actions are right that produce the greatest good for the greatest number of people. The fourth theory, respect for persons, maintains that people should be treated as an end and not as a means to an end and that actions are right if everyone adopts the moral rule presupposed by the action.

ETHICAL ISSUES IN BUSINESS

Social Contracts of Business

There are two themes relating to the role of business in society which in turn relate to the role of ethics in business. The first theme, often called the Old Contract of Business, states

2

that a business exists for the sake of the business and its stockholders. The ultimate account-ability is to the owner or stockholders. Consequently, this view emphasizes the bottom line.

The second theme, the Social Contract of Business, acknowledges that businesses are members of society and as such owe a degree of responsibility to society. However, although many corporations follow this contract, they may also follow the first contract in some of their operations. An example might be seen in the contradictory actions that lead a company to provide scholarships for minority students while continuing profit-motivated operations that pollute the environment. Current events are full of such examples of philosophical discrepancies: savings and loan fraud, corporate insider trading, university athletics scandals, and so on.

ETHICAL ISSUES IN INFORMATION SYSTEMS

The Relationship of IS and Ethics

Information systems (IS) embody all computerized systems associated with gathering, pro-cessing, and disseminating information. These systems are found on the smallest personal computers and on the largest supercomputers used by corporations and governments.

As discussed earlier, ethics refers to conduct concerning right and wrong. Since ethics deals with conduct and corporate decision making is inherently based on the conduct of the decision maker(s), it is safe to assume that ethical or unethical behavior is part of the cor-porate environment. Furthermore, since information systems are a major part of the corporate decision-making process, ethics and IS are very likely an integral part of corporate America. Thus, the relationship between ethics and information systems must be examined. This inves-tigation may be achieved from two viewpoints. First is the viewpoint that ethics have an impact on the design and implementation of information systems. The second viewpoint holds that information systems influence ethical decision-making processes.

For instance, in the design of an interest calculation program, ethical standards of fair-ness should guide the designers. However, the computerized information system can provide the opportunity to hide fraudulent actions easily, and thus the programmers might decide to add all fractions of a penny resulting from the program's calculations to their personal accounts.

Information Systems and Business

Before the introduction of computerized information systems, the major inputs to a com-pany's operations were management, manpower, machinery, materials, and money (the five Ms). Many ethical issues involve these inputs as they directly or indirectly influence the bottom line.

Today, because of the role of computers in corporate America, information has emerged as a major corporate resource. The information revolution and the nature of our service-oriented society has elevated information to the same level of importance as the five Ms. Consequently, the same types of ethical issues applied to the five Ms apply to information.

Areas of Ethical Concern in IS

The emergence of computerized information systems as a key component of an organization has expanded the scope of ethical concerns. Among these concerns are (1) the information system's role in the decision-making process, (2) the perceived opportunity (or lack thereof) to commit ethical or unethical activities, (3) issues of ownership and responsibility for information systems, and (4) the "shrinking world" issues caused by information systems and telecommunications systems.

THE PAPERS: CHAPTER 1

"A Behavioral Model of Ethical and Unethical Decision Making"

Bommer, Gratto, Gravander, and Tuttle develop a behavioral model that shows the relationship between factors that affect ethical and unethical decision making in organizations including social, legal, professional, and personal environments. Another component of the model discussed in this paper is the individual decision-making process as influenced by ethical and unethical behavior.

"A Question of Ethics: Developing Information Systems Ethics"

This paper studies ethics education in information systems classes. Three major concerns presented by the authors deal with (1) where ethics should be taught, (2) which pedagogical mechanism should be used, and (3) how to explore ethics issues in information systems.

"Education for the Moral Development of Managers: Kohlberg's Stages of Moral Development and Integrative Education"

The authors question the moral and ethical status of corporate management. They ask if ethical behavior or the lack thereof is the result of a proper education in ethics, and posit an alternative educational style. The paper concludes that the statement of mission of colleges and businesses should include the moral development of students.

THE PAPERS: CHAPTER 2

"Four Ethical Issues of the Information Age"

Mason introduces four cornerstone issues concerning "intellectual capital" in the information age: privacy, accuracy, property, and access. The paper focuses on the importance of the long-term impact of these social issues in the business world.

"Assessing the Ethical Standards and Policies in Computer-Based Environments"

Forcht surveyed the CEOs of the *Datamation* 100 companies to ascertain their assessments about the ethical standards that have been formally adopted by their organizations. Additionally, the author solicited opinions about the informal ethical environment that may be present in the respondents' organizations. The respondents also provided information about the most serious ethical dilemmas they had faced in their positions.

In choosing a sample population of CEOs, the author made this a particularly insightful paper. Generally the populations of these studies are composed of students and lower-level management personnel. The CEOs' responses provide unique information that readers should find interesting and useful.

"Preparing IS Students To Deal with Ethical Issues"

This paper discusses the importance of teaching ethics in IS courses. Couger points to unethical corporate practices, such as insider trading, and suggests that "unless professionals improve their ethical practices, legislation will force them to do so." Because of this situation, he proposes the use of scenarios in the classroom that require students to determine how they would act in various ethical situations.

"A Framework for the Study of Information Systems and Ethical Decision-Making Processes"

Dejoie, Fowler, and Paradice develop a framework for the study of information systems' influence on ethical decision-making processes. They present a review of prior research in information systems and ethical decision-making. Components of the framework are social impact, group differences, and technological effects.

"Why I Never Met a Programmer I Could Trust"

Shore presents an intriguing view of the programming world. He discusses the shortcomings of the profession and he suggests that a solution to the problem of distrust is the adoption of codes of ethics and certification and regulation of programmers.

REFERENCES

Harris, C. E., *Applying Moral Theories*. Belmont, CA: Wadsworth Publishing Company, 1986.

Chapter 1

Ethical Issues in Business

A Behavioral Model of Ethical and Unethical Decision Making

Michael Bommer, Clarence Gratto, Jerry Gravander, and Mark Tuttle

Originally published in *Journal of Business Ethics*, 6: 265–280, 1987. Copyright 1987 Kluwer Academic Publishers. Reprinted by permission of Kluwer Academic Publishers.

ABSTRACT

A model is developed which identifies and describes various factors which affect ethical and unethical behavior in organizations, including a decision-maker's social, government and legal, work, professional and personal environments. The effect of individual decision maker attributes on the decision process is also discussed. The model links these influences with ethical and unethical behavior via the mediating structure of the individual's decision-making process.

INTRODUCTION

Well-conceived schematic models are useful devices in understanding behavior, especially in situations where the individual is subjected to multiple forces. The decision-making dynamics of an individual faced with choices involving ethical issues are complex. However, current models of ethical and unethical behavior within organizations are generally not very helpful in understanding and explaining that behavior.

The absence of well-developed models of ethical and unethical behavior in organizations reflects a dearth of research on the factors affecting this behavior and on the ways in which these factors enter into the underlying decision process. Not only is there little relevant research, but what there is does not lend itself to model building. For example, business and professional ethics, a rapidly developing sub-discipline which concerns itself primarily with the social and professional aspects of ethical and unethical behavior in business and professional contexts, has seen little research directed toward uncovering the factors leading to ethical (and unethical) behavior in various situations. Instead, there is a considerable body of descriptive material of two main types: first, accounts of particular cases of actual decisions to act ethically or unethically (study of unethical actions predominates) and, second, surveys of managers about their attitudes toward certain ethical dilemmas, their perceptions about the circumstances within which these dilemmas currently must be resolved, and their beliefs about changes in these circumstances which would make resolution of the dilemmas easier. However, case studies do not always indicate why particular decisions were made, let alone indicate general causes behind ethical and unethical behavior. For example, Anderson et al. (1980) concluded in their study of the Bay Area Rapid Transit (BART) case that one could not be sure about what happened, much less that one could know who acted correctly and who incorrectly and why. Moreover, survey studies, like the one conducted by Flores (1982) about safety-related decisions in design and product development, typically stop with an account of what people say they would do in certain situations rather than determine directly which actual unethical and ethical behaviors would occur in those situations. Since this descriptive information does not identify the various environmental and individual factors which influence decisions to act ethically or unethically, it cannot indicate the relative importance of these factors in determining the outcomes of decisions.

The purpose of this paper is to propose and describe a conceptual model of ethical and unethical behavior in organizations. Although this model must be viewed as a first attempt to identify and relate the various factors which influence managers' decisions to act ethically or unethically, we believe that it will increase the understanding of such behavior as related to the many factors which affect the manager's decision-making process. We further believe that this conceptual model of the decision process underlying ethical and unethical actions would be of considerable use to those who are seeking to develop and implement programs which would facilitate ethical behavior on the part of decision makers, as well as to those who desire to turn their research from the descriptive study of ethical and unethical behavior to an investigation of the underlying structure of such behavior and the process leading to it.

A schematic diagram of the model appears as Figure 1. This model groups under several categories a wide range of factors which the literature lists as possible influences on managers' decisions when they are confronted by ethical dilemmas. These categories include a decision-maker's social environment, government and legal environment, professional environment, work environment, personal environment, and individual attributes. The model links these influences with ethical and unethical behavior via the mediating structure of the individual's decision-making process. The decision process in the model functions as a central processing unit with its own internal characteristics such as the individual's cognitive style, type of information acquisition and processing, and perceived levels of loss and reward that influence the decision. The model also distinguishes between the degree of influence which the decision maker perceives the various factors to have and the influence they actually have.

Given that the literature is scanty, it is at best suggestive about the influences on managers' ethical (and unethical) behavior, and it most definitely does not afford an exhaustive identification of the relevant factors nor of patterns of possible interaction among these. The categorization adopted for the model should thus be taken as tentative. Moreover, as each of the major categories of the model, along with the decision process function, are described and discussed in turn, the reader should remember both the paucity of relevant research and its ineptness for model building.

CONCEPTS AND DEFINITIONS

This paper is not prescriptive with respect to ethical and unethical behavior, that is, it does not attempt to establish which behaviors are objectively morally correct and incorrect in given situations. However, it does more than merely describe decision makers' beliefs and attitudes about their actions. It is an epidemiological investigation which aims to identify

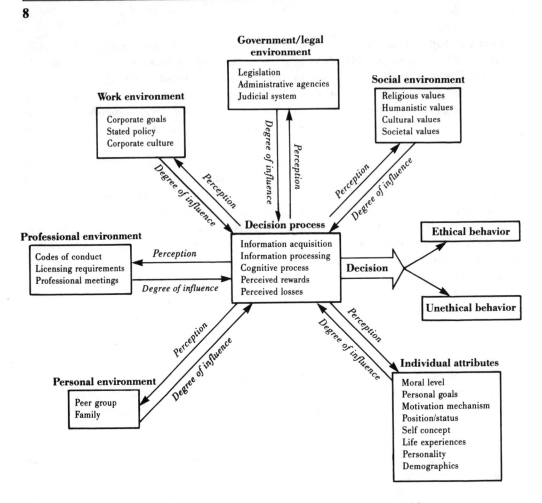

Fig. 1.   A behavioral model of ethical/unethical decision making.

the factors which influence decision makers to behave in certain situations, either ethically or unethically. Some of these factors enter into the decision makers' moral reasoning about the situations, whereas others do not. The paper will attempt to identify which factors play a role in decision makers' moral reasoning about the ethical situations in which they are involved, and it will suggest the nature of the role these factors play.

Clearly the key concepts involved in the paper are "ethical" and "unethical," and a central conceptual issue is how "ethical behavior" is identified and in what sense it is "ethical." There is a longstanding tradition in ethics which holds that "ethical behavior" is behavior which is shown to be objectively morally correct via appeal to a theory of morally correct (or permissible, obligatory, desirable, etc.) action, and that is "ethical" precisely because it is the behavior which is required by the theory. However, many ethicists maintain that the question of which ethical theory is correct is itself answered by appeal to certain ethical behaviors, that is, that some behaviors in certain situations are so clearly morally correct that they provide a moral intuition with which any theory must correspond if it is to be considered correct (see, for example, Bowie, 1982). This paper understands "ethical behaviors" to be those behaviors the correctness of which constitutes the moral intuition in business and the professions.

The remaining question is which behaviors the paper understands to be these litmus-test behaviors in the business and professional contexts. They are those which have been identified by experienced managers and professionals as clear and exemplary instances of "ethical behavior." Such instances are recorded and identified in, for example, the cases published by the Board of Ethical Review of the National Society of Professional Engineers, the awards given for exemplary ethics in engineering by the Institute for Electrical and Electronics Engineers, and the citations for ethics in business given by the Values in Business Management Program at the C. W. Post Center of Long Island University.

A final issue is what exactly is meant by saying environmental and individual factors influence a decision maker's selection of ethical and unethical behavior. This paper does not presuppose strict behaviorism. First, one of its objectives is to elucidate the patterns of moral reasoning used by decision makers and the way in which various factors enter into their decisions to choose ethical and unethical behavior. Second, although the model postulates that a variety of environmental and individual factors influence decisions, it does not assume that these factors are sufficient conditions for the selection of particular behaviors. On the contrary, the model assumes the factors are—individually and in various combinations— necessary conditions in the sense that were the factors impinging on any given individual to change, that individual's ethical and unethical behavior would be different. The environmental and individual factors establish a context within which decision makers must choose to act, and from this point of view the primary purpose of the paper should be interpreted as the identification of factors which are such that changing them would facilitate decision makers in choosing ethical over unethical behaviors in given situations.

SOCIAL ENVIRONMENT

The social environment of a manager is the set of humanistic, religious, cultural, and societal values generally shared by the members of his or her society, and in particular those values of that society's sub-groupings to which the manager belongs. Two aspects of the influence of the social environment on managers' decisions will be discussed in this section. First, although it is a truism that values affect behavior, evidence seems to indicate that with respect to ethical and unethical behavior on the job, many managers will not adhere to general social values unless these are also incorporated within their professional or work environment. Second, some ethicists have recently argued that some general social values are not necessarily appropriate guides to behavior in certain managerial and business situations. Brady (1985) has recently proposed a model to aid in the understanding of how a society's values and business interplay. Brady argues that often the type of ethical dilemma influences how strongly society's values affect the decision. In some situations (for example, equal employment) often a formalist view is taken where the decision maker does use society's value system in the decision-making process, while in other situations (for example, nuclear power or genetic engineering) individuals tend to be more pragmatic and concrete or do not use society's value systems as a guide.

Case upon case report on managers who make on-the-job decisions that violate general social values. Many critics take this as evidence that business and ethics do not mix, that is, that managers deliberately choose to abandon general social values in the conduct of their managerial duties. However, a manager's failure to follow his or her general social values while on the job is probably more complex than this. Managers do not appear to make on-the-job decisions that they believe are unethical within the job-related context in which the decisions are made, as can be concluded from the analysis of numerous cases of ethical and unethical behavior in the business context (see, for example, Fairweather, 1980; Cohan and Whitcover, 1980; Vandiver, 1980). In these cases, managers who have been accused of unethical on-the-job behavior will say such things as, "I am not that type of person. I am an elder in my church, active in community affairs, a good family man, a Boy Scout leader, and so on. I just thought this was the way you were supposed to act in this business." Such statements imply that managers are ethical segregationists, that is, that they segregate on-the-job ethical behavior from off-the-job ethical behavior and apply different sets of values to each. This implies, in turn, that managerial decisions will correspond more closely to the humanistic, religious, cultural, and societal values of society-at-large only when these values are made part of the job environment. This would occur either by incorporating these general social values into the codes of conduct which are part of managers' professional environment, including them in the corporate culture and policy of their work environment, or both.

Before general social values could be incorporated into managers' professional and work environment, the question of which social values are appropriate to the job context must be answered. The traditional answer from ethicists has been, "All of them." For example, some writers on professional ethics have argued that separate codes of conduct for the professions are unnecessary; all that is needed is the simple statement that generally held social values apply to professional decisions (Pavlovic, 1980; Oldenquist and Slowter, 1979). Recently this traditional wisdom has been challenged. For example, with respect to the value of truth-telling, some critics have argued that although truth-telling is a value that should have broad application in business, there are certain business and managerial situations to which it should not be applied (Carr, 1983; Gravander, 1982). They argue that there may be a species of business behavior which is properly labeled "business bluffing," which although it is not the truth, should not be condemned as a lie. This entire area of inquiry, however, needs more development before one could decide, first, how much of an exemption from general social values these critics want to give business and, second, whether their position is valid.

GOVERNMENT AND LEGAL ENVIRONMENT

Laws are values and mores of society that have the force of its formed authority. "Legal" and "ethical" are not necessarily synonymous. Nevertheless, the legal dimension is an important determinant in many ethical decisions. Some individuals are not dissuaded from a course of action by its illegality or the threat of punishment, but they are the exception. Most individuals feel compelled to refrain from an action which is specifically prohibited by law. This effect of legal considerations on managers' ethical decisions is due not just to the legal consequences which follow from breaking the law, but also the strong social stigma associated with the label "illegal," as well as the desire to comply with the moral force behind the law.

In order to be effective, laws need to be actively enforced. However, because of their complexities, business-related crimes by managers are often not rigorously prosecuted. It is frequently difficult for investigating officers, prosecutors, judges, and jurists to understand the intricacies of the offense. Further, since the harm is often of an economic nature rather than physical, and because the crime's victim may be an insurance company or other corporation that does not elicit sympathy, the cases may be given low priority by prosecutors (McGowan, 1983). Thus, the actual enforcement policy may result in low risk of detection, token enforcement and prosecution, and relatively light sentences with only short if any imprisonment in a minimum security institution (Geis and Stotland, 1980). In contrast to their relative legal insignificance, crimes by managers hold out the possibility of very large personal or corporate financial rewards. Thus, managers who refrain from business-related crime may be more motivated by the moral force behind the law and the social stigma of breaking it than by the legal consequences.

Crimes by managers cannot be attributed to ignorance of the law. It is true that from the perspective of the individual decision maker within a large organization, most of the law's institutions are remote. Consequently, the individual's perception of what the law requires has likely been obtained informally. For example, notions of what "the law" is come from conversations with other non-professionals, and many of the subtleties and reasons for the law are lost. Further, the individual's information is often dated. However, ignorance of what is required appears to be a factor in only a very few "white collar" crimes (Meier and Geis, 1982), and this finding can probably be extended to the full range of illegal actions open to managers.

Of greater influence on a manager contemplating committing a crime is the probability of detection. This influence stems from two distinct factors. First, expectations about the probability of an event's detection are more important in determining risk taking than is the magnitude of the expected consequence (Dickson, 1978). Thus, though the punishment for the crime might be small, the certainty of detection is a powerful deterrent. This may be due to the social stigma which is associated with detection, since even when managers escape severe punishment for their business-related crimes, they often become pariahs among their former friends and associates. Second, while the research indicates that there is a deterrent effect from rigorous prosecution of crime (Geis and Stotland, 1980), the converse undoubtedly is true, also. Lack of vigorous prosecution of certain violations indicates to the decision-maker that the particular conduct is being condoned. That is, low probability of detection due to lackadaisical enforcement robs the law of its moral force.

Of interest in connection with this latter point is the relative effect of governmental agencies. Because of their broad powers, they can change the probability of detection for certain crimes. For example, the FBI's enforcement priorities were shifted by the Reagan administration to reflect less concern with "white collar" crimes such as embezzlement and fraud. There was concern at the time in the Justice Department that wrongdoers would tailor their crimes so as to fall short of the amounts that would attract investigation by federal agents and, thus, that "white collar" crime would increase (Taylor, 1984).

PROFESSIONAL ENVIRONMENT

The professional environment of a manager is the institutionalized professional context within which a manager practices. This is quite different than the vague and informal identification of a person as "professional," by which is meant the person is competent and responsible. While persons who see themselves as professional in this sense may strive to bring high ethical standards to their decisions, such efforts are best understood as attempts by individuals to adhere to their personal values. Fields of activity are properly designated professions only if they are characterized by (a) professional associations, (b) established licensing procedures, or (c) both.

To say that a licensing procedure is established is to say that at least some aspects of the profession are closed to individuals who are not licensed via a formal licensing process. In a field with an established licensing procedure, individuals cannot identify themselves as members of that profession unless they hold a license. Though the possibility of loss of one's license is a powerful deterrent to unethical behavior, management is not a licensed profession.

Professional associations play an important role in both regulating the professions and controlling entry to them. For example, the American Bar Association and the major engineering professional associations accredit law and engineering degree programs, and it is impossible (in the case of law) or very difficult (in the case of engineering) to practice in these areas without graduating from an accredited program. Not all fields have professional associations which are this dominant, but even in those which do not the relationship between the individual and the professional organization is such that the individual has the self-image and social status of professional by virtue of membership in the association. Professional associations typically have formal and published standards of professional conduct (Flores, 1980; Layton, 1981), and recent court rulings have been based on the principle that the public perceives membership in a professional association as a guarantor of members' adherence to these standards (May, 1983).

Professional associations typically demand ethical behavior via formal codes of ethics. Some critics argue that these codes should be taken as merely suggestive of what various professions take to be morally important, since attempts to follow these codes forces professionals into unacceptable moral quandaries (Leugenbiehl, 1983). For example, engineering codes require that engineers be loyal to their clients and employers and also blow the whistle on them, and since it seems impossible to do both simultaneously, engineers are forced to choose between different violations of the code (Gravander, 1981). Moreover, it is not always clear what course of action complies with the codes in specific situations. A recent survey of chemical engineers revealed considerable differences of opinion about what was ethically correct when they were asked to apply their professional code of ethics to a set of case studies (Kohn and Hughson, 1980).

In spite of these difficulties with codes of ethics, professionals exhibit considerable interest in complying with the ethical standards established by their codes. For example, the National Society of Professional Engineers regularly publishes hypothetical cases in which its Board of Ethical Review applies the NPSE Code to the type of ethical problem encountered in engineering, and there has recently been considerable activity within the engineering community directed toward formulating a clear, "unified" code by which all engineers can easily regulate their professional conduct (Oldenquist and Slowter, 1979). Moreover, professional associations, especially in engineering, have increasingly taken to enforcing their codes via expulsion of violators (Martin and Schinzinger, 1983; Unger, 1982), and this sanction, even though it really involves only loss of status, has been perceived as so extremely undesirable by some members that presumably it has some general effectiveness in forcing compliance (see, for example, Fairweather, 1980). In addition to sanctions to force compliance with the codes, professional associations in engineering have begun developing support mechanisms for members who have followed the codes and in so doing have clashed with their employer's or client's wishes. Many advocates argue that such support mechanisms will be the decisive factor in tipping the balance toward ethical behavior (Unger, 1982; Broome, 1983).

Managers have a professional environment insofar as they are members of a profession. Several of the professional associations which are open to managers have formal codes of ethics and discuss ethics at meetings and in journals of their professional societies. Although it does not have developed enforcement procedures in the way that professional associations in other fields have, the American Assembly of Collegiate Schools of Business will only accredit programs that have significant course work dealing with "ethical considerations and social and political influences as they affect" business organizations (AACSB, 1983). Moreover, some managers are members of a second profession by virtue of being lawyers, accountants, engineers, and so on. When enforcing codes of ethics, these professions have not distinguished between managerial behavior on the one hand and legal, accountancy, and engineering behavior on the other. Therefore, for managers, especially those who are also members of another profession, the factors discussed in this section will be important determinants in their ethical behavior. Moreover, it is likely that this causal effect is not dependent on the individual's awareness of the extent to which he or she is affected by the professional environment, since the standards of the professional are internalized over time and followed implicitly without an explicit awareness of the sanctions which are a force behind compliance.

WORK ENVIRONMENT

Several factors in the work environment strongly influence managers' decisions on whether to act ethically or unethically. These are corporate goals, stated policy, and corporate culture. Unfortunately for the individual managers, these three factors can each support conflicting decisions in a given situation. For example, short-term corporate goals and the corporate culture may point in one direction, and long-term goals and stated policies point in another. Which direction managers turn often depends on which factor is more dominant in their work environment.

Short-term goals for profit and similar measures of performance are often emphasized in companies. When an acceptable rate of return on investment or similar monetary measure is the dominant goal, being ethical will be an important sub-goal only insofar as it does not detract from the primary goal. Yet an emphasis on short-term profitability which leads to unethical actions can have substantial long-term negative effects, to the point of threatening the corporation's very existence. Good examples of this can be found in the insufficient standards concerning the handling of asbestos by Johns-Manville and the operation of the Three Mile Island nuclear power plant (Wheelen and Hunger, 1984).

Many business entities have formal policies that prohibit unethical conduct and prescribe punishment for it. Statements of these are typically found in operating and policy manuals and in supervisors' workplace statements, and they are disseminated in training programs and posters in the workplace. What real effect do these have? Would those people who profess that they are affected by these statements have acted ethically anyway? Do the stated policies simply reinforce or restate values that the individuals have already internalized?

There is considerable evidence to support the notion that a company's stated policies do in fact foster and increase the frequency of ethical behavior. For example, in a simulated decision-making exercise, a letter from the fictitious company's president supporting ethical behavior and warning of dismissal for unethical behavior resulted in increased ethical behavior (Hegarty and Sims, 1979). Similarly a significant determinant as to whether purchasing officers accepted gratuities was the existence of a written company policy (Staff, 1979).

Several factors affect the efficacy of stated policies in leading managers to make ethical decisions (Mautz et al., 1979). First, the more decentralized the decision-making function, and consequently the less direct the supervision of managers, the greater the likelihood of inadvertent non-compliance. Some companies, for example those with outside sales forces, are inadvertently decentralized and run a greater risk of non-compliance with stated company policy. Second, the stated policies can be unclear, with the consequence that there are conflicting or incompatible messages. For example, the policies might set levels of performance and goals that are unattainable without the individual resorting to behavior that is prohibited by the policy. Third, organic changes in a company such as mergers, rapid growth, and the addition of foreign operations can lead to situations which the formulators of the policy did not have in mind. In such cases, the policies can no longer effectively guide action.

While stated policies on ethical behavior are generally voluntary, some are required by law. For example, the Securities and Exchange Commission Rule 17j-1 under the Investment Company Act of 1940 requires that registered companies and other certain closely associated entities must have written codes of ethics in which the companies articulate prohibited practices and implement detection and enforcement procedures (Gillis, 1981).

Corporations have their own cultures, just as societies do. The culture is reflected in the "... attitudes and values, management styles and problem-solving behavior of its people" (Schwartz and Davis, 1981). Corporate norms are the products of this culture. It is often contended that in a capitalist system humanistic, compassionate, and egalitarian values tend to be left behind as the business enterprise pursues its profit motive. Within this context the fact that business enterprises generally act only in their self-interest is not surprising. "As one comes across occasional corporate good works, it should not be forgotten that corporations are not eleemosynary (charitable) institutions and cannot be expected to act in ways contrary to their dominant ethos, which is profit" (Hodges, 1963).

The conduct of the Board of Directors, CEO and other senior management can signal subordinate managers as to which behaviors are acceptable. An individual's supervisor often has the capacity for rewarding and punishing and, therefore, is an authority figure for the individual in the work environment. Social psychologists (Freedman et al., 1981) have found that one way to maximize compliance to a set of norms is to put an individual in a well-controlled situation and make noncompliance difficult. The well known Milgram studies (1963, 1965) are examples of how authority figures can exert extreme pressure to comply to orders even when compliance is unethical.

Policies that have been suggested as encouraging ethical behavior include the presence of effective procedures for monitoring compliance to company policy and ascertaining what is actually occurring in those areas where policies have been established. These procedures need to be sufficient for determining or detecting when improper acts have taken place, as well as for identifying the transgressor. Since existence of easy opportunities to act unethically facilitates the occurrence of unethical acts, systems and controls need to be implemented that will both decrease the ease and eliminate the opportunities. Screening prospective employees for trust and responsibility and instituting appropriate limits on access to information and tangible items are also important (Mautz et al., 1979).

There are other organizational characteristics associated with a reduced frequency of unethical activity. The presence of systems to facilitate communications, both vertically and horizontally in the managerial hierarchy, is one. To be effective, such communication needs to be timely, clear, and accurate, as well as open and frank. Such channels of communication apparently help prevent senior management from becoming distant or insulated from wrong-doers at lower levels in the organization. Managers are thus more likely to know who is doing what and by which means. Under such circumstances it is more difficult for managers to ignore unethical behavior within their organizations (DeGeorge, 1978).

PERSONAL ENVIRONMENT

The variables in this segment of the model—the family and peer groups—relate to the individual's personal life outside of the organization. Although the research in this area is very limited, it raises a number of conceptual issues.

Research on the relation between an individual's family and occupational situations has focused almost exclusively on the influence of occupation on the family (Mortimer, 1980; Donald and Bradshaw, 1981). For example, Donald and Bradshaw (1981) found that work and occupational stress tends to produce family problems whereas there is little or no research on how the family affects on-the-job ethical and unethical behavior. McLean (1978) has taken a different approach to the relationship between the family and ethical and unethical behavior. His theory of reference groups stresses that ethicists have failed to account for the pressure which multiple roles exert on members of modern society when they undertake ethical analyses. He notes that one of the multiple roles not often taken into account is that of family member.

Peer group pressure seems to be a significant variable in predicting deviant behavior (Grasmick and Green, 1980; Burkett and Jensen, 1975) among adolescent youth. There seems to be a strong relationship between peer group attitude and behavior and the propensity of illegal activity by youthful offenders. Other research indicates that peer group pressure may cause the group to make faulty and often immoral decisions (Janis, 1972; Allison, 1971; Halberstam, 1972).

The individual's home environment also seems to guide moral development. Kagan (1984) has argued for a non-environmental approach. He advances a genetic explanation for the development of moral values, but at the present he seems to be in the minority. The opposing view, supported by a large body of literature within developmental psychology, postulates the theory that the individual's family and peers have a large influence on moral development (Bandura, 1971, 1977). The child goes through a complex socialization process which is an important determinant of moral thinking. The family and peer groups are both important in this process (Cohen, 1976; Clausen, 1968). Although the literature in the area emphasizes the child's moral actions, the individual's family and peer environment surely also has a continuing influence into adulthood. However, the lack of relevant research on many of the topics limits the conclusions that can be drawn.

INDIVIDUAL ATTRIBUTES

The individual component of the model comprises moral level, personal goals, motivation mechanisms, position/status, self concept, life experiences, personality, and demographic variables. The research connecting individual attributes with ethical and unethical behavior is fairly limited and tends to concentrate on moral level, demographics, motivation mechanisms, and self-concept.

Kohlberg's influence is found throughout most of the research on the individual and moral development. Kohlberg (1969, 1971) defines six stages of moral development, which he groups into three general categories, two stages per category. The first general category is the preconventional (or premoral). Individuals in this category do not base judgment of right and wrong on society's standards, but on their own physical needs. Fear of punishment is the main reason rules are followed by people in this category. Kohlberg's second category is the conventional level. Children usually reach this category around the age of ten, and it is also the most prevalent moral category for adults. The basic criteria for right and wrong in this category are the norms and regulations of society. Kohlberg's final category is the postconventional. An individual in this category does not reject the legitimacy of rules in society, but at times find society's prescriptions wanting. The postconventional individual has the capacity for reflection, logical reasoning, responsibility, and an inner source of morality and justice.

Kohlberg has developed an instrument for assessing an individual's level of moral reasoning. Many of the studies relating to the individual attributes in this segment of the model use a Kohlberg-type instrument to determine moral level and then study moral level as a dependent variable influenced by the other individual attributes as independent variables. Kohlberg-type instruments use a series of ethical dilemmas as an ambiguous stimulus for subjects who are then asked to describe how they would behave in the situation. The level of moral reasoning is determined from the rationale used in explaining the hypothetical actions.

Maqsud (1980), for example, studies the effect of the personality characteristic of locus of control on moral level. Locus of control refers to the degree one relies on oneself (internal) vs. others (external) for reinforcement (Rotter, 1966). Maqsud found a significant concentration of internal locus of control individuals in the postconventional (higher order) level of moral reasoning. Others (Adams-Weber, 1969; Johnson and Gormly, 1972) have reported similar findings. Other studies have used a variety of personality measures and related them to level of moral reasoning. Authoritarianism, neuroticism, and level of anxiety have all been related to differing indices of moral reasoning (Elliott, 1976).

Demographic variables, for example, sex, age, and education, have been used to predict moral reasoning in a number of studies. A number of authors (Lyons, 1982; Braverman et al., 1972) have studied the effect of sex differences on moral level. They found that females tend not to progress to postconventional morality as often as males because of differential societal pressures on females, even though at younger ages females tend to be more advanced in terms of moral reasoning (Freeman and Giefink, 1979). Age and education level also are related to moral reasoning. Older individuals tend to score lower on moral reasoning scales, while the more educated tend to score higher (Dortzbach, 1975; Rest, 1976; Crowder, 1976; Coder, 1975).

Ward and Wilson (1980) have studied the effect of motivational orientation (safety vs. esteem). They found that esteem-motivated individuals do not submit to group pressure, that is, they display a consistent moral posture across situations. Safety-motivated subjects tend to acquiesce to group pressure and exhibit inconsistent moral action. When acting as individuals, there was no difference between the moral actions of the safety and esteem subjects.

There have been many studies in criminology that attempt to identify characteristics that distinguish criminals from non-criminals (Lykken, 1957; Frost and Frost, 1962; Peterson et al., 1961). For example, Mednick and co-workers (1977) found that criminals exhibited the following characteristics: low intelligence, poorer impulse control, emotional immaturity, lack of ability to learn by experience, poorer work habits, and lower nervous activity. However, crime in corporations does not fit the profile of crime at large. So-called "white collar" crime is committed by people of high social status and, usually, high income level. Many of the other variables which identify criminals at large do not generalize to the corporate criminal, for example, low intelligence or personality disorganization. Different characteristics seem to identify the corporate criminal. For example, Aubert (1952) found that individuals at the corporate level who behave unethically have in general a negative attitude toward legal regulations, although they admit that certain types of law are necessary. Moreover, many who have been convicted of "white collar" crime do not perceive that they have behaved inappropriately (Geis, 1973).

Individual attributes do seem to relate to the level of moral reasoning. However, the research reported in this section does have a number of problems. First, the level of moral reasoning is the dependent variable in ethics research, not ethical behavior. This clearly assumes that it is obvious that the postconventional individual is going to act ethically. But does the capability for ethical reasoning guarantee ethical action or behavior? The real dependent variable should be ethical behavior, not level of moral reasoning. Second, the research is not realistic. Most of the research is done in academia, with little relevance toward ethics in the real world (especially the business world). Designs need to be developed that realistically simulate real world environments, and research needs to be done in more applied settings. Third, the research tends to focus on the isolated individual. However, there is some evidence (Nichols and Day, 1982) that individuals interacting in a group produce group decisions at a higher level of moral reasoning than the average of the individual members when acting alone. Since many business decisions relating to ethics are made in the corporate context, this effect needs further study.

DECISION PROCESS

In recent years a variety of different models have emerged which outline the major steps or functions involved in a rational decision-making process. Rationality here is defined as the best selection of means to achieve an objective consistent with the value system of the decision maker (Steiner et al., 1982). Most of the models encompass the following steps in one form or another: setting managerial objectives; searching for alternatives; evaluating alternatives; choosing an alternative; implementing the decision; and monitoring and controlling the results. Associated with each of these steps is the gathering and processing of information within a value construct and the cognitive limitations of the decision maker.

Ethical issues may arise in any step of the decision-making process. For example, in setting managerial objectives, it is necessary to consider ethical concerns relating to the choice of pursuing various directions. In comparing various alternatives, ethical considerations often arise as part of the valuation process. In the implementation step the potential consequences to resources (human and physical) which will be affected by the decision must be considered from an ethical perspective (Boulding, 1966).

In making these types of decisions involving ethical consideration a manager draws upon his/her basic personal values from his/her role in the environments previously discussed. In making these decisions value conflicts are inevitable, and the particular resolution of these conflicts depends on the relative degree of influence of the various environments on the decision maker. For example, at any point the values of the decision maker may conflict with the values of the organization. A study of 238 managers revealed that they "experience pressure, real or perceived, to compromise their personal moral standards to satisfy organizational expectations" (Carroll, 1975). A study by England (1967) revealed that managers place a great deal of importance on organizational goals and have a strong group orientation. A further study by Senger (1971) found that managers tend to evaluate their subordinates with respect to their degree of acceptance of organizational values. These findings would tend to support a hypothesis that in event of a conflict of values, organizational and group values may assume greater emphasis in comparison to personal values. However, in resolving this conflict between the personal values of the manager and the goals of the organization, Monsen et al. (1966) argue that the manager most frequently resolves this conflict by emphasizing his/her own personal goals. This seems to imply that in the event of a conflict, managers pursue a path that they perceive will enhance their own self interests especially with respect to career advancement.

In making various decisions at each step in the decision-making process the manager acquires and processes a myriad of information. Some of this information is problem specific whereas other information relates to the previously discussed environmental factors. This information ranges from hard data, such as laws and stated corporate policies, to soft data, such as an individual's self concept and peer group with a range of information in between

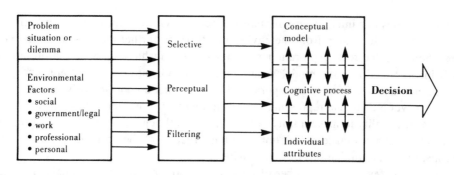

Fig. 2. The decision process.

these states. The manager must then synthesize and analyze this information to determine a rational decision to the problem situation. A simplified model of the more important elements in this process are depicted in Figure 2. The two information inputs—the parameters of the problem situation and the environmental factors impinging on the decision maker—are filtered by the manager in a selective perception process. The manager then builds a conceptual model, which goes through an iterative process affected by the individual attributes and mediated by the individual's unique cognitive process. Since environmental factors and individual attributes have been discussed in previous sections of this article, this section will focus on the remaining aspects of the decision process.

Hogarth (1980) notes that people have limited information-processing capacity. The consequence of this limitation affects the manager's (1) perception of information, (2) style of information processing, and (3) memory as follows:

1. Perception of information is selective. The decision maker, influenced by a number of different forces, may or may not select the information which is most relevant to the problem situation.
2. Since people cannot simultaneously integrate a great deal of information, processing is mainly done in a sequential manner. The sequence in which information is processed may bias a person's judgment and limit the evaluation of interrelated elements.
3. Finally, people have limited memory capacity. This limits the access to information which might be relevant to the problem.

Given this limited information-processing capacity, managers tend to select information and process it in a sequential manner. What we select depends on the information stimulus and on our internal representation of the problem situation.

As a way of dealing with the complexity of the situation, managers appear to form a conceptual model of the problem. Simon (1976) notes that decision makers cannot comprehend all alternatives, probabilities, consequences, values, and the evaluation of these and so constructs an internal representation or model of the situation. The model may be simplistic or complex, depending on the cognitive capabilities and capacity of the manager. New information modifies our internal representation model which, in turn, directs our activities to further sample information from the environment, which further modifies our internal representation, which directs exploration, etc., in a cyclical fashion. Only that information that fits is incorporated into the model. Features that fit well into the model are more readily selected and more likely to be incorporated than those that do not fit easily. In any case, the model is never a complete representation of the real world problem situation, which limits the manager's ability to make a truly rational decision (bounded rationality). Consequently, judgments or choices made reflect not only the structure of the problem situation but also the capabilities and limitations of the decision maker.

In the past few years a number of conceptual and empirical articles have appeared in the literature regarding the effect of a manager's cognitive style of problem solving and decision making (see, for example, Benbasat and Taylor, 1978; Blaylock and Rees, 1984; Henderson and Nutt, 1980; Kilman and Mitroff, 1976; and Taggart and Robey, 1981). Simon (1960, p. 72) defines cognitive style as "the characteristic, self consistent mode of functioning which individuals show in their perception and intellectual activities." There are many dimensions of cognitive style (Goldstein and Blackman, 1978) just as there are many dimensions of an individual's personality. The difference between the personality and cognitive style of an individual is "a distinction between what an individual thinks (personality) and the way the individual thinks (cognitive style)" (Pratt, 1980, p. 502). Although there is general acknowledgment that the construct of cognitive style is multidimensional, the number and identity of such dimensions and the relationship between these dimensions are not clear (Zmud, 1979).

In recent years there has been a surge of interest about the impact of cognitive style on managerial problem solving and decision making. Some of the most cited cognitive measures which would seem to affect ethical and unethical decision making include: Myers-Briggs Type Indicator (Myers, 1962); Witkin's Embedded Figures Test (Witkin, 1971); Cognitive Complexity (Bieri, 1966) and Tolerance of Ambiguity (Budner, 1962). The Myers-Briggs Indicator, which is based on Carl Jung's theory of type, purports to assess differences in behavior as to how an individual uses perception and judgment. Witkin's Embedded Figures test assesses whether one is more field dependent (relies more on external referents on behavior) or field independent (relies more on internal referents for behavior). Cognitive complexity is a measure of one's ability to evaluate multiple dimensions or aspects of a problem situation. Budner's Scale for Tolerance-Intolerance of Ambiguity assesses one's degree of tolerance for dealing with ambiguous, uncertain situations. Such factors as personality traits, psychological needs, self concept, demographic factors, value systems, as well as one's memory of experiences shape the selection process and internal representation of the problem situation. Actions become consistent with the internal cognitive process of an individual which is shaped by these many factors rather than by the reality of the problem situation.

In deciding whether or not to pursue a given course of action, the rational decision maker is further influenced by both the perceived consequences and the perceived risks involved. Many times an individual's perception of a consequence or risk differs significantly from the actual consequence or risk as a result of a minimization or exaggeration process. Few individuals have the luxury of perfect information when making a decision or even knowing the degree of information to which they are knowledgeable. The decision is further influenced by the subjective weights applied to the consequences according to the individual's unique value system of utility function.

Finally, in making a final choice or decision for the problem situation, the manager may or may not resort to using a decision tool or aid. In recent years a number of decision tools and aids have been developed ranging in complexity from highly structured computer-based models to simple rules of thumb. These aids provide the opportunity of extending the limited information processing cognitive capabilities of the managers.

The ultimate decision of choice (ethical or unethical) to a problem situation is dependent on a number of factors affecting the decision process. These factors include the available information (hard and soft), the individual attributes and cognitive capabilities of the managers, the perceived consequences and risks of a decision, the value or utility assigned to these consequences, as well as the degree of reliance on structured model by the manager.

CONCLUSIONS

The model developed in this article must be recognized as a first attempt to identify and relate the environmental factors and influences in decision making, where an individual is faced with a choice that has ethical implications. We expect this model to evolve as further research expands the body of knowledge relating to this field.

While substantial research has been done concerning ethical issues, clearly much more needs to be done. Most urgently needed is a series of empirical studies of specific decision-making situations involving ethical issues. The behaviors of individuals and their interaction with their environments should be systematically observed so as to determine which factors lead to a particular decision. Components of the model could be manipulated in order to ascertain the importance of each component. Undoubtedly such a complex undertaking would require substantial time and resources. The results of such a series of experiments would allow further refinement and understanding of the model and its components.

While this representation and description is preliminary, it can still provide valuable assistance in the understanding, development and evaluation of intervention and awareness programs in industry. Likewise it can be useful in academic settings, in courses that deal with ethical issues in business and industry, by providing a multidimensional framework to assist in the comprehension of the variety and magnitude of the factors that need to be considered.

REFERENCES

Adams-Weber, J.R.: 1969, "Generalized Expectancies Concerning Locus of Control Reinforcements and the Perception of Moral Sanction," *British Journal of Social and Clinical Psychology* 8, 340–343.

Allison, G.T.: 1971, *Essence of Decision: Explaining the Cuban Missile Crisis*, Boston: Little, Brown & Company.

American Assembly of Collegiate Schools of Business Acreditation Council Procedures and Standards: 1983, AACSB, St. Louis, MO.

Anderson, R., R. Perrucci, D. Schendel, and L.E. Trachman: 1980, *Divided Loyalties: Whistle Blowing at BART*, West LaFayette, IN: Purdue University Press.

Aubert, U.: 1952, "White-Collar Crime and Social Structure," *American Journal of Sociology* 58, 263–271.

Bandura, A.: 1971, "Analysis of Modeling Process" in A. Bandura ed.), *Psychological Modeling*, Chicago: Atherton, Aldine.

Bandura, A.: 1977, *Social Learning Theory*, Englewood Cliffs, NJ: Prentice-Hall.

Benbasat, I. and R.N. Taylor: 1978, "The Impact of Cognitive Styles on Information Systems Design," *Management Information Systems Quarterly* 2, 43–54.

Bieri, J., A.L. Atkins, S. Briar, R.L. Leaman, H. Miller, and T. Tripoldi: 1966, *Clinical and Social Judgement*, New York: Wiley.

Blaylock, B.K. and L.P. Rees: 1984, "Cognitive Style and the Usefulness of Information," *Decision Sciences* 15, 74–91.

Boulding, K.: 1966, "The Ethics of Rational Decision," *Management Science* 121, 161–169.

Bowie, N.: 1982, *Business Ethics*, Englewood Cliffs, NJ: Prentice-Hall.

Brady, F.N.: 1985, "A Janus-Head Model of Ethical Theory: Looking Two Ways at Business/Society Issues," *Academy of Management Review* 10(3), 568–576.

Broome, T.H.: 1983, "New Developments in Engineering Ethics: The AAES Plan," in V. Weil (ed.), *Beyond Whistle-blowing*, pp. 228–242, Chicago, IL: Illinois Institute of Technology.

Braverman, I., S. Vogel, D. Braverman, F. Clarkson, and P. Rosenkrantz: 1972, "Sex-Role Stereotypes: A Current Appraisal," *Journal of Social Issues* 28, 58–78.

Budner, S.: 1962, "Intolerance of Ambiguity as a Personality Variable," *Journal of Personality* 30, 29–50.

Burkett, S.R. and E. Jensen: 1975, "Conventional Ties, Peer Influence, and the Fear of Apprehension: A Study of Adolescent Marijuana Use," *Sociological Quarterly* 16, 523–553.

Carr, A.Z.: 1983, "Is Business Bluffing Ethical?" in B. Vincent (ed.), *Moral Issues in Business*, pp. 17–24, Belmont, CA: Wadsworth.

Carroll, A.B.: 1975, "Managerial Ethics; A Post-Watergate View," *Business Horizons* 18, 75–80.

Clausen, J.A.: 1968, "Perspectives on Childhood Socialization," in J. Clausen (ed.), *Socialization and Society*, Boston: Little, Brown & Company.

Coder, R.: 1975, *Moral Judgement in Adults*, Unpublished doctoral dissertation, University of Minnesota.

Cohan, R.M. and J. Whitcover: 1980, "A Heartbeat Away," in R. Baum (ed.), *Ethical Problems in Engineering: Cases*, 2nd edition, Vol. 2, pp. 52–57, Troy, NY: Rensselaer Polytechnic Institute.

Cohen, S.E.: 1976, *Social and Personality Development in Childhood*, New York: Macmillan.

Crowder, J.W.: 1976, *The Defining Issues Test and Correlates of Moral Judgment*, Unpublished master's thesis, University of Maryland.

DeGeorge, R.T.: 1978, *Ethics, Free Enterprise and Public Policy*, New York: Oxford Press.

Dickson, J.W.: 1978, "Perceptions of Risk as Related to Choice in a Two-Dimensional Risk Situation," *Psychological Reports* 44, 1059–1062.

Donald, J. and P. Bradshaw: 1981, "Occupational and Life Stress and the Family," *Small Group Behavior* 12, 329–375.

Dortzbach, J.R.: 1975, *Moral Judgment and Perceived Locus of Control: A Cross-Sectional Developmental Study of Adults, Aged 25–74*, Unpublished doctoral dissertation, University of Oregon.

Elliott, A.: 1976, "Fakers: A Study of Managers: Responses on a Personality Test," *Personnel Review* 5, 33–37.

England, G.W.: 1967, "Personal Value Systems of American Managers," *Academy of Management Journal* 10, 53–68.

Fairweather, V.: 1980, "$80,000 in Payoffs," in R.J. Baum (ed.), *Ethical Problems in Engineering: Cases*, 2nd edition, Vol. 2, pp. 50–51, Troy, NY: Rensselaer Polytechnic Institute.

Flores, A.: 1980, "The Problem of Professionalism: A Code of Ethics," in A. Flores (ed.), *Ethical Problems in Engineering: Readings*, 2nd edition, Vol. 1, pp. 1–6, Troy, NY: Rensselaer Polytechnic Institute.

Flores, A. (ed.): 1982, *Designing for Safety: Engineering Ethics in Organizational Contents*, Troy, NY: Center for the Study of the Human Dimensions of Science and Technology, Rensselaer Polytechnic Institute.

Freedman, J.L., D.O. Sears, and J.M. Carlsmith: 1981, *Social Psychology*, Englewood Cliffs, NJ: Prentice Hall.

Freeman, S.J.M. and J.W. Giefink: 1979, "Moral Judgment as a Function of Age, Sex, and Stimulus," *Journal of Psychology* 102, 43–47.

Frost, B.P. and R.K. Frost: 1962, "The Pattern of WISC Scores in a Group of Juvenile Sociopaths," *Journal of Clinical Psychology* 18, 354–355.

Geis, G.: 1973, "Deterring Corporate Crime," in R. Nader and M.J. Green (eds.), *Deterring Corporate Crime*, pp. 182–197, New York: Grossman.

Geis, G. and E. Stotland: 1980, *White-Collar Crime Theory and Research*, Beverly Hills, CA: Sage.

Gillis, J.G.: 1981, "Securities Law and Regulation," *Financial Analysts Journal* 37, 14.

Goldstein, K.M. and S. Blackman: 1978, *Cognitive Style: Five Approaches and Relevant Research*, New York: Wiley-Interscience.

Grasmick, H. and E. Green: 1980, "Legal Punishment, Social Disapproval, and Internalization as Inhibitors of Illegal Behavior," *Journal of Criminal Law and Criminology* 71, 325–335.

Gravander, J.W.: 1981. "The Origins and Implications of Engineers' Obligations to the Public Welfare," in P.D. Asquith and R.N. Giere (eds.), *PSA 1980*, Vol. 2, pp. 443–455, East Lansing, Michigan: The Philosophy of Science Association.

Gravander, J.W.: 1982, "When in Rome, Do as Who?" *The Liberal Studies Educator* 4, 23–28.

Halberstam, D.: 1972, *The Best and the Brightest*, New York: Random House.

Hegarty, W.H. and H. Sims: 1979, "Organizational Philosophy, Policies, and Objectives Related to Unethical Decision Behavior: A Laboratory Experiment," *Journal of Applied Psychology* 64, 331–338.

Henderson, J.C. and P.C. Nutt: 1979, "The Influence of Decision Style on Decision Making Behavior," *Management Science 26*, 371–386.

Hodges, L.: 1963, *The Business Conscience*, Englewood Cliffs, NJ: Prentice-Hall.

Hogarth, R.: 1980, *Judgment and Choice: The Psychology of Decision*, New York: John Wiley and Sons.

Janis, I.: 1972, *Victims of Groupthink*, Boston: Houghton Mifflin Co.

Johnson, C.K. and J. Gormly: 1972, "Academic Cheating: The Contribution of Sex, Personality, and Situational Variables," *Developmental Psychology* 6, 320–325.

Kagan, J.: 1984, *The Nature of the Child*, New York: Basic.

Kilman, R.H. and I.I. Mitroff: 1976, "Qualitative versus Quantitative Analysis for Management Science: Different Forms for Different Psychological Types," *Management Science* 22, 19–32.

Kohlberg, L.: 1969, "Stage and Sequence: The Cognitive Developmental Approach to Socialization," in D. Goslin (ed.), *Handbook of Socialization Theory and Research*, pp. 347–480, Chicago: Rand McNally.

Kohlberg, L.: 1971, "From Is to Ought (How to Commit the Naturalistic Fallacy and Get Away with It in the Study of Moral Development)," in T. Mischel (ed.), *Cognitive Development and Epistemology*, pp. 151–235, New York: Academic Press.

Kohn, P.M. and R.V. Hughson: 1980, "Perplexing Problems in Engineering Ethics," *Chemical Engineering* 75, 132–147.

Layton, E.T.: 1981, *The Revolt of the Engineers*, Cleveland, OH: Case Western Reserve University.

Leugenbiehl, H.C.: 1983, "Moral Education and the Codes of Ethics," in V. Weil (ed.), *Beyond Whistleblowing: Defining Engineers' Responsibilities*, pp. 284–299, Chicago, IL: Illinois Institute of Technology.

Lykken, D.T.: 1957, "A Study of Anxiety in the Sociopathic Personality," *Journal of Abnormal and Social Psychology* 55, 6–10.

Lyons, N.: 1982, *Conceptions of Self and Morality and Modes of Moral Choice*, Unpublished doctoral dissertation, Harvard University.

Maqsud, M.: 1980, "Locus of Control and Stages of Moral Reasoning," *Psychological Reports* 46, 1243–1248.

Martin, M. and R. Schinzinger: 1983, *Ethics in Engineering*, New York: McGraw-Hill.

Matthews, J.B., K.E. Goodpaster, and L.L. Nash: 1985, *Policies and Persons: A Casebook in Business Ethics*, New York: McGraw-Hill.

Mautz, R., R. Reilly, and M. Maher: 1979, "Personnel Failure: The Weak Link in Internal Control," *Financial Executive* 47, 22–25.

May, L.: 1983, "Professional Action and Professional Liability," in V. Weil (ed.) *Beyond*

Whistleblowing: Defining Engineers' Responsibilities, pp. 211–227, Chicago, IL: Illinois Institute of Technology.

McGowan, W.: 1983, "The Great White Collar Cover-up," *Business and Society Review*, 25–31.

McLean, S.D.: 1978, "Ethics, Reference Group Theory, and the Root Metaphor Analysis," *Andover Newton Quarterly* 14, 211–221.

Mednick, S.A., L. Kirkegaard-Sorensen, B. Hutchings, J. Knop, R. Rosenburg, and F. Schulsinger: 1977, "The Interplay of Socioenvironmental and Individual Factors in the Etiology of Criminal Behavior," in S. Mednick and K.O. Christiansen (eds.), *Biosocial Bases of Criminal Behavior*, New York: Gardner Press.

Meier, R.F. and G. Geis: 1982, "The Psychology of the White-Collar Offender," in G. Geis (ed.), *On White-Collar Crime*, Lexington, MA: Lexington.

Milgram, S.: 1963, "Behavioral Study of Obedience," *Journal of Abnormal and Social Psychology* 67, 317–378.

Milgram, S.: 1965, "Some Conditions of Obedience and Disobedience to Authority," *Human Relations* 85, 57–76.

Monsen, R.J., B.O. Saxberg, and R.A. Sutermeister: 1966, "The Modern Manager: What Makes Him Run?," *Business Horizons* 9, 23–24.

Mortimer, J.T.: 1980, "Occupational-Family Linkages as Perceived by Men in the Early Stages of Professional and Managerial Careers," *Research in the Interweave of Social Roles* 1, 99–117.

Myers, I.B.: 1962, *Manual for the Myers-Briggs Type Indicator*, Princeton, NJ: Educational Testing Service.

Nichols, M.L. and V.E. Day: 1982, "A Comparison of Moral Reasoning of Groups and Individuals on the 'Defining Issues Test'", *Academy of Management Journal* 25, 201–208.

Oldenquist, A.G. and E.E. Slowter: 1979, "Proposed: A Single Code of Ethics for All Engineers", *Professional Engineer* 49, 8–11.

Pavlovic, K.R.: 1980, "Autonomy and Obligation: Is There an Engineering Ethics?," in A. Flores (ed.), *Ethical Problems in Engineering: Readings*, 2nd edition, Vol. 1, pp. 89–93, Troy, NY: Rensselaer Polytechnic Institute.

Peterson, D.R., H.C. Quay, and T.L. Tiffany: 1961, "Personality Factors Related to Juvenile Delinquency," *Child Development* 32, 355–372.

Pratt, J.: 1980, "The Effects of Personality on a Subject's Information Process: A Comment," *The Accounting Review* 55, 501–506.

Rest, J.R.: 1976, *Moral Judgment Related to Sample Characteristics* (Final report to NIMH), Minneapolis: University of Minnesota.

Rotter, J.B.: 1966, "Generalized Expectancies for Internal versus External Control of Reinforcement," *Psychological Monographs*, 80 (Whole No. 609).

Schwartz, H. and S.M. Davis: 1981, "Matching Corporate Culture and Business Strategy," *Organizational Dynamics* 10, 36.

Senger, J.: 1971, "Managers' Perceptions of Subordinates' Competence as a Function of Personal Value Orientations," *Academy of Management Journal* 14, 415–423.

Simon, H.: 1960, *The New Science of Management*, New York: Harper and Row.

Simon, H.: 1976, *Administrative Behavior: A Study of Decision Making Processes in Administrative Organization*, New York: Free Press.

Staff: 1979, "Gifts to Buyers," *Purchasing*, April 11, 19.

Steiner, G., J. Miner, and E. Gray: 1982, *Management Policy and Strategy*, New York: Macmillan Publishing Company.

Taggart, W. and D. Robey: 1981, "Mind and Managers: On the Dual Nature of Human Information Procesing and Management," *Academy of Management Review* 6, 187–195.

Taylor, R.E.: 1984, "White Collar Crime Getting Less Attention," *The Wall Street Journal*, Vol. 203, No. 23, p. 27.

Unger, S.H.: 1982, *Controlling Technology: Ethics and the Responsible Engineer*, New York: Holt, Rinehart and Winston.

Vandiver, K.: 1980, "Engineers, Ethics, and Economics," in R.J. Baum (ed.), *Ethical Problems in Engineering: Cases*, 2nd edition, Vol. 2, pp. 136–138, Troy, NY: Rensselaer Polytechnic Institute.

Velasquez, M.G.: 1980, *Business Ethics: Concepts and Cases*, Englewood Cliffs, NJ: Prentice-Hall.

Ward, L. and J.P. Wilson: 1980, "Motivation and Moral Development as Determinants of Behavioral Acquiescence and Moral Action," *Journal of Social Psychology* 112, 271–286.

Wheelen, L. and J.D. Hunger: 1984, *Strategy Management*, Reading, MA: Addison-Wesley.

Witkin, H.A., P.K. Oltman, R.K. Ruskin, and S.A. Karp: 1971, *The Embedded Figures Test*, Palo Alto, CA: Consulting Psychologist Press.

Zmud, R.W.: 1979, "Individual Differences in MIS Success: A Review of the Empirical Literature," *Management Science* 25, 966–979.

A Question of Ethics: Developing Information Systems Ethics

Eli Cohen and Larry Cornwell

Originally published in *Journal of Business Ethics*, 8: 431–437, 1989. Copyright 1989 Kluwer Academic Publishers. Reprinted by permission of Kluwer Academic Publishers.

ABSTRACT

This study develops a pedagogy for the teaching of ethical principles in information systems (IS) classes, and reports on an empirical study that supports the efficacy of the approach. The proposed pedagogy involves having management information systems professors lead questioning and discussion on a list of ethical issues as part of their existing IS courses. The rationale for this pedagogy involves (1) the maturational aspects of ethics, and (2) the importance of repetition, challenge, and practice in developing a personal set of ethics. A study of IS ethics using a pre-post test design found that classes receiving such treatment significantly improved their performance on an IS ethics questionnaire.

It appears to me that in Ethics, as in all other philosophical studies, the difficulties ... are mainly due to ... the attempt to answer questions, without first discovering precisely what question it is which you desire to answer.
George Edward Moore, Principia Ethica [1903], preface

Moore's observation about the problem of ethics is certainly true for the teaching of information systems ethics; we have yet to determine what questions need to be asked.

This paper deals with three related concerns in teaching information systems ethics in MIS/IS classes. The paper first addresses the concern of where we should teach ethics in the curriculum. It then addresses the concern by what pedagogical mechanism might we teach ethics. The paper lastly provides suggestions for topics and questions that depict the issues in information system (IS) ethics.

But the paper does more than just address those three concerns; it shows how these concerns are interrelated. The core of these concerns is a desire to build in our students a personal code of ethics. In answering how best to build that code we answer all three of these concerns. That answer is by teaching IS ethics using the Socratic, question-asking method.

Having developed this framework for teaching IS ethics, the paper concludes by providing empirical support for this pedagogy.

Concern 1: Where Should Ethics Be Taught?

Ethics is addressed in many information systems (IS) curricula. In some IS curricula, ethics is taught separate from the rest of the curriculum as part of an isolated course. This approach has its advantages:

- Students may give the issue greater weight because of its recognition as a separate topic area, the equal of database and finance.
- Administrators can point out specific coverage of ethics in the IS curriculum, in response to queries by accreditation review teams.
- The course can be staffed by an instructor with specialized knowledge in ethics, such as a philosophy professor. This professor is in a better position to give the students the right answers.

An alternative approach, noted in a Carnegie Foundation report, calls for the integration of topics in curricula. Earnest L. Boyer, one of the report's authors, writes that such a coordination improves the students' ability to think in an integrated manner and thus serves their intellectual development (Boyer, 1981). Gandz and Hayes (1988) similarly argue that ethical instruction should be integrated throughout the curriculum. Instead of teaching the hand by having separate courses for each finger, the hand should be taught as a whole so as better to learn how to use it as a whole.

Integrating the exploration of ethical issues into all (or at least most) classes shows students that this topic is not "just one more topic," on an equal level with finance and database. Rather it stresses that ethics is an issue that pervades thinking in all areas, from finance to database.

Having ethics explored by different teachers helps students understand that there is no one right answer. Rather, what is important is the process of thinking about ethics. The process of thinking about ethics will lead students to develop their own code of ethics. Many, from government publications (*Computers: Crimes, Clues and Controls*, 1986) to research papers (Laczniak and Inderrieden, 1987), write of the importance of personal codes of ethics to the well-being of the organization. Such personal codes of ethics have two elements: (1) having a sense of right and wrong and (2) having a commitment to behave accordingly.

Concern 2: Which Pedagogical Mechanism Should Be Used?

For all these benefits of integrating ethics into the entire IS curriculum, a problem remains: many professors feel ill-equipped or uncomfortable in teaching ethics. This problem can be overcome, at least in part, by providing instructors of information system courses with an easy-to-follow set of instructions or discussion suggestions. The suggestion that this paper recommends is a list of ethical scenarios and questions to pose to students. The scenarios can be used to set the stage for the questions and present realistic work problems. These questions are designed to cause the students to think, consider and make moral judgments.

The viability of this approach is based on studies (Kohlberg, 1969) that ethics cannot be taught directly. Instead, the instructor should establish an atmosphere that promotes the natural maturation process. Here is the line of reasoning that supports this approach.

MORALITY AS A MATURATION PROCESS.   Studies on moral development of individuals show that people develop their moral thinking in stages (Reed and Hanna, 1982). Morality develops in a predictable pattern, and there is limited benefit from instructing students in what is right and wrong.

These studies then suggest that we cannot directly teach morality, since morality develops as a maturational process. Baxter and Rarick (1987) argue that by integrating ethics into the curriculum, such maturation can be encouraged. Questioning as a method for teaching ethical issues has the advantage that students can challenge their own thinking by hearing the responses of other students. Questioning creates an atmosphere conducive to ethical development.

Concern 3: Questions for Exploring the Ethics Issues in Information Systems

Information systems confront society with a variety of challenges of an ethical nature, some old and some new. Here is a list of some of the issues that might be explored throughout a student's college career, and questions to help explore those areas. The categories listed below are those derived from Parker (nd).

CONFIDENTIALITY.   Some graduates of IS classes will one day build systems for a living; all graduates will be users of information systems. Confidentiality of information is important for all information-using professions.

Some solutions to securing data, such as requiring the use of a password to access data and providing passwords only on a need-to-know basis are fairly straightforward. But concomitant ethical issues, such as deciding who needs to know, are not so simple to address. For example, should managers have access to their supervisee's medical records or psychological profiles? If one employee discovers that another employee contemplates suicide, should a supervisor be informed and whose supervisor? What is the proper response to a police request for information about an employee, vendor, or customer?

The possibility of matching of data from various databases confounds this issue. Database matching occurs when information is collected from more than one database to locate persons who match some criterion. For example, a state's welfare agency may query the balances in bank accounts assigned to social security numbers of welfare recipients (Davis, 1987). If the agency finds an offender using this computerized method, may it just send out a computerized letter notifying the offender of a cutoff of funds, or must it confront the accused in person? Was the harm that was incurred by the woman who unjustly lost her subsidy due to database matching worth the benefit to society? Is this a case of being presumed guilty unless proven innocent?

SOCIAL RESPONSIBILITY OF PROGRAMMERS AND OF THEIR MANAGERS.   An important ethical question that students should confront is whether programmers have an obligation to act in a socially responsible manner. Berkeley (1962) explores this issue in depth. May a free-lance programmer ethically work for a thief? If not, how about working on a computer project that is legal, but unethical, such as the one used to intern Americans of Japanese origin during the WW II? Is all that is legal ethical? Are all ethical decisions legal?

Consider the example of a programmer whose manager argues that there is not enough time to write the payroll properly. "We must have it in place on January 1 or we won't be able to implement the system until next year. You can add the audit trails later." May the programmer comply with this order and remain ethical? Is insubordination ever ethical? Should the programmer resign? What if the programmer would be fired for failing to comply? Did the manager breach ethics in making this request?

SOCIAL RESPONSIBILITY OF SYSTEMS ANALYSTS. An analyst's job is to design work flows that are efficient. One result of an analyst's work can be that people will lose their jobs. Is such conduct ethical?

Some jobs that analysts design, such as full-time VDT operators' jobs, are known to be highly stressful and cause harm to the worker (Cohen, 1988). Should analysts create such jobs?

Research has shown that computer monitoring of workers (number of keystrokes per hour, number of telephone calls responded to per hour) increases productivity of the worker. Is such activity an invasion of privacy? Should an analyst refuse to implement a system that creates computer monitoring or that involves privacy?

ISSUES COMMON TO ALL MANAGERS. Should information system managers refuse gifts from a vendor? Should the manager refuse a cup of coffee or a coffee cup? Is free literature to educate the manager legitimate? a free vendor course? a free course, travel paid, held in Hawaii?

What should you do if your boss appears to be making a bad business decision because of a bribe?

Is it legitimate to call home if you are going to be late? To call home over the lunch break, just to chat? To call your friends in town? in Hawaii?

DEALING WITH OTHERS. The various computer professional organizations, including Data Processing Management Association (DPMA) and Association for Computing Machinery (ACM) have set ethical standards for their members (DPMA, 1988; ACM, 1988). Three common elements in these codes are to (1) maintain competence, (2) disclose conflict of interest, and (3) maintain confidentiality of information even after employment ends.

What should you do if a co-worker is incompetent? If a colleague at another company calls, asking for your opinion of a former co-worker who was fired for incompetence, what should you do? Should companies reveal violations of ethical standards?

Should you forgo a good thing simply because you benefit from its use? (Should a professor not adopt his or her own book?)

If you write code for one employer, are you forbidden forever from using that code again for another employer? If so, how many times can you re-invent the wheel?

EXPLORING THE ETHICS ISSUES IN INFORMATION SYSTEMS: THE STUDY

The efficacy of the pedagogy described above, challenging students through questions, is tested by the following study. The study focuses on whether ethical instruction using a question-asking pedagogy changes students' attitudes.

Design

THE MEASURE.   Items were developed that have face validity in measuring information system ethics in its broader scope. These items query the respondents regarding their attitude toward software piracy, confidentiality of data, unauthorized use of computer equipment, and plagiarism. One such item reads "I think it is okay to look at (but not change) another student's grades on the computer."

The items were selected to replicate and build upon two earlier empirical studies. Questions from both the Schuster (1987) and Christoph et al. (1987/88) surveys were included in or adapted for the present study.

Respondents were given the choice of selecting the alternatives True, False, or leaving them blank. Even though items from the Schuster questionnaire were included in this study, this study uses this response scheme to overcome a difficulty in the Schuster study. Schuster explicitly included a "Don't Know" category for selected questions. Since in Schuster's survey a majority of the sample responded "Don't Know" for selected items, and since the present survey queries attitude, not knowledge, this study omits that category. Also, this study chose to word items parallel to one another, even at the cost of wording them differently at times from those items in the Schuster and Christoph studies. For those reasons, the survey methodology is not absolute replications of those earlier studies.

Table I shows inter-item and item-total correlations. Table II lists the items of the scale.

Item analysis showed the scale to have a reliability index alpha of 0.74.

The study was administered in January 1988 and again in February 1988 to students taking classes in the College of Business Administration at Bradley University. Three sets of classes were used. Two of these sets were similar in content. The third set involved students from a different college within the university. Classes were sample from disciplines that use computers.

TREATMENT.   The authors developed the broad outlines for ethical questions for the professions involving information processing. The questions were derived from the guidelines of the ethical standards as defined by the professional associations DPMA and ACM (DPMA, 1988; ACM, 1988). The topics for questioning included areas relating to confidentiality, social responsibility of programmers and systems analysts, and issues common to all managers.

The treatment consisted of using the ethical question-asking pedagogy described above. One set of classes received treatment, while the control did not. Pre- and post-tests were administered to all classes.

Table I Inter-Item and Item-to-Scale Correlation Matrix

Item	1	2	3	4	5	6	7	8	9	10
1	1.000	0.600	0.233	0.111	0.120	0.090	0.070	0.166	0.218	0.518
2		1.000	0.074	0.077	0.087	0.106	0.084	0.078	0.136	0.120
3			1.000	0.045	0.163	0.106	0.058	0.194	0.072	0.276
4				1.000	0.045	0.105	−0.025	0.037	−0.064	−0.006
5					1.000	0.126	0.067	0.055	0.054	0.023
6						1.000	0.085	0.089	0.163	0.057
7							1.000	0.041	0.325	0.110
8								1.000	0.104	0.218
9									1.000	0.125
10										1.000

Item	11	12	13	14	15	16	17	18	19	Total
1	0.111	0.170	0.139	0.251	0.170	0.156	0.065	0.200	0.281	0.449
2	0.057	0.148	0.044	0.354	0.159	0.117	0.078	0.143	0.200	0.368
3	0.087	0.227	0.151	0.163	0.190	0.076	−0.065	0.235	0.231	0.351
4	0.043	0.008	0.130	0.051	−0.008	0.060	0.077	0.047	0.046	0.105
5	0.195	0.214	0.435	0.072	0.212	0.029	0.062	0.047	0.261	0.317
6	0.066	0.125	0.065	0.066	0.115	0.111	0.246	0.130	0.120	0.236
7	0.367	0.075	0.101	0.114	0.002	0.228	0.171	0.051	0.018	0.236
8	0.076	0.089	0.040	0.046	0.075	0.073	0.058	0.214	0.153	0.264
9	0.207	0.097	0.096	0.088	−0.003	0.084	0.089	0.093	0.133	0.261
10	0.120	0.153	0.167	0.211	−0.029	0.148	−0.021	0.107	0.186	0.287
11	1.000	0.064	0.177	0.069	0.091	0.133	0.107	0.095	0.216	0.278
12		1.000	0.196	0.260	0.222	0.108	0.072	0.160	0.279	0.377
13			1.000	0.199	0.219	0.183	0.076	0.123	0.256	0.385
14				1.000	0.102	0.073	−0.018	0.190	0.254	0.372
15					1.000	0.003	0.591	0.174	0.254	0.295
16						1.000	0.414	0.111	0.160	0.277
17							1.000	0.013	0.193	0.199
18								1.000	0.287	0.327
19									1.000	0.494

The Item-to-Scale correlations are corrected for each item inclusion in the scale.

HYPOTHESES. The study tested the following hypotheses:

H_1: the mean for the treatment group will drop significantly after treatment; i.e. mean (treatment, pre) < mean (treatment, post)

H_2: no such change will occur for the control group; i.e. mean (control, pre) < mean (control, post)

H_3: the control and the treatment groups are drawn from the same population; i.e., mean (treatment, pre) − mean (control, pre) − mean (control, post).

Table II   Items Included in Scale

I think it is okay . . .

1. for people such as myself to copy commercial software instead of buying it.
2. for people such as myself to copy commercial software instead of buying it when we use it for educational purposes.
3. to use another student's computer account if the student agrees.
4. to use another student's computer account without the student's knowledge.
5. for faculty to use the University's computer for non-University activities.
6. for a student to look at, but not change, confidential student records.
7. for a student to look and change confidential student records.
8. for students to work together on computer assignments.
9. for students to give a copy of their work to another student to hand in.
10. for two students to share the work for a computer assignment and each hand in a copy.
11. for me to sell names and addresses from the University's phone directory.
12. for employees to take with them to their new job copies of programs they have written for the University.
13. for University employees to run programs for their social organization on the University's computer.
14. for employees to copy commercial software to evaluate it for possible purchase.

It is okay to use the University's computer for my personal benefit . . .

15. if it has no adverse effect on others.
16. if it has only minor adverse effects on others.
17. regardless of its effect on others.

It is okay to use University-owned software at home . . .

18. to complete University assignments.
19. for my personal use.

ANALYSIS.   The data were analyzed using a 2×2 Analysis of Variance design, pre/post $\times$ 2 classes, with post-hoc Scheffe paired comparison test of group means.

RESULTS

Two-hundred ninety nine (N = 299) questionnaires were obtained. These results are summarized below.

The results of an ANOVA by treatment and pre/post test condition are shown in Table III. We see statistically significant differences due to the treatment effect and between groups as well. No significant interaction effects were noted.

A Scheffe test, displayed as Table IV, shows that the pre-treatment group means (and post-treatment mean for the control group) are not statistically different from one another.

Table III   ANOVA Table

Source of Variation	Sum of Squares	DF	Mean Square	F	Significance of F
Main Effects	209.135	2	104.568	12.820	0.000
Treatment	119.973	1	119.973	14.709	0.000
pre/post	91.906	1	91.906	11.268	0.001
2-way interaction	17.019	1	17.019	2.087	0.150
Residual	2120.660	260	8.156		
Total	2346.814	263	8.923		

Table IV   Scheffe Test

	Test Condition	
Group	Pre-	Post-
Treatment	9.11 (151)	7.94 (113)
Control	8.82 (17)	8.83 (18)
Total		8.64 (299)

The number in parentheses represents the number of respondents, the number above it shows the mean score on the test.

Figure 1 graphically illustrates the results shown numerically in the above table; the group means on the ethics scale for the treatment group declined after treatment while the control group's mean did not.

Consequently, we cannot reject H_1, H_2, or H_3. This study provides evidence that supports the efficacy of the pedagogy of developing ethics among students through the use of question asking and discussion.

SUMMARY

The literature indicates that ethics are best taught and learned through integration into the curriculum. This creates the problem of what to teach as ethics and how to teach it.

This paper suggests that one solution is to pose ethical questions to the students and to discuss their responses. These questions deal with the real ethical problems of the area being studied. Literature indicates that ethical development may be enhanced through the maturational process of struggling with ethical questions. The empirical evidence presented here

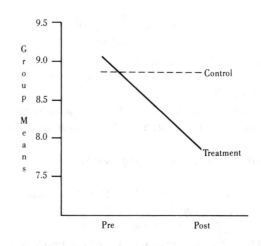

Fig. 1. The group means on the ethics scale for the treatment group declined after treatment while the control group's mean did not.

supports the conclusion that students are able to answer a questionnaire in a more socially acceptable way after being challenged by ethical questions and pursuant discussion. Derek Bok, president of Harvard University, asks "Can Higher Education Foster Higher Morals?" (Bok, 1988) This shows that indeed we can.

REFERENCES

Association of Computing Machinery's Code of Ethics, 11 West 42nd Street, New York, NY.

Baxter, G.D. and Rarick, C.A.: 1987, "Education for the Moral Development of Managers: Kohlberg's Stages of Moral Development and Integrative Education", *Journal of Business Ethics* **6**, pp. 243–248.

Berkeley, E.C.: 1962, *The Computer Revolution* (Doubleday & Co., Garden City, NY).

Bok, Derek: Summer, 1988, "Can Higher Education Foster Higher Morals?", *Business and Society Review* **66**, pp. 4–12.

Boyer, E.L.: 1981, "The Quest for Common Learning", *Common Learning*, Washington, DC: The Carnegie Foundation.

Cohen, E.: 1988, "A Call for VDT Job Restructuring", *Inside DPMA* **1**(1), p. 2.

Computers: Crimes, Clues and Controls. Government Printing Office, 1986, p. 33.

Richard Christoph, Karen Forcht, and Charles Bilbrey: Winter 1987/1988, "The Development of Information Systems Ethics: An Analysis", *The Journal of Computer Information Systems*, pp. 20–23.

Davis, Bob: August 20, 1987, "Abusive Computers", *Wall Street Journal*, p. 1.

Data Processing Management Association's Code of Ethics, *Inside DPMA* **1**(2), 1988, p. 14.

Gandz, Jeffery and Hayes, Nadine: September, 1988, "Teaching Business Ethics", *Journal of Business Ethics* **7**(9), pp. 657–669.

Kohlberg, L: 1969, "Stage and Sequence: the Cognitive-Developmental Approach to Socialization", in D. Grosling (ed). *Handbook of Socialization Theory and Research* (Chicago: Rand McNally).

Laczniak, G.R. and Inderrieden, E.J.: 1987, "The Influence of Stated Organizational Concern Upon Ethical Decision Making", *Journal of Business Ethics* **6**, pp. 297–307.

Parker, D.B., *Ethical Conflicts in Computer Science and Technology*, Arlington, VA: AFIPS Press.

Reed, E.M. and Hanna, P.: January, 1982, "Developmental Theory and Moral Education: Review Essay", *Teaching Philosophy* **5**:1.

William, V. Schuster, *Bootleggery, Smoking Guns and Whistle Blowing: a Sad Saga of Academic Opportunism*, presented at Western Educational Computing Conference, San Francisco, (October 1987).

Education for the Moral Development of Managers: Kohlberg's Stages of Moral Development and Integrative Education

Gerald D. Baxter and Charles A. Rarick

Originally published in *Journal of Business Ethics*, 6: 243–248, 1987. Copyright (c) 1987 by D. Reidel Publishing Company. Reprinted by permission of Kluwer Academic Publishers.

ABSTRACT

Recent management behavior such as the PINTO gasoline tank decision has received a great deal of notoriety. In fact, repugnant examples of management amorality and immorality abound. One is forced to ask a number of questions. Does such behavior reflect a lack of a proper education in moral behavior? Can education result in moral behavior? If so, what kind of education might that be? Answers to these questions might point a way out of the moral shadows giant corporations have cast over much of the world. An attempt to answer these questions, then, might be a worthwhile venture.

The PINTO gasoline tank decision received a great deal of publicity, notoriety, it might be suggested, that it richly deserved. There are other equally repugnant examples of management amorality that have received widespread attention. Most recently, top management of Film Recover Systems, Inc., were convicted of murder for allowing non-English-speaking employees to work around dangerous chemicals. Bizarre responses are not uncommon. For example, George M. Steinbrenner, who had served as chief executive officer of American Shipbuilding, Inc., was found guilty of using corporate funds to make illegal campaign contributions during the 1972 presidential campaign. His debt to society was repaid with fines totaling $15,000. After Steinbrenner's conviction of a felony he was presented with an engraved plaque by Speaker of the House Carl Albert at the 1975 Democratic Congressional Victory Dinner. The audience of prominent political figures gave the "businessman, sports lover, political fund raiser, and felon" a lengthy ovation (Wall Street Journal, 1974). Other, less-publicized behaviors have, seemingly, passed almost unnoticed. For example, Jack L. Clark, who founded Four Seasons Nursing Centers of America, Inc., defrauded stockholders of $200 million, served nine months of a one-year sentence in a minimum security prison and enjoyed the advantages of four three-day furloughs at home during his stay. He retired to an 1800 acre cattle ranch upon his release (The Daily Oklahoman, 1975). Pollution, Pentagon-waste and override cases are additional examples indicating the magnitude of the problem of moral crises. Such behavior reflects an absence of moral precepts, principles that might guide behavior. The management behaviors above, it might be said, tend to illustrate the lack of proper education in moral behavior. But, can education result in moral behavior? Are there stages one moves through in developing moral precepts, like acquiring increasingly complex ideas in mathematics or language behavior? Is there, in fact, a relationship between cognitive development and moral development? If the answer to these questions is "yes," then what kind of education can best bring moral maturity about? It is the purpose of this paper to attempt answers to these questions. Concerning moral evolution, fascinating speculation is available (Kohlberg, 1969). Kohlberg sought to determine whether there are universal stages in the development of moral judgments. He presented stories such as the following one to children and adults of various ages and cultural backgrounds.

In Europe, a lady was dying because she was very sick. There was one drug that the doctors said might save her. This medicine was discovered by a man living in the same town. It cost him $200 to make it, but he charged $2000 for just a little of it. The sick lady's husband, Heinz, tried to borrow enough money to buy the drug. He went to everyone he knew to borrow the money. But he could borrow only half of what he needed. He told the man who made the drug that his wife was dying, and asked him to sell the medicine cheaper or let him pay later. But the man said, "No. I made the drug and I'm going to make money from it." So Heinz broke into the store and stole the drug.

The subject is asked, "Should Heinz have done that? Was it actually wrong or right? Why?" By analyzing the answers to a series of stories of this type (each portraying a moral dilemma) Kohlberg arrived at six developmental stages of moral judgment grouped into three broad levels (see Table 1). The answers are scored as belonging to a certain stage not on the basis of whether the action is judged right or wrong but on the reasons given for decision. For example, agreeing that Heinz should have stolen the drug because "if you let your wife die, you'll get in trouble" or condemning him for his actions because "If you steal the drug, you'll be caught and sent to jail" are both scored at Stage 1. In both instances, the man's actions are evaluated as right or wrong on the basis of anticipated punishment. Kohlberg's studies indicate that the moral judgments of children who are 7 years old and younger are predominantly at Level 1—actions are evaluated in terms of whether they avoid punishment or lead to rewards. By age 13, a majority of the moral dilemmas are resolved at Level II—actions are evaluated in terms of maintaining a good image in the eyes of other people. This is the level of conventional morality. In the first stage at this level (Stage 3), one seeks approval by being 'nice', this orientation expands in the next stage (Stage 4) to include 'doing one's duty', showing respect for authority, and conforming to the social order in which one is raised.

According to Kohlberg, many individuals never progress beyond Level II. He sees the stages of moral development as closely tied to Piaget's stages of cognitive development, and only those who have achieved the later stages of formal operational thought are capable of the kind of abstract thinking necessary for postconventional morality at Level III. The highest stage of moral development (Level III, Stage 6) requires formulating abstract ethical principles and upholding them to avoid self-condemnation. Kohlberg reports that fewer than 10

Table I

Levels and Stages		Illustrative Behavior
Level 1	Preconventional morality	
Stage 1	Punishment orientation	Obeys rules to avoid punishment
Stage 2	Reward orientation	Conforms to obtain rewards, to have favors returned
Level II	Conventional morality	
Stage 3	Good-boy/good-girl orientation	Conforms to avoid disapproval of others
Stage 4	Authority orientation	Upholds laws and social rules to avoid censure of authorities and feelings of guilt about not "doing one's duty"
Level III	Postconventional morality	
Stage 5	Social-contract orientation	Actions guided by principles commonly agreed on as essential to the public welfare: principles upheld to retain respect of peers and, thus self-respect
Stage 6	Ethical principle orientation	Actions guided by self-chosen ethical principles (that usually value justice, dignity, and equality); principles upheld to avoid self-condemnation

percent of his subjects over age 16 show the kind of "clear principled" Stage 6 thinking exemplified by the following response of a 16-year-old to Heinz's dilemma: "By the law of society he was wrong but by the law of nature or of God the druggist was wrong and the husband was justified. Human life is above financial gain. Regardless of who was dying, if it was a total stranger, man has a duty to save him from dying" (Kohlberg, 1972, p. 14).

Kohlberg views children as "moral philosophers" who develop moral standards of their own; these standards do not necessarily come from parents or peers but emerge from the cognitive interaction of children with their social environment. Movement from one stage to the next involves an internal cognitive reorganization rather than a simple acquisition of the moral concepts prevalent in their culture (Kohlberg, 1972).

It is this internal cognitive reorganization that is the focus of this paper. More specifically, how can we educate managers to: (1) integrate moral reasoning and moral behavior: (2) consider long-range consequences of one's actions (rather than the immediate gain) and to integrate one's behavior accordingly; and, (3) put oneself in someone else's place, that is, to integrate one's own understandings, to motivate oneself to help. Note that the key word above is "integrate", parallelling the correlation Kohlberg cites between the stages of moral development and stages of cognitive development. Just so, it shall be argued that an educational package that contains a strong integrative element is suggested to educate managers, and especially, to be moral agents.

FRAGMENTATION OF KNOWLEDGE

The basic problem resulting from a lack of integration is fragmentation of knowledge. William J. Bennett recently wrote that "When the humanities (or any group of course offerings) are presented as a series of isolated disciplinary packages, students cannot possibly see the interrelatedness of great works, ideas, and minds." This "often contributes to a fragmented, compartmentalized curriculum instead of an integrated, coherent one" (Bennett, 1984). This fragmentation prevents a unified approach to both education and life, resulting in narrowness and parochialism, and contributes to amorality, as previously discussed. Specifically, Kohlberg's Punishment reward orientation of Preconventional morality and the Conformity of Conventional morality result from the lack of a world view of real life. In the words of Paul L. Dressel and Dora Marcus, "The fatal defect of the single disciplinary approach to phenomena is that the disparate facts and principles accumulated through the independent application of several disciplines to a problem or phenomenon cannot easily be conjoined into a coherent picture of the totality" (Dressel and Marcus, 1982, 17). Nor is this a newly recognized problem. Recognition occurred at least as long ago as 1916 when Alfred North Whitehead wrote in The Aims of Education, that

> The problem with education is to make the pupil see the wood by means of the trees. The solution which I am urging is to eradicate the fatal disconnection of subjects which kills the vitality of our modern curriculum. There is only one subject-matter for education and that is Life in all its manifestations . . . The best that can be said of it [a non-integrative educational system] is that it is a rapid table of contents which a deity might run over in his mind while he was thinking of creating a world, and had not yet determined how to put it together (Whitehead, 1929).

The spin-off of fragmentation is intellectual, and thereby, moral stunting. Overall, the link of cognitive and moral behavior, therefore, is reinforced. An integrated education provides a "world view" of life as a totality. Only such an education, we suggest, can foster Kohlberg's notion of "Postconventional morality".

The resultant problem is difficulty with abstractions. According to the Study Group on Conditions of Excellence in American Higher Education, failure to teach the ability to synthesize, a failure which an integrated curriculum tries to overcome, results in college students having "considerable difficulty with abstractions and models that are the grounds of advanced study in the disciplines . . ." (Study Group, 1984). And, it might be added, advanced moral behavior.

Another problem stemming from lack of integration is distrust and suspicion. A study by Paul Ciholas of Kentucky State University of their general education program found that fragmentation of educational offerings "all too often, generates an unacceptable level of distrust and suspicion. Students tend to view the university not so much as a community of learning but a supermarket of programs. They consider as acceptable certain forms of 'ignorance' in relationship to disciplines they regard as unessential for their professional training" (Ciholas, 1983). This distrust occurs not only among the students but also among the faculty. It is not unusual to hear faculty denigrate other disciplines or faculty members in other disciplines. Indeed, both faculty and students seem to fall prey to Kohlberg's "Good-boy/ good-girl" and "Authority" orientations.

BENEFITS OF INTEGRATION

There are a number of benefits that can accrue from the implementation of an integrated general education curriculum. Among the major benefits are the following (note the links to Kohlberg's ideations): First, integration helps us to focus the questions that we ask. In the introductory essay to a book on interdisciplinarity, Alvin M. White writes that such an approach "helps us to understand why a question may be crucial in one context and meaningless in another, and how insight and ideas in seemingly unrelated disciplines can illuminate" fundamental questions (White, 1981). Locating questions, in turn, is fundamental to locating principles.

Second, integration teaches the ability to synthesize. This provides for a unitary approach to education and life which "is necessary for the development of judgment and for the application of academic learning to real life situations" (Study Group, 1984). Joseph A. Pichler, President of Dillon Companies, Inc., helps to make this case for integration: "Business subjects are comparatively weak in developing a facility for generating opportunities, exploring their full implications, and orchestrating choices to form a coherent strategy . . . In general, business must rely upon the arts and sciences to develop creative and integrative dispositions of mind." In order to do this, according to Pichler, the teaching of the courses has to be integrative in nature. "Study of the humanities does not guarantee that an individual will develop creative and integrative qualities of mind. If the humanities are taught in a disintegrated fashion, their contribution will not be much different from technical training" (Pichler, 1983). Judgment is essential to those ethical considerations inextricably interwoven with Kohlberg's "Ethical principle orientation."

Third, there are advantages for faculty as well as students. Ciholas lists four advantages: relief from the tedium that often accompanies traditional offerings; an increase in intellectual curiosity and creative approaches to teaching; improvement in the understanding of other areas of learning and a decrease in interdepartmental distrust; and, better student-teacher relationships resulting from faculty serving as educational models. These advantages were echoed by the experience with an integrative core general education curriculum at St. Joseph's College in Indiana. Malcolm Parlett of the Higher Education Study Group, who visited St. Joseph's College on several occasions, reported that

> It seemed obvious to me that faculty members got a lot out of taking part in the Core. They are personally stimulated; they find it interesting in an intellectual way; they report, in casual conversations, that they have learned this or that in the Core

. . . In collaborating together, and dealing with each other over issues of substantive business. I suspect that they got to know each other well and that there are myriad small benefits from the community as a whole.

Geoffrey Vickers, in the White edited book on interdisciplinarity, asks, "Might not ever specialties be better taught if teachers saw the subject matter in the context of all the other specialties to which they contribute and which contribute to them? If so, the question raised is not so much the general education of the students as the general education of the faculty. This general education of faculty, as well as of the students, would provide educational role models for the students, stimulate cross disciplinary discussions, and provide an exciting opportunity for intellectual growth and development. In the spirit of Kohlberg, an Ethical, moral community can be created. Principles commonly agreed on as essential to the Public welfare are adhered to and, thus, Self-condemnation is avoided.

Finally, and most importantly, there is what seems to be persuasive evidence that an integrative approach benefits the intellectual growth of students. The best empirical study of this issue that we know of was reported in A New Case for the Liberal Arts. After looking at several different programs, they concluded that "Our strong impression, then, is that institutions that stress the integration of ideas, courses, and disciplines are the ones whose students show the greatest growth in critical thinking" (Winter et al., 1983). Turning to a study of a specific college, they report that:

> In a study of the effects of this integrative program, we gave the Test of Thematic Analysis to sixty-six students from the joint humanities program at both the beginning and the end of the group of courses. As a control, we also tested sixty-seven students in regular courses in the same general area, or covering some of the same material, at the same two times. While the program students started out scoring higher than the controls (average score of 1.66 versus 1.22), they also tended to show greater gains from before to after the courses (average increase of +.50 as compared to +.08 for the controls, part of the difference in gains <.10 in the predicted directions>). This suggests that the actual experience of having to integrate two or more disciplines at the same time, guided by faculty committed to and encouraging such integration, brings about greater cognition growth than does studying the same material in separate courses without the consciously-designed integrative rubric (pp. 165–166).

This increase in cognitive skills would seem to warrant the implementation of a significantly integrated general education curriculum. An increase in cognitive skills, as we have seen, means an increase in dealing with principles. By extension, skills in integrating principles means attaining the Universal ethical principles orientation. Consider: integrating principles means that one is able to compare and contrast ideas and cognitions. Integration is impossible without this ability; one cannot integrate unless one can pick and choose among alternative principles, by comparison and contrast. Importantly, if one can compare and contrast principles, one can pick and choose among ethical principles that supersede any laws or social agreements. This goes beyond the social contract or legalistic orientation. Significantly, there is room for changing the law in order to better society. One behaves at Kohlberg's Sixth stage.

CONCLUSION

In keeping with all of the other studies on higher education which call for the integration of the general education component, the Carnegie Foundation report entitled *Common Learning*, in the lead essay by Ernest L. Boyer, refers to the changes taking place in our society and states that "seeing 'the connectedness of things,' is, we conclude, the goal of common learning" (Boyer, 1981). We conclude, in turn, that "seeing the connectedness of things" is the source of moral development. Therefore, a college's and a school of business' "Statement of Mission" should reflect this philosophy. It should set out what our students are taught, and should be taught: "to gather, organize, analyze and synthesize information, to think coherently, and to speak and write clearly." It should then state that the integration of these skills, including the ability to synthesize, into all aspects of our curricula "is considered essential for developing a flexible, self-renewing learner." It seems as if the time has come to begin to provide our students with an integrated general education package which reflects the changes taking place in our society, reflects the best current thinking about general education, and reflects what a School of Business' and a University's "Statement of Mission" ought to be. John Maynard Keynes once wrote that "the difficulty lies, not in the new ideas, but in escaping from the old ones." The changes leading to the information era indicate that advancing technology has mandated the development of new ideas with regard to education for the future. Now seems to be the time to escape from the strictures of a discipline-based general education program. Not to do so is to be caught in a kind of "time warp" from which we cannot escape, a "shock" from technological innovation from which we cannot awaken, an amorality we can not resolve. How many PINTO incidents can our civilization, itself, survive?

REFERENCES

Bennett, William J.: (November 28) 1984, "To Reclaim a Legacy", *The Chronicle of Higher Education*.

Boyer, Earnest L.: 1981, "The Quest for Common Learning", *Common Learning*, Washington, D.C.: The Carnegie Foundation.

Ciholas, Paul: 1983, *Integrative Studies*, draft proposal of a report on the Kentucky State University General Education Program.

The Daily Oklahoman: (June 26) 1974, 2.

Dressel, Paul L. and Dora Marcus: 1982, *On Teaching and Learning in College*, San Francisco: Jossey-Bass.

Kohlberg, L.: 1969, "Stage and Sequence: The Cognitive-Developmental Approach to Socialization" in D. Grosling (ed), *Handbook of Socialization Theory and Research*, Chicago: Rand McNally.

Kohlberg, L.: 1972, "A Cognitive-Developmental Approach to Moral Education", *The Humanist* **4**, 13-16.

Pichler, Joseph A.: 1983, "Executive Values, Executive Functions, and the Humanities". Speech given at the Proceedings of the conference on "The Humanities and Careers in Business'', sponsored by the Association of American Colleges and National Endowment for the Humanities.

Study Group on the Conditions of Excellence in American Higher Education: (October 24) 1984, ''Involvement in Learning: Realizing the Potential of American Higher Education'', *The Chronicle of Higher Education*, 35–49.

Whitehead, Alfred North: 1929, *The Aims of Education*, New York: Macmillan.

White, Alvin M. (ed): 1981, ''Introductory Remarks'', *Interdisciplinary Teaching*, San Francisco: Jossey-Bass.

Winter, David G., David C. McClelland and Abigail J. Steward: 1982, *A New Case for the Liberal Arts*, San Francisco: Jossey-Bass.

Chapter 2

Ethical Issues in Information Systems

Four Ethical Issues of the Information Age

Richard O. Mason

Reprinted by special permission from the *MIS Quarterly*, Volume 10, Number 1, March 1986. Copyright 1986 by the Society for Information Management and the Management Information Systems Research Center at the University of Minnesota.

Today in western societies more people are employed collecting, handling and distributing information than in any other occupation. Millions of computers inhabit the earth and many millions of miles of optical fiber, wire and air waves link people, their computers and the vast array of information handling devices together. Our society is truly an information society, our time an information age. The question before us now is whether the kind of society being created is the one we want. It is a question that should especially concern those of us in the MIS community for we are in the forefront of creating this new society.

There are many unique challenges we face in this age of information. They stem from the nature of information itself. Information is the means through which the mind expands and increases its capacity to achieve its goals, often as a result of an input from another mind. Thus, information forms the intellectual capital from which human beings craft their lives and secure dignity.

However, the building of intellectual capital is vulnerable in many ways. For example, people's intellectual capital is impaired whenever they lose their personal information without being compensated for it, when they are precluded access to information which is of value to them, when they have revealed information they hold intimate, or when they find out that the information upon which their lives depends is in error. The social contract among people in the information age must deal with these threats to human dignity. The ethical issues involved are many and varied, however, it is helpful to focus on just four. These may be summarized by means of an acronym—PAPA.

> Privacy: What information about one's self or one's associations must a person reveal to others, under what conditions and with what safeguards? What things can people keep to themselves and not be forced to reveal to others?

> Accuracy: Who is responsible for the authenticity, fidelity and accuracy of information? Similarly, who is to be held accountable for errors in information and how is the injured party to be made whole?

> Property: Who owns information? What are the just and fair prices for its exchange? Who owns the channels, especially the airways, through which information is transmitted? How should access to this scarce resource be allocated?

Accessibility: What information does a person or an organization have a right or a privilege to obtain, under what conditions and with what safeguards?

PRIVACY

What information should one be required to divulge about one's self to others? Under what conditions? What information should one be able to keep strictly to one's self? These are among the questions that a concern for privacy raises. Today more than ever cautious citizens must be asking these questions.

Two forces threaten our privacy. One is the growth of information technology, with its enhanced capacity for surveillance, communication, computation, storage, and retrieval. A second, and more insidious threat, is the increased value of information in decision-making. Information is increasingly valuable to policy makers; they covet it even if acquiring it invades another's privacy.

A case in point is the situation that occurred a few years ago in Florida. The Florida Legislature believed that the state's building codes might be too stringent and that, as a result, the taxpayers were burdened by paying for buildings which were underutilized. Several studies were commissioned. In one study at the Tallahassee Community College, monitors were stationed at least one day a week in every bathroom.

Every 15 seconds, the monitor observed the usage of the toilets, mirrors, sinks and other facilities and recorded them on a form. This data was subsequently entered into a database for further analyses. Of course the students, faculty and staff complained bitterly, feeling that this was an invasion of their privacy and a violation of their rights. State officials responded, however, that the study would provide valuable information for policy making. In effect the state argued that the value of the information to the administrators was greater than any possible indignities suffered by the students and others. Soon the ACLU joined the fray. At their insistence the study was stopped, but only after the state got the information it wanted.

Most invasions of privacy are not this dramatic or this visible. Rather, they creep up on us slowly as, for example, when a group of diverse files relating to a person and his or her activities are integrated into a single large database. Collections of information reveal intimate details about a person and can thereby deprive the person of the opportunity to form certain professional and personal relationships. This is the ultimate cost of an invasion of privacy. So why do we integrate databases in the first place? It is because the bringing together of disparate data makes the development of new informational relationships possible. These new relationships may be formed, however, without the affected parties' permission. You or I may have contributed information about ourselves freely to each of the separate databases but that by itself does not amount to giving consent to someone to merge the data, especially if that merger might reveal something else about us.

Consider the story that was circulating during the early 1970's. It's probably been embellished in the retellings but it goes something like this. It seems that a couple of programmers at the city of Chicago's computer center began matching tape files from many of the city's different data processing applications on name and I.D. They discovered, for example, that several high paid city employers had unpaid parking fines. Bolstered by this revelation they pressed on. Soon they uncovered the names of several employees who were still listed on the register but who had not paid a variety of fees, a few of whom appeared in the files of the alcoholic and drug abuse program. When this finding was leaked to the public the city employees, of course, were furious. They demanded to know who had authorized the investigation. The answer was that no one knew. Later, city officials established rules for the computer center to prevent this form of invasion of privacy from happening again. In light of recent proposals to develop a central federal databank consisting of files from most U.S. government agencies, this story takes on new meaning. It shows what can happen when a group of eager computer operators or unscrupulous administrators start playing around with data.

The threat to privacy here is one that many of us don't fully appreciate. I call it the threat of exposure by minute description. It stems from the collection of attributes about ourselves and use of the logical connector "and." For example, I may authorize one institution to collect information "A" about me, and another institution to collect information "B" about me; but I might not want anyone to possess "A and B" about me at the same time. When "C" is added to the list of conjunctions, the possessor of the new information will know even more about me. And the "D" is added and so forth. Each additional weaving together of my attributes reveals more and more about me. In the process, the fabric that is created poses a threat to my privacy.

The threads which emanate from this foreboding fabric usually converge in personnel files and in dossiers, as Aleksandr Solzhenitsyn describes in The Cancer Ward:

> "... Every person fills out quite a few forms in his life, and each form contains an uncounted number of questions. The answer of just one person to one question in one form is already a thread linking the person forever with the local center of the dossier department. Each person thus radiates hundreds of such threads, which all together, run into the millions. If these threads were visible, the heavens would be webbed with them, and if they had substance and resilience, the buses, street cars and the people themselves would no longer be able to move ... They are neither visible, nor material, but they were constantly felt by man ...
>
> Constant awareness of these invisible threads naturally bred respect for the people in charge of that most intricate dossier department. It bolstered their authority." (Solzhenitsyn, 1968, p. 221).

The threads leading to Americans are many. The United States Congress' Privacy Protection Commission, chaired by David F. Linowes, estimated that there are over 8,000 different record systems in the files of the federal government that contain individually identifiable data on citizens. Each citizen, on average, has 17 files in federal agencies and administrations. Using these files, for example, Social Security data has been matched with Selective Service data to reveal draft resisters. IRS data has been matched with other administrative records to tease out possible tax evaders. Federal employment records have been matched with delinquent student loan records to identify some 46,860 federal and military employees and retirees whose pay checks might be garnished. In Massachusetts welfare officials sent tapes bearing welfare recipients' Social Security numbers to some 117 banks to find out whether the recipients had bank accounts in excess of the allowable amount. During the first pass some 1600 potential violators were discovered.

Computer matching and the integration of data files into a central databank have enormous ethical implications. On the one hand, the new information can be used to uncover criminals and to identify service requirements for the needy. On the other hand, it provides powerful political knowledge for those few who have access to it and control over it. It is ripe for privacy invasion and other abuses. For this reason many politicians have spoken out against centralized governmental databanks. As early as 1966 Representative Frank Horton of New York described the threat as follows:

> "The argument is made that a central data bank would use only the type of information that now exists and since no new principle is involved, existing types of safeguards will be adequate. This is fallacious. Good computermen know that one of the most practical of our present safeguards of privacy is the fragmented nature of present information. It is scattered in little bits and pieces across the geography and years of our life. Retrieval is impractical and often impossible. A central data bank removes completely this safeguard. I have every confidence that ways will be found for all of us to benefit from the great advances of the computermen, but those benefits must never be purchased at the price of our freedom to live as individuals with private lives . . ." (U.S. House of Representatives, 1966, p.6)

There is another threat inherent in merging data files. Some of the data may be in error. More than 60,000 state and local agencies, for example, provide information to the National Crime Information Center and it is accessed by law officers nearly 400,000 times a day. Yet studies show that over 4% of the stolen vehicle entries, 6% of the warrant entries, and perhaps as much as one half of the local law enforcement criminal history records are in error. At risk is the safety of the law enforcement officers who access it, the effectiveness of the police in controlling crime, and the freedom of the citizens whose names appear in the files. This leads to a concern for accuracy.

ACCURACY

Misinformation has a way of fouling up people's lives, especially when the party with the inaccurate information has an advantage in power and authority. Consider the plight of one Louis Marches. Marches, an immigrant, was a hard working man who, with his wife Eileen, finally saved enough money to purchase a home in Los Angeles during the 1950's. They took out a long term loan from Crocker National Bank. Every month Louis Marches would walk to his neighborhood bank, loan coupon book in hand, to make his payment of $195.53. He always checked with care to insure that the teller had stamped "paid" in his book on the proper line just opposite the month for which the payment was due. And he continued to do this long after the bank had converted to its automated loan processing system.

One September a few years ago Marches was notified by the bank that he had failed to make his current house payment. Marches grabbed his coupon book, marched to the bank and, in broken English that showed traces of his old country heritage, tried to explain to the teller that this dunning notice was wrong. He had made his payment he claimed. The stamp on his coupon book proved that he had paid. The teller punched Marches' loan number on the keyboard and reviewed the resulting screen. Unfortunately she couldn't confirm Marches' claim, nor subsequently could the head teller, nor the branch manager. When faced with a computer generated screen that clearly showed that his account was delinquent, this hierarchy of bankers simply ignored the entries recorded in his coupon book and also his attendant raving. Confused, Marches left the bank in disgust.

In October, however, Marches dutifully went to the bank to make his next payment. He was told that he could not make his October payment because he was one month in arrears. He again showed the teller his stamped coupon book. She refused to accept it and he stormed out of the bank. In November he returned on schedule as he had done for over 20 years and tried to make his payment again, only to be told that he was now two months in arrears. And so it went until inevitably the bank foreclosed. Eileen learned of the foreclosure from an overzealous bank debt collector while she was in bed recovering from a heart attack. She collapsed upon hearing the news and suffered a near fatal stroke which paralyzed her right side. Sometime during this melee Marches, who until this time had done his own legal work, was introduced to an attorney who agreed to defend him. They sued the bank. Ultimately, after months of anguish, the Marches received a settlement for $268,000. All that the bank official who testified could say was, "Computers make mistakes. Banks make mistakes, too."

A special burden is placed on the accuracy of information when people rely on it for matters of life and death, as we increasingly do. This came to light in a recent $3.2 million lawsuit charging the National Weather Service for failing to predict accurately a storm that raged on the southeast slope of Georges Bank in 1980. As Peter Brown steered his ship— The Sea Fever—from Hyannis Harbor toward his lobster traps near Nova Scotia, he monitored weather conditions using a long range, single sideband radio capable of receiving weather forecasts at least 100 miles out to sea. The forecasts assured him that his destination area near Georges Bank, although it might get showers, was safe from the hurricane. The storm that the weather bureau had predicted would go far to the east of his course. So he kept to his course. Soon, however, his ship was engulfed in howling winds of 80 knots and waves cresting at 60 feet. In the turbulence Gary Brown, a crew member, was washed overboard.

The source of the fatal error was failure of a large-scale information system which collects data from high atmosphere balloon satellites, ships, and a series of buoys. The data is then transmitted to a National Oceanographic and Atmospheric Administrative computer which analyzes it and produces forecasts. The forecasts, in turn, are broadcast widely.

The forecast Peter Brown relied on when he decided to proceed into the North Atlantic was in error because just one buoy—station 44003 Georges Bank—was out of service. As a result the wind speed and direction data normally provided were lost to the computer model. This caused the forecasted trajectory of the storm to be canted by several miles, deceiving skipper Peter Brown, and consequently sending Gary Brown to his death.

Among the questions this raises for us in the information age are these: "How many Louis Marches and Gary Browns are there out there?" "How many are we creating every day?" The Marches received a large financial settlement; but can they ever be repaid for the irreparable harm done to them and to their dignity? Honour Brown, Gary's widow, received a judgment in her case; but has she been repaid for the loss of Gary? The point is this: We run the risk of creating Gary Browns and Louis Marches every time we design information systems and place information in databases which might be used to make decisions. So it is our responsibility to be vigilant in the pursuit of accuracy in information. Today we are producing so much information about so many people and their activities that our exposure to problems of inaccuracy are enormous. And this growth in information also raises another issue: Who owns it?

PROPERTY

One of the most complex issues we face as a society is the question of intellectual property rights. There are substantial economic and ethical concerns surrounding these rights; concerns revolving around the special attributes of information itself and the means by which it is transmitted. Any individual item of information can be extremely costly to produce in the first instance. Yet, once it is produced, that information has the illusive quality of being easy to reproduce and to share with others. Moreover, this replication can take place without destroying the original. This makes information hard to safeguard since, unlike tangible property, it becomes communicable and hard to keep it to one's self. It is even difficult to secure appropriate reimbursements when somebody else uses your information.

We currently have several imperfect institutions that try to protect intellectual property rights. Copyrights, patents, encryption, oaths of confidentiality, and such old fashioned values as trustworthiness and loyalty are the most commonly used protectors of our intellectual property. Problem issues, however, still abound in this area. Let us focus on just one aspect: artificial intelligence and its expanding subfield, expert systems.

To fully appreciate our moral plight regarding expert systems it is necessary to run back the clock a bit, about two hundred years, to the beginnings of another society: the steam energy-industrial society. From this vantage point we may anticipate some of the problems of the information society.

As the industrial age unfolded in England and Western Europe a significant change took place in the relationship between people and their work. The steam engine replaced manpower by reducing the level of personal physical energy required to do a job. The factory system, as Adam Smith described in his essay on the pin factory, effectively replaced the laborer's contribution of his energy and of his skills. This was done by means of new machines and new organizational forms. The process was carried even further in the French community of Lyon. There, Joseph Marie Jacquard created a weaving loom in which a system of rectangular, punched holes captured the weaver's skill for directing the loom's mechanical fingers and for controlling the warp and weft of the threads. These Jacquard looms created a new kind of capital which was produced by disembodying energy and skill from the craftsmen and then reembodying it into the machines. In effect, an exchange of property took place. Weaving skills were transferred from the craftsman to the owner of the machines. With this technological innovation Lyon eventually regained its position as one of the leading silk producers in the world. The weavers themselves, however, suffered unemployment and degradation because their craft was no longer economically viable. A weaver's value as a person and a craftsman was taken away by the new machines.

There is undoubtedly a harbinger of things to come in these 18th century events. As they unfolded civilization witnessed one of the greatest outpourings of moral philosophy it has ever seen: Adam Smith's *Theory of Moral Sentiments* and his *Wealth of Nations*; the American revolution and its classic documents on liberty and freedom; the French revolution and its concern for fraternity and equality; John Stuart Mill and Jeremy Bentham and their ethical call for the greatest good for the greatest number, and Immanuel Kant and his categorical imperative which leads to an ethical utopia called the "kingdom of ends." All of this ethical initiative took place within the historically short span of time of about 50 years. Common to these ideas was a spirit which sought a new meaning in human life and which demanded that a just allocation be made of social resources.

Today that moral spirit may be welling up within us again. Only this time it has a different provocator. Nowhere is the potential threat to human dignity so severe as it is in the age of information technology, especially in the field of artificial intelligence. Practitioners of artificial intelligence proceed by extracting knowledge from experts, workers and the knowledgeable, and then implanting it into computer software where it becomes capital in the economic sense. This process of "disemminding" knowledge from an individual, and subsequently "emminding" it into machines transfers control of the property to those who own the hardware and software. Is this exchange of property warranted? Consider some of the most successful commercial artificial intelligence systems of the day. Who owns, for example, the chemical knowledge contained in DENDRAL, the medical knowledge contained in MYCIN, or the geological knowledge contained in PROSPECTOR? How is the contributor of his knowledge to be compensated? These are among the issues we must resolve as more intelligent information systems are created.

Concern over intellectual property rights relates to the content of information. There are some equally pressing property rights issues surrounding the conduits through which information passes. Bandwidth, the measure of capacity to carry information, is a scarce and ultimately fixed commodity. It is a "commons." A commons is like an empty vessel into which drops of water can be placed freely and easily until it fills and overflows. Then its capacity is gone. As a resource it is finite.

In an age in which people benefit by the communication of information, there is a tendency for us to treat bandwidth and transmission capacity as a commons in the same way as did the herdsmen in Garrett Hardin's poignant essay, "The Tragedy of the Commons," (subtitled: "The population problem has no technical solution; it requires a fundamental extension in morality"). Each herdsman received direct benefits from adding an animal to a pasture shared in common. As long as there was plenty of grazing capacity the losses due to the animal's consumption were spread among them and felt only indirectly and proportionally much less. So each herdsman was motivated to increase his flock. In the end, however, the commons was destroyed and everybody lost.

Today our airways are becoming clogged with a plethora of data, voice, video, and message transmission. Organizations and individuals are expanding their use of communications because it is profitable for them to do so. But if the social checks on the expanded use of bandwidth are inadequate, and a certain degree of temperance isn't followed, we may find that jamming and noise will destroy the flow of clear information through the air. How will the limited resource of bandwidth be allocated? Who will have access? This leads us to the fourth issue.

ACCESS

Our main avenue to information is through literacy. Literacy, since about 1500 A.D. when the Syrians first conceived of a consonant alphabet, has been a requirement for full participation in the fabric of society. Each innovation in information handling, from the invention of paper to the modern computer, has placed new demands on achieving literacy. In an information society a citizen must possess at least three things to be literate:

One must have the intellectual skills to deal with information. These are skills such as reading, writing, reasoning, and calculating. This is a task for education.

One must have access to the information technologies which store, convey and process information. This includes libraries, radios, televisions, telephones, and increasingly, personal computers or terminals linked via networks to mainframes. This is a problem in social economics.

Finally, one must have access to the information itself. This requirement returns to the issue of property and is also a problem in social economics.

These requirements for literacy are a function of both the knowledge level and the economic level of the individual. Unfortunately, for many people in the world today both of these levels are currently deteriorating.

There are powerful factors working both for and against contemporary literacy in our organizations and in our society. For example, the cost of computation, as measured in, say, dollars per MIPS (millions of instructions per second), has gone down exponentially since the introduction of computers. This trend has made technology more accessible and economically attainable to more people. However, corporations and other public and private organizations have benefited the most from these economies. As a result, cost economics in computation are primarily available to middle and upper income people. At the same time, computer usage flourishes among poor people who have no direct access to the more efficient computational technology and who have little training in its use.

Reflect for a moment on the social effects of electronically stored databases. Prior to their invention, vast quantities of data about publications, news events, economic and social statistics, and scientific findings have been available in printed, microfilm, or microfiche form at relatively low cost. For most of us access to this data has been substantially free. We merely went to our public or school library. The library, in turn, paid a few hundred dollars for the service and made it available to whomever asked for it. Today, however, much of this information is being converted to computerized databases and the cost to access these databases can run in the thousands of dollars.

Frequently, access to databases is gained only by means of acquiring a terminal or personal computer. For example, if you want access to the *New York Times Index* through the Mead Corporation service you must first have access to a terminal and communication line and then pay additional hook-up and access fees in order to obtain the data. This means that the people who wish to use this service possess several things. First, they know that the database exists and how to use it. Second, they have acquired the requisite technology to access it. And third, they are able to pay the fees for the data. Thus the educational and economic ante is really quite high for playing the modern information game. Many people cannot or choose not to pay it and hence are excluded from participating fully in our society. In effect, they become information "drop outs" and in the long run will become the source of many social problems.

PAPA

Privacy, accuracy, property and accessibility, these are the four major issues of information ethics for the information age. Max Plank's 1900 conception that energy was released in small discrete packets called "quanta" not only gave rise to atomic theory but also permitted the development of information technology as well. Semiconductors, transistors, integrated circuits, photoelectric cells, vacuum tubes, and ferrite cores are among the technological yield of this scientific theory. In a curious way quantum theory underlies the four issues as well. Plank's theory, and all that followed it, have led us to the point where the stakes surrounding society's policy agenda are incredibly high. At stake with the use of nuclear energy is the very survival of mankind itself. If we are unwise we will either blow ourselves up or contaminate our world forever with nuclear waste. At stake with the increased use of information technology is the quality of our lives should we, or our children, survive. If we are unwise many people will suffer information bankruptcy or desolation.

Our moral imperative is clear. We must insure that information technology, and the information it handles, are used to enhance the dignity of mankind. To achieve these goals we must formulate a new social contract, one that insures everyone the right to fulfill his or her own human potential.

In the new social contract information systems should not unduly invade a person's privacy to avoid the indignities that the students in Tallahassee suffered.

Information systems must be accurate to avoid the indignities the Marches and the Browns suffered.

Information systems should protect the viability of the fixed conduit resource through which it is transmitted to avoid noise and jamming pollution and the indignities of "The Tragedy of the Commons."

Information systems should protect the sanctity of intellectual property to avoid the indignities of unwitting "disemmindment" of knowledge from individuals.

And information systems should be accessible to avoid the indignities of information illiteracy and deprivation.

This is a tall order; but it is one that we in the MIS community should address. We must assume some responsibility for the social contract that emerges from the systems that we design and implement. In summary, we must insure that the flow of those little packets of energy and information called quanta, that Max Plank bequeathed to us some 85 years ago, are used to create the kind of world in which we wish to live.

REFERENCES

Solzhenitsyn, Aleksandr I., *The Cancer Ward*, Dial Press, New York, New York, 1968.

U.S. House of Representatives, *The Computer and Invasion of Privacy*, U.S. Government Printing Office, Washington DC, 1966.

Assessing the Ethical Standards and Policies in Computer-Based Environments

Karen A. Forcht

Current address: Department of Information and Decision Sciences, College of Business, James Madison University, Harrisonburg, VA 22807, (703) 568–6889/6812. Printed by permission of Karen A. Forcht.

ABSTRACT

This chapter reports the results of a questionnaire mailed to the chief executive officers of the *Datamation* 100 companies to ascertain their assessments concerning the ethical standards that have been formally adopted by their organizations and to seek their opinions about the informal ethical environment that may be present in their organizations. The respondent's personal opinions concerning the ethical use of computers was evaluated, using a Likert scale. In addition, miscellaneous information is reported on the respondents' opinions concerning the most serious ethical dilemma they have personally faced on their job, how public figures aid in the development of ethical standards in our society today, whether the respondent's organization has a formal ethics policy, how the respondents rate themselves in terms of moral conduct, ethical behavior, and law-abiding citizen.

The data analysis indicates that, for the most part, the CEOs responding adhere to a very high standard of personal ethical conduct of computer use. Furthermore, and most importantly, they expect (and require) that their employees follow ethical standards. This ethical attitude is reinforced by ethics codes, ethics awareness programs, and sanctions/reprimands of offending employees.

INTRODUCTION

The subjects of computer security and computer-based crime have been the focus of substantial debate during the past decade; however, the issues involved are far from resolved. A variety of measures have been instituted, enforced, and monitored to ensure that computer centers are not vulnerable to human intervention—whether accidental or intentional. Unfortunately, this physical interpretation of security represents only one facet of a complex problem. The misuse of computer software and stored data and information may ultimately prove to be the more significant concern. In short, it is not yet clear to all parties involved in computer use just what acts should be considered as computer crime.

In the past few years, interest in the issue of ethics has been heightened as we now focus on the "people side" of computer security. The copying of a software program for a friend,

56

while in direct violation of copyright laws and, therefore, technically a crime, may not be considered as serious to the user as stealing a physical system component or sabotaging a system for profit or revenge. The paramount question then becomes one of, "What are the definitive responsibilities of computer center employees or persons having access to software and information to the public they serve—the ultimate user or owner of information—in creating an 'environment of security' and in practicing solid ethical standards in regard to the valuable data they use when performing their jobs?"

DEFINING ETHICAL STANDARDS

"Ethics can be defined as the science of social survival; what is ethical promotes the survival of individuals and civilizations, cultures, and societies" (Bernier, 1985). Every culture, no matter how civilized or primitive, has an ethical code. Some codes tend to be rather formal and are entered into, unknowingly, at birth as they are a definite part of the social culture. Other ethical codes develop as we grow, becoming a vital part of our personal and professional lives. Our ethical code is formed and shaped "by experience (especially historical experience), experiment, and measurement" (Bernier, 1985). Throughout our lives, we are constantly faced with the dichotomous dilemma of right versus wrong, good versus bad.

Legal Versus Ethical Versus Moral

When asked to identify the parameters that govern our lives, three key areas generally emerge: laws, ethics, and morals. The delineation between the three becomes "cloudy" as they tend to overlap, depending on the particular situation and the individual's interpretation. (See Figure 1.)

Many laws enforce ethical standards in our civilized society and prohibit citizens from "acting out of their own volition," thus insuring and promulgating a sense of social structure. On the other hand, many acts that are considered to be immoral or unethical are not necessarily illegal. Laws are enacted to ensure that a society has definite rules of behavior—those persons violating acceptable rules are to be punished or dealt with according to our estab-

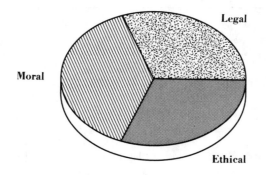

Figure 1. Parameters Governing Our Lives

lished sanctions. Even though laws vary from one locality to the next and over periods of time, they do serve as an absolute—a known. The real dilemma is in defining or clarifying morality and ethics. "Morality, generally speaking is the attempt to control humanity's most powerful social forces—sex, money, and power—while ethics is the philosophic or objective study of abstractions called 'the good or right conduct' " (Levine, 1986). Our religious convictions tend to provide our moral fiber and separate the good from the bad.

Ethics, conversely, is a cultural conditioning that builds on our religious convictions and is influenced by our societal beliefs, our family background, our geographic bearing, etc. Ethics then becomes the "melting pot" of those gray areas not covered with formal sanctions, such as laws, or religious convictions.

If we were to develop a quadrant theory of acceptable behavior (see Figure 2), ethics would be a factor in all quadrants as a certain amount of interpretation and assimilation takes place in any situational analysis.

The most simplistic, easy-to-accept quadrant would be the legal and moral (B). If a person donates to a charity, it would be considered both legal and moral. The issue of ethics may not be a valid consideration in this example as the situation is somewhat "clear-cut." To further explain the theory, a person might view an act such as robbing a bank as falling into quadrant C—without question. The act is both immoral and illegal as we adhere to the religious doctrine of "Thou Shalt Not Steal" and also known legal sanctions concerning theft of someone else's property.

On the other hand, not fully divulging information for income tax purposes may fall

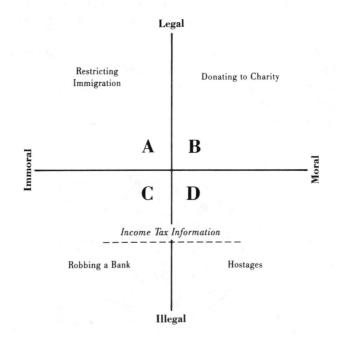

Figure 2. Quadrants of Acceptable Behavior

between quadrants C and D—illegal, but moral—at least in some people's minds, as they tend to rationalize that "everyone does it," thus absolving themselves of personal guilt.

A situation that may fall into the A quadrant—legal, but immoral—could be a country's policy on restricting immigration quotas. The laws currently in effect may enforce limitation, but morally, we face the dilemma of right versus wrong.

Realistically, people are much more complex than this quadrant theory implies. Our ethics and moral "space" become a matter of personal conjecture—we accept a code we can live with comfortably.

The constant dilemma of deciding between what is legal and ethical is a "cloudy" one that pervades all facets of our personal and professional lives. This "cloudiness" is further compounded by an ever increasing complexity of our environment.

The Information Age

As our society moves into an Age of Information, more and more people are involved in collecting, handling, distributing, and using information than previously thought imaginable. John Naisbitt's prediction in *Megatrends* that "the new source of power is not money in the hands of few but information in the hands of many" (Naisbitt, 1982) is becoming increasingly a reality of our "high-tech" society. The tremendous impact of information is also noted by Richard Mason in his statement, "information forms the intellectual capital from which human beings craft their lives and secure dignity" (Mason, 1986). Mason further postulates that the four ethical issues of the Information Age are:

Privacy

What information about one's self or one's association must a person reveal to others, under what conditions and with what safeguards? What things can people keep to themselves and not be forced to reveal to others?

Accuracy

Who is responsible for the authenticity, fidelity and accuracy of information? Similarly, who is to be accountable for errors in information and how is the injured party to be made whole?

Property

Who owns information? What are the just and fair prices for its exchange?

Who owns the channels, especially the airways, through which information is transmitted? How should access to this scarce resource be allocated?

Accessibility

What information does a person or an organization have a right or a privilege to obtain, under what conditions and what safeguards?

Mason's four issues form a composite nucleus of the major issues facing our information society—not an easy solution or a "quick fix." He states that:

Our moral imperative is clear. We must insure that information technology, and the information it handles, are used to enhance the dignity of mankind. To achieve these goals, we must formulate a new social contract, one that insures everyone the right to fulfill his or her own human potential (and) . . . create the kind of world in which we wish to live.

Mason's beliefs may well serve as a guide in establishing ethical behavior patterns that are not only acceptable, but plausible.

Sieber (1986) states that "simple control of employees does not constitute sufficient personnel politics. The application of adequate safety measures and the honest behavior of employees will also be influenced by their *motivation*." Sieber further postulates that the following measures should be instituted:

employee counseling and security briefings to develop awareness of risks
development of a good business atmosphere, fair practices, and an aura of a privileged elite
positive examples of moral leadership by directors

Computer-Related Legislation

Many states have enacted laws dealing with computer crime; however, there is a substantial difference between what the individual states define as illegal, the significance of the act (misdemeanor or felony), and the punishments prescribed. The Computer Security Act of 1987, which was passed by the United States Senate and the House of Representatives, should add impetus to the problem of coping with computer security violations. The general intent as stated in the opening paragraph is that:

The Congress declares that improving the security and privacy of sensitive information in Federal computer systems is in the public interest, and hereby creates a means for establishing minimum acceptable security practices for such systems, without limiting the scope of security measures already planned or in use. (Computer Security Act of 1987)

Jay BloomBecker, the founder and Director of the National Center for Computer Crime Data in Los Angeles, addresses the need for the development of ". . . computer ethics as a solution to the nebulous computer crime problem" (Leinfus, 1986). BloomBecker also points out that there is virtually no way of knowing how much computer crime goes unreported as companies are often reluctant to report a violation and, thereby, alerting the general public to the vulnerability of their system.

Crimes of Technology and Intellect

The paramount problem with relying on legal sanctions to protect information and punish violators is that our legal system responds to human activity/violations, rather than serving as a predictor—a reactive, rather than a proactive approach.

The crimes of technology and intellect, warned Edwin H. Sutherland in the 1940s, are potentially far more serious than the crimes generally associated with the poor and the under-educated (Bequai, 1978). How prophetic this statement was to become as the legal community and general public had no way of knowing that within the next 40 years, misuse of information, hacking, theft of vital data, diversion of funds, etc., would become a reality. As the general public becomes increasingly "computer literate," the gap between technology versus intellect shrinks considerably. Computers are no longer high-powered machines for the knowledgeable few, but tools for the enlightened many. The danger is real that the computer abuse problem will possibly reach epidemic proportions by the year 2000 if not curtailed by legal sanctions—coupled with the adoption of accepted standards of ethical conduct.

CODE OF ETHICS

Many professional groups are attempting to formulate some definitive guidelines in this computer "sea of uncertainty" by proposing formal Codes of Ethics. "The current concept today in evaluating a computer security program is 'prevention on the front end—not just punishment on the back end'" (Forcht and Pierson, 1987). This "preventative maintenance" concept should be practiced by ALL members of the organization—users included—to be truly effective.

Objectives of Ethics Codes

Johnson and Snapper (1985) state in *Ethical Issues in the Use of Computers* that ethics codes should emphasize five basic objectives:

Inspirational—to inspire members to be more "ethical" in their conduct.
Sensitivity—to alert professionals to the moral aspects of their work.
Disciplinary—to enforce certain rules of the profession on its members and defend integrity.
Advising—to offer guidance in cases of moral perplexity about what to do.
Awareness—to alert prospective clients and employees to what they may and may not expect by way of service from a member of the profession concerned.

If a company or organization decides to develop an ethics awareness program or adopt a formal code, several factors should be considered, including:

Certification—an affirmation by a governmental or private organization that an individual has met certain qualifications.
Licensing—the administrative lifting of a legislative prohibition.
Accreditation—an affirmation by a governmental or private organization that an educational institution meets certain standards.
Ethics—a standard of conduct drawn up by an organization to protect the consumer and competition against "unfair" practices.

Accepted Codes of Ethics

At the present time, there are five widely accepted Codes of Ethics in the computer profession: the British Computer Society (BCS) *Code of Conduct,* the Data Processing Management Association (DPMA) *Code of Ethics, Standards of Conduct and Enforcement Procedures,* the Association for Computing Machinery (ACM) *Professional Conduct and Procedures for the Enforcement of the ACM Code of Professional Conduct,* the Institute of Electrical and Electronics Engineers (IEEE) *Code of Ethics,* and the Institute for Certification of Computer Professionals (ICCP) *Codes of Ethics and Good Practices.* While there are many similarities and major points of emphasis in the individual codes, there are some basic differences based primarily on the nature of computer-related projects being conducted by the members of each organization.

RESEARCH METHODOLOGY

The purpose of the research described in this paper was to determine the opinions of Chief Executive Officers of the *Datamation* 100 (June 15, 1988, listing) concerning ethical use of computers in their organizations.

The research method consisted of a survey in which questionnaires were mailed to the 100 CEOs of the *Datamation* 100 companies. To protect the privacy of the individual, the questionnaires were not coded and no follow-up was sent to non-respondents. The *Datamation* 100 listing was chosen as it represents the world-wide companies that deliver a global menu of tools for today's technology managers. In 1987, the *Datamation* 100 were responsible for IS revenue of over $208 billion, which represents 80% of the world IS industry's total sales.

To explore the opinions of the CEOs of these companies concerning their opinions and corporations' policies concerning the ethical use of computers, the following areas/topics were presented:

Demographic Information—including number of employees in their company, the title of the respondent, total number of years' experience within information, systems/computer-related position, and respondent's age

Respondent's Personal Opinions Concerning Ethical Use of Computers—twenty statements rated on a 1–5 Likert scale, covering various types of computer-related abuse, misuse, questionable actions, etc.

Miscellaneous Information—most serious ethical dilemma facing respondents on their job *at the present time* (narrative comments), how can public figures aid in the development of ethical standards in our society today (narrative comments), whether their company has a formal ethics policy (Yes or No), and personal rating of moral conduct, ethical behavior, law-abiding citizen (High, Average, Low).

SURVEY RESULTS

During the spring of 1989, questionnaires were sent to the CEOs of the *Datamation* 100 companies worldwide.

The following analysis was based on 30 responses, representing a return rate of 30%. Three responses were incomplete and, therefore, unusable, making the total number of valid responses 27. As stated earlier, no follow-up or coding of questionnaires was utilized so that complete anonymity was guaranteed in a survey of such a private nature.

DEMOGRAPHIC SAMPLE CHARACTERISTICS

Over 80% of the respondents reported that their organizations had more than 1,000 employees (83.3%). The respondents, being Chief Executive Officers of large organizations, tended to have a lengthy experience level within information systems/computer-related positions. Over 60% (18 respondents) reported more than 14 years experience. Most of the respondents were between the ages of 31–60, with 23.3% reporting 31–40 years, 26.7% reporting 41–50 years of age, and 30.0% reporting 51–60 years of age. A very small percentage were under 30 (6.7%) and only 3.3% were over 60. Over 80% of the respondents were male (24).

RESPONDENTS' OPINIONS CONCERNING ETHICAL USE OF COMPUTERS

The respondents were asked to respond to twenty statements concerning their opinions on various ethical issues relating to computer usage. The respondent was asked to reflect his/her *personal opinions only*—not necessarily the official corporate policy. A Likert scale as follows was used:

Strongly Agree (5)
Agree (4)
No Opinion (3)
Disagree (2)
Strongly Disagree (1)

For clarification in evaluating the results, the opinions were grouped into three categories as follows.

MISUSE OF COMPUTERS

Copying Proprietary Software

In response to the statement, "it is acceptable for employees to copy proprietary software to evaluate for future purchase," 50% (15) strongly disagreed, and 33.3% (10) disagreed. Hopefully, this indicates an effort on the part of CEOs to recognize the copyright infringement that is occurring today in many organizations and to instill policies to thwart/deter illegal copying.

Copying Software for Personal Use

Response to the statement, "if your company has purchased/developed proprietary software for use in the office, it is acceptable for employees to copy this software for personal use at home," indicated that over 60% strongly disagreed and 30% disagreed. This response reinforces the opinions given previously regarding the copying of proprietary software for future purchase evaluation.

Using Company's Computer for Personal Benefit

The statement, "it is fair to use your company's computer for your personal benefit if it has no adverse effect on other users," indicated responses that were more spread out with 23.3%

(7) strongly disagreeing, 30% (9) disagreeing, 16.7% (5) having no opinion, 13.3% (4) agreeing, and 3.3% (1) strongly agreeing. While the predominant number (over 50%) do not approve of using a company's computer facilities for personal benefit, a significant number approve of the idea or have no feeling against this practice. Perhaps the company's policies should be reassessed and shared with employees so that an acceptable policy can be followed by all employees.

"Snooping" Through Files

When asked, "it is acceptable to 'snoop' through other people's files if they do not take adequate password protection and access is relatively easy," over 85% disagreed (43.3% [13] strongly disagreed and 33.3% [10] disagreed.) The ethics of 'snooping' are obviously an act that these CEOs view with disfavor.

Using Computers in "Off" Hours

In response to the statement, "using an organization's computer to run a profit-generating business (private consulting, contract programming, etc.) is acceptable if done on 'off' hours," nearly 85% of the respondents disagreed (53.3% [16] strongly disagreed and 30.07% [9] disagreed). Many companies are recognizing that any unauthorized use of computer facilities can cause serious vulnerabilities in their authorized programs/applications, therefore, only preauthorized applications are allowed.

Computer Piracy

In response to the statement, "computer piracy is as serious an offense as driving while intoxicated," the responses were varied with 16.7% strongly disagreeing, 20.0% disagreeing, 16.7% having no opinion, 23.3% agreeing, and 10.0% strongly agreeing.

HUMAN FACTORS

Importance of Human Factor

When asked, "in information systems processing, the human factor is considered to be less critical than the technology factors," 23.3% (7) strongly disagreed and 43.3% (13) disagreed, thus pointing out that the human side of technology is still in the forefront of the high-tech information explosion.

Requiring an Ethics Oath

When asked whether, "companies should require all employees to sign an ethics oath before beginning work," 3.3% (1) strongly disagreed, 13.3% (4) disagreed, 16.7% (5) had no opinion, 40.0% (12) agreed and 16.7% (5) strongly agreed. With over 50% of the respondents indicating that they agreed to the required signing of an ethics oath, it is evident that companies are putting some degree of emphasis on ethical practices by their employees.

Authorized Use of Electronic Surveillance

In response to the statement, "employers should be authorized to use electronic surveillance to monitor employees' performance," the responses were varied with 23.7% (7) strongly disagreeing, 20.0% (6) disagreeing, 23.3% (7) indicating no opinion, 16.7% (5) agreeing, and 6.7% (2) strongly agreeing. These varied responses would seem to indicate that further clarification on the use of electronic monitoring, from both a legal and ethical perspective, is needed in order to standardize a very questionable use of technology.

Scrutinizing Computer Center Employees

In response to the statement, "computer center employees should be more closely scrutinized than other employees as they have more access to information," nearly half of the respondents agreed (33% [9] and 13.3% [4] strongly agreed). This statement is quite controversial as many IS employees feel they should not be held more accountable than the other employees. Many companies, however, do require computer center employees to sign, and adhere to, an additional ethics oath.

Sanctioning/Reprimanding Employees

In response to the statement, "my company follows acceptable procedures in sanctioning/ reprimanding employees who violate ethical procedures," over 50% (56.7) agreed and 23.3% strongly agreed.

Ownership of Created Product

The statement, "employees should be allowed to recreate a product/program/design for another company if they change jobs and are no longer employed by the company who paid them to create it," showed that 60% (18) strongly disagreed and 16.7% (5) disagreed. Many employees are required to sign an agreement when beginning employment to waive their rights to ownership of the products they create while employed by the company. The agreements are usually found in favor of the company when challenged in court.

Using Consultant's Work

In response to the statement, "it is acceptable for a client, after they have paid the consultant, to use the consultant's work without his/her knowledge," nearly 40% (36.7) agreed and 20% strongly agreed. This issue tends to be somewhat controversial as consultants' "intellectual creations" are involved. Consequently, most companies (and many consultants) sign an agreement prior to starting a project to ensure the legality of the consultant's work for hire.

Termination of Unethical Employees

The statement, "employees should be immediately terminated if they perform an unethical act," showed that over 40% disagreed and over 40% agreed (6.7% [2] strongly disagreed, 26.7% [8] disagreed, 33.3% [10] agreed, and 13.3% [4] strongly agreed). Many times, termination involves questions of legal issues, discrimination, just cause, proof, and personnel departments are somewhat reluctant to terminate employees on ethical issues alone. Legal factors and considerations involving the definition of unethical acts help to divide this issue of termination.

Violation of Employee's Civil Rights

In response to the statement, "when employees are required to sign a pledge to the company concerning the ethics policy of the firm, it is a violation of the employee's civil rights," almost 90% disagreed (33.3% [10] strongly disagreed, 50.0% [15] disagreed). This response reinforces an earlier statement concerning the required signing of an ethics oath where over 50% of the respondents agreed with the signing of an oath. The CEOs responding felt that the employees' civil rights are not being violated.

Punishment of Many Attitudes

When responding to the statement, "most employees are ethical in their job performance and companies tend to overact, punishing the many for the crime of the few," 10% (3) strongly disagreed, 26.7% (8) agreed, 20.0% (6) had no opinion, 26.7% agreed and only one respondent strongly agreed. This varied response may be indicative of an attitude of "the punishment must fit the crime." Many companies are very intolerant of unethical behavior and will reprimand or terminate employees immediately. Others take a much less drastic measure and will merely warn the employee.

Formal Ethics Policy

Twenty-four respondents (80%) reported that their organizations have a formal ethics policy.

Ethics Awareness Programs

In response to the statement, "Companies/organizations should develop and administer an ethics awareness program for ALL employees," over 75% agreed (33.3% [10] agreeing, 43.3% [13] strongly agreeing). Today, many companies are developing and administering ethics awareness programs so that ALL employees are oriented to the company's policies, thus insuring a positive step "in the right direction."

TEACHING ETHICS

Teaching Ethical Behavior

The respondents' opinion on the statement, "it is not really possible to teach ethical behavior in a classroom—it must be learned 'on the job,' " varied. Approximately 70% of the respondents felt that ethics could be acquired in a classroom setting (20% [6] strongly disagreed and 46.7% [14] disagreed). Perhaps educators should take a stronger stance and incorporate ethics in our existing programs to foster this base. The American Assembly of Collegiate Schools of Business (AACSB) has suggested that *all* business schools provide a separate ethics course or incorporation of ethics into existing courses in the curriculum.

Teaching Ethics in the Classroom

In response to the statement, "colleges and universities should incorporate an ethical use of computers course in their present curriculum," almost half (46.77) agreed and 20% (10) strongly agreed. This response reinforces an earlier statement where almost 75% agreed that ethical behavior can be taught in the classroom. Again, instructors would be wise to devote a portion of their course time to the teaching of ethics.

CONCLUSION

The objective of this study was to examine the opinions of Chief Executive Officers concerning the ethical use of computers in their organizations. It would appear that the CEOs responding hold some very high ethical standards personally and expect their companies to abide by these same standards. The reader is cautioned, however, about drawing conclusions or forming inferences about the responses. A much more detailed questionnaire would be required to delineate the responses more thoroughly. It is very encouraging to note that CEOs are willing to respond to such a vital topic and share their opinions. Perhaps, if industry and education can work more closely together to develop and reinforce ethical attitudes in students and employees, the end result will be a very acceptable outcome.

The unique and varied challenges we face in this age of information are truly unprecedented. How we achieve a balance between intellectual/professional growth and ethical compromise — and yet remain in the competitive "ballpark" — is indeed the paramount challenge.

An information systems professional's responsibility to themselves, as well as to their profession and industry, is constantly under close scrutiny as our "moving target" environment is in constant flux and change. Our challenge is indeed a unique and special one—we can follow no lead, but must forge our own path to ethical enlightenment and responsibility. Individual, societal, organizational, and professional ethics must be combined cohesively in order for any business to prosper in an acceptable manner.

If corporations follow a responsibility philosophy, based on personal as well as corporate growth, ethical conduct can be readily practiced without compromise. A person's computer output is their product—we must make sure that we can give it our personal stamp of approval, just as craftsmen do on their creations.

REFERENCES

Bayles, Michael, D., *Professional Ethics*, Belmont, California: Wadsworth, Inc., 1981.

Becker, Hal B., *Information Integrity: A Structure for Its Definition and Management*, New York: McGraw-Hill, 1983.

Bequai, *Computer Crime*, Heath and Company, 1978, p. 3.

Bernier, Charles L., "Ethics of Knowing," *Journal of the American Society for Information Sciences*, May, 1985, pp. 211–212.

Bologna, Jack, *Corporate Fraud: The Basics of Prevention and Detection*, Stoneham, Mass.: Butterworth Publishers, 1984.

Computer Security, Time Life Books, Alexandria, Virginia, 1986.

Computer Security Act of 1987, Congressional Record—U.S. House of Representatives, Washington, D.C., June 22, 1987, H5339.

Computer Security Institute, *Computer Security Handbook: The Practitioner's "Bible,"* 4th ed., Northborough, Mass., 1987.

Cressey, Donald R., and Charles A. Moore, *Corporation Codes of Ethical Conduct*, Santa Barbara, California: University of California Press, 1980.

Cromer, Robert, *Review Course Text for CDP Candidates, Data Processing Management Association*, Park Ridge, Illinois, 1987.

Electronic Data Processing Security Standards and Practices for Departments and Agencies of the Government of Canada, GES/NGI-14/DO3–1986–02–11, February, 1986.

Fisher, Royal P., *Information Systems Security*, Englewood Cliffs, N.J.: Prentice-Hall, 1984.

Flaherty, David H., Terence J. Donohue, and Peter J. Harte, *Privacy and Data Protection: An International Bibliography*, White Plains, N.Y.: Knowledge Industry Publications, 1984.

Forcht, Karen A., and J. K. Pierson, "Developing Computer Security Awareness," *IRM Bulletin*, November, 1987, p. 2.

Guidelines for Computer Security Certification and Accreditation, AFIPS Pub. 102, U. S. Department of Commerce, National Bureau of Standards, Washington, D.C., September 17, 1983.

Johnson, Deborah G., and John W. Snapper, *Ethical Issues in the Use of Computers*, Belmont, California: Wadsworth Publishing Company, 1985, pp. 11–12.

"Legislature Report," *Data Management*, October, 1985, pp. 42–43.

Leinfus, Emily, "Computer Crime: How Deep Does It Go? Much of It Goes Undetected, Unreported," *Management Information Systems Week*, February 10, 1986, p. 41.

Levine, Marilyn M., "Ethical Space," *Information Express*, July, 1986.

McCoy, Charles S., *Management of Values: The Ethical Differences in Corporate Policy*, Marshfield, Mass., Pitman Publishing, Inc., 1985.

MIS Training Institute, Inc., *The MIS Information Security Resource Manual*, Framingham, Mass.: 1986.

Manning, George, Kent Curtis, *Ethics at Work*, Cincinnati, Ohio: South-Western Publishing Company, 1988.

Martin, James, *Security, Accuracy, and Privacy in Computer Systems*, Englewood Cliffs, N.J.: Prentice-Hall, 1973.

Mason, Richard O., "Four Ethical Issues of the Information Age," *MIS Quarterly*, March, 1986, pp. 5–12.

Moulton, Rolf T., *Computer Security Handbook: Strategies and Techniques for Preventing Loss or Theft*, Englewood Cliffs, N.J.: Prentice-Hall, 1986.

Naisbitt, John, *Megatrends*, New York: Warner Books, 1982.

Norman, Adrian R.D., *Computer Insecurity*, New York: Chapman and Hall, 1983.

Perry, William E., *Computer Control and Security: A Guide for Managers and Systems Analysts*, New York: Wiley, 1981.

Perry, William E., *Management Strategies for Computer Security*, Stoneham, Mass.: Butterworth Publishers, 1985.

Sieber, Ulrich, *The International Handbook on Computer Crime*, New York: Wiley, 1986.

Solomon, Robert C., and Kristine R. Hanson, *Above the Bottom Line: An Introduction to Business Ethics*, New York: Harcourt Brace Jovanovich, 1983.

U.S. Department of Commerce, Computer Science and Technology, National Bureau of Standards, *Overview of Computer Security Certification and Accreditation*, NBS Special Publication 500-109, Washington, D.C.: U. S. Government Printing Office, 1989.

U.S. Department of Commerce, National Bureau of Standards, *Guideline for Computer Security Certification and Accreditation*, FIPS 102, Springfield, VA.: NTIS, 1983.

U.S. Department of Defense, *Trusted Computer System Evaluation Criteria*, Fort George G. Meade, MD: Computer Security Center, 1983.

U.S. Department of Justice, Bureau of Justice Statistics, Superintendent of Documents, *Computer Crime: Computer Security Techniques*, Washington, D.C., U.S. Government Printing Office, 1985.

Vallabhaneni, S. Rao, *Auditing Computer Security*, New York, Wiley, 1989.

Van Duyn, Julia, *The Human Factor in Computer Crime*, Princeton, N.J.: Petrocelli Books, 1985.

Ward, Gerald M. and Harris, Jonathan D., *Managing Computer Risk: A Guide for the Policymaker*, New York: Wiley, 1986.

Wood, C. C., W. W. Banks, S. B. Guarro, A. A. Garcia, V. E. Hampel, and H. P. Sartorio, *Computer Security: A Comprehensive Controls Checklist*, New York: Wiley, 1987.

Preparing IS Students to Deal with Ethical Issues

J. Daniel Couger

Reprinted by special permission from the *MIS Quarterly,* Volume 13, Number 2, June 1989. Copyright 1989 by the Society for Information Management and the Management Information Systems Research Center at the University of Minnesota.

ABSTRACT

The recent series of ethics violations in business (e.g., insider trading) has caused a number of firms to begin courses in ethics for employees. Unless professionals improve their ethical practices, legislation will force them to do so. The ACM and DPMA curriculum recommendations include ethics topics. An important issue is the proper education of IS students to deal with on-the-job ethical situations. Unfortunately, ethics education gets lost among the myriad of subjects to be taught in IS courses. But there is an effective pedagogical approach for this material. The approach requires students to determine how they would act in various ethical scenarios. This "personalization" method may be the first step toward proper ethical behavior in the workplace. While not a rigorous scientific treatment of the subject, the classroom experiences reported here may be helpful for IS faculty and IS trainers as they develop improved ethics instruction.

INTRODUCTION

> I never thought ethics was something that could be formally taught. I thought ethics was something you learned growing up at home, in school, and in church.

Robert Fomon, chairman of E.F. Hutton and Company, made the above comment while discussing his company's guilty plea to 2,000 counts of fraud because of checking-account overdrafts. E.F. Hutton now sends its employees to a course on ethical practices (*Business Week,* 1985). The Boesky case and other insider trading cases have elevated interest in business ethics to a new high. However, the surge in interest in ethical issues is not confined to the financial industry. The computer industry has been plagued with problems for many years, to the extent that legislation has been introduced to try to control the problem. The "hackers" legislation is only one example. One would hope that professionals in the field would take personal responsibility in applying ethics to their daily activities, rather than be forced through external pressures (i.e., legislation) to conform to a code of ethics.

Buck Bloombecker, director of the National Center for Computer Crime Data in Los Angeles, frequently lectures on ethics to computer classes around the country. Recently a student commented during his lecture that "being ethical only allows other people to take advantage of you ... but I'm not a computer criminal." Bloombecker (1988) says such attitudes prevail in schools where there is no ethics in the computer curriculum. "Faculty members praise me," he says, "for coming in to town to speak about computer ethics. They explain that with all the important changes in technology, they just don't have the time to teach that subject" (p. 17).

Both the ACM and DPMA curriculum committees include ethical issues in the recommended curriculum for IS majors. Both committees debated whether a full course on the subject was justified in light of all the other material needing coverage. For that reason, I was one of the ACM committee members who believed that a full course was unnecessary. But I do include two one-hour sessions on ethics in the capstone course for undergraduate IS majors. However, I experimented with a variety of approaches before I found one that effectively personalizes what many students view to be an abstract subject. This article will cover three approaches to teaching ethics materials and then concentrate on one that appears to be the most successful. My definition of success includes both pedagogical methods and behavioral results.

Before discussing pedagogy, however, it is useful to review the computer-specific ethical issues that arise as a result of the roles of computers, such as:

1. Repositories and processors of information. Unauthorized use of otherwise unused computer services or of information stores in computers raise questions of appropriateness or fairness.
2. Producers of new forms and types of assets. For example, computer programs are new types of assets, subject to the same concepts of ownership as other assets.
3. Instruments of acts. To what degree must computer services and users of computers, data, and programs be responsible for the integrity and appropriateness of computer output?
4. Symbols of intimidation and deception. The images of computers as thinking machines, absolute truth products, infallible, subject to blame, replacements for human errors, and as anthropomorphic in nature should be carefully considered.

These roles of computers have been carefully documented at SRI International in a study of over 550 reported cases of intentionally caused losses associated with computer science and technology (Parker, 1980). These cases serve as a good starting basis for developing a pedagogy for conveying ethics to students majoring in IS. The evolution of my own pedagogical approaches is provided next.

PEDAGOGICAL APPROACH #1

"Studying ethics is like taking a flu shot," according to one of my students. "You know it is necessary, but there is no way to make it enjoyable." I heard that comment following my initial pedagogical approach to the subject. Students weren't very excited by my introducing the subject with a lecture on the code of ethics for the IS profession. I began with a dictionary definition of ethic: "a principle of right or good conduct, or a body of such principles." The "body" of principles appropriate to our field has been clearly defined in the ACM and DPMA codes of ethics (Appendices A and B).

After a brief lecture on the need for ethics in the field, students were asked to compare the two codes of ethics to determine differences. This comparison generated good discussion on what had been included in the code and why. Nevertheless, the approach failed to force students to review their own codes of ethics in light of the professional codes. They did not internalize the material. A change in pedagogy was needed.

PEDAGOGICAL APPROACH #2

For my second evolutionary stage in teaching ethics in IS, I decided to concentrate on examples that would show students how professionals in the field behave in real-life ethical situations. *Computerworld* proved to be a good source of articles on violations of ethics codes. In discussing the cases in class, one group of students was asked to take the position of the guilty person and rationalize the behavior. Another group played the role of an ACM code of ethics committee evaluating the behavior. The approach improved student involvement and generated some interesting discussions.

A few students began to personalize the ethics issues as a result of the revised pedagogical approach. But the majority did not, based on classroom discussion. It was obvious that another approach was needed to try to cause each student to evaluate his or her own ethical code against the professional codes.

PEDAGOGICAL APPROACH #3

Six years ago, my third evolutionary stage of teaching ethics to IS majors began. This approach proved successful in getting each student to personalize the topic. The topic was initiated with the follow question:

> You have purchased a microsoftware package to use at work. You paid for it personally. The license agreement stipulates "you may use the program on a single machine." You want to make a copy to use on your home computer. You will make sure that you are the only person using the package. This approach appears to adhere to the "spirit" though not the "letter" of the license agreement. Is this consistent with the code of ethics of our profession?

Starting the discussion on the issue of copying of software makes it immediately relevant to all students. It perks their attention. However, the ethics codes contain nothing on this specific issue. The DPMA code provides a general statement: "In recognition of my obligation to society I shall support, respect and abide by the appropriate local, state, provincial and federal laws." The ACM code has only one canon that relates to this issue, also quite general: "An ACM member shall act at all times with integrity."

Since this particular case requires personal interpretation of the code, discussions become quite heated. I explain that, by signing the license agreement, individuals are obligated to avoid copying the software. The majority of students oppose that view. They rationalize copying software for a myriad of reasons—all of which dodge the issue.

As follow-up, I use two cases from *Ethical Conflicts in Computer Sciences and Tech-*

nology. The author, Donn Parker (1980), is the foremost authority on computer crime. The book contains the ethics codes of ACM, the Institute for Certification of Computer Professionals, and the British Computer Society. However, the key content is a series of ethics scenarios for the computer field, along with evaluation of each ethics issue by a panel of experts. There are 47 scenarios, each one page in length. Under the auspices of the AFIPS (American Federation of Information Processing Societies), 35 persons were selected to develop opinions on each scenario. After studying the facts of a case, each person decided whether it represented ethical conduct, unethical conduct or was not an ethical issue. These persons were "leaders in the computer field, lawyers and experts in ethical philosophy." Next, a workshop of these persons was held to discuss the results. The results were intended as a way for individuals or groups to benchmark their views against those of experts in the field.

Two scenarios in the book are especially appropriate for IS students. Each student is asked to read the scenarios and then make a decision about the issues. I tabulate the results and report them to the class. Each student is then asked to compare his or her own decision with the class mean and with the AFIPS panel of experts. The result is a real eye opener for students, because they differ so much from the panel of experts.

The two scenarios are provided below with results of student ratings over the past five years. What is surprising is the wide differences from year to year, with no particular trend in evidence. The term "practitioner" instead of "panel of experts" is used to simplify presentation.

A first scenario deals with misuse of the campus computer:

A university student used the campus computer time-sharing service as an authorized user. The director announced that students would receive public recognition if they successfully compromised the computer system from their terminals. Students were urged to report the weaknesses they found. This created an atmosphere of casual game playing and one-upmanship in attacking the system.

The student found a means of compromising the system and reported it to the director. However, nothing was done to correct the vulnerability and the student continued to use his advantage to obtain more computer time than he was otherwise allowed. He used his time to play games and continue his attacks to find more vulnerabilities (Parker, 1980, p. 20).

Table 1 shows the differing views of the experts and the students.[1] The panel of experts clearly understands the behavior as misuse; students rate it very differently, following the campus code of ethics. The essence of the campus code is "beating the system is the name of the game."

When the results of this scenario are reviewed, student opposition concerning copying software begins to diminish. Their discrepancy with the panel of experts is a sobering experience for students.

---

[1] Because of space limitations, I have only presented the results on the decision related to the students' ethics. The scenario also calls for students to rate the director's behavior, first for encouraging compromise and second for not correcting the vulnerability.

Table 1   The First Scenario: Exploiting Vulnerabilities

Participants	Unethical	Percent Believing Student Was: Not Unethical	No Ethics Issue
IS Practitioners	75%	17.5%	7.5%
IS Students			
1983	36%	50%	14%
1984	61%	26%	13%
1985	67%	23%	10%
1986	38%	54%	8%
1987	67%	13%	20%

The class is more cautious in evaluating the second scenario:

A programming manager received a directive to develop a set of programs that would circumvent the normal accounting controls in his employers' business. It was explained to him the purpose was only to test new business functions. He protested to his senior manager, but was told that the dangers of circumventing the controls had been assessed and a decision had been made to proceed as planned. The manager implemented the programs (Parker, 1980, p. 133).

Again, the class mean varied a great deal (see Table 2). Only the 1984 and 1987 classes were similar to the panel of experts. Also, 29% and 33% from those classes, respectively, believed no ethics issue was involved, compared to 17% of the panel of experts.

COMPARISON OF CASES TO CODES OF ETHICS

The initial lecture and two cases are covered in the first class. The second class continues the discussion, after students have had an opportunity to reflect on the results for several days. First, students realize that issues of this type do require more attention. It was shocking to them to realize how far they differed from the panel of experts—and from each other.

Second, students are more motivated to read the code of ethics carefully to try to find whether the issues in the two scenarios are covered. One point in the code clearly relates to the first scenario. It states that: "I shall not exploit the weakness of a computer system for personal gain or personal satisfaction."

Also, after each scenario, the Parker book provides a statement of "general principles" that apply to the case. For example, after the first scenario, the general principle is "the existence of temptation does not justify irresponsible action. For example, absence of a lock does not justify theft. Reporting knowledge of a system weakness does not remove the ethical responsibility not to exploit the weakness" (pp. 20–21).

Students learn, by examining the code in depth, that it applies quite well to the situations being evaluated. For example, in the second scenario, students recognize that the 17% of the panel of experts who said no ethics issue was involved did not clearly examine the situation

Table 2 The Second Scenario: Developing Programs Without Adequate Controls

| | **Percent Believing Programming Manager Was:** | | |
| | | **Not** | **No** |
Participants	**Unethical**	**Unethical**	**Ethics Issue**
IS Practitioners	20%	63%	17%
IS Students			
1984	27%	44%	29%
1985	41%	28%	31%
1986	50%	27%	23%
1987	20%	47%	33%

against the code or overlooked that part of the code. The DPMA code states: "In recognition of my obligation to my employer, I shall protect the proper interest of my employer at all times." Parker raises a general principle at the end of the scenario: "An individual responsible for business computer programs is also responsible to assure that there are adequate controls to protect the business against loss" (p. 133).

MODIFICATIONS TO PEDAGOGY

Having found a pedagogy that motivates students, I have introduced only slight refinements. The weighting on the final exam now includes 5 percent for coverage of ethics content. That small weighting is sufficient to get students to perform another review of the material. Another reinforcement approach is to ask students to bring in newspaper clippings or to describe personal incidents involving ethical issues.

We also discuss ethics programs in companies. Students are given the *IBM Business Conduct Guidelines* (1983) and asked to contrast this very detailed listing versus the Hewlett-Packard "high-trust" approach, where there are few guidelines. Unfortunately, we are able to spend very little time on this additional material, small in proportion to the value gained by maintaining the emphasis on the subject throughout the semester.

CONCLUSION

The discussion above concentrates on one of the two aspects in teaching ethics, instructor emphasis on the importance of the subject. The second objective is to try to motivate students to incorporate the code of ethics into their behavior. The first step in this process is to motivate them to personalize the issues discussed in class. The pedagogical process discussed above is successful in causing students to think about how they personally would handle these issues. But does it change their behavior?

One positive piece of evidence is the reduction in cheating in the course. It never was a wide-spread problem—only a few persons were disposed to cheating. The discussion of the second scenario provides a natural entre to the subject of enforcement of the code of ethics. The DPMA code states: "In recognition of my obligation to my fellow members and the profession, I shall take appropriate action in regard to any illegal or unethical practices that come to my attention." Many students oppose an honor system because it requires them to "rat" on their colleagues. When they read that the code of ethics for their profession includes enforcement clauses, they began to revise their views on reporting "honor code" violations. Although there is no honor code system in my university, the code of ethics establishes an honor code environment for the course.

I tried to introduce an honor code in my classes a number of years ago. It was not successful; students continued to come by my office from time to time to complain about cheating. They asked me to change my practice of leaving the room during quizzes and exams because some students were cheating, taking unfair advantage of the honest students. I complied. Since introduction of the topics of ethics and the professional code of ethics for the IS field, I have resumed the practice of leaving the room during quizzes and exams. Students enforce the honor system. There has been only one incident of cheating reported to me in the past five years. I personally grade all quizzes and exams and rarely find evidence of cheating. Several students have discussed with me how cheating was observed in a class and how members of the class immediately reprimanded the individual. Thereafter, cheating was no longer a problem, according to students.

There is another aspect of the course that allows observation of honesty. The course has a large system project where students are encouraged to work together for the first half of the project but are asked to complete the latter half without assistance from others. It is very easy to determine if they colluded on the second part—it would be more difficult to disguise work done in common than to do the work alone. Reduction in collusion has occurred for the project as a result of the ethics addition to the curriculum.

Increasingly, managers in firms who hire our IS graduates have asked for on-site presentations on the subject of ethics in the IS profession. Most of this interest has been from our IS alumni who are employees of these firms.

Of course, the ultimate test on whether students have incorporated ethics into their behavior is how they act on the job. This is difficult for an academician to measure. I keep close contact with employers of my students and have not heard of any unethical practices. In other words, none have been caught!

"Once they graduate, will students miraculously become more ethical?" This was the question of Thomas Roberts, a consultant who frequently writes on the issue of illegal copying of software. He says his surveys of students reveal that they are "aware that they are ripping off intellectual property but don't much care. Their attitude can best be summed up by the phrase, 'Everyone else does it, so why shouldn't I?'" (Roberts, 1987, p. 48).

Students do not wait until graduation to begin to attain some skills in the tools and techniques in the IS curriculum. Nor should they wait to begin to apply their newfound knowledge about professional ethics.

Unfortunately, the IS literature is almost void of articles on the topic; my literature search reveals only two other publications (Couger, 1984; Johnson, 1984). The index for *MIS Quarterly* does not include a section for this topic. However, there are references from the general ethics literature that are useful to the IS academician. One is a recent book on business ethics by Robert Jackall (1988) entitled *Moral Mazes: The World of Corporate Managers*. Another is *Essays on Ethics in Business and the Professions* by Jack Behrman (1988). Also, there are two good publications related to pedagogy in business. The first is *Ethics in the Education of Business Managers* by Charles Powers and David Vogel (1980). The second is *Ethics in the Business Curriculum* by George Pamental (1980).

The approaches used in this project do not conform to a specific research paradigm. Since the ethics issue is expanding in importance for our profession, there may be others who would build on this research. For these researchers, I recommend development of a questionnaire for students to complete to enable statistical analysis of the quality of their learning in this subject area.

It is hoped that the above discussion will be of benefit to IS faculty who want to include the ethics topic in the curriculum but must economize among all the topics to cover for majors. It should also be useful to the IS trainer who is attempting to include more ethics instruction for the career development of IS practitioners.

REFERENCES

Behrman, J.N. *Essays on Ethics in Business and the Professions,* Prentice-Hall, Inc. Englewood Cliffs, NJ, 1988.

Bloombecker, B. "Computer Ethics for Cynics," *Computerworld,* February 29, 1988, pp. 17–18.

Business Week. "Where Business Goes to Stock Up on Ethics," October 14, 1985, pp. 63–66.

Couger, J.D. "Providing Norms on Ethics to Entering Employees," *Journal of Systems Management* **35**(2), February 1984, pp. 40–43.

IBM, *Business Conduct Guidelines,* Armonk, NY, 1983.

Jackall, R. *Moral Mazes: The World of Corporate Managers,* Oxford University Press, New York, NY, 1988.

Johnson, D.G. and Snapper, J. *Ethical Issues in the Use of Computers,* Wadsworth, Belmont, CA, 1984.

Pamental, G.L. *Ethics in the Business Curriculum,* University Press of America, Lanham, MD, 1988.

Parker, D. *Ethical Conflicts in Computer Science and Technology,* AFIPS Press, Reston, VA, 1980.

Powers, C.W. and D. Vogel. *Ethics in the Education of Business Managers,* Hastings Center, Hastings-on-Hudson, NY, 1980.

Roberts, T. "The Absence of Ethics," *Computerworld Focus,* December 2, 1987, p. 48.

Appendix A
Bylaw 19, ACM Code of
Professional Conduct

PREAMBLE

Recognition of professional status by the public depends not only on skill and dedication but also on adherence to a recognized code of Professional Conduct. The following Code sets forth the general principles (Canons), professional ideals (Ethical Considerations), and mandatory rules (Disciplinary Rules) applicable to each ACM Member.

The verbs "shall" (imperative) and "should" (encouragement) are used purposefully in the Code. The Canons and Ethical Considerations are not, however, binding rules. Each Disciplinary Rule is binding on each individual Member of ACM. Failure to observe the Disciplinary Rules subjects the Member to admonition, suspension or expulsion from the Association as provided by the Procedures for the Enforcement of the ACM Code of Professional Conduct, which are specified in the ACM Policy and Procedures Guidelines. The term "member(s)" is used in the Code. The Disciplinary Rules of the Code apply, however, only to the classes of membership specified in Article 3, Section 5, of the Constitution of the ACM.

CANON 1

An ACM member shall act at all times with integrity

Ethical Considerations

EC1.1 An ACM member shall properly qualify himself when expressing an opinion outside his areas of competence. A member is encouraged to express his opinion on subjects within his area of competence.

EC1.2 An ACM member shall preface any partisan statements about information processing by indicating clearly on whose behalf they are made.

EC1.3 An ACM member shall act faithfully on behalf of his employers or clients.

Disciplinary Rules

DR1.1.1. An ACM member shall not intentionally misrepresent his qualifications or credentials to present or prospective employers or clients.

DR1.1.2. An ACM member shall not make deliberately false or deceptive statements as to the present or expected state of affairs in any aspect of the capability, delivery, or use of information processing systems.

78

DR1.2.1. An ACM member shall not intentionally conceal or misrepresent on whose behalf any partisan statements are made.

DR1.3.1 An ACM member acting or employed as a consultant shall, prior to accepting information from a prospective client, inform the client of all factors of which the member is aware which may affect the proper performance of the task.

DR1.3.2. An ACM member shall disclose any interest of which he is aware which does or may conflict with his duty to a present or prospective employer or client.

DR1.3.3. An ACM member shall not use any confidential information from any employer or client, past or present, without prior permission.

CANON 2

An ACM member should strive to increase his competence and the competence and prestige of the profession.

Ethical Considerations

EC2.1. An ACM member is encouraged to extend public knowledge, understanding and appreciation of information processing, and to oppose any false or deceptive statements relating to information processing of which he is aware.

EC2.2. An ACM member shall not use his professional credentials to misrepresent his competence.

EC2.3. An ACM member shall undertake only those professional assignments and commitments for which he is qualified.

EC2.4. An ACM member shall strive to design and develop systems that adequately perform the intended functions and that satisfy his employer's or client's operational needs.

EC2.5. An ACM member should maintain and increase his competence through a program of continuing education encompassing the techniques, technical standards, and practices in his fields of professional activity.

EC2.6. An ACM member should provide opportunity and encouragement for professional development and advancement of both professionals and those aspiring to become professionals.

Disciplinary Rules

DR2.2.1. An ACM member shall not use his professional credentials to misrepresent his competence.

DR2.3.1. An ACM member shall not undertake professional assignments without adequate preparation in the circumstances.

DR2.3.2. An ACM member shall not undertake professional assignments for which he knows or should know he is not competent or cannot become adequately competent without acquiring the assistance of a professional who is competent to perform the assignment.

DR2.4.1. An ACM member shall not represent that a product of his work will perform its function adequately and will meet the receiver's operational needs when he knows or should know that the product is deficient.

CANON 3

An ACM member shall accept responsibility for his work.

Ethical Considerations

EC3.1. An ACM member shall accept only those assignments for which there is reasonable expectancy of meeting requirements or specifications, and shall perform his assignments in a professional manner.

Disciplinary Rules

DR3.1.1. An ACM member shall not neglect any professional assignment which has been accepted.

DR3.1.2. An ACM member shall keep his employer or client properly informed on the progress of his assignments.

DR3.1.3. An ACM member shall not attempt to exonerate himself from, or to limit his liability to clients for his personal malpractice.

DR3.1.4. An ACM member shall indicate to his employer or client the consequences to be expected if his professional judgement is over-ruled.

CANON 4

An ACM member shall act with professional responsibility.

Ethical Considerations

EC4.1. An ACM member shall not use his membership in ACM improperly for professional advantage or to misrepresent the authority of his statements.

EC4.2. An ACM member shall conduct professional activities on a high plane.

EC4.3. An ACM member is encouraged to uphold and improve the professional standards of the Association through participation in their formulation, establishment, and enforcement.

Disciplinary Rules

DR4.1.1. An ACM member shall not speak on behalf of the Association or any of its subgroups without proper authority.

DR4.1.2. An ACM member shall not knowingly misrepresent the policies and views of the Association or any of its subgroups.

DR4.1.3. An ACM member shall preface partisan statements about information processing by indicating clearly on whose behalf they are made.

DR4.2.1. An ACM member shall not maliciously injure the professional reputation of any other person.

DR4.2.2. An ACM member shall not use the services of or his membership in the Association to gain unfair advantage.

DR4.2.3. An ACM member shall take care that credit for work is given to whom credit is properly due.

CANON 5

An ACM member should use his special knowledge and skills for the advancement of human welfare.

Ethical Considerations

EC5.1. An ACM member should consider the health, privacy, and general welfare of the public in the performance of his work.

EC5.2. An ACM member, whenever dealing with data concerning individuals, shall always consider the principle of the individual's privacy and seek the following:

- To minimize the data collected
- To limit authorized access to the data.
- To provide proper security for the data.
- To determine the required retention period of the data
- To ensure proper disposal of the data.

Disciplinary Rules

DR5.2.1. An ACM member shall express his professional opinion to his employers or clients regarding any advance consequences to the public which might result from work proposed to him.

Appendix B
DPMA Code of Ethics, Standards of Conduct and Enforcement Procedures

CODE OF ETHICS

I acknowledge:

That I have an obligation to management, therefore, I shall promote the understanding of information processing methods and procedures to management using every resource at my command.

That I have an obligation to my fellow members, therefore, I shall uphold the high ideals of DPMA as outlined in its International Bylaws. Further, I shall cooperate with my fellow members and shall treat them with honesty and respect at all times.

That I have an obligation to society and will participate to the best of my ability in the dissemination of knowledge pertaining to the general development and understanding of information processing. Further, I shall not use knowledge of a confidential nature to further my personal interest, nor shall I violate the privacy and confidentiality of information entrusted to me or to which I may gain access.

That I have an obligation to my employer whose trust I hold, therefore, I shall endeavor to discharge this obligation to the best of my ability, to guard my employer's interests, and to advise him or her wisely and honestly.

That I have an obligation as a personal responsibility and as a member of this association. I shall actively discharge these obligations and I dedicate myself to that end.

Standards of Conduct

These standards expand on the Code of Ethics by providing specific statements of behavior in support of each element of the Code. They are not objectives to be strived for, they are rules that no true professional will violate. It is first of all expected that information processing professionals will abide by the appropriate laws of their country and community. The following standards address tenets that apply to the profession.

IN RECOGNITION OF MY OBLIGATION TO MANAGEMENT I SHALL:

- Keep my personal knowledge up to date and insure that proper expertise is available when needed.
- Share my knowledge with others and present factual and objective information to management to the best of my ability.

- Accept full responsibility for work that I perform.
- Not misuse the authority entrusted to me.
- Not misrepresent or withhold information concerning the capabilities of equipment, software or systems.
- Not take advantage of the lack of knowledge or inexperience on the part of others.

IN RECOGNITION OF MY OBLIGATION TO MY FELLOW MEMBERS AND THE PROFESSION I SHALL:

- Be honest in all my professional relationships.
- Take appropriate action in regard to any illegal or unethical practices that come to my attention. However, I will bring charges against any person only when I have reasonable basis for believing in the truth of the allegations and without regard to personal interest.
- Endeavor to share my special knowledge.
- Cooperate with others in achieving understanding and in identifying problems.
- Not use or take credit for the work of others without specific acknowledgement and authorization.
- Not take advantage of the lack of knowledge or inexperience on the part of others for personal gain.

IN RECOGNITION OF MY OBLIGATION TO SOCIETY I SHALL:

- Protect the privacy and confidentiality of all information entrusted to me.
- Use my skill and knowledge to inform the public in all areas of my expertise.
- To the best of my ability, insure that the products of my work are used in a socially responsible way.
- Support, respect and abide by the appropriate local, state, provincial and federal laws.
- Never misrepresent or withhold information that is germane to a problem or situation of public concern nor will allow any such known information to remain unchallenged.
- Not use knowledge of a confidential or personal nature in any unauthorized manner or to achieve personal gain.

IN RECOGNITION OF MY OBLIGATION TO MY EMPLOYER I SHALL:

- Make every effort to ensure that I have the most current knowledge and that the proper expertise is available when needed.
- Avoid conflict of interest and insure that my employer is aware of any potential conflicts.
- Present a fair, honest and objective viewpoint.
- Protect the proper interests of my employer at all times.
- Protect the privacy and confidentiality of all information entrusted to me.
- Not misrepresent or withhold information that is germane to the situation.

- Not attempt to use the resources of my employer for personal gain or for any purpose without proper approval.
- Not exploit the weakness of a computer system for personal gain or personal satisfaction.

ENFORCEMENT PROCEDURES

1. Filing a Complaint

1.1 Any complaint against any Regular or Honorary Member of the Association shall be in writing, signed by the complainant, properly notarized and submitted by certified or registered mail to the Executive Director at International Headquarters. At a minimum, the complaint must include:

    1.1.1 a concise statement of the facts on which the complaint is based;

    1.1.2 citations to the section of the Code of Ethics and Standards of Conduct that were allegedly violated;

    1.1.3 a statement that the facts are true to the best of the complainant's knowledge and belief;

    1.1.4 a statement that the complainant is willing to appear at the expense of DPMA at a hearing with the accused, if requested.

1.2 Charges may be initiated only by a Regular or Honorary member in good standing of the Association.

A Framework for the Study of Information Systems and Ethical Decision-Making Processes

Roy M. Dejoie, George C. Fowler, and David B. Paradice

INTRODUCTION

Computer-based information systems are a growing part of the average person's daily existence. Whether making an airline reservation, paying a traffic fine, reviewing a bank statement, or selecting a seat for an upcoming opera performance, individuals face ever-increasing levels of interaction with computer-based information systems. In spite of this trend, little is known about the ethical decision-making processes of persons creating these systems or how information systems influence ethical decision-making behavior.

Rigorous investigation of any field requires some guiding notion of topics worthy of investigation. The scientific method dictates that one first formulates a theory of the relationships between certain domain variables, collects data on those variables and relationships, analyzes the data, and then determines whether the data supports the theory. This process is relatively straightforward in many of the "formal" sciences (e.g., chemistry, physics, and biology), but it can become quite difficult in disciplines where the focus of study is a behavioral trait of a human.

When human behavior is being studied, clear notions of what to study and why to study it become essential. Without a well-developed theory to guide an investigator, irrelevant data may be collected or spurious relationships may be analyzed. Scientific theory provides a road map to what is known about a subject.

The MIS field needs such a theory in order to guide the development of our knowledge of how information technology affects ethical decision-making processes. There are several reasons why a theory does not currently exist:

- MIS is a relatively young discipline, there are many areas in MIS that are not theory based
- the study of ethical behavior has only recently developed theory that supports scientific study
- information technology is evolving so rapidly that there has been little stable basis for developing theory

In this environment, one may begin theory development by analyzing the smaller, more focused research efforts that have been executed earlier. This analysis provides a framework for theory development, typically by (1) providing a taxonomy for categorizing prior studies, (2) summarizing the results of those studies, and (3) proposing hypotheses for future investigation.

ETHICS STUDIES IN MIS

Research in ethics and information systems may be categorized into three areas (Tables 1–3). One of these considers the social implications of ethics and information systems. A second area is the research that looks at ethical issues that pertain to identifiable groups of individuals. In other words, do accountants look at moral issues differently than MIS managers? etc. The third research area deals with the effects of technology on ethical decision making.

Social Issues

Research into the social aspects of computer technology is relatively new. Additionally, this area is currently lacking in empirical studies. The majority of the research actually consists of papers positing the possibilities and areas of social impact that computer technology is likely to affect. Table 1 summarizes the research done regarding the social aspects of computer technology.

Earlier research began in the late 1960s when Sackman (1967) developed a general theory and philosophy of man-machine systems. Little work was pursued for the next decade, until several events in the 1980s occurred. Throughout the 1980s, Computer Professionals for Social Responsibility (CPSR) provided a focal organization for those interested in the social and ethical impacts on computer technology. Douglas Johnson (1984) outlined the characteristics for a computer society ethic. Deborah Johnson (1985a, 1985b) identified ethical issues regarding computer use including the equal access to computing and computing expertise. Richard Mason (1986) identified privacy, accuracy, property, and access as four ethical issues that warranted special consideration in the information age. LaChat (1986) posited questions of the ethical issues concerning artificial intelligence research and experimentation in terms of medical experimentation. M. Mitchell Waldrop (1987) addressed the relationship between man and artificially intelligent machines. Paradice and Dejoie (1991) presented research that suggests that the presence of computer-based information systems in an ethical dilemma might lead to more socially oriented decision-making processes in resolving the dilemma.

Investigations in this area are relatively recent, but a movement in understanding the social aspects of computer technology is gaining momentum. The area of human factors is a related, growing area. A better understanding of prior studies helps us comprehend the origin of social aspects study and the direction it is headed.

Summary of Research in Social Aspects

Sackman's 1967 development of a general theory and philosophy of man-machine systems included the tenet of "humanistic automation." Sackman stated that computer systems existed to meet human needs and serve *social* well-being. Given Sackman's theory, automation was not required to assume the role so drudgingly depicted in Fritz Lang's masterpiece *Metropolis*. Sackman also observed that ethics and values could be treated as research hypotheses and could therefore be examined scientifically.

Table 1 Categories of MIS/Ethics Social Aspects Research

Reference	Description
Sackman (1967)	Developed a general theory and philosophy of man-machine systems.
Johnson (1984)	Outlined the characteristics for an ethic for a computer society.
Johnson (1985a, 1985b)	A philosopher identified ethical issues regarding computer use from a contemporary philosophical viewpoint.
Mason (1986)	Identified privacy, accuracy, property, and accessibility as four ethical issues of the information age.
LaChat (1986)	Constructed the premise of a "personal" AI entity and questioned AI experimentation in terms of medical experimentation.
Waldrop (1987)	Addressed the relationship between man and artificially intelligent machines.
Paradice & Dejoie (1990)	Presented research that suggested that the presence of a computer-based information system in an ethical dilemma might lead to more socially oriented decision-making processes in resolving the dilemma.
Computer Professionals for Social Responsibility	An alliance of computer professionals concerned about the impact of computer technology on society. Publishers *CPBR Newsletter.*

Douglas Johnson (1984) addressed ethical issues involving the proliferation of computer-based information. He focused primarily on the need for modification of existing rules governing human behavior. His work outlined the characteristics that an "ethic for a computer society" should exhibit.

Deborah Johnson (1985a, 1985b) presented the idea that while computers have not currently caused a fundamental change in our social institutions they will "pose new versions of standard moral problems and moral dilemmas, exacerbating the old problem, and forcing us to apply ordinary moral norms in unchartered realms" (Johnson 1985a, p. 1). She suggested that the computer transforms the context in which professional-ethical issues arise. Additionally, Johnson addressed the concerns of equal access to computing and computing expertise, including the role that computers will play in the distribution of rights and benefits in the future information society.

Richard Mason (1986) addressed ethical behavior in terms of privacy, accuracy, property, and accessibility. Mason states there exist certain data items which individuals have a right (1) to keep private, (2) to ensure are accurate, (3) to own, and (4) to access. He noted that "information forms the intellectual capital from which human beings craft their lives and secure dignity" (p. 5). However, information technology may be misused in each of these four critical areas, reducing an individual's intellectual capital.

Michael LaChat (1986) approached the topic of artificial intelligence research from a philosophical and medical standpoint. He constructed the premise of a "personal" AI entity, one with consciousness and awareness. After constructing this premise he then questioned the morality of AI experimentation in terms of medical experimentation ethics. He also questioned the possibility and capacity of such an entity making moral decisions.

M. Mitchell Waldrop examined the future relationship of man and machine. In his 1987 book, *Man-Made Minds: The Promise of Artificial Intelligence,* he envisioned the possible future of computer technology and drew parallels between the invention of the printing press in Renaissance times and the advent of computer technology in our present times. He also addressed the trend of automation and gave possible alternative workstyles and lifestyles by varying automation scenarios. He confronted the degree of responsibility that should be given to computers in our society. He posited the possibility of artificially intelligent entities that interacted in man's society and the degree to which these machines should be given various responsibilities. His theory of machine ethics created rules to govern moral and ethical behavior of AI entities among their human counterparts.

Paradice and Dejoie (1991) researched the influence of information systems on ethical decision-making processes. They used the Defining Issues Test (DIT), developed by James Rest (1979, 1986, 1987), and a modified version of the Defining Issues Test (which included a computer-based information system). The DIT presents moral dilemmas to subjects followed by a list of issues that a person might consider in resolving the dilemma. Paradice and Dejoie found people are more likely to consider more socially oriented issues when attempting to solve an ethical dilemma when a computer is present.

A recently formed organization, Computer Professionals for Social Responsibility (CPSR), emphasizes the ethical responsibilities of computer industry professionals. CPSR's main focuses have been privacy rights and computers and the military. They have, however, also addressed many other social and ethical issues including responsibility for faulty computer programming, computers and South Africa, viruses, voting, and education. The organization is comprised of many noteworthy individuals and has made great strides in introducing legislation to protect individuals' rights as well as opposing legislation it believes threatens those rights.

Future Research Issues in Social Aspects

Many future research areas regarding the social aspects of computer technology exist. In light of Douglas Johnson's work regarding the characteristics of a computer society ethic, one might compare the evolving computer society ethic to the society ethic that evolved during the Industrial Revolution. Deborah Johnson's work could be extended with comparative studies of the disparity between socio-economic classes, education levels, races, genders, and so forth with regard to computing access.

Richard Mason's research provides a basis for further investigations into the areas of privacy, accuracy, property, and access. Research concerning the ownership of information, national databases, responsibility, information maintenance, copyright laws, ownership, liability, and equal access to information are specifically needed to ensure that individuals' rights are considered in the information age.

More speculative pieces, like Michael LaChat's article, are needed to provide interdisciplinary focus. The area of medicine has already experienced moral and ethical conflicts, for example in genetic engineering. Parallels between the moral and ethical challenges in the medical field and computer field should be investigated.

M. Mitchell Waldrop's theory of machine ethics could be explored more. If conscious AI entities are possible there must be some means for conveying and instilling ethics and morality into their artificially intelligent minds. Even if nothing comes of the study of machine ethics, Waldrop asserts that the knowledge gained will be more than worth the effort.

A longitudinal study is needed to determine whether socially oriented decision-making processes continue as computer technology is assimilated into society. Also, researchers must determine whether the introduction of any new technology produces the same type of socially-oriented decision-making processes.

As stated earlier, many social aspects of computer technology are discussion-oriented. As the technology is assimilated into society these issues will become more empirically measurable. Until that time, these issues must not be shunned just because they do not easily lend themselves to empirical testing. Through the discussions of the possibilities today we may be able to avoid problems tomorrow.

MIS Group Differences

Research into the interpretation of ethical dilemmas by different groups of individuals is relatively new. Table 2 presents an overview of the research done in this area as of the writing of this book. As can be seen, the research goes back to 1971 when Weinberg first put forth the idea that data processing managers faced ethical dilemmas in managing programmers. His research was followed by Parker in 1979. Parker found that professionals varied widely in their perceptions of ethical dilemmas. In his research, Parker used short scenarios that posed ethical dilemmas that professionals interpreted. The next major event following Parker's published research was the Bentley College ethics conference of 1981. This conference marked the first time that computer technology and ethics were discussed by such a prominent group of individuals. Although the proceedings show a variety of views and even some differences in perceptions of ethical behavior, the group differences issue was not investigated further until 1988 by Shim and Taylor. They used ethical issues related to microcomputer software piracy as their vehicle for analyzing differences between faculty groups. They used IS faculty from several disciplines: MIS, statistics/OR/MS and others in their study. In 1989, Shim and Taylor extended their study with IS managers as the respondent group. Their paper in this book compares these studies. Paradice and Dejoie expanded on the results of Parker and Shim and Taylor and in 1989 used ethical scenarios to determine if group differences could be determined between students that were MIS majors and those that were

Table 2   Categories of MIS/Ethics Group Differences Research

Date	Source	Professional Affiliation	Research Hypothesis
1971	Weinberg	IS Faculty	Ethical dilemmas exist for data processing managers.
1979	Parker	Senior consultant, SRI	Used ethical scenarios and found group differences in perceived ethical behavior.
1981	Hoffman & Moore	Director of Center for Business Ethics	Conference discussed. Showed differences in perceived ethical issues.
1988–1989	Shim & Taylor	IS Faculty	Compared IS faculty, from different disciplines, and compared IS managers on the ethical issues involved in software copying.
1989–90	Paradice & Dejoie	IS Faculty Ph.D. Student	Used scenarios to study differences in ethical decision-making between MIS and non-MIS students.
1990	Shim & Taylor	IS Faculty	Compared faculty's ethical perceptions about software copying to those of IS managers.

non-MIS majors. Their research also examined empirically, for the first time, the impact that computers have on ethical decision-making.

Although only 20 years old, the area of research has made important progress and interest in it is gaining rapidly.

Summary of Research in Group Differences

Weinberg (1971) noted in his book that ethical dilemmas were faced by data processing managers. Although he did not address group difference issues, he identified ethical dilemmas were present in the data center. In doing so, his book brought attention to the idea that perception of ethical dilemmas needed to be considered for different groups of people.

This need to look at ethical issues from the perspective of identifiable groups was finally addressed nearly a decade after Weinberg's writings. Parker (1979) published the findings of his research in a book called *Ethical Conflicts in Computer Science and Technology*. Parker's research was driven by his belief that "We should get a consensus on the application of ethics to the computer field before we start writing codes of ethics, rather than after" (Parker 1981, p. 49). Thus, Parker assembled a group of professionals (technologists, managers, ethical philosophers, lawyers, and others) and asked them to evaluate short hypothetical ethical dilemmas presented in the form of short stories. The dilemmas that were used fell into six categories: (1) contractual issues, (2) rights to product (ownership) issues, (3) privacy issues, (4) personal morality and organization loyalty, (5) responsibility for computer applications, and (6) responsibility for information accuracy. Interestingly, several of these classifications parallel the issues (privacy, accuracy, property and access) discussed by Mason in his 1986 article, "Four Ethical Issues of the Information Age."

Parker observed that the professionals' ability to identify ethical issues varied widely. This study was the first time empirical evidence verified this variance in perceived ethical issues in a computer technology setting. While differences were seen, the professionals were still not grouped homogeneously (e.g., all MIS professionals in a group).

The interest developing in this research area led in part to more studies. In 1981 the book *Ethics and the Management of Computer Technology* was published. This book includes the papers and discussions made at the Fourth National Conference on Business Ethics sponsored by the Center for Business Ethics at Bentley College. The very nature of the conference spoke loudly to the importance of ethics and information technology. One of the many participants was Donn Parker, whose research is noted above. Although the conference did not address the group difference issues that Parker's previous research had investigated, the varied backgrounds of its participants (computer specialist, lawyers, ethicist and others) and topics (privacy, education, human values and business strategy) added credence to the importance of research into group differences in the perception of ethical behavior.

In 1988, Shim and Taylor addressed the issue of homogeneous professional groups and ethical attitudes. Their study dealt with school faculties partitioned into MIS, accounting, marketing, business policy, statistics/MS/OR and other groups. The thrust of their study dealt with microcomputer software copying: who was more likely to do it and who perceived it as unethical behavior. Their results showed ninety percent (90%) of faculty believed their colleagues copied software. And, while faculty believed it was unethical to do so, they themselves copied software. However, faculty differed on how unethical copying was depending on why it was copied. Sixty-seven percent (67%) felt it was unethical to copy software to be used for teaching. Six percent more or seventy-three percent (73%) said it was unethical to copy software for use in research activities and yet fourteen percent more (87%) felt copying software for use in consulting was unethical.

Shim and Taylor also found that male faculty tend to copy software more often than female faculty. Also, junior faculty copied more often than senior faculty and MIS faculty and statistics/MS/OR faculty copied more often than other faculty.

In another study of ethical perceptions between professional groups, Paradice and Dejoie (1991) examined differences of MIS majors versus non-MIS majors. Their studies, like Parker's, made use of short ethical scenarios and asked the respondents to identify unethical behavior. However, their scenarios were based on the work done by Rest (1979, 1986, 1987) which built on Kohlberg's work by developing the Defining Issues Test (DIT). The DIT presents written moral dilemmas to subjects followed by a list of issues that a person might consider in resolving the dilemma. Paradice and Dejoie found that MIS subjects' ethical decision-making processes are different and that they consider societal effects more often than non-MIS majors. Their results also show that computer-based information systems may influence ethical decision-making processes. This second finding was very interesting in that it suggests that ethical behavior differs if computers are introduced into the scenario.

Future Research into Group Differences

Since this area of research is relatively young, many avenues are available for meaningful research. Parker's studies provide a basis for further research in that much could be learned if the scenarios were evaluated by homogeneous groups such as MIS managers, MIS faculty, accountants, and others. The work started by Paradice and Dejoie opens a new research area. The idea that computers affect ethical decision-making had never been investigated before their work. They point out that since their work was breaking new ground, replication should be done by other researchers. They pose questions like ''Is there something about the MIS curriculum that would help explain the results?'' And ''Why does a computer-based information system seem to influence ethical decision-making?'' Research should also be done using respondents from business. Will we see the same results as Paradice and Dejoie? Evidence shows that a person's ethical framework is correlated with academic experience. Therefore, since Paradice and Dejoie used seniors in their study one would expect to get the same results using adults with similar education levels. One longitudinal study might involve testing the hypotheses that ethical maturity is reached by the time a student enters the workplace and does not continue to develop. What about students that return for advanced degrees? What about graduate students? What about faculty? Since faculty are still in an academic environment, does their ethical maturity differ from their counterparts in industry? After all, Shim and Taylor's results seem to say that ethical behavior is different between IS faculty and IS managers.

Many questions need to be answered and in fact many questions still need to be asked. Research will prove to be fruitful for the person interested in the reasons for differences in perceived ethical behavior. The groundwork is just being laid but much more needs to follow in order to understand the relation of ethics and information systems.

Technological Impact

The impact of technology on sociological aspects of the human condition has drawn much attention, as discussed above. More recently, Jastrow (1987) addressed the growth of computing power and related this growth to man's evolution. He suggested the future may consist of a symbiotic relationship where computers minister to man's social and economic needs.

Similarly, much work has occurred in studying the impact of technology on criminal activity. Sheridan (1987), for example, describes computer crime phenomena and asks whether an information system's presence directly impacts criminal activity. Laudon (1986), in a paper included in this book, examines another side of the criminal justice issue. He demonstrates that while computer-based technology can facilitate criminal record management, a potential risk exists wherein erroneous records may be used to justify arrests of innocent persons. A recent consequence of unjustified intervention by law enforcement authorities has been the expansion of the Computer Professionals for Social Responsibilty (CPSR) Civil Liberties and Computing Project aided by Mitch Kapor (Lotus founder) and Steve Wozniak (Apple co-founder).

Taylor and Davis (1989) investigated levels of concern associated with different types of computer-based information. They concluded that the subjects they studied were more concerned about individuals/groups obtaining access to certain categories of data than about the collection of each type of data. The researchers feel this result reflects more concern over a lack of control over the information than a concern for its maintenance and use.

Table 3   Categories of MIS/Ethics Technology Effects Research

Reference	Description
Jastrow (1987)	Suggests symbiotic relationship between man and machine.
Sheridan (1987)	Considers impact of computer presence on criminal activity.
Bommer et al. (1987)	Hypothesized that information fiiltering and presentation affects ethical behavior.
Parker (1979, 1981)	Focused on dilemmas involving computer technology.
Coates (1985)	Argues that current corporate ethics policies are inadequate in light of information technology's impact on organizational functions.
Taylor & Davis (1989)	Investigated levels of concern associated with computer-based information.
Paradice & Dejoie (in press)	Manipulated the existence of computer-based information in ethical dilemmas.

Paradice and Dejoie (1991) manipulated the existence of computer-based information in a study of ethical decision-making choice. They presented subjects with two versions of ethical dilemmas. One version presented a dilemma in which the main actor received information from a computer-based system. The other version presented a similar dilemma, but the actor received information from a person or some other noncomputer-based source. The study results showed weak confirmation of the hypothesis that obtaining computer-based information influences ethical decision-making processes.

Aside from these few studies, however, little empirical work has investigated the impact of computer-based technology on ethical decision-making processes. As observed by Bommer (1987, p. 275), managers acquire and process information from many sources at each decision process stage. Information selection and filtering at each stage is likely to have considerable impact on the ultimate decision made. Each of these situations implies that computer-based information systems influence actions. Yet no study has actually investigated this hypothesis.

Future Research Issues in Technology Impact

Any number of studies could be replicated with a computer-based focus. Hegarty and Sims' (1978, 1979) classic studies involving ethical managerial decision-making dilemmas exemplify the type of research that is needed. In these studies, subjects that received letters expressing a policy of corporate support for ethical behavior acted more ethically than subjects who received a letter that did not support ethical behavior. Barnett and Karson (1987) used vignettes to study subjective values and decision responses. They found older executives and workers in non-quantitative areas exhibited more ethical behaviors. An important question needing resolution is whether the same results would be obtained in computer-based environments.

Some MIS research has addressed the impact of technology on decision-making processes. When communication between organizational decision makers is discouraged, dysfunctional approaches to decision making characterized by high levels of cohesiveness and conformity (i.e., "groupthink") may begin. Group decision support systems research (Nunamaker et al. 1987, Straub and Beauclair 1988, DeSanctis and Gallupe 1987) is aimed directly at mitigating the ill effects of group decision-making processes while retaining and enhancing its advantages. Although dysfunctional group processes have been observed, to our knowledge no one has focused on ethical decision-making behavior in computer-based group decision-making situations.

SUMMARY

In summary, theory-based empirical investigation of computer industry professionals' ethical decision-making behavior is scarce. Understandably, given the nature of the research questions at hand, manipulating ethical decision-making behavior in actual field studies would be unacceptable (Trevino 1986, p. 601). Thus, empirical studies in ethics research are difficult. De George (1987) observed that frameworks and hypotheses need to be tested, however, to move business ethics research beyond discussions of morality to a point where tangible results that can impact organizational behavior can be identified.

REFERENCES

Barnett, J.H. and Karson, M.J. "Personal Values and Business Decisions: An Exploratory Investigation." *Journal of Business Ethics,* Vol. 6, No. 5, 1987, pp. 371–382.

Bommer, M., Gratto, C., Gravander, J. and Tuttle, M. "A Behavioral Model of Ethical and Unethical Decision Making." *Journal of Business Ethics,* Vol. 6, No. 4, 1987, pp. 265–280.

Coates, J. "Computers and Business: A Case of Ethical Overload." *Philosophy, Technology, and Human Affairs,* L. Hickman, editor, College Station: Ibis Press, 1985.

DeGeorge, R.T. "The Status of Business Ethics: Past and Future." *Journal of Business Ethics,* Vol. 6, No. 3, 1987, pp. 201–211.

DeSanctis, G. and Gallupe, R.B. "A Foundation for the Study of Group Decision Support Systems." *Management Science,* Vol. 33, No. 5, May 1987, pp. 589–609.

Ethics and the Management of Computer Technology. Proceedings of the Fourth National Conference on Business Ethics, Bentley College, 1981.

Hegarty, W.H. and Sims, H.P., Jr. "Organizational Philosophy, Policies, and Objectives Related to Unethical Decision Behavior: A Laboratory Experiment." *Journal of Applied Psychology*, Vol. 64, No. 3, 1979, pp. 331–338.

Hegarty, W.H. and Sims, H.P., Jr. "Some Determinants of Unethical Decision Behavior: An Experiment." Journal of Applied Psychology, Vol. 63, No. 4, 1978, pp. 451–457.

Jastrow, R. "Toward an Intelligence Beyond Man's." In *Information Systems for Management: A Book of Readings*. Watson, H.J., Carroll, A.B., and Mann, R.J., editors. Plano: Business Publications, Inc. 1987, p. 512–514.

Johnson, D.G. *Computer Ethics*. Englewood Cliffs: Prentice-Hall, 1985a.

Johnson, D.G. "Equal Access to Computing, Computer Expertise, and Decision Making About Computers." *Business and Professional Ethics Journal,* Vol. 4, Nos. 3 & 4, 1985b, pp. 95–103.

Johnson, D.W. *Computer Ethics: A Guide for the New Age*. Elgin, IL: The Brethren Press, 1984.

Laudon, K. "Data Quality and Due Process in Large Interorganizational Record Systems." *Communications of the ACM,* Vol. 29, No. 1, 1986, pp. 4–11.

LaChat, M.R. "Artificial Intelligence and Ethics: An Exercise in the Moral Imagination." *AI Magazine,* Vol. 7, No. 2, 1986, pp. 70–79.

Mason, R.O. "Four Ethical Issues of the Information Age." *MIS Quarterly,* Vol. 10, No. 1, March 1986, pp. 4–12.

Nunamaker, J.F., Applegate, L.M., and Konsynski, B.R. "Facilitating Group Creativity: Experience with a Group Decision Support System." *Journal of Management Information Systems,* Vol. 3, No. 4, 1987, pp. 5–19.

Paradice, D.B. "Ethical Attitudes of Entry-Level MIS Personnel," *Information and Management,* Vol. 18, 1989, pp. 143–151.

Paradice, D.B. and Dejoie, R.M. "The Ethical Decision-Making Processes of Information Systems Workers," *Journal of Business Ethics,* Vol. 10, 1991, pp. 57–77.

Parker, D.B. *Ethical Conflicts in Computer Science and Technology*. AFIPS Press, 1979.

Parker, D.B. "Ethical Dilemmas in Computer Technology." *Ethics and the Management of Computer Technology*. Proceedings of the Fourth National Conference on Business Ethics, Bentley College, 1981.

Rest, J.R. *Development in Judging Moral Issues*. Minneapolis: University of Minnesota Press, 1979.

Rest, J.R. *DIT: General Information*. Available from the Center for the Study of Ethical Development, University of Minnesota, 1987.

Rest, J.R. *Moral Development—Advances in Research and Theory*. New York: Praeger, 1986.

Sackman, H. *Computers, System Science, and Evolving Society*. New York: John Wiley and Sons, 1967.

Sheridan, J.H. "Is There a Computer Criminal Working for You?" in *Information Systems for Management: A Book of Readings*. Watson, H.J., Carroll, A.B., and Mann, R.J., editors. Plano: Business Publications, Inc. 1987, pp. 499–511.

Shim, J.P. and G.S. Taylor: 1988, "Business Faculty Members' Perceptions of Unauthorized Software Copying" *OR/MS Today*, 15(5), 30–31.

Shim, J.P. and G.S. Taylor: 1989, "Practicing Managers' Perception/Attitudes Toward Illegal Software Copying" *OR/MS Today,* 16(4).

Straub, D.W. and Beauclair, R.A. "Current and Future Uses of Group Decision Support Technology: Report on a Recent Empirical Study." *Journal of Management Information Systems,* Vol. 5, No. 1, Summer 1988, pp. 101–116.

Taylor, G.S. and Davis, J.S. "Individual Privacy and Computer-Based Human Resource Information Systems." *Journal of Business Ethics,* Vol. 8, 1989, pp. 569–576.

Trevino, L.K. "Ethical Decision Making in Organizations: A Person-Situation Interactionist Model." *Academy of Management Review,* Vol. 11, No. 3, 1986, pp. 601–617.

Waldrop, M.M. "A Question of Responsibility." *AI Magazine,* Vol. 8, No. 1, 1987, pp. 29–39.

Waldrop, M.M. *Man-Made Minds, The Promise of Artificial Intelligence,* New York: Walker and Company, 1987.

Weinberg, G.M. *The Psychology of Computer Programming,* New York: Van Nostrand Reinhold Company, 1971.

Why I Never Met a Programmer I Could Trust

John Shore

John Shore is the author of *The Sachertorte Algorithm, and Other Antidotes to Computer Anxiety,* published by Penguin and available through the CPSR National Office. He works for Entropic Processing, Inc., in Washington, D.C., and is a CPSR member. He wrote this piece for the *CPSR Newsletter.* Reprinted by permission of Computer Professionals for Social Responsibility.

Human lives and human society depend daily on many technologies. Of all such technologies, I can think of one that is virtually free from government and professional regulation: computer technology.

Computer professionals are well aware of the risks associated with computer technology, and we have fought for years to control them. But our fight has been a technical fight, because it's natural that technologists try to control technical risks by means of technical forces. Technical forces, however, cannot do the job alone. The control of technical risks requires social forces as well as technical forces.

I believe that it follows from human nature that the fight against computer risks will remain unsuccessful until we marshal social forces as well as technical forces. This will happen eventually, but we should put some of our professional energy into making it happen sooner rather than later.

THE "SOFTWARE CRISIS" ISN'T ONE

crisis, n., 1. the turning point in the course of a disease, when it becomes clear whether the patient will recover or die.

After almost twenty years of battling the software crisis, it's time to admit that we're not doing so well. When you consider the unsatisfactory state of software engineering, and when you consider that our profession now includes people after the term "software crisis" became popular, it's clear that the software crisis is less a turning point than a way of life.

It's not that there hasn't been progress. But our software ambitions have grown at least as fast as our abilities, and software technology doesn't scale well. Moreover, our rate of progress in extending software technology is dwarfed by the rate at which the public is becoming dependent on computer systems, the net result being that the public depends on fragile systems.

In Code We Trust?

The software crisis used to be merely a struggle for program correctness. Today we ask more. It's not enough the software be correct; it should also be reliable, safe, and trustworthy—as though acceptance testing includes a Boy Scout oath.

Returning home from a software conference last year, I was amused to realize how much time we had on linguistic arguments rather than technical arguments. We argued incessantly about "correctness," "reliability," "safety," and "trustworthiness." Some said, "It's more important that software be trustworthy than safe." Other said, "How can it be trustworthy if it's not reliable?"

Instead of discussing solutions to software problems, we dissected the language used to pose the problems. We thought of ourselves as software engineers, but we acted like Talmudic scholars. In doing so, we gave evidence for the propositions that progress in software engineering has slowed.

This *nouvelle cuisine* of software rhetoric has some advantages. I especially like the language of trust, since it reminds us that trustworthy software requires trustworthy programmers.

What Do The Lawyers Say?

Perhaps the most telling evidence of our failure to resolve the software crisis is a legal document known as the software license. Many of you are acquainted with these things, perhaps because you've arm-wrestled with a lawyer over one. Here's my favorite example, which won a prize in a contest run by *Abacus* magazine. It is said to be a real license.

> We don't claim Interactive EasyFlow is good for anything—if you think it is, great, but it's up to you to decide. If Interactive EasyFlow doesn't work, tough. If you lose a million because Interactive EasyFlow messes up, it's you that's out the million, not us. If you don't like this disclaimer, tough. We reserve the right to do the absolute minimum provided by the law, up to and including nothing.
>
> This is basically the same disclaimer that comes with all software packages, but ours is in plain English and theirs is in legalese.

Quite right, this is basically the same disclaimer that comes with all software. It inspires a variation of that joke about the three most frequent lies:

(1) The check's in the mail.
(2) Of course I'll still respect you in the morning.
(3) The software works.

How can we trust people who lie constantly?

Sometimes I think the net effect of battling the software crisis is that twenty years ago only professionals knew how hard it is to write trustworthy software, whereas today everyone knows. To paraphrase something attributed to Ambrose Bierce, I offer the First Law of Software Economics:

A programmer's word is worth its weight in gold.

CONFESSIONS OF A LAPSED SOFTWARE ENGINEER

One of the reasons for my current cynicism about the software crisis is that I've become part of the problem. About two years ago I left the Naval Research Laboratory (NRL) for Entropic Processing, Inc. (EPI), a private company whose products include software, both standalone and embedded. I knew a fair amount about software engineering, and I vowed that software development within the company would be done "right." Company management was convinced, and they also vowed to do it "right."

At NRL I had participated in a project, led by David Parnas, that developed a successful requirements methodology for real-time avionics software. So it was natural to use the methodology for the real-time telecommunications software we were developing at EPI. After a considerable effort, however, we had to admit that the methodology didn't fit exactly and we didn't have time to figure out how to adapt it. We pressed on, determined at least to maintain software engineering rigor in our software design, development, and documentation efforts. Eventually, however, these efforts began to deteriorate in the face of financial, competitive, and corporate pressures. We haven't given up, and we do retain substantial software discipline, but our efforts are increasingly similar to those we had disparaged. I am told that the first labor laws in England resulted in part from the efforts of those who wanted fair labor laws but who could not compete unless all businesses were required to meet the same standards. There are parallels in today's software industry.

While still at NRL, I wrote:

> Within the computer industry today, the software crisis is widely recognized and widely battled, except by a few who accept it as a fixture along with cancer, venereal disease, and budget deficits.[1]

Today, I suspect that the few are in fact many and that I have become one of them. When the pressure is on, I throw up my hands, throw out the methodology, close the door, and hack. I have become a lapsed software engineer, a member of Hackers Anonymous.

Knowing How Isn't Enough

When I say, "We didn't have time to do it right," others say, "You didn't take the time." Strictly speaking, they're right, but I was as well-motivated as anyone—the pressures were simply too great. The critics also say, "In the long run you'll be sorry," and, again, they're right, but they overlook the fact that the short run comes before the long run, especially in companies like ours.

The problem here is that knowledge and good intentions are sufficient for success. This is not just true of software. Those of you who understand nutrition and want to lose weight, can you count on a successful diet? And how many of you who modify your homes always do so according to applicable building codes?

---

[1] *The Sachertorte Algorithm,* Penguin, 1986, p. 163.

Software Idealism Isn't Enough

Software idealists argue that personal inspiration and market forces will suffice. They say that software producers should resist selling hasty software—those that don't will suffer in the long run. And they say that software consumers should resist buying hasty software—those that don't deserve what they get. They imply that regulation is somehow unnecessary or wrong. This is like being a rabid, no-nuke peacenik who doesn't believe in arms control regulations, as though the belief in peace should be sufficient. It's like being against alcohol and drugs but not believing in any form of regulation. By this way of thinking we should have Edsger Dijkstra tour our nation's schools with the Reverend Jesse Jackson, preaching to future programmers before their exposure to corruption, and pinning on their chests buttons that urge:

SOFTWARE DISCIPLINE REQUIRES ENFORCEMENT

Much of what is known about the production of quality software can be summarized in a single word: *discipline*. Unfortunately, our experience with human nature shows that discipline requires enforcement. Now there are a few Saints of Programming out there whose self-discipline is sufficient—sort of Digital Gandhis who never seem tempted to write bad code. The rest of us, however, need more than an inner force. It's not that we are the software heathen; indeed, many of us are true believers. But we are software sinners, and like sinners everywhere we respond best to the threat of punishment.

As for what would work, I'm not sure. One general approach is to license individuals. We could require that certain types of software be "signed off" by licensed software engineers, and hold those engineers accountable. Another general approach is to specify software building standards that would have to be met by certain types of software, which would be subject to regular inspections.

Advancing the state of the art attracts us all, but we should admit that the introduction of appropriate regulation is probably the single most effective thing that can be done today to raise the average quality of software.

Code for the First Software Dynasty

For inspiration, we can look to the history of regulation in the building industry. In his fine book, *To Engineer is Human*,[2] Henry Petroski cites the Code of Hammurabi, a 4,000-year-old collection of laws from the First Dynasty of Babylon. Included are perhaps the world's first building regulations, so it seems reasonable to start with them. To make them relevant we need only apply a simple linguistic transformation, substituting "programmer" for "builder," and "program" for "house."

I was able to apply this transformation without the aid of an AI program, with the following results:

---

[2] St. Martin's Press, 1982.

Updated Hammurabi Code
for the First
Software Dynasty

If a programmer build a program for a man and do not make its construction firm, and the program which he has built collapse and cause the death of the owner of the program, that programmer shall be put to death. If it cause the death of the son of the owner of the program, they shall put to death a son of that programmer.

Some Other Lessons from History?

Eighteenth-century French warships were the best in the world. Their dominance arose not only because of new technical developments, but also because these developments coincided with the professionalization of French shipbuilders.[3]

Certification or regulation of software professionals would bring social forces to bear on a problem for which technical forces have proven to be insufficient. I'm not sure why we tend to ignore the need for such social forces. I suspect that it's because, as technological professionals, we want to believe that technical solutions will obviate regulation. They won't. Indeed, nothing in the history of science and technology suggests that the ability to build safe systems is sufficient to result in safe systems.

Large buildings in the United States have a pretty good track record. They tend not to fall down, and if you recall the movie *The Towering Inferno,* you'll also recall that serious fires are extremely rare. This good record exists not just because we know how to make buildings safe, but because we know how and are not permitted to do otherwise.

We have building codes for buildings, why not for software? We trust elevators, but they must be approved on installation and inspected regularly thereafter. You might think that the "regular inspection" analogy shouldn't apply to software, but software under maintenance does degrade. (Note the contrast: elevators degrade if they are not maintained; software degrades if it is maintained.)

We require certification for doctors, lawyers, architects, civil engineers, aircraft pilots, automobile drivers, and even hair stylists. Why not for software engineers engaged in building systems on which the public depends?

Consider automobile safety. Were market forces or legislation responsible for safety glass and seat belts? Consider aircraft safety. Would you be in favor of extending airline deregulation to aircraft certification and maintenance?

It Will Happen

Even if you are not in favor of regulating the software industry, I can guarantee one thing: it will happen. Just look at the history of all forms of technology on which society depends. This history also shows the legislative constraints are lightest on those who regulate themselves. So let's do it ourselves before they do it to us. And let's make sure that when it does happen—and it will—that it has a sound and useful technological basis.

---

[3]James Pritchard, "From Shipwright to Naval Constructor: The Professionalization of 18th Century French Naval Shipbuilders," *Technology and Culture,* January, 1987, pp. 1–25.

A Role for CPSR

It's one thing to believe that some form of professional regulation is needed. It's quite another to know what to do. In many respects, regulating software will be more difficult than implied by the historical analogies I have mentioned. The complexity is greater, and the practical application of the relevant mathematics is harder.

There's an important and difficult technical challenge in this, and one that I think is well suited for CPSR. After all, the introduction of appropriate regulations would not only improve software quality, but it would do so by encouraging computer professionals to accept their social responsibility.

Part II

Traditional Issues and Information Systems

HISTORICAL PERSPECTIVE

Historically certain rights have been considered intrinsically human. Society has perpetuated these human rights by promoting generally acceptable ethical behavior. Some of these "inalienable rights," life, liberty, and the pursuit of happiness, were expressed by Thomas Jefferson in the Declaration of Independence.

Two centuries later the inalienable rights still hold true; however, they have donned new faces. For instance, Jefferson probably never imagined that his words would also be associated with the right to life and right to death movements of the latter decades of the twentieth century. Issues such as abortion and "suicide machines" have given new meaning to the ethical issue of the right to life.

A closely related ethical issue is the right to freedom. In Jefferson's day this was primarily the right of political freedom. Today this issue includes the right to political freedom as well as economic freedom, individual freedom of choice, and the freedom to pursue knowledge. Without these freedoms, the issue of right to life (and death) would be moot since one must have freedom of choice in order to pursue the right to life (or death).

The rights to life and freedom help to secure the right to happiness or well-being. Once again, without either a right to life or a right to freedom, the issue of the right to pursue happiness is moot.

Freedoms, rights, and ethical behavior are intermingled. One does not exist without the others. Without the rights to pursue these freedoms one can't fully obtain them. Unethical behavior also deprives persons of freedoms and rights.

FOUR ETHICAL ISSUES PERTAINING TO "INALIENABLE RIGHTS"

Four traditional areas regarding human rights include privacy, accuracy, property, and access. By protecting these individual rights, we are indirectly providing protection of inalienable rights. The traditional issues are interwoven in the fabric of society. Although the readings for this part focus on these issues in terms of computers and information, they are also pertinent to noncomputer arenas.

In terms of noncomputer issues, privacy, accuracy, property, and access refer to such topics as (1) the right of the government and individuals concerning search and seizure, (2) issues of surveillance, (3) access to an education, (4) security of property and data, (5) the right to disclosure and review of personal records, and (6) the right of compensation for one's efforts.

Concerning computers and information systems, these issues take on a different flavor. Among the computer-related issues of privacy, accuracy, property, and access are (1) exposure by minute description, (2) the right to disclosure and review of an individual's *computerized* database records and relationships, (3) the context in which data is presented, viewed, or processed and the accuracy of that data, (4) the right to access information (which includes the economic disparity issue of being able to access information), (5) responsibility for the accuracy of computer programs and applications, and (6) copyright laws and software ownership.

The topics of privacy, accuracy, property, and access have not changed much over the years in terms of their essence; however, they have changed with regard to the specific situations in which they must be viewed. The Information Age has not changed the basic issues involved; instead it has provided new challenges and viewpoints.

THE PAPERS: CHAPTER 3

"Why Privacy Is Important"

Rachel's paper examines the issues associated with privacy. He discusses reasons why privacy is important in our lives: (1) the need to protect people's interests in competitive situations, (2) the need to keep things private to avoid embarrassment, (3) the need to keep medical records private, and (4) the need to limit disclosure of information only to that which is pertinent to the situation. He also talks about the idea that the individual's right to privacy is a group of rights that intersect with other clusters of rights (e.g., the right of owning property).

"Computers and Privacy"

Miller deals with the many issues involved in data collection, analysis, and dissemination and how these processes are influenced by computer technologies. His discussion ranges from the impact of recent court rulings on the constitutional bases of privacy to the tendency we have to collect all the data we can just because we have the means even if we don't need it. This is the idea that data grow to fill the capacity of the storage medium.

Miller believes that regulation is needed to protect the individual's right to privacy while still allowing the benefits that extensive data collection provides. Laws should require the dating of information and the destruction of data after some identified period of time. The practice of selling and combining information would be restricted. Stricter practices of data verification and accuracy would also be covered by law.

"Computer Monitoring: A Threat to the Right to Privacy?"

This speech was presented by Karen Nussbaum, founder and executive director of the National Association of Working Women, at the 1989 Computer Professionals for Social Responsibility (CPSR) Annual Meeting. The speech focuses on the growing incidence of corporate monitoring of employees. Nussbaum discusses techniques such as subliminal suggestions and monitoring of the workplace via LANs.

"Data Quality and Due Process in Large Interorganizational Record Systems"

Laudon addresses the problems associated with the computer's ability to store and maintain large volumes of data. The problem of data quality and integrity is also discussed. His point is that the computer's ability to store and then provide data provokes a much more severe problem of individual privacy. His particular example is the criminal record system of the United States. A system of this type, which contains inaccurate, incomplete, or ambiguous information, not only violates society's notion of being fair to individuals but also threatens specific due process rights guaranteed by the Constitution.

"Vulnerable on All Counts: How Computerized Vote Tabulation Threatens the Integrity of Our Elections"

This excerpt from "An Election Watch Report," which appeared in the *CPSR Newsletter,* primarily discusses the inherent problems and possibilities of abuse of computerized vote tabulation. The article outlines the problems with a particular focus on accuracy and suggests possible solutions. The article also warns that our voting rights are being eroded by these inaccuracies.

THE PAPERS: CHAPTER 4

"The Effect of Demographic Factors on Attitudes Toward Software Piracy"

Solomon and O'Brien identify those factors that may or may not be associated with attitudes toward software piracy. These factors include both personal and organizational variables. The organizational variables include the environment, perceived attitudes of colleagues and superiors, opportunity, and level of expertise. The personal demographic variables tested include age, college major, work experience, and individual's income level. The authors sampled MIS and CIS students at two public institutions. Their results suggest that software piracy is viewed as socially and ethically acceptable. Students seem to excuse the piracy because there was a perceived lack of software provided by the institutions for class assignments. Students also seem to feel justified in copying software because the attitude of their faculty seems to condone it.

"A Psycho-Social Model of Software Piracy: The Development and Test of a Model"

Eining and Christensen describe the development and testing of a behavioral model to identify factors influencing the decision-making process with regard to software piracy. The factors in their model include (1) attitude toward computers, (2) material consequences, (3) normative expectations, (4) social-legal attitudes, and (5) effective or emotional factors. Demographic data was also collected for the study: age, marital status, employment status, and year in school.

They tested their model by administering the questionnaire to a sample of upper-division business majors. Their results showed that people who copy software do not believe that their actions are wrong nor do they believe that their friends view it as wrong. They also found that those people who had more positive attitudes toward computers were less likely to engage in piracy activities.

"A Comparative Study of Unauthorized Software Copying: Information System Faculty Members' vs. Practicing Managers' Perceptions"

Shim and Taylor explore the perceptions of two distinct IS groups, faculty and managers, about software piracy. They found these perceptions to differ. Although their analysis of the data did not clearly support all their hypotheses, their results are still interesting. They found that perceptions differed in the frequency in which colleagues were perceived to copy software. They also found that faculty seem to think that copying software for teaching and research is not as unethical as copying for consulting purposes.

"CPSR Responds to the Internet Computer Virus"

With the alarming increase in the number and destructive potential of viruses, CPSR drafted a formal statement on computer viruses. This statement was in response to the November 2, 1988 Internet "worm" that affected approximately 6,000 computers nationwide. Although the drafters of the statement believe that viruses and worms should not be condoned since they have the potential to destroy personal property, they also believe that strict regulation of computer networks is not the correct solution, since this would limit the free flow of ideas, which "are the ingredients of scientific advancement and technological achievement."

"Computer Accessibility for Federal Workers with Disabilities: It's the Law

Ladner outlines the guidelines and regulations of Section 508 of the Rehabilitation Act Amendments of 1986. He additionally describes reactions to the guidelines and regulations and discusses challenges for the future in meeting the computer accessibility needs of users with disabilities.

This paper addresses the physical access issues of computing. That is, handicapped individuals also need to be able to work in an electronic environment, implying a need for items like alternative I/O devices, braille, and large screens.

"Equal Access to Computing, Computing Expertise, and Decision Making about Computers"

Johnson addresses the social impact of computers. In particular she focuses on the concerns of equal access to computing and computer expertise. She also examines the role of computers in our future society and the impact that they will have on the distribution of rights and benefits. Society should strive for increased access to computers and computer expertise.

"Computers in Education"

This article is a summary of a panel discussion at the 1989 Computer Professionals for Social Responsibility Annual Meeting, entitled "Computers in Education: Mixed Agendas and Uncertain Outcomes." Pierce and Murray summarize the panel's discussions concerning issues of computer access. The panel approaches the access issue from the same viewpoint of Richard Mason and Deborah Johnson, i.e., from the socially oriented view of equal access to information and computing expertise in our educational system.

Chapter 3

The Traditional Issues of Privacy and Accuracy

Why Privacy Is Important

James Rachels

Philosophy & Public Affairs, 4, No. 4, Summer 1975. Copyright © 1975 Princeton University Press. Reprinted with permission of Princeton University Press.

According to Thomas Scanlon, the first element of a theory of privacy should be "a characterization of the special interest we have in being able to be free from certain kinds of intrusions." Since I agree that is the right place to begin, I shall begin there. Then I shall briefly comment on Judith Jarvis Thomson's proposals.[1]

I

Why, exactly, is privacy important to us? There is no one simple answer to this question, since people have a number of interests that may be harmed by invasions of their privacy.

1. Privacy is sometimes necessary to protect people's interests in competitive situations. For example, it obviously would be a disadvantage to Bobby Fischer if he could not analyze the adjourned position in a chess game in private, without his opponent learning his results.
2. In other cases someone may want to keep some aspect of his life or behavior private simply because it would be embarrassing for other people to know about it. There is a splendid example of this in John Barth's novel *End of the Road*. The narrator of the story, Jake Horner, is with Joe Morgan's wife, Rennie, and they are approaching the Morgan house where Joe is at home alone:

> "Want to eavesdrop?" I whispered impulsively to Rennie. "Come on, it's great! See the animals in their natural habitat."
>
> Rennie looks shocked. "What for?"
>
> "You mean you never spy on people when they're alone? It's wonderful! Come on, be a sneak! It's the most unfair thing you can do to a person."
>
> "You disgust me Jake!" Rennie hissed. "He's just reading. You don't know Joe at all, do you?"
>
> "What does that mean?"
>
> "Real people aren't any different when they're alone. No masks. What you see of them is authentic."

---

[1] Judith Jarvis Thomson, "The Right to Privacy," *Philosophy & Public Affairs,* **4**(4), Summer 1975, 295–314.

. . . Quite reluctantly, she came over to the window and peeped in beside me.

It is indeed the grossest of injustices to observe a person who believes himself to be alone. Joe Morgan, back from his Boy Scout meeting, had evidently intended to do some reading, for there were books lying open on the writing table and on the floor beside the bookcase. But Joe wasn't reading. He was standing in the exact center of the bare room, fully dressed, smartly executing military commands. About FACE! Right DRESS! Ten-SHUN! Parade REST! He saluted briskly, his cheeks blown out and his tongue extended, and then proceeded to cavort about the room — spinning, pirouetting, bowing, leaping, kicking. I watched entranced by his performance, for I cannot say that in my strangest moments (and a bachelor has strange ones) I have surpassed him. Rennie trembled from head to foot.[2]

The scene continues even more embarrassingly.

3. There are several reasons why medical records should be kept private, having to do with the consequences to individuals of facts about them becoming public knowledge. "The average patient doesn't realize the importance of the confidentiality of medical records. Passing out information on venereal disease can wreck a marriage. Revealing a pattern of alcoholism or drug abuse can result in a man's losing his job or make it impossible for him to obtain insurance protection."[3]

4. When people apply for credit (or for large amounts of insurance for jobs of certain types) they are often investigated, and the result is a fat file of information about them. Now there is something to be said in favor of such investigations, for business people surely do have the right to know whether credit-applicants are financially reliable. The trouble is that all sorts of other information goes into such files, for example, information about the applicant's sex-life, his political views, and so forth. Clearly it is unfair for one's application for credit to be influenced by such irrelevant matters.

These examples illustrate the variety of interests that may be protected by guaranteeing people's privacy, and it would be easy to give further examples of the same general sort. However, I do not think that examining such cases will provide a complete understanding of the importance of privacy, for two reasons.

First, these cases all involve relatively unusual sorts of situations, in which someone has something to hide or in which information about a person might provide someone with a reason for mistreating him in some way. Thus, reflection on these cases gives us little help in understanding the value which privacy has in *normal* or *ordinary* situations. By this I mean situations in which there is nothing embarrassing or shameful or unpopular in what we are doing, and nothing ominous or threatening connected with its possible disclosure. For example, even married couples whose sex-lives are normal (whatever that is), and so who have nothing to be ashamed of, by even the most conventional standards, and certainly

---

[2]John Barth, End of the Road (New York, 1960), pp. 57–58.
[3]Dr. Malcolm Todd, president of the A.M.A., quoted in the *Miami Herald,* 26 October 1973, p. 18-A.

nothing to be blackmailed about, do not want their bedrooms bugged. We need an account of the value which privacy has for us, not only in the few special cases but in the many common and unremarkable cases as well.

Second, even those invasions of privacy that *do* result in embarrassment or in some specific harm to our other interests are objectionable on other grounds. A woman may rightly be upset if her credit-rating is adversely affected by a report about her sexual behavior because the use of such information is unfair; however, she may also object to the report simply because she feels—as most of us do—that her sex-life is *nobody else's business*. This, I think, is an extremely important point. We have a "sense of privacy" which is violated in such affairs, and this sense of privacy cannot adequately be explained merely in terms of our fear of being embarrassed or disadvantaged in one of these obvious ways. An adequate account of privacy should help us to understand what makes something "someone's business" and why intrusions into things that are "none of your business" are, as such, offensive.

These considerations lead me to suspect that there is something important about privacy which we shall miss if we confine our attention to examples such as [1–4]. In what follows I will try to bring out what this something is.

II

I want now to give an account of the value of privacy based on the idea that there is a close connection between our ability to control who has access to us and to information about us, and our ability to create and maintain different sorts of social relationships with different people. According to this account, privacy is necessary if we are to maintain the variety of social relationships with other people that we want to have, and that is why it is important to us. By a "social relationship" I do not mean anything especially unusual or technical; I mean the sort of thing which we usually have in mind when we say of two people that they are friends or that they are husband and wife or that one is the other's employer.

The first point I want to make about these relationships is that, often, there are fairly definite patterns associated with them. Our relationships with other people determine, in large part, how we act toward them and how they behave toward us. Moreover, there are *different* patterns of behavior associated with different relationships. Thus a man may be playful and affectionate with his children (although sometimes firm), businesslike with his employees, and respectful and polite with his mother-in-law. And to his close friends he may show a side of his personality that others never see—perhaps he is secretly a poet, and rather shy about it, and shows his verse only to his best friends.

It is sometimes suggested that there is something deceitful or hypocritical about such differences in behavior. It is suggested that underneath all the role-playing there is the "real" person, and that the various "masks" that we wear in dealing with some people are some sort of phony disguise that we use to conceal our "true" selves from them. I take it that this is what is behind Rennie's remark, in the passage from Barth, that, "*Real* people aren't any different when they're alone. No masks. What you see of them is authentic." According to this way of looking at things, the fact that we observe different standards of conduct with different people is merely a sign of dishonesty. Thus the cold-hearted businessman who reads poetry to his friends is "really" a gentle poetic soul whose businesslike demeanor in front of his employees is only a false front; and the man who curses and swears when talking to his friends, but who would never use such language around his mother-in-law, is just putting on an act for her.

This, I think, is quite wrong. Of course the man who does not swear in front of his mother-in-law may be just putting on an act so that, for example, she will not disinherit him, when otherwise he would curse freely in front of her without caring what she thinks. But it may be that his conception of how he ought to behave with his mother-in-law is very different from his conception of how he may behave with his friends. Or it may not be appropriate for him to swear around *her* because "she is not that sort of person." Similarly, the businessman may be putting up a false front for his employees, perhaps because he dislikes his work and has to make a continual, disagreeable effort to maintain the role. But on the other hand he may be, quite comfortably and naturally, a businessman with a certain conception of how it is appropriate for a businessman to behave; and this conception is compatible with his also being a husband, a father, and a friend, with different conceptions of how it is appropriate to behave with his wife, his children, and his friends. There need be nothing dishonest or hypocritical in any of this, and neither side of his personality need be the "real" him, any more than any of the others.

It is not merely accidental that we vary our behavior with different people according to the different social relationships that we have with them. Rather, the different patterns of behavior are (partly) what define the different relationships; they are an important part of what makes the different relationships what they are. The relation of friendship, for example, involves bonds of affection and special obligations, such as the duty of loyalty, which friends owe to one another; but it is also an important part of what it means to have a friend that we welcome his company, that we confide in him, that we tell him things about ourselves, and that we show him sides of our personalities which we would not tell or show to just anyone.[4] Suppose I believe that someone is my close friend, and then I discover that he is worried about his job and is afraid of being fired. But, while he has discussed this situation with several other people, he has not mentioned it at all to me. And then I learn that he writes poetry, and that this is an important part of his life; but while he has shown his poems to many other people, he has not shown them to me. Moreover, I learn that he behaves with his other friends in a much more informal way than he behaves with me, that he makes a point of seeing them socially much more than he sees me, and so on. In the absence of some special explanation of his behavior, I would have to conclude that we are not as close as I had thought.

The same general point can be made about other sorts of human relationships: businessman to employee, minister to congregant, doctor to patient, husband to wife, parent to child, and so on. In each case, the sort of relationship that people have to one another involves a conception of how it is appropriate for them to behave with each other, and what is more, a conception of the kind and degree of knowledge concerning one another which it is appro-

---

[4]My view about friendship and its relation to privacy is similar to Charles Fried's view in his book *An Anatomy of Values* (Cambridge, Mass., 1970).

priate for them to have. (I will say more about this later.) I do not mean to imply that such relationships are, or ought to be, structured in exactly the same way for everyone. Some parents are casual and easy-going with their children, while others are more formal and reserved. Some doctors want to be friends with at least some of their patients, others are businesslike with all. Moreover, the requirements of social roles may change: the women's liberation movement is making an attempt to redefine the husband-wife relationship. The examples that I have been giving are drawn, loosely speaking, from contemporary American society; but this is mainly a matter of convenience. The only point that I want to insist on is that *however* one conceives one's relations with other people, there is inseparable from that conception an idea of how it is appropriate to behave with and around them, and what information about oneself it is appropriate for them to have.

The point may be underscored by observing that new types of social institutions and practices sometimes make possible new sorts of human relationships, which in turn make it appropriate to behave around people, and to say things in their presence, that would have been inappropriate before. "Group therapy" is a case in point. Many psychological patients find the prospect of group therapy unsettling, because they will have to speak openly to the group about intimate matters. They sense that there is something inappropriate about this: one simply does not reveal one's deepest feelings to strangers. Our aspirations, our problems, our frustrations and disappointments are things that we may confide to our husbands and wives, our friends, and perhaps to some others—but it is out of the question to speak of such matters to people that we do not even know. Resistance to this aspect of group therapy is overcome when the patients begin to think of each other not as strangers but as *fellow members of the group*. The definition of a kind of relation between them makes possible frank and intimate conversation which would have been totally out of place when they were merely strangers.

All of this has to do with the way that a crucial part of our lives—our relations with other people—is organized, and as such its importance to us can hardly be exaggerated. Thus we have good reason to object to anything that interferes with these relationships and makes it difficult or impossible for us to maintain them in the way that we want to. Conversely, because our ability to control who has access to us, and who knows what about us, allows us to maintain the variety of relationships with other people that we want to have, it is, I think, one of the most important reasons why we value privacy,

First, consider what happens when two close friends are joined by a casual acquaintance. The character of the group changes; and one of the changes is that conversation about intimate matters is now out of order. Then suppose these friends could *never* be alone; suppose there were always third parties (let us say casual acquaintances or strangers) intruding. Then they could do either of two things. They could carry on as close friends do, sharing confidences, freely expressing their feelings about things, and so on. But this would mean violating their sense of how it is appropriate to behave around casual acquaintances or strangers. Or they could avoid doing or saying anything which they think inappropriate to do or say around a third party. But this would mean that they could no longer behave with one another in the way that friends do and further that, eventually, they would no longer *be* close friends.

Again, consider the differences between the way that a husband and wife behave when they are alone and the way they behave in the company of third parties. Alone, they may be affectionate, sexually intimate, have their fights and quarrels, and so on; but with others, a more "public" face is in order. If they could never be alone together, they would either have to abandon the relationship that they would otherwise have as husband and wife or else behave in front of others in ways they now deem inappropriate.[5]

These considerations suggest that we need to separate our associations, at least to some extent, if we are to maintain a system of different relationships with different people. Separation allows us to behave with certain people in the way that is appropriate to the sort of relationship we have with them, without at the same time violating our sense of how it is appropriate to behave with, and in the presence of, others with whom we have a different kind of relationship. Thus, if we are to be able to control the relationships that we have with other people, we must have control over who has access to us.

We now have an explanation of the value of privacy in ordinary situations in which we have nothing to hide. The explanation is that, even in the most common and unremarkable circumstances, we regulate our behavior according to the kinds of relationships we have with the people around us. If we cannot control who has access to us, sometimes including and sometimes excluding various people, then we cannot control the patterns of behavior we need to adopt (this is one reason why privacy is an aspect of liberty) or the kinds of relations with other people that we will have. But what about our feeling that certain facts about us are "simply nobody else's business"? Here, too, I think the answer requires reference to our relationships with people. If someone is our doctor, then it literally is his business to keep track of our health; if someone is our employer, then it literally is his business to know what salary we are paid; our financial dealings literally are the business of the people who extend us credit; and so on. In general, a fact about ourselves is someone's business if there is a specific social relationship between us which entitles them to know. We are often free to choose whether or not to enter into such relationships, and those who want to maintain as much privacy as possible will enter them only reluctantly. What we cannot do is accept such a social role with respect to another person and then expect to retain the same degree of privacy relative to him that we had before. Thus, if we are asked how much money we have

---

[5]I found this in a television program-guide in the Miami Herald, 21 October 1973, p. 17:

> "I think it was one of the most awkward scenes I've ever done," said actress Brenda Benet after doing a romantic scene with her husband, Bill Bixby, in his new NBC-TV series, "The Magician."

> "It was even hard to kiss him," she continued. "It's the same old mouth, but it was terrible. I was so abnormally shy; I guess because I don't think it's anybody's business. The scene would have been easier had I done it with a total stranger because that would be real acting. With Bill, it was like being on exhibition."

I should stress that, on the view that I am defending, it is *not* "abnormal shyness" or shyness of any type that is behind such feelings. Rather, it is a sense of what is appropriate with and around people with whom one has various sorts of personal relationships. Kissing *another actor* in front of the camera crew, the director, and so on, is one thing; but kissing *one's husband* in front of all these people is quite another thing. What made Ms. Benet's position confusing was that her husband *was* another actor, and the behavior that was permitted by the one relationship was discouraged by the other.

in the bank, we cannot say, "It's none of your business," to our banker, to prospective creditors, or to our spouses, because their relationships with us do entitle them to know. But, at the risk of being boorish, we could say that to others with whom we have no such relationship.

III

Thomson suggests, "as a simplifying hypothesis, that the right to privacy is itself a cluster of rights, and that it is not a distinct cluster of rights but itself intersects with the cluster of rights which the right over the person consists of, and also with the cluster of rights which owning property consists of." This hypothesis is "simplifying" because it eliminates the right to privacy as anything distinctive.

"The right over the person" consists of such "un-grand" rights as the right not to have various parts of one's body looked at, the right not to have one's elbow painted green, and so on. Thomson understands these rights as analogous to property rights. The idea is that our bodies are *ours* and so we have the same rights with respect to them that we have with respect to our other possessions.

But now consider the right not to have various parts of one's body looked at. Insofar as this is a matter of *privacy,* it is not simply analogous to property rights, for the kind of interest we have in controlling who looks at what parts of our bodies is very different from the interest we have in our cars or fountain pens. For most of us, physical intimacy is a part of very special sorts of personal relationships. Exposing one's knee or one's face to someone may not count for us as physical intimacy, but exposing a breast, and allowing it to be seen and touched, does. Of course the details are to some extent a matter of social convention; that is why it is easy for us to imagine, say, a Victorian woman for whom an exposed knee would be a sign of intimacy. She would be right to be distressed at learning that she had absent-mindedly left a knee uncovered and that someone was looking at it—if the observer was not her spouse or her lover. By dissociating the body from ideas of physical intimacy, and the complex of personal relationships of which such intimacies are a part, we can make this "right over the body" seem to be nothing more than an un-grand kind of property right; but that dissociation separates this right from the matters that make *privacy* important.

Thomson asks whether it violates your right to privacy for acquaintances to indulge in "very personal gossip" about you, when they got the information without violating your rights, and they are not violating any confidences in telling what they tell . . . She thinks they do not violate your right to privacy, but that if they do "there is trouble for the simplifying hypothesis."

This is, as she says, a debatable case, but if my account of why privacy is important is correct, we have at least some reason to think that your right to privacy can be violated in such a case. Let us fill in some details. Suppose you are recently divorced, and the reason your marriage failed is that you became impotent shortly after the wedding. You have shared your troubles with your closest friend, but this is not the sort of thing you want everyone to know. Not only would it be humiliating for everyone to know, it is none of their business. It is the sort of intimate fact about you that is not appropriate for strangers or casual acquaintances to know. But now the gossips have obtained the information (perhaps one of them innocently overheard your discussion with your friend; it was not his fault, so he did not violate your privacy in the hearing, but then you did not know he was within earshot) and now they are spreading it around to everyone who knows you and to some who do not. Are they violating your right to privacy? I think they are. If so, it is not surprising, for the interest involved in this case is just the sort of interest which the right to privacy typically protects. Since the right that is violated in this case is not also a property right, or a right over the person, the simplifying hypothesis fails. But this should not be surprising, either, for if the right to privacy has a different *point* than these other rights, we should not expect it always to overlap with them. And even if it did always overlap, we could still regard the right to privacy as a distinctive sort of right in virtue of the special kind of interest it protects.

Computers and Privacy

Arthur R. Miller, Harvard Law School

Reprinted by permission of the Author.

I am here to talk to you very quietly and benignly and unemotionally about a revolution. I call it the "Privacy Revolution." It is not a revolution fought with guns and tanks and planes. Rather, it is a revolution that has been going on in people's minds, in their feelings, in their attitudes, in their values and what is very interesting for me as a lawyer, it is a revolution that has been going on within the legal system.

I use the world "revolution" in part because, as a lawyer, I am used to things happening very, very slowly. For example, one of my fields of interest happens to be the Law of Copyright—intellectual and artistic property. And in that field of the law, prior to 1978, we had been operating under a federal statute that was passed in 1909. Nobody thought it was important enough to address the fact that we had developed such things as motion pictures, the phonograph record industry, radio, television, computers, satellite communication. In the eye of the law, it was enough to stumble along with a 1909 statute and make guesses as to what the law should do. So the word "revolution" as I am using it connotes the fact that, in less than twelve years, the legal system has become somewhat revolutionized in terms of this value we call the "right of privacy."

Starting with the brouhaha about the National Data Center in about 1967, there has been a preoccupation, a focusing, an attention to various individual rights that we can bring under this amorphous umbrella known as the "right of privacy." And in that time, in the space of less than fifteen years, what has happened? Congress has enacted the Fair Credit Reporting Act. What is the Fair Credit Reporting Act? It is an act designed to protect the privacy, quality of information, and information flow in the consumer reporting industry, which embraces retail merchants, employers, and banks. In that same period Congress has enacted the Educational Privacy Act—the Buckley Amendment, which, for the first time in American history, represents a federal, and I underscore the word *federal*, presence on the campus, every campus, from primary school to postgraduate school, from public education to private education, from secular schools to religious schools. Every school in these United States is now under a congressionally enacted mandate to handle student files with a federal degree of care: what can be recorded, who can see it, auditing, document destruction policy, and a number of other things. I consider that statute, just by way of an aside, one of the most amazing pieces of legislation ever enacted in our federalist country, particularly since people like Strom Thurmond sit in key positions in the legislative branch. That's statute number two.

Statute number three is the Fair Information Practices Act of 1974, a massive federal statute controlling governmental data collection, governmental data maintenance, and governmental data dissemination. And there are little Fair Information Practices Acts that have sprouted, like weeds, at the state level throughout the country, Minnesota being the leader in that regard, Massachusetts being somewhat, but not too far, behind. These state statutes control state governmental information around the country. Those are three massive statutes in less than fifteen years.

In addition the United States Supreme Court, in *Roe v. Wade*, which is thought of as the Abortion Decision, recognized very clearly, very precisely, that the right of privacy in this country is constitutionally based. The Justices of the Supreme Court had a little bit of difficulty finding the privacy right in any particular part of the Constitution, so it is one of those "We-got-it-by-osmosis" kinds of things. But it's there; that's what the Justices say. True, it dealt with privacy of the body; and that is a unique type of privacy, but when you patch the Roe case together with other Supreme Court decisions dealing with freedom of ideology, freedom of association, freedom of protest, speech and dissent, it all comes together as a broadly based right of privacy.

And we've had some amazing judicial decisions stemming from *Roe v. Wade*. Some of them are a bit humorous. You can look at pornography in the home, courtesy of your constitutional right of privacy. You can smoke pot in the home, courtesy of your constitutional right of privacy. On a serious note, you have a right to die. The New Jersey Supreme Court, in a decision involving Karen Ann Quinlan, allowed a hospital to take her off a respirator; this is a privacy case. Her right to privacy was held to embrace her right to die, which is being exercised for her by her parents. The right to die—a strange aspect of privacy. More germane to this conference, I suppose, is a California Supreme Court decision that says the constitutional right of privacy embraces freedom from governmental surveillance on the campus. Now I say again: from a legal perspective, this is a revolution. This is a legal revolution of the first order.

Why did this come about? Privacy is not a new problem. Privacy has been significant and threats to it have existed ever since two people existed. Adam and Eve probably had some need for privacy. The catalyst for the issue, of course, is the computer. We had barely any organized law of privacy prior to the computer. And if you start tracing it out, you begin to see the sensitivity about privacy starting to take a gradual and then escalating upward turn with the development of electronic data processing.

Part of it has been the expanded use of digits. I used to live in Brooklyn, New York. I am now told that, no, I didn't live in Brooklyn, New York, I lived in area code 212. I *think* I live in Cambridge. And, no, I am told I live in zip code number 02138. My telephone number used to be "Digby." Digby. That has a ring to it. Boy, I know a Digby when I see a Digby, but now I am told no, that old telephone number is now 344 or something or other. I used to think I was Arthur Miller. And now I'm told I'm really my Social Security number. People don't like that. It may be a psychological problem rather than a factual one, but people think of themselves as humans, not code numbers. We have been brought up to think in terms of names and places and identifiers that are not a data or digit stream.

Think about it and imagine a high school prom, the year 1984: a peach-fuzzed young man walks up to a young lady and says, "Hi, I'm 127–26–7378." And she blushes and replies, "Oh, it's so nice to meet you. I'm 097–12–8394." He shrinks back and says, "Funny, you don't look Jewish."

An allegory, nothing but an allegory. But it's the computer, the oversell of the computer, the constant movement to numerology in the sixties, that started the apprehension among all sorts of people, that somehow their right of privacy, their right of individuality, their right of autonomy, their sense of self, their notions of control over themselves and their fortunes, was threatened. This is what produced the reaction I am terming the Privacy Revolution. And privacy has deep roots in our society, although legally we haven't had to deal with it very much. We had, after all, in the eighteenth and nineteenth centuries an open frontier, a high rate of illiteracy, and no technology to record data. The mobility of American society prevented that data from being much of a threat to anyone. As Horace Greeley said, "Go West, young man, go West." I suspect he meant not only that there were economic opportunities on the frontier, but that it was a way to escape a bankruptcy record or a carping spouse back East. There was the ability to escape, there was no sense of closure in society. All of that is being threatened. To say to someone, "Go West, young man, go West," today is a cruel joke; the computer will have your files in San Francisco seven hours before you get there.

Let me try to describe these apprehensions. I am the first to admit that some of them are psychological, not objective. But some of them are very real and not mere figments of paranoid imaginations. Whatever their reality, these concerns exists. And they must be responded to because you don't tell a million, two million, five million people, or however many there are who are concerned about data collection in this society, "Oh, you're crazy, we're going to ignore you." Any data manager worth his or her salt must face the reality that there is a great deal of popular concern. And every public opinion poll taken in the last five or eight years shows a constant, upward swing in public attention to privacy. This used to be considered to be nothing but a white, middle-class value in the mid-sixties. The current surveying suggests this is no longer true, that over the last fifteen years, there has been enormous attention to this issue. I think we can divide the apprehensions, the privacy concerns of people, into four discrete categories.

First is the cliché: We live in an information-based society. More and more institutions are collecting more and more data about more and more people and more and more of their activities. That's Apprehension Number One. There's too damn much data collection going on in this society. Too many people are asking too many questions and maintaining too many files. Stated in this way, it's a truism. I don't think anyone in his or her right mind will doubt the proposition that there's more data collection going on in this society than ever before. All you have to do is pull out the IRS Form 1040, which is what you fill out when you pay your taxes. To those of you who keep records, take out a 1040 from ten years ago and this year's, and lay the two IRS forms side by side. You'll be stunned at the increase in data collected from us by the IRS for the privilege of paying our taxes. The fine graining of the questions, the new categories of questions; any decent information scientist looking at somebody's 1040 can prepare a very extensive profile on that person. Not only do you have all of the taxpayer's financial dealings laid out, but you have all of the taxpayer's medical problems laid out if he takes the medical deduction; and you have all of the taxpayer's ideological and charitable associations laid out if he takes the charitable deduction.

Every time you get on an airplane, every time you rent a car, every time you check into a hotel, you create a file. Every time you apply for a job, every time you seek a credit card, every time you want insurance, every time you think you're eligible for a governmental benefit, you create a file. Those are not transient files. Most of them are permanent or semi-permanent files. The airline doesn't erase your travel record when you step off in Washington, D.C.; it is maintained and, increasingly, is a source of monitoring by the so-called organized crime strike forces to analyze travel patterns of suspects. And remember, those airline reservation services don't simply tell which flight you were on; if you stop and think about it, they obviously contain everybody else who was on that plane. If you're traveling with somebody, it will indicate that; if you've given a contact number at either end of your trip, it will show that; if you've rented a car or a hotel through your agent of the airline, it will show that as well. This type of file didn't exist ten years ago, before there was a thing called the computer. It is the computer that has enabled this constantly upward spiraling pattern of data collection in our society to exist. Why does the IRS ask so many questions? Why do social service agencies ask so many questions? Because they now have the technological capacity to record that data and, presumably, to use it.

I like to think of it as a variant on Parkinson's Law. Namely, any institution that gets a computer inevitably figures out ways to fill the capacity of that computer. And when it's filled the capacity of that computer, like in Parkinson's Law, it goes out and gets itself another computer. And since organizational power in so many parts of our society has as its vortex the computer and the ability to control and manage the computer, it is like a dog constantly chasing its tail.

You find the most incredible quantities of data collected. Why? Because the capacity to store it exists. Why? Because somebody always says, "Gee, since we're doing a survey, we might as well ask these additional questions because someday we might need the information." That seems to be the wail of the longitudinal researcher. "We might as well ask that, we might as well ask this, we might as well ask this," and so on. The net result is: surveys multiply, elongate, and people have the overwhelming sense that they are being subjected to more and more information extractions—to use the dental analogy—as part of daily life in this country. And many of them don't like it. But worse, in my judgment, is that many people are getting used to it because we're becoming anesthetized to any sense of individuality about our informational profile. And that's Apprehension Number One.

Apprehension Number Two is also, I think, a truism. It's this: more and more decisions about us are being made on the basis of files. And when I use the word "files" I'm talking about manila files as well as computer files. Decision making is less and less based on a face-to-face dynamic. We don't deal, as we once did on the frontier and in the rural environment at the turn of the century, across the table with a banker, or a credit grantor, or an admission office, or a governmental agency. Today the question is whether your file falls within the right decision-making parameter—what a fateful word! If you want to get credit, to get a job, to get insurance, or to get a benefit, you are increasingly dependent on what is in the files; more and more decision-making occurs by file. The phenomenon surrounds us. And even though we are sitting here in the gentility of an academic community, we are not free of it. Have you ever considered how you get into many professional schools these days?

Let's take a big, hypothetical professional school. Perhaps one that gets 8,000 applications a year. There can't possibly be any face-to-face dynamic. So what happens? Let's take an average twenty-two or twenty-three-year-old breathing, aspiring, fresh, flesh and blood college senior, and assume he or she wants to go to law school. After getting an application from our hypothetical school our senior sits, night after night, filling out the forms recording the events of his or her twenty-two years, including the essay, "Why I Want to Go to Law School" or "The Greatest Book I Ever Read." Our applicant sits there, night after night, writing part fact, part fiction. A tear drops here, a whimsical smile there. But the entire life of that applicant is embodied in that application form, which is then entrusted to the United States postal system and eventually, we hope, comes to our hypothetical law school. Then, our twenty-two-year-old breathing applicant, now represented by the application of that applicant, is opened up, a few entries made in books at the admissions office, and the forms are shot off, you know where? To the Educational Testing Service in New Jersey.

Upon arriving at ETS it is handed over to the data processors who immediately take the transcript and keypunch it into the machine. Now, this is not just an ordinary machine. It is a very sophisticated computer because if the school is at all adept at the admissions process, there is a program in ETS's computer that adjusts the transcript. You realize that they don't just "adjust the transcript," because there's a twenty-two-year-old in back of that transcript. It's the applicant who is being adjusted, essentially lobotomized. The adjustments take the form of kicking out certain courses—perhaps Military Science or Music Appreciation—and a new grade point average is computed. The transcript is then further adjusted because many law schools have developed an experience base showing how students from numerous undergraduate institutions perform at their school. The truth is that an "A" average from Cal Tech is very different from an "A" average from Siwash U, at least as far as admissions officers are concerned. So this marvelous computer program augments or discounts the already adjusted transcript, depending on where that applicant went to school.

So let's take a simple example—an adjusted grade point average, according to ETS's computer, of 3.5. This is then multiplied by an arbitrary weighting number, let's say 200, producing 700. To which is added the applicant's Law School Aptitude Test grade. The Law School Aptitude Test is thought by many to be another one of society's depersonalizations. They believe it is somebody's cruel joke as to what characteristics go into making a lawyer because it was not prepared by lawyers, and most lawyers would laugh at it if they saw it. In any event, let's take another simple number—700 on the Law School Aptitude Test. So we have an adjusted grade point average weighted to 700, and we have a Law School Aptitude Test score of 700. We now have what is euphemistically called a Predictor Index Score of 1400, which is supposed to indicate whether this human being can make it at the law school. ETS sends the number 1400 back to the admissions office of the hypothetical law school.

Let's see where we are. We have taken the twenty-two-year-old college senior, reduced him or her to a formal application, and then taken the formal application and reduced it to a number—1400. But we're not done. When the number 1400 arrives at the admissions office it is taken by some functionary over to a wall chart. A floor to ceiling wall chart—a scattergram. And where the axes show a Predictor Index Score of 1400, our admissions office functionary carefully puts a dot. Our twenty-two-year-old aspiring, flesh and blood applicant is now a fly speck, a dot on the wall.

Then about this time every year, the high priests and priestesses of the admissions office, garbed in the appropriate dress, engage in something like a crypto-religious rite of spring. They go to the great wall chart, as one would go the Oracle at Delphi, and they draw two parallel lines. Now, if you, or should I say your dot, appears above the top line, you are automatically admitted. If your dot appears below the bottom of the two lines, you are automatically rejected. If your dot appears between the two lines, you are in a hold category and someone probably will go to the manila folders and see if they can differentiate you, rather, your dot, from someone else's dot. In all three cases, the applicant's admit, reject, or hold letter is produced by computer.

People don't like that kind of decision making. It may be necessary in a mass society such as ours, but that doesn't make people like it any more. It takes much of the humanity out of life. It makes one feel as if he or she is completely at the mercy of the data handlers. How does an individual know what the so-called "parameters" of decision making are, the criteria of admission or rejection? How does the individual know which elements in the data stream are germane and which are irrelevant to the decision maker? How does the individual even know that the decision maker has the right data, that it is factual, that it is accurate, current, and verified, not hearsay or gossip, that it has been programmed correctly? I often worry that my credit files around the country are littered with the debris of other Arthur Millers. That's Apprehension Number Two.

And now Number Three. We have talked about increased data collection, we have talked about decision making by data. Now I want to talk about the risks of "data out of context." And I am not talking about misplaced digits or errors in the data. I am talking about the fact that data generally is created in an environment, for a purpose, by a group with particular standards relating to its objectives. The police have standards in generating arrest records. Universities have standards in establishing grading scales. The military has standards in terms of efficiency reports on its personnel. Every organization that generates data does so for a purpose, and under standards germane to it.

And that is perfectly acceptable in a data environment in which the information is static: it is generated, posted, stored, and doesn't move. But we know that is not reality in the 1980s. The computer and communications technology have completely obliterated any time or space limitation on data movement during the last twenty years. There is no such thing as localized data anymore. We can shoot data to the moon and back in seconds. We bring television signals in from Teheran in seconds. We send credit reports transcontinentally in seconds. And we can send medical data transcontinentally or intercontinentally in seconds. Scientists have placed a lot of emphasis on the time-space configuration of data movement and data transfer. But thus far very little consideration has been given to the fact that when you move data from one context to another, there is no reason to believe that the receiver has the foggiest notions of the purpose, the standards, or the inferences to be drawn from that data, because he, she or it didn't generate it and may be 8,000 miles away from the point of initiation. That's what I mean by "data out of context." The fact is that our great technologies can make the data available anywhere, but no one has educated people to understand the data beyond the superficialities of "Oh, it's an A" or "Oh, he's been arrested" or "Oh, he has this physical characteristic." Maybe that particular physical characteristic was germane to the employer that created the file because the company operates in a high dust-producing environment, but it's totally irrelevant for working in a bank 3,000 miles away or for granting credit.

Let me give you an example—arrest records. They circulate in most parts of this country freely. Not, supposedly, in Massachusetts; Massachusetts is one of the few states in the nation that has put limitations on the movement of criminal justice information. But, generally speaking, arrest records circulate. Now, if they only circulated within the law enforcement community, that would be one thing. We can more or less take the risk that law officers, whether they be in Los Angeles or Boston, view life from much the same perspective. They know why an arrest file is generated, what it means, and why a particular entry was made.

But no one in this room should have any doubt as to the ability to move arrest information beyond the law enforcement community. I trust you've all been reading the newspapers and watching television, where every criminal justice entry relating to Mr. Hinckley has been recounted for days. Indeed, all that information was generated and publicized within hours of the offense. To the extent that the law enforcement community needs the technological capacity to move information nationally or internationally to promote law and order, I am with them. That sounds terrific to me. I don't want a Massachusetts state trooper's head blown off on the turnpike because he doesn't know he has stopped someone more dangerous than a speeder, somebody who has outstanding warrants for bank robbery, murder, and arson. There are things he can check out through his vehicle's communication gear, which is tied to the computer terminal at headquarters. And certainly I want the Secret Service, the FBI, and all the rest to find out about Mr. Hinckley within minutes of the shooting of the president. The crime is that they didn't find out about Mr. Hinckley before, but that's another story.

You've all seen the program The FBI on television—the original with Efrem Zimbalist, Jr., as Inspector Erskine. They're hot on the trail of some suspect and he says to another neatly dressed, brush-cut agent: "Check him out in NCIC." Well, NCIC isn't the figment of television's imagination. NCIC is the National Crime Information Center. It is an on-line computer-based system that makes available all arrest records and outstanding warrants to anyone with a terminal attached to NCIC, and there are thousands of those terminals throughout the nation.

However, its users go beyond law enforcement. To be a beautician in Florida, you get checked out in NCIC; to be a croupier in Vegas, you get checked out in NCIC. Remember, these are mostly arrest records. But an arrest is a charge, it is proof of nothing, a fact that seemingly has escaped many employers in this country. "Have you ever been arrested?" This strikes me as an impermissible question, yet the answer is coming out of NCIC. The statistics show that almost 40 percent of the data in NCIC are raw arrest records, not convictions. Yet they are on preemployment investigations and credit checks and insurance inquiries. That is data out of context.

Let me give you some real rap sheets. Arrested: June 5th, 1943. Charge: Felony. Indicted. Tried: January 4th, 1944. Convicted. Sentenced: Three years, Leavenworth. Served: Six months, probation. That's a rap sheet of a *convicted* felon. Remember, 80 percent of them just say "Arrested." No disposition data is provided and the subject may have been exonerated. So there you are, sitting in the great corporate empire in the sky, deciding whether this "convicted felon" is to get a job. Better safe than sorry, you might say, reject him, and call for the next applicant. Do you stop to ask what the crime was? It's not on that data stream. The reality is that it was conscientious objection, World War II. And the conviction was under a standard since struck down as unconstitutional in the Muhammed Ali case. The applicant really isn't a felon at all. Oh well, next file.

I'll give you another one a little closer to home, looking around this room. Arrested: Meridian, Mississippi, April 5, 1957. Charge: Criminal Trespass. Convicted. Sentenced: Six months probation. Boy, that's a bad apple. That's one of those violent vandal kids, right? No job for that punk. Criminal trespass sounds bad! But it really was a civil rights demonstration; the conviction was reversed on appeal as being an impermissible intrusion on First Amendment protected conduct. How are you going to know that? I am not blaming you for not knowing it. All I am pointing out is the danger of relying on foreign data without any sense of what it means.

Let me describe another phenomenon. In the late sixties there was a back-office crunch in the brokerage houses of Wall Street. What that meant was that the trading pace exceeded the capacity to handle the transactions. So a number of stock certificates disappeared. To this day we don't know whether it was just accounting errors, whether they were misplaced, or whether there was massive fraud or embezzlement. The New York State Legislature reacted, as all legislatures, all policymakers, do in a crisis; they panicked. They passed a statute. From now on, the statute provided, before anyone could work in the brokerage industry, he or she had to go through Arrest Record Clearance. That starts with fingerprinting, just like they do, you know, in those bad countries. Then they check the prints out in NYSIIS. NYSIIS isn't so nice. It's the New York State Intelligence and Investigation Service; this is a computer system, New York's equivalent to the FBI's NCIC. If the system showed an arrest, the odds were you didn't get the job. Better safe than sorry (think in terms of the mentality of the bureaucrats who make the decisions on hiring stock boys or girls and messengers).

Now let me give you a few statistics. I hate statistics but occasionally they are illuminating. If you're black, if you're male, if you're a late teenager (eighteen or nineteen), if you come out of Bedford-Stuyvesant or Harlem in the City of New York, the odds are between eight in ten and nine in ten you have an arrest record—not a conviction record, an arrest record. Inner-city police know how to keep the lid on in the summer—a little sweep down 125th Street. Maybe the kids are just rolling craps in the alley, but take them in, just keep them off the street, book them, throw them back out when it's late enough at night so they'll just go home. Better safe than sorry. Eight out of ten, nine out of ten teenage black males have an arrest record in the city of New York. How are they going to get jobs in the securities industry? What happened to our commitment to equal opportunity in employment? The right hand doesn't know what the left hand is doing. That is data out of context.

Fourth apprehension. This, in my humble judgment, is the most important one of them all because it goes to the roots of what you want in a democratic society. It is the apprehension about governmental data collection which creates the feeling that "the government knows too much about me"; that I am no longer in control of my informational profile; that to do anything with the government involves a data extraction—whether it's paying my taxes, getting a mortgage on a house, or applying for some governmental benefit. And add to the general phenomenon of increasing data collection by governmental agencies the picture of domestic surveillance by the government, as we had during the Viet Nam War, when the Quakers were infiltrated, let alone the SDS, and the crazies. At that time if you went to a rally, you ran the risk of being photographed and posted in a Rogue's Gallery. If you signed a petition, there was a pretty good chance that every name on that petition would go into some file, somewhere.

Ask yourself whether that type of data collection and surveillance is at all consistent with notions of democracy and freedom, let alone consistent with the expressed constitutional guarantees of free speech, assembly, protest, and dissent set out in the First Amendment to the Constitution. Why do I have to be posted in a file just because I sign a petition about Viet Nam? Or about the abolition of the Legal Services Corporation? Or on nuclear power? Why does my government take down that fact and how are they going to use it? That is the apprehension.

We tend to react badly in crisis. Every civil liberties mistake we have made in our history was made at a time of crisis: the Alien and Sedition Laws in 1798, the suspension of the Writ of Habeas Corpus during the Civil War, the imprisonment of the Japanese-American population during World War II, the McCarthy Era, the activation of the domestic military intelligence network by President Johnson, who was reacting to the inner city riots, the Enemies List prepared by Mr. Nixon. These are all abuses of our civil liberties *justified* because of a "crisis."

Now let's look at a certain, I think fairly obvious, psychological fact. Many of us are emotional Spartans; we don't give a damn about having our names taken, our pictures taken. If we believe something, we will pursue that cause, that belief, that ideology, whatever. But certainly many of us are not. Countless among us may be deterred from going to a rally if we believe that our names or our picture will be taken and put into a file, especially since we don't have the foggiest notion what that file will be used for and by whom. What we are talking about is what some psychologists refer to as the Record Prison Syndrome: people surrounded by files and data collection begin to lose sense of themselves as individuals; they believe that they are in a record prison themselves; they begin to react by always wanting the records to reflect well on them; and then they act accordingly. And you know what those words "act accordingly" amount to? They describe behavior modification. If you are not going to go to the rally because you don't want to run the risk of looking bad in the government's eyes, you have had your behavior modified by your government. And that is exactly why, when the FBI decided to engage in surveillance of the Quakers, they did it overtly. I used to think it was the *covert* surveillance that was the big problem. It turns out that overt surveillance is just as threatening.

The FBI may have done it to the Beacon Press following the publication of *The Pentagon Papers*; they come into Boston with this big campaign, "We're going to find out how the papers got to the Beacon Press." Knowledgeable people say they already knew where Dan Ellsberg was at that point. Big headlines in the *Globe*: "FBI to Examine Financial Records of the Beacon Press," and at that time it was part of the Universalist-Unitarian Church. This may sound crazy to you, but people stopped going to church. Attendance at the churches dropped. Contributions, other than in cash, dried up for months. That's behavior modification. That isn't consistent with anything I know about what this country is supposed to be all about. I hate to use the image of *1984*, but it's apt. Surveillance is Big Brother on the television screen, watching us. You know what the true, the ultimate, lesson of *1984* and its notion of Big Brother on the television screen is? It's that it doesn't matter whether there actually is a Big Brother on the television screen. It doesn't matter at all whether somebody is, in fact, watching you. The only thing that matters is that you *think* that there's somebody watching you. You'll do the rest to yourself. We're human beings; we react. We don't even know we're reacting, that we are modifying our behavior.

Privacy Revolution. That is why public consciousness about privacy is as high as it is right now. And this is not a kooky phenomenon; this is not a Howard Hughes–Greta Garbo syndrome; this is not a lefty, ACLU, civil liberties phenomenon. I remind you of the co-sponsorship of the Federal Fair Information Practices Act: Ed Koch and Barry Goldwater, Jr. Ed Koch, then the liberal Democrat from New York and Barry Goldwater, Jr., the ultra-conservative congressman from Orange County, California. That is a marriage made in heaven. Why? For the liberal, it's civil liberties, for the conservative, it's anti-big government philosophy.

There are five themes. First, I think increasingly we are beginning to recognize an important ethical and moral principle: if you can't get people's attention through basic ethics and morality, eventually you begin to legislate. I think we are recognizing the proposition that every data collector and every data handler and user in our society owes what the law calls a fiduciary obligation—which you can translate into a humanistic notion of good faith, fair dealing—to the data subject. The obligation applies whether you're talking about a credit data operation, a bank, an employer, a university, a hospital, a governmental agency. The information handler *owes the subject* a duty of care to make sure that the information is germane, that it is current, and that it is verified. And we've already had cases in the courts about how we make people who are not satisfying that fiduciary obligation compensate those who are injured. That is theme Number One.

Theme Number Two: Increasingly I think we are seeing recognition of a notion that certain kinds of information should not be collected at all. AT ALL. Don't collect it even though the longitudinal researchers say they might be interested in the data eight years down the pike. Some of it is fairly obvious: political affiliation, religious association, ideology. More and more, people are beginning to understand that you must have a pretty good reason for encroaching on those areas of individual privacy. People are beginning to think about what it is they *really* need to know, as opposed to what it is they'd *like* to know, let alone what they might have some morbid curiosity about.

Principle Number Three is primarily administrative and technological. Namely, it's the notion that systems require safeguards. We will never achieve fail-safe; there has never been a lock without a key. But that does not mean that we cannot reduce the possibility of breaches of confidentiality. We must use access coding audit trails, have ombudsmen, indoctrinate data handlers as to the values of privacy and the importance of confidentiality. I, for one, am much more inclined to give information when, in return, I get a pledge of confidentiality that I can rely on. This objective requires a combination of technological, administrative, and educational efforts.

The Fourth Theme is almost a universal right now, probably the most advanced of all these principles. It is the recognition of the right of the data subject to gain access to his or her own file. The data subject used to be the one person excluded from the file. Psychologically that is foolish in terms of an institution's relationship with that individual. It is foolish because a data collector or user has no interest in having bad information, and who is in a better position to make sure a file is accurate than the data subject? I view this as almost a due process right, certainly in the context of relationships with governmental agencies. I have a due process right to see what you've got on me and to correct it if it is wrong. To be sure, there is a lot of mindless chatter about the system's privacy, or, "Oh no, we can't tell him about his mental condition. He's going to jump out of the fifth floor." That is the reaction of part of the medical fraternity. The answer to that is easy: "How many people have jumped out of the fifth floor window lately upon seeing their file?" Moreover, using a third party to screen the data is the obvious solution in any situation in which there is a legitimate reason not to let the actual data subject see the file; there is always an intermediary who can verify the information.

Finally, the Fifth Theme. In many ways information has a life cycle. You can be very anthropomorphic about it. Information is born, just the way we are, when it's generated; it grows, as we do; it gets married to other files, and, like at least half the population, information gets divorced when you separate bits of information and scatter them in different directions; and information, like all of us, gets older. But unlike us, information *never* seems to die. That's the Fifth Principle: death to information! We have got to stop being so anal retentive. We must begin to get information out of operating systems and at least into the archives; some of it must be expunged. And I know that word "expungement" just drives the historians, and the anthropologists, and the archivist up the wall. But at least get it out of the operating systems so that it doesn't sit there like an informational time bomb.

I recognize that I have spoken rather sharply about this subject. It's a subject I feel strongly about. And I'm always reminded of a line by e. e. cummings, the great American poet—"progress is a comfortable disease." We all get benefits from data technology. We could not run our Social Security system without it. (We may not be able to run it with it, but at least we have a fighting chance!) We could not enjoy the benefits of high-speed communication and high-speed transportation, flying would be an infinitely more hazardous job if we didn't have data technology. We receive wonderful benefits from the computer. And progress is a terribly comfortable disease because we tend to become anesthetized to the fact that, like any technology humankind has ever come up with, from fire to the wheel to the internal combustion engine, the computer has deleterious side effects. And I am not here as a nineteenth-century Luddite arguing that we should axe the machines but, rather simply, to talk about the need to engage in the classic cost-benefit, plus and minus analysis with regard to computer and information technology that we use in other contexts. Maximize its social utility, yes, but minimize its deleterious side effects. Above all, keep a weather eye out for the information managers because that is a subculture all to itself that will proceed down life's pathway to the beat of its own drummer, not necessarily in pursuit of society's best overall interests. I am not suggesting they are malevolent. Everyone in life is mission oriented and sees the world through their own eyes. And all of us are astigmatic to some degree. So let's not wake up one day and find that the information-management subculture is so much in control of the technology that they, in effect, are making decisions about people in the name of what's good for the data system. (How many times have human practices been adjusted to the fact that the machine only takes five digits, or something like that?) Because if we do wake up one day and find that kind of mentality at the wheel of the ship of state, we will have a dictatorship of dossiers and data banks, rather than hobnail boots. But don't kid yourselves, it will still be a dictatorship.

DISCUSSION

Question: Picking up on what you said about the fiduciary relationship of the computer manager or computer person and putting that together with what has been reported, one of the things that bothers me about that legislation is that it's only when you inquire about whether or not information about you is in the bank that they are obligated to tell you or show you. But in essence this seems to be totally inadequate because in order to find out whether or not this information is there, I have to write a bunch of long letters. Shouldn't the person who maintains a data bank be obligated, in good faith, to inform you that they've got information about you?

Miller: There are at least two immediate answers to that. First, as you can imagine, any piece of legislature is a vectoring of forces, and the people upon whom privacy legislation has been imposed have been fighting it tooth and nail. When you get into the legislative environment and you say to a consumer reporting agency, a credit bank, "Hey! You're going to have to give notice to every person you open a file on, and give them notice every time there's a change in the file," they immediately go to "the-foundations-of-the-republic-are-crumbling" type of argument—namely, that you have put such an administrative burden on us that we cannot operate, we will die, and everybody in society will lose the benefit of the credit environment. Or, they will say, "The cost of doing that is going to double the cost of credit screening, which will double the cost of borrowing money." So, in a sense, it was a pragmatic judgment to abandon the notion of automatic notice to each person every time a file was created. On a cost-benefit analysis, creating those files was thought to be unworkable.

Notice is a wonderful right in the abstract. The truth of the matter is that for every hundred notices you send out, maybe one, two, or three people will actually look at it. This fact, coupled with the cost of sending the notice, was enough to scuttle it.

Question: Some of the Europeans, particularly the Scandinavians, have been extremely active in legislating for protection of privacy. Do you think that will be the way with Americans in the future?

Miller: Probably the perfect example is found in Sweden. The Swedish data protection act is the first in the world; it is probably among the most comprehensive, and is a relatively benign law. We should bear in mind that Sweden has a basically homogeneous population. It is not as fractured as American society with alienated subcultures. In addition, it has had over a hundred years of peace; its citizens have had several centuries of rather good relations with the government. In other words, the people place a great deal of faith in the Swedish government and their society. It is, for all practical purposes, a socialist state, heavily dependent upon government largesse, and in that kind of environment you can develop information legislation a lot more easily than you can in a country like the United States. That is simply by way of explanation of "Why the Swedes?"

My own judgment as to what is going on in the United States right now is that we are in a holding pattern. We have had, as I said, fifteen years of intense activity. We are now unlikely, particularly given the cost-conscious, anti-regulation political climate of the day, to escalate the privacy revolution to a second stage, which would have to go after such things as corporations, the medical profession, the hospital industry, and the insurance industry. What I see happening is a ten- or fifteen-year period of experience building up under the existing regime with a fresh look being taken at the time. The climate just wouldn't tolerate increased regulation of the private sector now.

I see that also with the judiciary, by the way. The U.S. Supreme Court has taken some basic steps in recognizing privacy. But since the decision in *Roe v. Wade*, the basic abortion case, it has really not moved in the field of informational privacy. The U.S. Supreme Court seems to be in a holding pattern also. (And one of the ironies of the day is that if you really want to push for civil rights or civil liberties, whether in the area of environment, race, sex, or privacy, you are much better off at the state level in many parts of this country.) I think we are in a digestive pattern now of trying to absorb everything that has happened over the last decade.

Question: The post office is about to put out twenty million ZIP codes; there are just under eighty million addresses in the United States. That would work out to one ZIP code for every four of us. More likely, there would be about a hundred people in one ZIP code area. If this were enacted, it would have a massive impact on data generation. I'm assuming everyone in the room here would be forced to take into consideration the new data generation. I see nothing in print that leads me to believe that very much consideration of privacy is being given.

Miller: I think that's right. I think the debate—and that dignifies it—about the nine-digit ZIP has been totally oblivious to privacy thus far. It is just the way, in its formative stage, that the debate over the National Data Center took place in the mid-sixties. That went on with total obliviousness to the potential privacy implications of that proposal. By the way, the Social Security number probably is not an effective individual identifier, and you could go to a nine-digit ZIP and convert it into a personal identification number without too much further work. But nobody seems to be talking about it. What you see in the media is more humorous than serious.

Question: Is there any legislation giving employees the right of access to their files in their country?

Miller: There were proposals by the President's National Commission to Study Privacy that went in that direction, but I don't know of any legislation that is likely to succeed. Just a little footnote to that: I do get some sense that labor unions are beginning to see the privacy issue as something that is germane to the labor-management dynamic. But as I said a few minutes ago, I don't think it's realistic to anticipate federal legislation on private company employment files.

Comment: Just in the larger context, in Belgium the Royal Decree of 1973 not only gives to work councils the right to company data but also, through work councils, gives employees the right to their own personnel files, a right which exists through codetermination legislation in Germany, in the Netherlands, in Sweden, Denmark, and Norway already. Whether it will come in the States, in an environment which is moving away from regulation, is still an open question. The models are in place, and the strongest one is the Royal Decree of 1973 in Belgium.

Comment: I agree with you that one of the toughest legislative issues arises when you propose that people have access to all their data, including medical data. And the medical establishment always contends that this could cause anxiety that would be damaging to patients' life or health. However, there was one study in a psychiatric hospital where patients and staff shared the records, and the results were that nobody was harmed by having access to their psychiatric data. These patients were hospitalized; no one was harmed, and the staff even decided that some patients benefited from having a frank discussion of their condition, which was stirred by having access to files.

Question: The business community came out badly on several ethical counts in some of our discussions. What sort of ethical considerations are built into the work that is done now at Harvard in educating lawyers?

Miller: I just had a *deja vu* of an appearance I made on the Phil Donahue Show recently, which was one hour of "When-will-you-stop-beating-your-wife?" People always seem to take the opportunity to list the number of lawyers involved in Watergate. If the law schools today are much more attentive to ethical problems, it's called professional responsibility in our context. The truth is that Watergate caused the profession a great deal of anxiety, and a great deal of pressure was put on the academic side of the legal profession by the American Bar Association. And a lot of pressure was internally generated to try and deal with problems of ethics, morality, and social responsibility inside the legal curriculum.

Most law schools today have a required course or at least one elective in ethics as such, or pursue these matters as part of one of the traditional courses, such as criminal law, which is earmarked as a professional responsibility course. One of the basic objectives is to make the law student see every major issue in criminal law not simply from the adversarial model perspective, but also from ethical, moral and social responsibility perspectives. This is a formal requirement that now exists in every first-class law school I can think of. Beyond that I can only speak autobiographically and by projection to those colleagues in the law-teaching business I am close to. I think there is a greater sense on the part of the individual law teacher that his or her job includes the teaching of professionalism—and not simply the rule of land transfer or the rule of making a tort liability, but, for example, the professionalism of how you represent clients in a disadvantaged environment. Each of us to some degree has augmented our own courses with discussions about what I loosely call professionalism. Again, I am just being autobiographical at this point, inferring from the way I teach my basic course in court procedure these days. I teach it much more from the perspective of the system and the system's needs, namely, society and society's needs, rather than purely as an exercise in the advocate's role. So I think a lot has been done educationally. Whether between the ages of twenty-two and thirty, and therefore are reasonably formed ethically, is, of course, uncertain.

Question: What do you think about what the complexities of the computing issue are doing to court procedure? In *IBM v. Memorex,* an antitrust case, the judge decided that the jury was incompetent to decide what was going on. There are some very complex issues out there, and I wonder if you feel that perhaps the complexities are going over the heads of the juries.

Miller: The answer is yes and no. There is no doubt that any new technology presents the legal system with enormous new challenges and questions. The issue of whether software should be copyrightable or patentable is a public policy decision. The problem is not unique to the computer. The same kinds of problems occur with atomic energy and satellite communication. With regard to the issues of high technology that come into the courts for litigation, yes, you're dealing, by definition, with judges and juries who reached maturation in the generation before the technology. So you've got at least a generation of catch-up before your judges begin to live on intimate terms with the computer—which they're doing now because there's a computer-based legal research system that is available in most of the major courts in the country. Yes, they have difficulty; they have always had difficulty. They had difficulty when Watt developed the steam engine; they had difficulty, I am sure, when the first oxcart ran somebody down on the public highway. That's inherent in the movement of society. We have always lived with the curious notion that one of the bastions of generalism in our society is the judge. But once you start making judges specialists, you are losing all sorts of human and social dimensions. You just have to bite the bullet and say, "Hey, you, generalist judge! You've seen life from beginning to end! I'll trust you with this software question, or antitrust question, rather than give it to a blindered telescopic-sighted specialist in economics or in computer technology!" That is a value judgment we have made.

A footnote: There is a raging controversy in this country about the jury system; I'm interested that you put your finger on it. We have been committed in this country since 1791 to lay justice through the jury system; trial by peers is in our Constitution. And now we've reached 1981 and people ask: "How can you give a lay group of twelve people, twelve average people, twelve Johnny Carson viewers, problems of high technology?" And some courts say that they're not going to give these problems to the jury because they are beyond the jury's competence. Other judges take the position that it is in the Constitution, and we have no power to override the Constitution. The United States Supreme Court is going to resolve this issue one day.

I'd like to tell you a little anecdote. I was conducting a seminar of federal judges on jury trial, and we reached this issue of whether we were at the point of such complexity in science and technology that the jury system had broken down. During a break a seventy-year-old federal judge from North Carolina told me this little story. He was trying a jury trial case in North Carolina—a six-person jury, which is now more common than the twelve-person jury. The issues in the case involved extraordinary technical questions about metallurgy and metal fatigue. A huge truck drive-train had gone haywire, and the claim was that it had been negligently manufactured. An enormous drive-train had been set up in the courtroom for the experts to testify about, and the experts went on for hours and hours and hours. The judge said to me: "Frankly, Arthur, I didn't know what the hell they were talking about! After we took a break and came back to the courtroom, there were the six jurors around the drive-train. They were assembling and disassembling it, with no supervision. So I called over the experts and I said, 'Do you know what the hell they're doing?' And the experts said, 'Judge, they're doing it absolutely perfectly!' That renewed my belief in juries." So who knows where intelligence begins and ends? And who knows what is beyond the compass of any human being?

Computer Monitoring
A Threat to the Right to Privacy?

Karen Nussbaum

Reprinted by permission of Computer Professionals for Social Responsibility.

The following speech was the luncheon address at the 1989 CPSR Annual Meeting in Washington, D.C., given by Karen Nussbaum, founder and executive director of the National Association of Working Women, also known as 9to5. [The views below are those of Ms. Nussbaum and do not reflect an official or unofficial position of CPSR.—ed.]

The king has note of all they intend
By interception which they dream not of. . . .

Shakespeare was talking about Henry V, but he could have been referring to today's legions of managers who are verily obsessed with methods of interception.

Monitoring is not new—they say spying is the second oldest profession. But new technology creates capabilities in computer monitoring which make it qualitatively different from supervision in the past.

Today I'll talk about why workplace surveillance is increasing; what's wrong with computer monitoring; and what can be done about it.

WHY SO MUCH SURVEILLANCE

Monitoring is one of a growing list of surveillance techniques used in the workplace. The congressional ban on polygraphs last year only heightened the scramble for other methods, including drug testing, handwriting analysis, and "honesty tests."

"When lie detector tests were banned," according to *The New York Times,* "a Miami bank substituted a new employee screening program—a written honesty test, a urinalysis and a thorough background check before hiring an employee."

What's the panic? Especially when so many experts point to the questionable value of these methods—drug tests have up to a 40% error rate; handwriting is considered to have no correlation to job success. And what *is* an "honesty test" anyway? Look for the expanded application of Ouija boards or astral projection in the personnel office.

Some say there's no call to draw so much attention to computer monitoring, since management has monitored workers with or without computers forever.

There's truth in that.

American management has a history of relying on control as the primary management tool. With the rise of industry in the late 19th century, management wrested control of the work process from the shop floor.

"Scientific management" was developed here and has remained popular for nearly a century. Work was broken down into its smallest possible components, taking particular care to separate manual from mental tasks, with hierarchies of supervisors overseeing the work process.

Though we may laugh at the excesses of Frederick Winslow Taylor today (and Taylor himself admitted that he had recurring nightmares that he had to work in the system he created), scientific management is still the underlying management theory.

But there's a resurgence of management control today—almost a fetish—with managers attributing the need for it to rising competition and falling productivity.

Competition *is* rising—from countries such as Japan and Sweden with their more productive workers, to countries such as Korea and Mexico with their low-wage workers.

One response would be to compete by creating a high-skilled, high value-added workforce—where technology was used to enhance the jobs of an educated, well-trained workforce.

Instead, the dominant business strategy has been to cut labor costs through lower wages and benefits. We see this across the board.

For example, what's known as the "contingent" workforce has skyrocketed here. These are the part-time, temporary, and contracted workers who typically earn less, enjoy few benefits, and have no job security. They now make up one third of the workforce.

More part-time jobs than full-time jobs are being created every year. Wages are falling.

Less than half of employees are covered by pensions and that has been declining steadily. Today, thirty million workers are not covered by health insurance.

Employees are being trained to change our expectations of job security, to free management of responsibility.

A management strategy characterized by this lack of commitment to and faith in the workforce requires a supervision style based on control and fear. Surveillance and control now take the place of supervision, commitment, and training.

Monitoring isn't a technological fluke—it is the logical extension of these changes in the economy.

WHAT IS MONITORING?

Monitoring isn't simply the benign use of computers to collect data. It is different in three important ways: it monitors not just the work, but the worker; it measures work in real time; and it is constant.

It effectively provides a permanent time study not simply to gather data, but to pace and discipline the workforce. And the scope for this is quite broad.

Truck drivers are an example. What job gives you more of a sense of independence and freedom from supervision than long-haul truckers? Imagine a trucker barrelling across Wyoming completely independent.

Well, completely independent until the trucker pulls into a barn in Denver and a little computer tape is removed from the engine. The tape tells a supervisor how many stops the driver made; what the average gas mileage was; where the stops took place; and lots more.

Or consider the airline reservation clerks. When you called to make your reservation for this conference, the reservation agent was timed on the exact seconds she took per caller; the number and length of her breaks; and the time between calls. And your conversation may have been listened in on.

As one executive put it, "I count everything that moves."

This represents a fundamental shift—from relying on a worker's individual professionalism to relying on electronic control. In a study for the Office of Technology Assessment, Dr. Michael Smith finds:

> Electronic monitoring may create adverse working conditions such as paced work, lack of involvement, reduced task variety and clarity, reduced peer social support, reduced supervisory support, fear of job loss, routinized work activity, and lack of control over tasks.

If that's too much to remember, I can summarize it in one word: fear.

Mary Williams is a case in point. In a now-famous case, Mary Williams was disciplined by United Airlines for comments she made to a co-worker. She was courteous to an obnoxious customer and handled him well—management had no quarrel with her there. But after this three-minute call, which was monitored, she complained to a co-worker. Management, listening in to this discussion among co-workers, put her on probation for her remark, then sent her to the company psychiatrist when she complained, and ultimately fired her.

Or take the case of Toni Watson. Toni works for another airline which strictly enforces a 12-minute limit on bathroom breaks. When Toni went over by two minutes, she was disciplined. The pressure on her job finally put her out of work with a nervous disorder.

A data processor in New York told me that her screen periodically flashed "You're not working as fast as the person next to you!"

Others are bitter that their work speed and productivity are publicly posted daily or hourly.

An ad in *PC Week* magazine for networking software boasts to management that

> Close-Up LAN brings you to a level of control never before possible. It connects PCs on your network giving you the versatility to instantly share screens and keyboards.

The ad continues:

> You decide to look in on Sue's computer screen. . . . Sue won't even know you are there! . . . All from the comfort of your chair.

A secretary from Florida told us that the thing she found most offensive about her generally abusive boss in her small office was that he calls up on *his* VDT the work she's doing while she's doing it.

A personnel director of a big company in North Carolina called and told us she quit her long-term job because she thought the use of computer monitoring was sadistic.

And computer monitoring isn't limited to terminal operators and truck drivers.

The maids at the hotel you are staying at are probably monitored. Your maid punches a code in the phone when she enters and leaves your room, providing a detailed log of her speed and a record of her movements for the entire day.

Don't get sick, because nurses are monitored. They carry boxes on their belts which track the amount of time used for each procedure with a patient. So don't be surprised if they lack bedside manner.

And the "higher professions" are being hit too. One reporter told me as she was typing in her story, her computer flashed "I don't like that lead"—a surreptitious supervisor butting in on a first draft.

I've *never* heard a worker say that he or she appreciated this "feedback," though I have heard management representatives that claim it. The workers we hear from feel humiliated, harassed, and under the gun.

As a leading maker of monitoring software programs says, "Monitoring helps employees. It's the only way we can get everything on the permanent record." To workers that sounds frightening.

Employees object to monitoring for several reasons. They don't always know if they are being monitored. They don't know how the information is being used. And basic rights are compromised—the "right to know"; privacy; due process; and health and dignity.

A survey by the Massachusetts Coalition for New Office Technology collected responses from over 700 union and non-union monitored office workers. Here are a few of their findings:

- 62% of respondents were not informed they would be monitored prior to hiring;
- Three-quarters feel they are being spied upon;
- Three-quarters say that monitoring lowers morale;
- 80% say that monitoring makes their jobs more stressful.

A back office bank worker in the survey was mystified as to how her supervisor was gaining access to highly specific personnel information. At her six-month review her supervisor started quizzing her about her bathroom breaks—that's when her co-workers filled her in on monitoring capabilities on her computer.

This survey shows deep alienation from the process. And these feelings are substantiated by study after study.

SUBLIMINAL SUGGESTION

Those are the electronic capabilities workers are aware of. Even more frightening is the marketing of tools for subliminal suggestion.

Mind Communication, Inc., markets subliminal suggestion audio tapes to order for just $249. Among their customers are AT&T, Kimberly-Clark, Procter and Gamble, and Honeywell. Behavioral Engineering Corporation offers "Subliminal Sound." And Greentree Publishers produces computer software called "Subliminal Suggestion and Self-Hypnosis," with everything from feel-good messages to more pointed commands like "work faster."

Monitoring is the ultimate expression of lack of trust. Supervisors don't trust their workers to do their jobs. Workers don't trust their supervisors to be fair. Upper level management doesn't trust lower level management to handle basic supervision.

WHAT'S THE RESPONSE?

Does anyone care? Is monitoring a threat to privacy? *Workers think so.*

Workers are filing privacy suits against their employers in unprecedented numbers. Between 1984 and 1987, *twenty times* as many workplace privacy suits were decided by U.S. courts than in the three years before. Jury verdicts in favor of workers averaged $316,000— compared to 1979 and 1980 when no workers won compensation.

9to5 started a hotline last year, providing counselling for office workers with job problems. When *Ms.* magazine ran a short notice that we wanted to hear from people who were being monitored, we were flooded with calls. Hundreds of women called, mostly from airlines and non-union phone companies.

Some called whispering. Some called saying they had been appointed by their co-workers to call the hotline. One woman specifically called on her monitored phone so her supervisor would know! Many told us they were having meetings in the parking lot, or at their homes, to talk about what to do. They all talked about being violated, humiliated.

An airlines reservationist in Texas said, "This is America! If I wanted to live like this I'd move to Beijing!" She described paranoia so intense that people whispered in the parking lot and assumed the public phone in the lunchroom was monitored.

Unions are bargaining in language to respond. For instance, at Ohio Bell in Cleveland the union has won language preventing secret monitoring. And though management can collect individual data on customer service reps, it has agreed it will use the data only in aggregate.

The courts are mixed. Out of four key cases, two assert workers' rights (*Watkins v. Berry,* 1983, and *U.S. v. Harpel,* 1974) and two found for management (*Epps v. St. Mary's,* 1986, and *James v. Newspaper Agency Corp.,* 1979).

The Congress is concerned. The Office of Technology Assessment, the congressional research arm, published a report on monitoring in 1987 which said:

> There are strong arguments that the present extent of computer-based monitoring is only a preview of growing technological capabilities for monitoring, surveillance and worker testing on the job.

If this is the case, then there may be a need for a new balance between workers' rights to privacy or autonomy in the workplace and management requirements for information.

Legislation is pending at the federal and state levels. For example, the Privacy for Consumers and Workers Act (HR 2168, Clay, Edwards, Williams, Gilman) provides for right-to-know and privacy protections. The California Assembly passed legislation prohibiting subliminal suggestion in the workplace, ultimately vetoed by the governor. Many states are considering comprehensive monitoring bills, including Connecticut, Massachusetts, Minnesota, New Jersey, Rhode Island, and Oregon. And New Mexico and New York are both considering "beep bills."

WHAT YOU CAN DO

So why am I telling you all this? You are the creators of this wonderful technology. But it is misused. And there is no one with more credibility than you to speak out against this misuse.

We want you to know how we experience monitoring. We want you to work with us to design alternatives. We ask you to join us in preventing abuse and to help us make the most of these fantastic tools. Thank you.

Information about computer monitoring and other subjects under research at 9to5 are available from 9to5, 614 Superior Ave., N.W., Cleveland, OH 44113.

Data Quality and Due Process in Large Interorganizational Record Systems

Kenneth C. Laudon

Author's present address: Kenneth C. Laudon, Computer Applications and Information Systems Area, Graduate School of Business, New York University, New York, NY 10003. Communications of The ACM, Vol. 29, No. 1, 1986, pp 4–11. Copyright © 1986, Association for Computing Machinery, Inc., reprinted by permission.

ABSTRACT

As societies have become more dependent on information systems to conduct and record transactions between organizations and individuals, interorganizational computer systems have become a widely used method of coordinating the actions of independent organizations. This article examines the quality of data in one important interorganizational system—the criminal-record system of the United States.

Since the late 1960s, state and federal governments have built a number of interorganizational computer-based information systems to service the needs of the criminal-justice system [23]. Decisions concerning pre-trial release and bail, career-criminal prosecution, and "selective incapacitation" of individuals thought likely to commit a crime in the future (on the basis of a criminal record) rely heavily on computerized criminal-history record systems. Similarly, police street detentions are often based on computerized warrant systems, and increasingly, securing employment in many occupations may depend on a criminal-record check [8, 17]. This article will focus on the quality of information in these systems, and how it can affect a person's constitutional rights.

The Privacy Act of 1974, along with other federal regulations, has firmly established the importance of maintaining accurate, complete, and unambiguous information in computerized record systems. Likewise, the concept of due process assumes that organizations will not treat individuals arbitrarily, capriciously, or with malice. Thus, information systems containing inaccurate, incomplete, or ambiguous information not only violate society's notion of fairness in dealing with individuals, they also threaten specific due-process guarantees that are afforded by the Constitution and statute [13].

The problem of maintaining high-quality records in an information system is magnified in an interorganizational computer system. Some interorganizational systems only permit the sharing of *voluntarily* submitted information or notices—as in an electronic bulletin board. In this instance, there is no central authority or management, few standards for the content and format of the information, weak incentives for compliance with system rules, and little concern for accuracy. Other interorganizational systems are based on a central library model where there is strong management control over data entry, active management of files, powerful incentives for participants to comply with system standards, and sanctions for noncompliance.

Systems also differ in terms of their relation to the public: Some inform on decisions of critical life importance, whereas others involve individual convenience. A national criminal-history system, for example, affects matters of critical life importance; an airline-reservation system deals with matters of convenience; a credit-reporting system may fall in between.

Systems vary in terms of their visibility and openness to the public. An airline-reservation system operates in such a way that erroneous information can be spotted easily, but national criminal-history systems are not as equally visible to the individuals involved. Exactly what information is on file and who used it—when and where—are questions not easily answered by criminal-record systems.

The obvious connection between the structural characteristics of interorganizational systems and the nature of the decisions they inform is that systems dealing with matters of critical life importance—and which are less "open" or "visible" to the public—should be structured as central libraries with strong central management controls. Systems dealing with matters of convenience may be operated as bulletin boards—if only because they are more self-correcting.

DUE PROCESS REQUIREMENTS

Over the years, the courts and legislatures have addressed the problems caused by poor-quality records in administrative processes. The findings of Townsend versus Burke in the U.S. Supreme Court illustrate the position of the courts:

> This petitioner was sentenced on the basis of assumptions concerning his criminal record which were materially untrue. Such a result, whether caused by carelessness or design, is inconsistent with due process of law and such a conviction cannot stand . . . . It is the careless or designed pronouncement of sentence on a foundation so extensively and materially false, which the prisoner had no opportunity to correct by the services which counsel would provide, which renders the proceeding lacking in due process. [Townsend versus Burke, 334 U.S., 1948]

More recent court rulings reflect the pervasive use of the criminal records in bail and other proceedings:

> Plaintiffs are clearly and systematically being deprived of due process in violation of the Fourteenth Amendment to the U.S. Constitution, and of the right of effective assistance of counsel as guaranteed by the Sixth Amendment, whenever rap sheets containing erroneous, ambiguous, or incomplete data with respect to prior arrests and dispositions are submitted to courts at arraignment sessions for use in connection with bail determination. The Eighth Amendment right to reasonable bail is also thus denied . . . neither plaintiff nor their counsel is capable, as a practical matter, of correcting errors, resolving ambiguities, or supplying missing information to cure defects contained in rap sheets . . . the result is frequently the impositions of bails in amount exceeding those which would be set if complete and accurate information were available to the courts. [16]

Such concerns for the accuracy and completeness of criminal-record information are reflected in federal regulations calling for complete records that "must contain information of any dispositions occurring within a state within 90 days after the disposition has occurred" [to prevent dissemination of "arrest only" data] (Title 28, U.S.C.). These regulations also call for minimal errors in records and procedures to ensure this result by a "process of data collection, entry, storage, and systematic audit that will minimize the possibility of recording and storing inaccurate information . . . and upon finding inaccurate information [the state or federal record system] shall notify all criminal justice agencies known to have received such information" [Title 28, United States Code of Federal Regulations, 1975].

Despite the growing importance of data quality in large record systems, methodologies for examining record quality have not been established, and few systematic research efforts have attempted to ascertain empirical levels of data quality. An exception is the state and federal benefit programs where Congress has mandated specific error levels and where agencies have undertaken extensive "quality assurance" programs to analyze record and decision-making qualities (United States Senate, 1984 and [2]). These studies focus on payment errors and are not applicable to other systems—such as criminal records.

In the absence of empirical research, legislative bodies have been forced to rely on vague and ambiguous directives such as those found in the Privacy Act of 1974, which direct all federal agencies to "maintain all records which are used by the agency in making any determination about any individual with such accuracy, relevance, timeliness, and completeness as is reasonably necessary to assure fairness to the individual in the determination" (P.L. 93–579: The Privacy Act of 1974, Section 3, [e] and [6]). With the exception of arbitrary standards adopted by legislative bodies for benefit programs, there are no really enforceable standards of data quality, accuracy, or completeness in governmental systems [7].

TYPES OF CRIMINAL RECORDS AND RECORD SYSTEMS

In this article, we will examine two kinds of criminal record systems: computerized criminal-history (CCH) records and computerized warrant records (Wanted-Person System—WPS). A criminal-history record is a record of arrests, court dispositions, and sentencing. It is originated by the police at arraignment; other record segments are supposed to be submitted by the courts and correctional agencies. There are about 195 million criminal-history records in the United States: 40 million records are maintained by the states, 32 million by federal agencies, and the rest by local agencies. About 18.6 million records are computerized at state and federal levels [8, 11]. About one-third of the labor force has a criminal-history record [18].

As of 1984, 36 states operate CCH systems, and the Federal Bureau of Investigation (FBI) operates two systems: the National Crime Information Center CCH (NCIC-CCH) System and the Identification Division (Ident). NCIC-CCH is an on-line file of approximately 2 million records. Ident is a semiautomated, largely manual file of 22–24 million records.

In addition to their use in law enforcement programs, CCH records are increasingly being used for screening employees in both the public and private sector. In some states, this is the fastest growing use. At the federal level, 53 percent of Ident's use of records is for employment screening [8].

A second kind of record is the computerized warrant. Currently, 35 states operate computerized WPSs, and the FBI operates a national WPS (NCIC-WPS). The federal system contains 127,000 warrants for arrests issued by local, state, federal and military agencies.

Warrants are issued by the police or the courts, either because the police have a reason to believe the person was involved in a crime, or because the courts have determined that the person is in violation of judicial process (e.g. failure to appear, jumped bail, violated parole). Warrants are supposed to be removed from systems when the person is arrested or when the warrant is "vacated" or canceled. As we will see below, failing to remove invalid warrants from WPSs is a critical weakness.

Warrant systems are used primarily by police in both prearrest and postarrest situations, and by prosecutors in determining bail. Due to advances in telecommunications, police in most jurisdictions now have access to local, state and federal wanted warrant systems from the patrol car. WPSs are socially significant because they directly affect the behavior of police at a critical moment in the arrest process. The arrest event, as described by many authors, is at times fraught with ambiguity and danger for both the police officer and the individual [15, pp. 45–48; 22]. The availability of warrant to police officers on the beat may increase the frequency of "stop and question" behavior, which may be perceived by individuals as harassment. Moreover, stopping and questioning individuals can turn into a lengthy detention as police officers check a variety of wanted and stolen property files. This, in turn, places a strain on Fourth Amendment protections from unreasonable police searches. While a 5-minute stop on the street sounds reasonable, stops of 50 minutes or five hours are less reasonable, but increasingly common (People versus McGaughran, 1979; People versus Harris, 1982). On the other hand, the ready availability of warrant and wanted information directly contributes to the ability of the police to remove dangerous criminals from the street, and to return them to a jurisdiction where they are wanted for criminal actions.

RESEARCH BACKGROUND

The research reported in this article was carried out from 1979 to 1984 and was funded by the Office of Technology Assessment (U.S. Congress). A preliminary assessment had already established in 1978 that a critical drawback to developing a national CCH system was the allegation that existing state and federal record systems contained high levels of inaccurate, ambiguous, and incomplete information [10]. Congress was especially concerned that the FBI's computerized WPS contained a significant number of cleared, vacant, or inaccurate warrants that potentially could lead to false arrests and the violation of individual rights of due process. My research sought to empirically and systematically establish the levels of data quality in the FBI's nonautomated Ident (containing 22–24 million criminal-history records); the automated NCIC-CCH system (containing 1.9 million CCH records); the criminal-history record systems of a western, a midwestern, and a southern state; and the NCIC-WPS. (The three state CCH systems were included in the data-quality research because any future national CCH system will depend on the criminal-history information generated initially by the states. Thus it is important to obtain estimates of the levels of record quality in these state systems.)

METHODOLOGY

The three methods generally used to examine data quality in large files are surveys of end users or clients, samples of entire record files, and samples of active or current cases. Surveys of end users typically measure "perceptions" of data quality and are fraught with problems of recall, self-report bias, and serious underestimates [14]. Surveys of entire files carried out by large agencies also contain inherent errors. Many persons on file are no longer active, some are deceased, and the method fails to account for eligible persons erroneously denied benefits [4].

Given the purpose of this research—which is understanding the quality of information currently being used by criminal-justice decision makers—the preferred method is a survey of active cases. For each of the systems examined, a sample of current cases was taken, and the records were compared to hard-copy original documents of known accuracy. The FBI Ident, NCIC-CCH, and NCIC-WPS samples were essentially random samples of around 400 cases each. In the three states, approximately 500 of the most recent prosecuted cases were selected from the files of district attorneys and state record systems. In some cases, this involved reviewing the prosecutions for an entire year (for a more detailed description of the methodology and procedures to protect the privacy of individuals, see [5] and [8]).

Dimensions of Record Quality in Criminal-History Systems

Previous research [3], as well as over 100 interviews I conducted with criminal-justice personnel at the state, local and federal level, has identified the following significant dimensions of record quality for criminal-record systems:

RECORD COMPLETENESS.   Criminal records that indicate an arrest but no formal court disposition recorded within one year of the arrest date are considered "incomplete" records. This was believed to be the single largest form of record-quality problem and is singled out in the tables as "No court disposition." Other forms of incomplete records are those that show conviction of "attempt," but where the specific crime is not stated; records that show sentencing information, but fail to indicate conviction information; and records in which correctional data are missing, but other data are present.

RECORD INACCURACY.   Records are inaccurate when the arrest, court disposition, or sentencing information on a CCH record does not correspond with the actual manual court records.

RECORD AMBIGUITY.   A record is ambiguous when it shows more charges than dispositions or more court dispositions than charges. Other ambiguities that also arise are dates that do not correspond, or a number of arrest charges followed by a single court disposition where it is not clear for which particular crime the individual was convicted.

Record Quality in Warrant Systems

The record-quality analysis of the NCIC-WPS focused on the extent to which warrants listed in the computerized file were still *active* warrants (meaning that the local agency that submitted the warrants to the federal system still wanted the person). If the computerized record correctly reflected that a warrant was indeed outstanding, it was labeled a *warrant outstand-*

ing. If the local agency had cleared or vacated the warrant (meaning that the person had already been arrested for that crime or that, for one reason or another, the local agency no longer wanted the person), the warrant was considered *cleared/vacated* and an invalid warrant—that is, a warrant that should not be listed on the automated national file. Other record-quality problems encountered during the course of the research were that the originating local agency had no record of ever having issued a warrant for the person listed on the automatic file, and, in other instances, that the person was wanted by a local agency, but no warranty for a specific crime could be located. These warrants are also considered invalid.

Generalization

The results from Ident are technically generalizable to the approximately 2.3 million annual requests from state/local agencies; the NCIC-CCH findings to the 1.8 million annual disseminations; the NCIC-WPS to the 127,500 persons resident on the file. The state findings, because they are not representative samples of state systems, can best be thought of as indicative of the kinds of record levels actually occurring in large urban areas of the states examined.

In the federal CCH systems, it was impossible to verify each of the arrests on each record because of resource constraints. Therefore, the first arrest event more than one year old was verified per record. This permitted the federal system a minimum of one year to obtain court disposition, sentencing, and related information. In the state systems, all arrest events more than one year old were verified.

In making inferences from the samples to the respective populations, the confidence interval is given by

$$\pi = P \pm 1.96 \times \sqrt{(PQ \div N)}$$

where

    P = the observed sample proportion,
    Q = 1-P
    1.96 = the value of Z (standard error measure) appropriate to a 95 percent confidence interval, and
    N = the number of responses to a given measure.

FINDINGS

FBI Criminal-History Files

The results of the data-quality study of FBI criminal-history files are presented in Table I. As noted above, the statistical results presented here reflect current disseminations from both the NCIC/CCH and the FBI Ident. At the time of our survey (summer, 1979), there were 2.35 million disseminations to state and local agencies from the Ident and approximately 360,000 disseminations from the NCIC/CCH file.

Table I. Data Quality of FBI Criminal-History Systems: NCIC-CCH and Ident
Criminal-History Records

	NCIC-CCH	Ident criminal-history records
Arrests in sample	400	400
Positive verification	256	235
Response rate	64.0%	58.5%
Arrests not verifiable because		
Pending or sealed	6	19
No record locatable*	54	37
No prosecution of arrest	10	7
Fugitive		1
No arrest data	24	—
	95 (37.1%)	64 (27.2%)
Total arrest cases verified	161	171
Characteristics of verified arrest case		
No disposition reported	27.9% (45)	40.9% (70)
Incomplete record	0.6% (1)	2.3% (4)
Inaccurate record	16.8% (27)	10.5% (18)
Ambiguous record	2.5% (4)	6.4% (11)
Combined problems	6.2% (10)	14.1% (24)
Complete, accurate, and unambiguous	45.9% (74)	25.7% (44)
Total	100.0% (161)	100.0% (171)

*In situations of "no record locatable," this generally reflected a police disposition of the arrest, for example, the person was released prior to presenting to a district attorney. This was removed from further analysis even though it might have been included as a "no disposition recorded"; hence, estimates of record characteristics are conservative.

1. If *no disposition* was reported ("record blank"), the data analysis exempted the record from further consideration even though it might have other problems of accuracy and ambiguity. Estimates of these features are therefore conservative.
2. A record was *incomplete* if it failed to record conviction or correctional data.
3. A record was *inaccurate* if it incorrectly reflected the court records of disposition, charges, or sentence.
4. A record was *ambiguous* if it indicated more charges than dispositions, but did not specify charges of conviction; *or* if a record indicated more dispositions than charges; or if for a number of reasons the record was not interpretable (see text).
5. A record had *combined problems* if it indicated more than one of the four logically possible permutations of incompleteness, inaccuracy, or ambiguity.

Our analysis indicates that 25.7 percent of the Ident records were complete, accurate, and unambiguous, whereas 74.3 percent of the records exhibited some significant quality problems. Translated to the population of 2.35 million annual disseminations, our results indicate that 1.75 million (plus or minus 6 percent) of the disseminations had a significant quality problem. The most common problem was lack of court disposition information, followed by inaccurate recording of court disposition information (where present at all), ambiguity of record, or some combination of the above.

Our analysis of the NCIC-CCH system found 45.9 percent to be complete, accurate, and unambiguous, and 54.1 percent with some significant quality problem. Translated to the entire population of 360,000 disseminations, approximately 165,240 (plus or minus 6 percent) were incomplete and/or inaccurate. Here, as in the manual criminal-history file of Ident, the most frequent problem involves the lack of disposition data followed by the accuracy of the disposition recorded.

FBI WPS

The statistical results of the WPS study reflected the condition of the Wanted-Persons File at the time of the study, although there is little reason to believe (with respect to the data-quality characteristics outlined here) that the results vary from month to month (see Table II). Our research found the following:

- Of the warrants, 11.2 percent were no longer valid. Generalized to the population of warrants in the entire file, 14,280 (plus or minus 3 percent) were invalid by virtue of being vacated/cleared, having no local record, or being not specifiable.
- Of the warrants, 93.7 percent were accurate in their classification of offense, and 6.6 percent were inaccurate. Generalized to the population of warrants, approximately 8,033 (plus or minus 3 percent) were inaccurate in this respect.
- A significant number of warrants appear to be nonprosecutable on the basis of age. Of the warrants, 23.9 percent are more than three years old, and 15.1 percent are more than five years old. It is generally believed by the district attorneys interviewed in this research that warrants more than five years old are not capable of prosecution because of deceased and/or missing witnesses, as well as other difficulties. Warrants not considered prosecutable will not lead to extraditions, although they can lead to arrest or detention.

Our research also found that 74.4 percent of the warrants (in the population, 94,960 plus or minus 4 percent) were for nonindex crimes ("index crimes" are those generally considered by the FBI and others as the "most serious crimes": murder, manslaughter, rape, robbery, aggravated assault, burglary, larceny, and motor-vehicle theft). Only 25.6 percent of the warrants found in the FBI system involve index crimes. Many nonindex crimes are serious (probation/parole violation, drug crimes, kidnapping, etc., are indeed serious), yet the appearance in this sample of warrants for traffic violations, child neglect, property destruction, cruelty to animals, abandonment, etc., leads to the conclusion that perhaps as much as 7 percent of the warrant file (8,925 warrants plus or minus 5 percent) are sufficiently nonserious that the apprehension of the suspect would in all likelihood not lead to extradition or prosecution. Nevertheless, the outstanding warrant could lead to an arrest or detention if the suspect was stopped by the police.

Table II. Wanted-Persons-File Summary Analysis

Population of warrants	127,500
Sample size	405
Originating agency response	394
Valid responses (complete information)	374
(20 agencies were unable to account for the date on which warrants cleared)	
Response rate	92%

Validity of Warrants

	Sample statistics	Population estimates
Valid warrants (affirmed to be outstanding or cleared during OTA research)	88.8% (332)	113,220 (±3.2%)
Invalid warrants (cleared or vacated or not verifiable by agency)	11.2% (42)	14,280 (±3.2%)
Total 100.0% (374)		

Breakdown of Validity

	Sample statistics	Population estimates
Valid warrant	85.8% (332)	—
Invalid warrant	11.2% (42)	—
Warrant cleared but still on file*	6.1% (23)	7,841 (±2.4%)
Agency had no record on warrant	4.3% (16)	5,483 (±2.0%)
Wanted but no warrant locatable	0.8% (3)	1,020 (±1.0%)

Accuracy of Offense Classifications

	Sample statistics	Population estimates
Compared to originating agency records, NCIC offense calculation was		
Accurate	93.7% (342)	119,468 (±3%)
Inaccurate	6.3% (23)	8,033 (±3%)
Total	100.0% (365)	

Summary—Age of Warrants

	Sample statistics	Population estimates
Less than one year old	29.0% (114)	36,975 (±5%)
One to three years old	47.0% (185)	59,925 (±5%)
More than three years old	23.9% (94)	30,473 (±5%)
More than five years old	15.1% (59)	19,253 (±4%)
Five years or less old	84.9% (334)	108,248 (±4%)

*Warrant was cleared or vacated one year prior to sample date.

Three State Criminal-History Systems

The findings of the state data-quality studies parallel those at the federal level. In the three state systems examined, the level of data quality ranges from only 12.2 percent of recently disseminated criminal-history records being accurate, complete, and unambiguous in a southeastern state, to 18.9 percent in a western state, to 49.4 percent in a midwestern state (see Table III). In all states, the most significant problem involves lack of disposition information, followed by incomplete records, inaccuracy of recorded dispositions, and ambiguity of information.

Table III.   CCH Record Quality in Three State Systems

	Western state	Midwest state	Southern state
Individuals in sample	500	502	498
Total prior arrests	2733	985	1345
Total in-country arrests	2172	739	1002
Arrests not verifiable because			
Case pending	1	3	3
Record sealed	0	0	0
Docket not locatable	0	47	1
Municipal court disposition	8	—	0
Total in-country			
arrests verified	2163	689	998
Characteristics of CCH verified arrests			
No disposition reported	915 (42.3%)	107 (15.5%)	390 (39.1%)
Incomplete	531 (24.5%)	93 (13.5%)	215 (21.5%)
Inaccurate	16 (0.7%)	91 (13.2%)	2 (0.2%)
Ambiguous	57 (2.6%)	22 (3.2%)	32 (3.2%)
Combined problems	236 (10.9%)	35 (5.1%)	237 (23.7%)
Complete, accurate and unambiguous	408 (18.9%)	341 (49.4%)	122 (12.2%)
Total	2163 (100.0%)	689 (100.0%)	998 (100.0%)

Notes:

1. Arrests were verified against local court records only if the arrests occurred within the prosecutorial district where the sample of individuals was drawn. See Task II for detailed analysis of coding sheets and samples.
2. If *no disposition* was reported on a CCH ("record blank"), the data analysis exempted the record from further consideration even though it might have other problems of accuracy and ambiguity. Hence, estimates of these features are conservative.
3. A record was *incomplete* if it failed to record conviction or correctional data.
4. A record was *inaccurate* if it incorrectly reflected the court records of disposition, sentence, or charges.
5. A record was *ambiguous* if it indicated in response to multiple charges a single plea of guilty, but did not specify of which charge (more charges than dispositions); or if more dispositions were recorded than charges; *or* if the record was for a number of reasons not interpretable (see text for explanation).
6. A record had *combined problems* if it reflected one or more of the four logically possible permutations of incompleteness, inaccuracy, or ambiguity.

There is a considerable range in data quality among the states. However, the data-quality problems in state systems are far larger than is commonly known and more significant than heretofore imagined.

INTERPRETATION OF FINDINGS

We recognize the limitations of our sampling methods, their limited geographic coverage, and the lack of "benchmark" criteria. The most conservative interpretation of our research is that it is reasonable to believe that (1) constitutional rights of due process are not well protected in either manual or computerized criminal-history systems and federal wanted-person systems, and (2) the efficiency and effectiveness of any law enforcement or criminal-justice programs that use or rely on such records must be considerably impaired. The maintenance of due process standards cannot be assured in administrative processes that rely on fundamentally incomplete, ambiguous, and inaccurate information. Dissemination of incomplete records that indicate stigmatizing arrests but not exonerating dispositions tends to overstate the proven criminality of individuals and may result in denial of employment with little justification in law [8, 17]. With large variations in record quality from state to state, it would appear that constitutional protections apply unequally. Whatever faith existed before this study in individual access, review, and challenge mechanisms to protect the rights of privacy and due process must surely be weakened. Despite the availability of these legal remedies to individuals, it is clear that criminal-record systems are continuing to operate with considerable error.

The findings of our research on the NCIC-WPS are perhaps even more indicative of how a poorly managed national information system can affect constitutional guarantees of due process. Information in this file, unlike the information in a criminal-history file, can be and is routinely used as grounds for arrest or detention of individual citizens. It also should be noted that the FBI has in recent years prior to our research taken significant actions to improve the currency and accuracy of the Wanted-Persons File by systematically requesting originating agencies at the state and local levels to verify the currency and accuracy of warrants they have placed on the NCIC Wanted-Persons File. Nevertheless, the following facts have emerged from our research:

- In excess of 14,000 persons are at risk of being falsely detained and perhaps arrested, because of invalid warrants in this system.
- Eight thousand persons are at risk of being detained, and perhaps arrested, but subsequently neither extradited nor prosecuted because of the nonserious nature of their indicated offense.
- Nineteen thousand persons whose outstanding warrants are valid, but more than five years of age, are at risk of being detained, and perhaps arrested, but neither prosecuted nor extradited due to the age of the outstanding warrant.

Statistics such as these have provided the substance for a steady stream of newspaper articles and anecdotes reporting that the NCIC-WPS and related systems operated by most states violate the constitutional rights of a significant number of individuals.

MANAGING INTERORGANIZATIONAL RECORD SYSTEMS

The criminal-record system in the United States provides a potent example of problems with data quality in large interorganizational record systems and reflects the need for organizations to reduce uncertainty by sharing data on one another's actions.

It is apparent that the FBI systems described here are not appropriately structured. The FBI systems require the cooperation of more than 60,000 criminal-justice agencies throughout the country to properly update, correct, and verify record segments. Neither self-interest nor shared interest is present to bring about voluntary compliance. The Constitution segments power among police, prosecutors, courts, and correctional agencies; it further disperses power among local, state, and federal levels of government. History provides ample examples of conflict, not cooperation, among such agencies [5, 9, 15], and few will argue that the various agencies should be consolidated into a single national justice agency—as has been done in many European countries—for the sake of administrative convenience and efficiency. Interorganizational systems are supposed to provide a functional equivalent to bureaucratic centralization, yet it is obvious that this alternative carries with it the risk of exceptionally poor data quality and the potential for Constitutional harm.

Knowing the risks and consequences of operating in this milieu, one might expect the nominal managers of these computerized criminal-record systems, the FBI and the Department of Justice, to initiate strong management controls in the area of data quality. Some simple first steps would eliminate arrest records that did not contain a court disposition within one year of arrest (the state of Minnesota follows this rule). This would solve the problem of incompleteness. The FBI could initiate frequent data-quality audits (especially of the warrant file), reduce the gargantuan national criminal-history files by focusing only on serious offenders, and occasionally exercise the statutory authority of the attorney general to eliminate agencies and states from participation in information systems when they fail to comply with system standards [8].

However, even a moderately strong management posture would carry with it significant political risks. States might reject such actions as a violation of federalism—an illegitimate intrusion by the federal government into an area that the Constitution grants to the states. A worse consequence could result for the FBI if the individual states established their own interstate criminal-record network—essentially beyond federal controls—something they almost accomplished in the early 1970s [9]. At stake then is the FBI's historic place at the center of national criminal-record systems, a role that began in the 1920s.

Given this uncertain political environment, the FBI has imposed few data-quality controls over participants in its criminal-record systems. Despite severe congressional criticism over the years, the FBI did not conduct a comprehensive audit of its record systems [11, 12] until 1984. Owing partly to the findings of the research presented here, in 1984 the FBI began a limited program of audits in selected states of the "hot files"—such as Wanted Persons (warrants). Although the FBI has been highly critical of my research findings, its own findings, released in August 1985, found that about six percent of the warrants were invalid in 12 selected states. On a national basis, the FBI estimates that 12,000 invalid warrants are sent out per day [1]. This error rate is approximately one-half of that measured in our national sample. Like our own research, the FBI's investigations discovered enormous irregularities. In Mobile, Alabama, of 453 warrants supplied to NCIC during the FBI's audit, 338 listed the height as 7 feet 11 inches, the weight as 499 pounds and the hair as "XXX" [1].

Unlike the Social Security Administration, which conducts a 20,000-case sample of beneficiary records each month in order to control payment and process quality, the FBI does not know the quality of its own records [20]. From its inception in the 1920s, the accuracy and completeness of FBI criminal-history files have been entirely the responsibility of local contributing agencies. Computerization of these records in the 1970s did not change this management position. Every outgoing record from the FBI system clearly states that it is the responsibility of the user agency to verify the accuracy of records. Although never stated as a matter of public policy, the FBI operates in essence an electronic bulletin board [19, pp. 202–203, 368–374].

The FBI claims not to be responsible for the accuracy, currency, or completeness of the data it collects, stores, and disseminates. Yet, in the rush to arrest, prosecute, judge, and penalize the approximately 9 million criminal offenders arrested each year, verification by users is rarely undertaken. Numerous interviews with criminal-justice decision makers established that the records are taken "as is" and used directly in the decision-making process ([8] and Tatum versus Rogers, 1971). Although some jurisdictions have adopted (under court pressure) regulations requiring police to verify information, and to obtain a high degree of correspondence between computerized warrants and identification supplied by citizens, most jurisdictions do not have limitations on a police officer's use of computerized records. Following a class action suit initiated in 1980, the Los Angeles City Council agreed in 1984 to require a 72 percent correlation between a computer-listed warrant and a detained suspect before officers could gain access to a full warrant record (see [21]).

Public attitudes will be crucial in determining whether or not the FBI will exercise strong management controls over the interorganizational systems it nominally operates. Although most Americans want serious felons to be effectively brought to justice, most do not want a system where individuals are routinely denied due process. Most Americans mistakenly believe that the criminal-record systems apply only to a small group of violent felons and social outcasts. With 36 million persons (about one-third of the labor force) having such a record, we must recognize that criminal-record systems are apt to contain our own name and the names of our relatives. In the future, these record systems will become even more extensive. As one California official noted, "Soon nearly everyone in their lifetime will produce a criminal record of some kind, and the mere possession of a record will not mean much per se. It will be like a credit record" [8]. When this comes to pass, public attitudes may change as we begin to see how the records pertain to our own lives.

REFERENCES

1. Burnham, D. FBI says 12,000 faulty reports on suspects are issued each day. *New York Times* (Aug. 25, 1985).
2. Comptroller General of the United States, General Accounting Office, *How Criminal Justice Agencies Use Criminal History Information*. U.S. Government Printing Office, Washington, D.C., 1974. Comptroller General of the United States, General

Accounting Office, *Complete and Accurate Information Needed in Social Security's Automated Name and Number Files.* U.S. Government Printing Office, Washington, D.C., 1982.

3. Doernberg, D.I., and Ziegler, D.H. Due process versus data processing: An analysis of computerized criminal history information systems. *New York Univ. Law J.55* (Dec. 1980).

4. Federal Bureau of Investigation, Washington, D.C., 1975.

5. Laudon, K. *Computers and Bureaucratic Reform.* Wiley, New York, 1974.

6. Laudon, K. Data quality in criminal history and wanted person systems. Rep. Office of Technology Assessment, United States Congress, Washington, D.C., 1980.

7. Laudon, K. Privacy and federal databanks. *Society* (Jan. 1980).

8. Laudon, K. *Dossier Society: Value Choices in the Design of National Information Systems.* Columbia University Press, New York. To be published.

9. Marchand, D. *The Politics of Privacy, Computers and Criminal Justice Records.* Information Resources Press, Washington, D.C., 1980.

10. Office of Technology Assessment, United States Congress, *Preliminary Assessment of the National Crime Information Center and the Computerized Criminal History System.* Office of Technology Assessment, United States Congress, Washington, D.C., 1978.

11. Office of Technology Assessment, United States Congress. *An Assessment of Alternatives for a National Computerized Criminal History System.* Office of Technology Assessment, United States Congress, Washington, D.C. 1982.

12. Office of Technology Assessment, United States Congress. Interview with Fred Wood. Office of Technology Assessment, United States Congress, Washington, D.C. July 31, 1985. (Wood was one of the principal authors of the 1982 OTA report and follows developments at the FBI.)

13. Privacy Protection Study Commission. *Personal Privacy in an Information Society.* U.S. Government Printing Office, Washington, D.C., 1977.

14. Project Search, Search Group. The American criminal history record. Tech. Rep. 14, Project Search, Search Group, Sacramento, Calif., 1976.

15. Skolnick, J.H. *Justice without Trial.* Wiley, New York, 1967.

16. Tatum versus Rogers. 75 Civ 2782 (CBM), U.S. District Court, Southern District of New York, 1979.

17. United States Department of Justice. *Criminal Justice Information Policy—Privacy and the Private Employer.* Bureau of Justice Statistics, U.S. Department of Justice, Washington, D.C., 1981.

18. United States Department of Labor. *A Study of the Number of Persons with Records of Arrest or Conviction in the Labor Force.* U.S. Department of Labor, Washington, D.C., 1979.

19. United States Senate. *Hearings Before the Subcommittee on Constitutional Rights of the Committee on the Judiciary.* United States Senate, 93rd Congress, Washington, D.C., Mar. 1974.

20. United States Senate. *Hearings Before the Special Committee on Aging.* United States Senate, 98th Congress, Washington, D.C., Nov. 29, 1983.

21. Vollmer, T. City agrees to new warrant methods to cut false arrests. *Los Angeles Times* (Aug. 22, 1984).

22. Westley, W. Violence and the police. *Am. J. Sociol.* 59 (1953), 34–41.

23. Zimring, F.E. Research agendas, information policies, and program outcomes. In *Information Policy and Crime Control Strategies.* A.F. Westin, Ed. U.S. Department of Justice, Washington, D.C., 1984.

Vulnerable on All Counts

How Computerized Vote Tabulation Threatens the Integrity of Our Elections: An Election Watch Report

Reprinted by permission of Computer Professionals for Social Responsibility.

I know of no safe depository of the ultimate powers of society but the people themselves ...
—*Thomas Jefferson*

The advent of computerized vote counting over the past two decades has created a potential for election fraud and error on a scale previously unimagined.

The complex systems that tally the votes of 55 percent of our electorate are badly designed, hard to monitor and subject to a host of technological threats. Worse yet, detection of error or sabotage is more difficult than in traditional elections.

This report identifies some of the ways in which electronic voting systems are vulnerable to error, both accidental and deliberate, and proposes a comprehensive solution that returns control of elections to citizens.

The plan would make election fraud much more difficult to accomplish and more certain of detection.

PART I:

A No-Confidence Vote for Computer Election Systems

Thirty-one percent of American counties representing 55 percent of our voters now use computerized systems to tally votes and declare election winners. These systems have been quietly introduced over the past twenty years without public understanding of the implications of this change.

Decisions to use computers in vote counting have usually been made by appointed election officials, guided by vendors in the business of selling hardware and software for election systems.

The sales pitch has been that computers are more accurate than people: that election results will be more secure once the human factor is minimized, and above all that election results will be available more rapidly.

Instead, the introduction of computerized vote tallying has made it much easier to compromise elections and much more difficult to detect errors. Today's computerized vote-tallying systems are extremely vulnerable to every kind of threat, error and manipulation possible to perpetrate in computer systems.

Our Voting Rights Are at Issue

When we vote, we expect our votes to be counted—once—for the candidates or issues we've chosen. We expect that only those registered voters who turn up on Election Day (or send absentee ballots) will have their votes counted. We expect that election officials representing diverse political viewpoints will protect our voting rights.

If and when suspicion arises, we expect a recount will expose culprits and lead to a correct election outcome.

Today's computerized voting systems can't guarantee these basic rights. Lawsuits in Indiana, Florida, Maryland and West Virginia have alleged fraud in computerized elections. Each case involves vote-counting systems from the same vendor, whose products dominate the market and are vulnerable to most of the threats outlined in this article.

Have the courts been able to resolve these cases? Not yet: because the computer programs that count our votes are poorly designed, contain proprietary information, cannot produce reliable recounts, and do not retain audit information that could confirm—or disprove—whether fraud actually occurred.

Our Election Officials Have Left Their Posts

What makes computerized election systems vulnerable to error or tampering? The fundamental answer is that control of elections no longer rests with identifiable and accountable local election officials.

The officials are still there: but after purchasing computer vote-tallying systems, many officials find the technology impossible to understand, operate or supervise. So they turn to computer experts for help. These experts usually work for the same vendors who supplied the vote-counting equipment.

There is no reason why computerized election systems have to be so obscure. But the companies that design and sell the voting systems have had little incentive to make their products intelligible to average citizens.

In the Electronic Voting Booth

In the most commonly used computer vote-counting system, the voter steps into a voting booth and inserts a punched-card ballot behind a printed cardboard booklet listing candidates and issues. The citizen votes by inserting a stylus into holes beside the appropriate names or issues, punching out corresponding holes on the ballot card.

Special vote-tallying computer programs then analyze the ballots by counting the holes which correspond to each candidate and issue. At the end of Election Day, the computer is supposed to report final winners and losers.

Can voters be sure they marked their ballot correctly? Can they be sure their votes will be counted for the candidates and issues they chose? Can they be sure their ballots will actually be counted? Often not.

Not-So-Benign Ballots

It is all too easy for ballots used in today's computerized elections to be mismarked or misread.

The booklet that indicates which candidates or issues go with which holes can be misprinted, deliberately or accidentally. Since most computer voting systems don't print the names of candidates and issues on the ballot itself—only on the booklet, which stays in the booth—the voter has no way of knowing whether the marked ballot really indicates the candidates and issues he or she selected. The voter can't even check for simple mistakes.

Punched card ballots can be invalidated simply by the addition of an extra punch or two. Bogus ballots can be added to the system (or others removed). Punched-out dots from punched cards can fall into the next ballot in the stack, filling a hole and erasing a vote.

Ballots that are marked like standardized tests carry orienting marks which tell the computer how they should be read. These marks can be misprinted or mispunched, for example, to throw each vote for the first candidate to the second, for the second to the third, and so on.

Of course, someone might question why the first candidate received no votes, so anyone intending to change the orienting marks would do so only for a fraction of the ballots—just enough to change the results in a close race. Elections in California, with its millions of voters, have been won and lost by as little as 100,000 votes.

Sabotaging the Vote-Counting Software

A computer vote-tallying program consists of a precise set of instructions the computer is expected to follow. Any change in the program means the computer will behave differently. In a computerized election system, the program can secretly be changed to:

- Add extra ballots
- Cast invalid ballots a particular way
- Discard a portion of ballots cast for a particular candidate or issue
- Misread some or all of the ballots
- Turn off the computer's record-keeping system
- Change how election results are reported

Any of these threats can be accomplished by a single computer expert or, in many instances, by a non-professional.

Quite recently the public has become aware of the vulnerability of computer systems to phenomena such as "viruses," "trapdoors," "time bombs" and "Trojan horses," any of which can be—and already have been—used to disrupt complicated computer programs. The potential use of these tricks in computerized vote tallying has received very little public attention.

The September 26, 1988, *Time* magazine cover story on computer viruses explained how these self-replicating programs penetrate and damage massive computer systems. Election systems weren't even mentioned, but, as it stands now, viruses may be able to do more harm in elections with less chance of detection than in the systems *Time* magazine described.

A trapdoor, or hidden sequence of steps in vote-tallying instructions, could allow an election operator to slip by the computer's security system with a secret password. Once into the program, anything can be modified: the operator could, for example, program the computer to count votes for one candidate as votes for another. After enough votes have been changed to swing the election, the trapdoor can be closed—with no record that it ever existed.

Trapdoors take someone on site to activate them. But with a time bomb, the computer program will act up at a certain time—say, on Election Day. The time bomb could instruct the computer to add five hundred dummy votes while the perpetrator relaxed thousands of miles away.

Just like the ploy the Greeks used, Trojan horses can sneak trouble into election computers by hiding inside another appealing program, perhaps one that prints up election results as bar charts.

Once election officials open the gates by using the bar chart program, the Trojan horse can let out its software soldiers and manipulate the vote-counting procedure, first turning off the computer's record-keeping system or audit trail so that no later inspection of the election will turn up the subversion.

Surely computerized election systems, like bank computers, have protections against these threats? Not yet.

What Security Systems?

An unscrupulous computer programmer could insert a Trojan horse, time bomb or numerous other software threats into our vote-counting systems simply by working at the right computer, unsupervised.

This could happen when the vote-counting software is designed, when it is modified for local precincts, or on Election Day, when the software program needs help from a human operator.

Who would ever know? Private businesses supply all of today's vote-counting software and specify the hardware on which it is to run. Only these vendors double-check their products for accuracy. There is no independent review that could assure election officials that the programs do exactly what they are supposed to do, and nothing else.

Furthermore, the programs do not lend themselves to examination. When Princeton computer scientists Howard Strauss and Jon Edwards reviewed the most common computer vote-tallying system (EL-80, which runs the Votomatic system that dominates the market), they found the software so poorly designed that it was virtually impossible to guarantee its functions.

Another computer scientist has called EL-80 "a bucket of worms," referring to its over 4,000 confusing, badly written instructions, all of which must work perfectly for the election results to be properly tallied and reported.

A Convenient Lapse of Computer Memory

One defense against software manipulation is the computer's audit trail, which makes a record of every step the computer takes, every keystroke entered, every ballot analyzed. With a complete audit trail, any attempt to change the computer's programmed operation would be recorded. Problem elections could be reconstructed to identify what happened, and when. Errors could be corrected.

But the audit trails of most election systems can be turned off. This means that, if the audit trail were turned off on Election Day, by error or intent, it would be impossible later to reconstruct the election if the results were challenged. This would be like trying to find the cause of a mysterious airplane crash without the cockpit "black box" recorder.

Manipulating Computer Hardware

The election computer itself can be violated. With access to the computer, its peripheral equipment, or cables that network election computers, a computer expert could alter the computer or tap into its operations on Election Day.

Through hardware manipulation, votes can be added or modified, an operator could be permitted to bypass the computer's security system, or the entire election could simply be muddled beyond repair.

This is possible whenever election hardware is left unsecured, or tended by a single person; by the use of unsecured networks linking election computers; and by the addition of modifications to the specialized computer equipment that most election systems now require.

Don't we lock up our election computers, like the lever machines of old? Not necessarily.

For example, in 1987, someone gained unauthorized access to the Voter Registration Board office in Burlington, Vermont and tampered with its computer. The unknown culprit managed to wipe the names of as many as 1,000 voters off the official voter checklist, which is used to confirm voter eligibility at the polls.

Some Enlightening Errors

There are many other deliberate tricks known to computer experts, and computerized vote-counting systems are vulnerable to just about all of them.

Since these tricks can be designed to destroy evidence of their existence, there are no confirmed reports of their use in elections. Two of the lawsuits mentioned above were dismissed because of lack of evidence which could prove or disprove fraud; another because the software manufacturer successfully asserted that his programs were "trade secrets" and could not be examined. The fourth, in Indiana, is still active.

But the chilling possibilities of deliberate fraud in computer vote-tallying can be understood by examining the chaos wrought by mistakes, which by their unplanned nature are far more likely to be discovered than fraud.

In the 1980 presidential primary, a programming error led Orange County, California, election computers to count 15,000 votes for Jimmy Carter and Ted Kennedy as votes for Lyndon Larouche and Jerry Brown.

In Gwinnet County, Georgia, a computer hardware error affected hundreds of votes in a close race. A complete recount reversed earlier results in which a candidate had apparently won by eight votes out of about 13,000.

In Moline, Illinois, a faulty timing belt slipped intermittently on one card reader. This led to a miscount where the wrong candidate actually assumed office and later had to give it up.

A 1988 National Bureau of Standards report lists some recent difficulties in 26 computerized elections.

How much worse can it get?

A De Facto Monopoly

In any given election district, the company that supplied the vote-counting system usually provides the experts needed to operate the system. Since the software received no independent review, and since election officials feel helpless to supervise the on-site experts, this kind of access means that a single computer programmer bent on mischief can secretly alter any election outcome.

Moreover, while there are about a dozen vendors of computerized election systems, one vendor alone supplies the programs which count more than one-third of the nation's votes in local, state and federal elections. This *de facto* monopoly could spell enormous trouble were any of this company's personnel tempted to play with our votes.

Such a concentration of power in the hands of computer experts is astonishing. Today's procedures make it absurdly easy for a person so inclined to meddle with election computers and their software. And there is little chance of detection later.

A Call to Action

America's fundamental democratic institution is ripe for abuse.

Election officials depend on a few computer experts who are unaccountable to voters.

A handful of private companies monopolize the technology that counts our votes.

Vote-counting programs, ballots and equipment are known to be vulnerable to various types of threats, yet current election procedures fail to protect them.

Many machine-readable ballots aren't readable by voters trying to confirm that the punched holes correspond to their choices.

And the election computer may never document that someone has tampered with it, because its audit trail can be turned off.

It is ridiculous for our country to run such a haphazard, easily violated election system. If we are to retain confidence in our election results, we must institute adequate security procedures in computerized vote tallying, and return election control to the citizenry.

It is our hope that this report will result in very constructive dialogue and action leading to reform of electronic voting in the United States.

PART II:

A Secure Solution

We have the technology and the knowledge right now to develop secure computerized election systems. Any computer system can be undermined by fraud or error, but there are methods that will make such threats difficult to perpetrate and likely to be detected.

Princeton computer scientists Howard Strauss and Jon Edwards have designed a plan for secure elections which could be implemented within two years. Their proposal balances the interests of software vendors with the public's need for accurate and verifiable vote counts. Whether or not this particular plan is adopted, it is urgent that the issue be publicly discussed and a competent, comprehensive election security plan adopted.

Independent Review of Software

A crucial element in the Strauss-Edwards proposal is independent review of vote-counting software by impartial computer scientists.

States and local election districts have the primary responsibility for ensuring that elections are properly conducted. When most voting was done with paper ballots and lever machines, the expertise required to manage an election could be readily obtained on a local level.

Electronic elections, however, require the development of specifications for election software, selection of software and hardware and verification that the systems will do what they are supposed to do and nothing else. To have each state obtain the expertise needed for these tasks would be expensive and indefensibly duplicative.

Strauss and Edwards propose, therefore, that a national review panel of computer scientists, *unaffiliated with any election software vendors,* be empowered to certify computer programs and equipment for use in all elections. The vendors would be required to provide software that could be readily analyzed.

Once these tasks are completed, the remainder of the election process—ballot creation, vote tabulation, reporting of results—can be done readily and cost effectively at the local level.

A Separation of Powers

The Strauss-Edwards proposal relies on the separation of functions, with checks and balances throughout the election system. This minimizes the opportunity for any one person or group to undermine election results, either accidentally or intentionally.

The separation of software development from software review has already been described. Another group would be charged with distributing that software to local precincts and election officials. This group would double-check the work of the software developers and software review personnel.

At the election level, the Strauss-Edwards proposal would separate ballot creation, precinct elections, election analysis and the determination of final election results.

Impartial officials representing all major and minor candidates would be needed to run each part of the election system. No one affiliated with the software vendor should be involved in any other part of the election system.

Putting Citizens Back in Control

A key tenet of the Strauss-Edwards plan is the return of election control to citizens. Citizens, not computer experts, should run our elections.

Software vendors have had no incentive to spend extra money on the kind of complex programming that would make their software "user friendly" for local election officials. Nor have election officials realized that they could or should demand programs that could be operated by a non-expert.

The Strauss-Edwards proposal would require vendors to develop software which local officials can use. The officials would simply have to be able to turn on the computer.

Hands Off the Keyboard on Election Day

Many strategies to undermine computerized elections require someone to gain access to the vote-counting equipment on Election Day. Strauss and Edwards propose an elegant solution: vote-counting programs that require no human interaction.

Invalid ballots offer one type of opportunity for people to interact with the election vote-counting computers. The computer vote-counting operation sometimes stops counting when it encounters an invalid ballot, and asks the human operator what to do with it.

This may open the gates, allowing the operator not only to choose how the ballot is cast (for his or her preferred candidate?), but also to confuse or mislead the vote-counting program. An operator could, for example, introduce a Trojan horse that would add just enough ballots to throw a close election.

Strauss and Edwards propose a system that does away with invalid ballots entirely: by requiring that ballots be checked for validity at the precinct *before* they are turned in and counted. This could be accomplished with special software and what Strauss and Edwards call the Ballot Validation Computer. Voters whose ballots were invalid would be given another chance to vote. Their original, invalid ballots would be logged and destroyed.

Let Ballots Be Ballots

Voters must be able to confirm that the votes indicated on their ballots represent the candidates or issues they wanted to select. The Strauss-Edwards proposal calls for all ballots to include the names of candidates and descriptions of issues so that the voter is assured his will has been correctly entered on the ballot.

Controlling the number of ballots has always been an issue in traditional, paper elections. Ballot security is even more important in electronic elections, since the computer's own records may be unable to reconstruct the election to permit a recount. Strauss and Edwards suggest that, in addition to physical security measures, each ballot be marked with a precinct number to ensure that stray ballots could be accurately voted in accord with their own local slate.

Since the orienting marks on each ballot determine how the computer will read the card, Strauss and Edwards also propose that local officials ensure that punched cards have proper orienting punches before being given to the voter, and that the printing of all other machine-readable ballots be carefully controlled to ensure accurate orientation when counted.

Off-the-Shelf Software and Hardware

Strauss and Edwards propose that all computerized election systems be designed to operate only on generic equipment, using generic programs which can be bought from commercial vendors. This allows all precincts and election analysis centers to buy their own "fresh" equipment for use in the election.

Even then, *Time* magazine reports an instance of a computer virus being unwittingly spread through a piece of commercial software.

A System Which Never Forgets

Probably the simplest, yet most important, security measure to take is to ensure that we have a complete record of all computerized elections. This can be accomplished by ensuring that the audit trail in computerized vote-tallying software can never be turned off. That way, when allegations of error or subversion arise, every single step of the election can be replayed—including errors or tricks in the software instructions.

Overseeing the System

Elections are the province of local and state government. But in our technological age, municipalities turn to national clearinghouses for advice on the best ways to manage traffic, pollution, housing, redevelopment, and other civic responsibilities.

It appears necessary that some national, publicly accountable body assume responsibility for ensuring voting rights in computerized elections. Strauss and Edwards propose a Citizens Election Commission (CEC) composed of impartial citizens of the highest personal integrity and computer scientists of comparable stature.

The CEC would be responsible for appointing the groups that review and distribute election software; for setting specifications and certifying hardware and software for use in local elections; and for developing and overseeing security measures in the entire election system.

Just how such a body is to be created, how it would respond to the states while being fashioned at a federal level, and who would join its august ranks remain complex political problems. But it is a surmountable obstacle, given the urgency of our current situation.

CONCLUSION

The election plan presented by Strauss and Edwards forces election officials to be responsible for the election process, minimizes the chances of fraud and mishap at each level, detects and records subversion that gets by anyway and produces an election which can be audited.

It should disturb us all that these relatively simple procedures are not already in place.

We do not believe that current voting methods are adequate. We urge lawmakers and all interested parties to do all that they can, if not to promote the precise measures that we recommend, then to guarantee that comprehensive guidelines and procedures that take our concerns into consideration are put into place and required of all election jurisdictions.

REFERENCES

Election Administration Reports (Washington, D.C: October 26, 1987), p. 5.

Philip Elmer-DeWitt, "Invasion of the Data Snatchers!" *Time.* September 26, 1988, pp. 62–67.

Lance J. Hoffman, *Making Every Vote Count: Security and Reliability of Computerized Vote-Counting Systems,* (Washington, D.C.: George Washington University, 1987).

Roy G. Saltman, *Accuracy, Integrity, and Security in Computerized Vote Tallying,* (Gaithersburg, MD: National Bureau of Standards Publication 500–158 1988).

Howard Jay Strauss and Jon R. Edwards, "Ensuring the Integrity of Electronic Elections," (Princeton, NJ, 1988).

"Voters Wiped Out," *Vanguard Press,* Burlington, VT, December 17, 1987.

Voting System Standard Program (Draft), Federal Election Commission, Washington, D.C., 1987–88.

Ethical Scenarios

Scenarios marked with an asterisk are adapted from Parker (1979).

*1. A student had access to the university computer system because a class she was taking required extensive computer usage. The student enjoyed playing games on the computer, and frequently had to request extra computer funds from her professor in order to complete her assignments.

Was the student's use of the computer to play games acceptable, questionable, or unacceptable?

2. A "virus" program is a program that performs tasks that a user has not requested, or does not want to perform. Some virus programs erase all files on a disk, some just print silly messages. Virus programs always copy themselves on other disks automatically, so the virus will spread to unsuspecting users. One day, a student programmer decided to write a virus program that caused the microcomputer to ignore every fifth command entered by a user. The student took his program to the university computing lab and installed it on one of the microcomputers. Before long, the virus had spread to hundreds of users.

Was the student's action infecting hundreds of users' disks acceptable, questionable, or unacceptable?

If the virus program output the message "Have a nice day," would the student's action infecting hundreds of users' disks have been acceptable, questionable, or unacceptable?

If the virus erased files, would the student's action infecting hundreds of users' disks have been acceptable, questionable, or unacceptable?

*3. A student suspected and found a loophole in the university computer's security system that allowed him to access other students' records. He told the system administrator about the loophole, but continued to access others' records until the problem was corrected two weeks later.

Was the student's action in searching for the loophole acceptable, questionable, or unacceptable?

Was the student's action in continuing to access others' records for two weeks acceptable, questionable, or unacceptable?

Was the system administrator's failure to correct the problem sooner acceptable, questionable, or unacceptable?

4. A university student obtained a part-time job as a data entry clerk. His job was to enter personal student data into the university's database. Some of this data was available in the student directory, but some of it was not. He was attracted to a student in his algebra class and wanted to ask her out. Before asking her, though, he decided to access her records in the database to find out about her background.

Were the student's actions in accessing a fellow student's personal information acceptable, questionable, or unacceptable?

*5. A manager of a company that sells computer processing services bought similar services from a competitor. She used her access to the competitor's computer to try to break the security system, identify other customers, and cause the system to "crash" (cause loss of service to others). She used the service for over a year and always paid her bills promptly.

Were the manager's actions acceptable, questionable, or unacceptable?

6. A telephone system employee saw an advertisement in a newspaper about a car for sale. The car sounded like a good buy to the employee. The advertisement listed the seller's telephone number, but not the seller's address. The telephone system employee knew he could determine the seller's address by accessing the seller's telephone records. He did this and went to the seller's house to discuss buying the car.

Was the telephone system employee's action acceptable, questionable, or unacceptable?

If you know that the seller wanted to screen potential buyers over the phone, was the telephone system employee's action acceptable, questionable, or unacceptable?

*7. A programmer at a bank realized that he had accidentally overdrawn his checking account. He made a small adjustment in the bank's accounting system so that his account would not have an additional service charge assessed. As soon as he made a deposit that made his balance positive again, he corrected the bank's accounting system.

Was the programmer's modification of the accounting system acceptable, questionable, or unacceptable?

8. An MIS employee at the county courthouse had access to all the county records in the county database. Over the past few weeks, she had become suspicious about her neighbor's buying habits. The neighbor had purchased new lawn furniture, had the house painted, and had purchased an expensive new car. The MIS employee decided to access her neighbor's records to determine how the neighbor could afford these purchases.

Was the MIS employee's action acceptable, questionable, or unacceptable?

If the MIS employee suspected that the neighbor might be involved in criminal activity, would that make her actions acceptable, questionable, or unacceptable?

9. The FBI would like to build a database to maintain information about all persons convicted of a crime. Any person convicted of a crime would be required by law to provide the information requested by the FBI. The data would be maintained for the life of the person.

Would this FBI action be acceptable, questionable, or unacceptable?

Suppose the FBI wanted to maintain information on all persons charged with a crime. Any person charged with a crime would be required by law to provide the information requested by the FBI. The data would be maintained for the life of the person.

Would this FBI action be acceptable, questionable, or unacceptable?

Suppose the FBI wanted to maintain data on all persons with a Ph.D. Their reason is that these persons represent a significant national resource that may be desperately needed in times of crisis. Any person who earned a Ph.D. would be required by law to provide the information requested by the FBI.

Would this FBI action be acceptable, questionable, or unacceptable?

REFERENCE

Parker, D. B. *Ethical Conflicts in Computer Science and Technology.* AFIPS Press, 1979.

Chapter 4

The Traditional Issues of Property and Access

The Effect of Demographic Factors on Attitudes Toward Software Piracy

Susan L. Solomon and James A. O'Brien

Originally published in *Journal of Computer Information Systems,* Volume XXX, Number 3, 40–46. Reprinted by permission of *Journal of Computer Information Systems.* Copyright 1990.

ABSTRACT

Although few individuals will admit guilt, it is generally acknowledged that software piracy is rampant in most PC-using organizations today. From the vendor's perspective, software piracy means lost revenue and less incentive to develop new products. From the point of view of management in the PC-using organization, software piracy means the threat of costly litigation on the one hand, balanced against the reduced expense for additional software if illegal copies are used. It is the individual computer user, however, who ultimately makes the decision whether or not to attempt to copy protected programs. If it were possible to identify demographic factors which weigh in this decision, perhaps all parties involved could exercise more informed control over the copying of software.

The goal of this research was to identify those factors which do or do not seem to be associated with a variety of possible attitudes toward software piracy. The factors include personal characteristics such as age, college major, work experience, and the income level of the individual and his/her family. Other factors concern the organizational environment, particularly the perceived availability of adequate legal copies of software, and the perceived attitude of colleagues and superiors toward software piracy. Opportunity factors may also be involved. Level of expertise, for example, may prevent a novice computer user from making illegal copies even if s/he would be inclined to do so. Similarly, a prospective software pirate who does not have access to a source copy of the software and/or a willing temporary donor may be thwarted in the attempt.

A range of possible attitudes toward software piracy can be defined, from very willing to copy software for a variety of reasons, to totally opposed to copying software for a variety of reasons, to indifferent to the whole subject. Once the demographic factors and possible attitudes have been defined, it remains to evaluate statistically whether or not there is any association between various factors, attitudes and actions.

Chi-square contingency tests were performed on data taken from a sample of 267 students enrolled in management information systems or computer information systems classes at various levels at two public universities in different Western states. Some fairly obvious and some rather surprising statistical results were significant enough to be considered in future policy decisions regarding software acquisition and supervision.

BACKGROUND

Having taught at quite a few universities during their academic careers, the authors were struck by apparent large-scale differences in the attitudes of students and faculty toward software piracy at the several institutions. At some, unauthorized copies of software seemed to be offered as a gesture of friendship as casually as an invitation to lunch. At others, no one mentioned illegal copying of software. At still others, published policies opposing software piracy were stringently enforced by the staff.

Some of these universities used public-domain software or "shareware" almost exclusively, while others adopted major-brand software packages for classroom use. Some were better endowed than others in terms of computing resources such as number of PCs, number of minicomputer/mainframe terminals, ratio of students to hardware units, ratio of students to legal copies of classroom software, adoption of texts with coordinated student versions of major-brand software, and charges or time limits restricting student use of computer facilities.

Some initial hypotheses were that:

1. Influential members of the organization set the tone for student attitudes toward software piracy;
2. Organizations in which hardware and software are more scarce, or which do not use public-domain software, are more likely than others to foster software piracy;
3. Wealthier individuals are less likely to be software pirates;
4. Majors in management information systems, computer information systems and other business fields should oppose software piracy because of their business backgrounds, consequent understanding of the probable effect of piracy on software developers, and the ethical issues involved; and
5. Older students are more mature and less prone to the "hacker" outlook, as well as better able to afford their own legal copies of software, so they should show less tendency toward software piracy.

Our hypotheses about all these factors proved to be incorrect!

PRIOR RESEARCH AND PUBLICATIONS ON SOFTWARE PIRACY

The Readers' Guide to Periodical Literature cites references to unauthorized use of software dating from 1982, the year after the IBM PC was introduced, and about six years after the first appearance of microcomputers. Prior to that time software piracy was not an issue for several reasons. First, minicomputer and mainframe software was already accessible by multiple users with hardware authorization. Second, business software, at least, often would not run on other brands of equipment because it was written in assembly language. Third, few users had their own systems to which software could be ported. Fourth, much business software was custom written and tailored to the needs of the purchasing organization rather than general purposes. Fifth, there were just not that many computers and that much software around and available for scrutiny. Finally, few computer users were skilled enough to pirate software from minicomputer and mainframe systems with sophisticated operating systems, editors and communications capabilities.

It is easy to assume that the notion of software piracy came from young "hackers," with considerable time and imagination but little cash or sense of ethics, who had early Apple and Radio Shack computers in high school or at home. However, the necessity of completing class assignments or business tasks in the face of scarce computing resources appears to be just as likely a motivation for software piracy. Illegal copying of software has become so rampant that a widely quoted unofficial statistic suggests that there are twice as many illegal copies of WordStar, the first business word processing package for the IBM PC, as legal copies. Micropro, the vendor of WordStar, is reputed to view this dismal statistic in a positive way, given the company's continuing success. Although bootlegged copies of software usually have little or no documentation, they give the user a taste of the capabilities of the software. Those who like it will tend to purchase legal copies with documentation, upgrades and support, this view contends. Nevertheless, the prevalence of third-party paperback texts and short courses suggests that many "illegals" do not go on to purchase legal copies of the software. Thus, bootlegged copies of the expensive WordStar package helped mightily to make it the original word processing standard for the IBM PC.

The Association of Data Processing Service Organizations (ADAPSO) was formed by software vendors to fight software piracy as a group, by public persuasion, advertising, development of new types of software protection and by litigation. Companies as large and profitable as IBM, Apple, Lotus, Aston-Tate, Microsoft and WordPerfect have funded undercover investigations of software piracy in U.S. businesses, on college campuses, and even overseas [19, 20, 21].

Some software industry consultants believe that software piracy is more prevalent in academia than in business, and that in fact, guilty teachers and administrators encourage students to emulate their behavior [20]. ADAPSO and its constituent members, particularly Lotus Development Corp., have initiated pilot lawsuits to try to discourage piracy. While some of these lawsuits have been successful, a major setback was the recent decision (BV Engineering vs. UCLA) that state agencies could not be sued for copyright infringement because of a technicality—only federal courts handle copyright infringement cases, and a state may not be sued in a federal court. Unless the verdict is overturned at the appellate level, this means that academics and administrators from elementary school through college who are state employees can continue to promulgate the unauthorized copying of software without fear of reprisals, if they choose to do so. Their proteges will not be equally protected in the business workplace, but even there, widespread prosecution of software pirates has not occurred yet.

Highland [14] profiles the computer criminal as typically young, skilled and knowledgeable, overqualified for his or her position, elitist, and believing that their use of the computer does not really harm anyone who can't afford it or doesn't deserve to be harmed. The "Robin Hood syndrome" [14, p. 12] causes computer criminals to see organizations at best as sterile objects and at worst as enemies of the people rather than as groups of people themselves. It may seem incredible that this view can extend from the liberal Far Left to the ranks of business majors, business educators and business executives. Apparently the software pirate of today does not visualize himself or herself as the software vendor of tomorrow.

Educators and business executives point to unrealistic licensing practices by vendors as incentives to cheat. For example, only recently did site licensing become widespread among vendors who feared for their market share. Still, many licensing agreements tie individual machines. In an educational microcomputer laboratory or a business microcomputer processing center it is an overwhelming burden to make sure that specific diskettes are used only on specific machines by specific operators [14]. The vendors reply that they need to recoup their research and development costs with individual sales and that those who use the fruits of their efforts ought to pay a fair price for them. The alternatives, of course, are to deal with vendors who are of a different mindset, to develop custom software, or to use public-domain products.

Cook [7, 8] suggests that students are primed for software piracy because they are not:

1. told what is and is not expected of them with respect to hardware and software use;
2. acquainted with laws concerning software piracy; and
3. confronted with ethical issues in general.

Green and Gilbert [11] cite EDUCOM's policy on intellectual rights:

> A respect for intellectual labor and creativity is vital to academic discourse and enterprise. This principle applies to works of all authors and publishers in all media. It encompasses respect for the right to acknowledgement, right to privacy, and right to determine the form, manner, and terms of publication and distribution.
>
> Because electronic information is volatile and easily reproduced, respect for the work and personal expression of others is especially critical in computer environments. Violations of authorial integrity, including plagiarism, invasion of privacy, unauthorized access, and trade secret and copyright violations, are grounds for sanctions against members of the higher education community. [11, p. 48]

How does this ex ante and ex post theorizing about software piracy actually relate to the on-campus attitudes and experiences of contemporary students? The responses to our questionnaire illuminate these and suggest some possible remedies.

SUMMARY OF DEMOGRAPHIC ATTRIBUTES OF SURVEY SUBJECTS

Appendix A shows the questionnaire which was distributed to 149 students at University 1 and 117 students at University 2, along with the percentage responses for each possible answer. These students, both graduate and undergraduate, were enrolled in various Management Information Systems (M.I.S.) or Computer Information Systems (C.I.S.) courses. The two designations are used for approximately the same coursework at the two different universities in the sample. Some of the courses were designed for M.I.S./C.I.S. majors, some for general business majors, and some were open to any student regardless of major. We will briefly review the descriptive characteristics of the respondents as a group.

Sixty-seven percent of the respondents were upper-division students, with the remainder about evenly split between lower-division and graduate students. Ages ranged from under 19 to over 40, with a grouped median of 23 years and 7 months. Nearly 60% of the respondents were male.

A near-majority (47.2%) said their family's economic background was middle-class, with about twice as many upper-income families represented as lower-income families. The modal class expected personal income of under $5,000 this year, but the median personal income was estimated to be $8,233.00 from all sources.

Almost 40% had worked between five and ten years. Only 5% had never held a job.

Almost 50% of the group were M.I.S. or C.I.S. majors.

Median grade-point average in the sample was 3.1 on a four-point scale.

Most of the students rated themselves as intermediate-level or experienced computer users, with only about 25% novices and almost no self-defined experts.

SUMMARY OF ATTITUDES OF SURVEY SUBJECTS

Almost half (44%) of the students selected one or the other of two responses which showed qualified approval of unauthorized copying of software for a valid purpose. Seventeen percent felt the software vendors were taking financial advantage of their market position. Fourteen percent expressed opposition to unauthorized copying either for ethical reasons or out of fear of reprisals. Sixteen percent believed the issue of software piracy was dull or unimportant. Finally, about six percent voiced the "hacker" perspective that copying protected software was mainly an exciting challenge.

Over half the surveyed students (52.8%) admitted having made unauthorized copies at some time. Even though the respondents were assured of confidentiality of replies and no identifiers of any kind were placed on returned questionnaires, very probably this figure understates the true percent of the group which had made bootleg copies because most people are reluctant to admit guilt, even anonymously.

Twenty-seven percent admitted to having allowed someone else to make copies of protected software which they personally owned, and sixty-five percent had been specifically asked by someone for permission to copy their software. Sixty-seven percent had been offered copies of protected software. Only 16% had been offered or asked to use illegal software copies on the job, a result consistent with prior research suggesting that software piracy was more prevalent in academia than in the workplace. A large majority (70.4%) were confident that it was very unlikely that software pirates would be caught and punished. Nearly 70% believed that software piracy occurs "quite a bit" or "very often." About 25% of the group had heard a college faculty member encourage or condone unauthorized software copying, while over half had heard a faculty member speak in opposition to software copying. A plurality of both groups was not interested enough in the topic to be affected by the remarks of the faculty member. Among the rest there was no clear effect of the remarks by the faculty member on the preceding attitude of the student.

Sixty-six percent of the students rated the availability of legally purchased copies of software for classroom use at their university as adequate or better. Twenty-one percent described it as mediocre, and 12% as poor.

The views of the students on the future course of copy protection were quite mixed. The largest group (32.2%) saw prices of software falling such that unauthorized copying would no longer be an attractive option. The next largest group (22.8%) expected software market conditions to remain about the same as they are now.

STATISTICAL ASSOCIATIONS BETWEEN DEMOGRAPHICS AND ATTITUDES

Frequency counts and crosstabs for the sample of 267 students were run using SPSS-X on the Cyber 170 system. Each demographic variable was tested for possible association with each attitudinal variable using a Chi-Square contingency test. When necessary, categories were combined to eliminate or reduce to less than 15% of all cells in the test, those cells with expected frequencies less than 5. In such cases only categories which could logically be grouped together were combined. An example might be, for perceived availability of software, the combination of responses of "fair" and "poor" into "mediocre."

Appendix B shows a list of statistically significant (.10 level or lower) relationships between variables, with a brief description of the pair of associated variables, the relevant question numbers from the questionnaire, and the level of significance.

The Chi-Square contingency test suggests an association between two variables but does not indicate the nature or direction of the association. One reason for this is that categories for this test may be nominal rather than ordinal. Nevertheless, sometimes it is possible to suggest the principal nature or major direction of significance informally by examining the difference between observed and expected values in the cells of the table. Some apparent trends will be discussed when the nominal category titles are quasi-ordinal, i.e., for software availability, "excellent," "good," "fair" and "poor," a clearly decreasing ranking of desirability.

Students who felt it was "very unlikely" to be caught making illegal copies were much more prone to make such copies than those who felt being caught was "somewhat likely" or "somewhat unlikely."

The high degree of significance in the pairs "made illegal copies" vs. "someone asked to copy," "made illegal copies" vs. "someone offered copies," and "made illegal copies" vs. "someone offered copies at work" suggests that either those who engage in software piracy make themselves known to others of like mind, or work in an environment which encourages or lends itself to software piracy. Supporting this position, those who made illegal copies consistently ascribed a strong prevalence to copying by others. Finally, software piracy is particularly prevalent where software availability is rated "mediocre" ("fair" or "poor") rather than "excellent," "good" or "adequate."

The association between "age," "how long working," and "major" vs. "made illegal copies" may be a matter of simple exposure and necessity. A young person working as an order-taker at a fast-foods restaurant has little need for software, whereas an entry-level accounting clerk might. Younger people with little job experience might not have the financial resources to have their own computers at home and, therefore, would have less need or desire for software. A college freshman taking general education classes probably would not feel pressure to copy software that might fall upon an M.I.S./C.I.S. major who needs the materials to complete class assignments.

CONCLUSIONS

The most important conclusions from this study are that software piracy is a widespread phenomenon among business students taking M.I.S./C.I.S. courses, and that it is viewed as socially and ethically acceptable by a significant proportion of such students. There is some suggestion that it is viewed as necessary because of inadequate provision of computer resources on campus for class assignments. However, at one of the universities in this study, the use of public-domain software rather than higher-priced commercial packages is actively encouraged by providing copies of word processing, database and spreadsheet shareware on diskettes at cost. Still, there is no statistically significant difference between the two colleges in the incidence of software piracy or student attitudes toward it, as measured by responses to the questionnaire. Apparently, students make illegal copies of software for purposes other than classroom use, and they do so irrespective of their ability to purchase legal copies as measured by their personal income and length of time employed.

A final disturbing feature of the survey results is that nearly half the students had never heard a faculty member speak against illegal copying, or even worse, that 25% of the sampled students had heard a faculty member condone the copying of protected software. Of these 25%, a further 25% were sufficiently influenced by the remarks to soften their own attitudes toward software piracy. In view of the importance ascribed to the teaching of ethics in today's business curriculum, M.I.S./C.I.S. instructors might be advised to consider their remarks on software piracy more carefully.

BIBLIOGRAPHY

1. Altman, J., "Copyright Protection of Computer Software," *Computer Law Journal,* V. 5, No. 3, Winter, 1985, pp. 413–432.
2. Altman, J., "Remedies in Software Copyright Cases," *Computer Law Journal,* V. 6, No. 1, Summer, 1985, pp. 1–33.
3. Barney, Douglas, "1-2-3 Sue! Lotus vs. Clones," *Computerworld,* V. 21, January 19, 1987, pp. 1–2.
4. Bebditch, David, "Pirate's Paradise: Shopping for Software, Bootlegged or Basic, Can Be a Real Experience in Hong Kong," *Datamation,* V. 32, September 1, 1986, pp. 71–72.
5. Bloombecker, A.J., "New Federal Law Bolsters Computer Security," *Computerworld,* October 27, 1986, pp. 55–59.
6. Buckeley, William M., "Courts Expand the Copyright Protection of Software, but Many Questions Remain," *Wall Street Journal,* November 18, 1986, pp. 35, 37.
7. Cook, Janet M., "Defining Ethical and Unethical Student Behaviors Using Departmental Regulations and Sanctions," *ACM SIGCSE Bulletin,* 19:1, February 1987, pp. 462–468.
8. Cook, Janet M., "What C.S. Graduates Don't Learn About Security Concepts and Ethical Standards Or—'Every Company Has Its Share of Damn Fools. Now Every Damn Fool Has Access to a Computer,' " *ACM SIGCSE Bulletin,* 1986, pp. 89–95.

9. Davis, George R., "Tougher Copyrights Will Boost Innovation," *Datamation,* V. 32, November 1, 1986, p. 18.

10. Faidhi, J.A.W., and S.K. Robinson, "An Empirical Approach for Detecting Program Similarity and Plagiarism within a University Programming Environment," *Computers and Education,* V. 11, No. 1, 1987, pp. 11–19.

11. Green, Kenneth C., and Steven W. Gilbert, "Software Piracy: Its Costs and the Consequences," *Change,* January–February, 1987, pp. 47–49.

12. Harper, Robert M., "Software Licensing for Installations with Multiple Microcomputers," *Computers in Education,* V. 9, No. 3, 1985, pp. 165–170.

13. Haugness, C.A., "Copyright and Computer Software," *AEDS Monitor,* V. 24, Nos. 1–2, July/August, 1985, pp. 13–14.

14. Highland, Harold J., "Protecting Your Microcomputer System," New York, Wiley, 1984.

15. Howe, Charles L., "Circling the Wagons: The Industry is Turning to Litigation in an Attempt to Stem the Hemorrhage of Pirated Intellectual Properties," *Datamation,* V. 32, May 15, 1986, pp. 42–45.

16. Johnson, Douglas W. *Computer Ethics: A Guide for the New Age,* Elgin, IL, The Brethren Press, 1984.

17. Kanzler, Stephen, "Software Protection Changes to Affect Site Licensing Plans," *PC Week,* V. 3, July 15, 1986, pp. 1–2.

18. Karon, Paul, "Software Industry Groups Set Sail Against Pirates in Academe," *PC Week,* V. 3, December 9, 1986, pp. 61–62.

19. Krauss, Leonard I., and Aileen MacGahan, *Computer Fraud and Countermeasures,* Englewood Cliffs, Prentice-Hall, 1979.

20. Machrone, Bill, "The Copyright Fight," *PC Magazine,* V. 8, February 12, 1987, pp. 81–82.

21. Pallette, John, "Software and the Law," *PC Week,* V. 3, October 7, 1986, pp. 79–84.

22. Parker, Rachel, "Coalition to Combat Software Piracy: Publishers Pursue Hong Kong Counterfeiters," *Infoworld,* December 7, 1987, p. 5.

23. Parker, Rachel, "Publishers Take on Software Piracy in Academia," *Infoworld,* October 19, 1987, p. 49.

24. Pepper, Jon C., "User, Software Firms Continue to Debate Copy-Protection Issues," *PC Week,* V. 3, April 8, 1986, pp. 52–55.

25. Posner, Ronald S., and George T. DeBakey, "Software Piracy Limits U.S. Export Growth," *Business America,* V. 9, June 9, 1986, p. 50.

26. Risher, C.A., "Copyright and Computer Software: A Question of Ethics," *AEDS Monitor,* V. 22, Nos. 9–10, March/April, 1984, pp. 23–24.

27. Ruby, Daniel, "Breaking the Copy-Protection Barriers," *PC Week,* V. 3, April 8, 1986, pp. 45–49.

28. Sanger, David E., "A Divisive Lotus 'Clone' War," *New York Times,* V. 136, February 5, 1987, p. 25.

29. Schneider, Jerry, "Users Must Take Responsibility to Control the Illegal Copying of Software," *Infoworld,* October 5, 1987, p. 56.

30. Seymour, Jim, "Costs of Copy Protection Hit Software Maker, Too," *PC Week,* V. 3, May 20, 1986, p. 66.

31. Shattuck, Petra T., "Public Perceptions of the 'Intellectual Property Rights' Issue," Washington, D.C., Office of Technology Assessment of the U.S. Congress, 1985.

32. Sterne, R.G., and P.J. Snidman, "Computers and Law: Copying Mass-Marketed Software," Byte, 10:2, February, 1985, pp. 387–390.

33. Swartz, Herbert, "Rise in Lawsuits over Illegal Software Use Prompts Companies to Revamp Usage Policies," *EDN,* V. 30, December 12, 1985, pp. 307–310.

34. Ticer, Scott, "Software Pirates Beware: Borkin is Out for Blood," *Business Week,* June 16, 1986, p. 83.

35. Wilson, D.S., "Software Rental Piracy and Copyright Protection," *Computer Law Journal,* V. 5, No. 1, Summer, 1984, pp. 125–141.

Appendix A

Questionnaire*
Student Views on Unauthorized Copying of Software

This questionnaire deals with attitudes toward and experience with unauthorized copying of computer software programs. This does not include copying of "shareware" or public domain software whose duplication is unrestricted by the provider and which can be copied without special permission. It also does not include the copying of original diskettes to produce backup copies allowed by the provider.

Your reply will be kept anonymous and used only as part of a group of responses from several universities as input to a faculty research project.

Please circle the response to each question which most closely reflects your views.

DEMOGRAPHIC INFORMATION**

1. I am a:
   a. Lower-division student   40 (15.0%)
   b. Upper-division student   180 (67.4%)
   c. Graduate student   47 (17.6%)
2. My age is:
   a. Under 19   8   (3.0%)
   b. At least 19 but less than 21   23   (8.6%)
   c. At least 21 but less than 23   87 (32.6%)

---

* Includes actual frequency and percent of responses.
** Percentages do not necessarily total 100% for each question due to missing responses.

     d. At least 23 but less than 25   49 (18.4%)

     e. At least 25 but less than 30   57 (21.3%)

     f. At least 30 but less than 40   36 (13.5%)

     g. 40 or older   6   (2.2%)

3. I am:

     a. Male   155 (58.1%)

     b. Female   99 (37.1%)

4. My family's economic background is:

     a. Poor   8   (3.0%)

     b. Working-class   38 (14.2%)

     c. Middle-class   126 (47.2%)

     d. Upper-middle-class   88 (33.0%)

     e. Wealthy   5   (1.9%)

5. I have worked full-time or part-time for:

     a. 0 years   14   (5.2%)

     b. Some work but less than two years   31 (11.6%)

     c. At least two years but less than five years   65 (24.3%)

     d. At least five years but less than ten years 105 (39.3%)

     e. Ten years or more   52 (19.5%)

6. My major is:

     a. Management Information Systems or Computer Information

         Systems   128 (47.9%)

     b. Other Business Field   106 (39.7%)

     c. Computer Science or Engineering   10   (3.7%)

     d. Other Scientific Field   4   (1.5%)

     e. Liberal Arts or Social Sciences   6   (2.2%)

     f. Other   13   (4.9%)

7. My personal income before taxes this year, including grants from relatives, friends, and governmental agencies, will probably be approximately:

     a. Under $5,000   85 (31.8%)

     b. At least $5,000 but less than $10,000   75 (28.1%)

     c. At least $10,000 but less than $15,000   48 (18.0%)

     d. At least $15,000 but less than $25,000   33 (12.4%)

     e. At least $25,000 but less than $50,000   24   (9.0%)

     f. $50,000 or more   2   (0.7%)

8. My grade-point average overall is approximately:

     a. Less than 2.0   3   (1.1%)

     b. Between 2.0 and 2.5   35 (13.1%)

     c. Between 2.6 and 3.0   94 (35.2%)

     d. Between 3.1 and 3.5   92 (34.5%)

     e. Over 3.5   43 (16.1%)

9. In terms of my computer literacy and experience, I consider myself:
   a. A novice   54 (20.2%)
   b. An intermediate-level user   103 (38.6%)
   c. An experimental user   87 (32.6%)
   d. An expert   9 (3.4%)

10. *Attitudes toward Unauthorized Software Copying*
    The statement which most closely describes my attitude toward unauthorized copying of software is:
    a. The software marketers are making big bucks, far in excess of the cost of production, when they sell software. They deserve to get stung occasionally.   9 (3.4%)
    b. The software producers are making big bucks, far in excess of the cost of production, when they sell software. A few unauthorized copies won't hurt them.   37 (13.9%)
    c. I enjoy the challenge of seeing whether I can copy protected software, even if I don't plan to use it. I don't see anything wrong with it.   15 (5.6%)
    d. I think it's basically okay to copy protected software if a person has access to it and has a use for it, but the idea makes me feel a little nervous or guilty.   67 (25.1%)
    e. I consider it justified to copy protected software only if there is a truly pressing need for it, such as to complete an assignment at work or school, and there is no other feasible way to get the job done.   50 (18.7%)
    f. An unnecessary amount of fuss is made over this issue. I really don't care much either way.   44 (16.5%)
    g. I am completely opposed to unauthorized copying of software because it is unethical, a form of stealing intellectual property.   32 (12.0%)
    h. I am completely opposed to unauthorized copying of software because I worry about the penalties if I were caught.   6 (2.2%)

11. Have you ever made unauthorized copies of software without proper consent or procedure provided by the vendor?
        Yes 141 (52.8%)   No 125 (46.8%)

12. Have you ever allowed another person to copy software which you had purchased and on which the vendor had placed copy restrictions?
        Yes 73 (27.3%)   No 191 (71.5%)

13. Have you ever heard a college or university faculty member encourage or condone unauthorized software copying?
        Yes 68 (25.5%)   No 199 (74.5%)

    If you answered "Yes" to Question 13, please answer Question 14. Otherwise, skip to Question 15.

14. How did the views of the faculty member affect your attitude toward unauthorized software copying?
    a. I wasn't interested in the topic.   38 (14.2%)

    b. I became more tolerant and understanding of unauthorized software copying.   18 (6.7%)

    c. I engaged in the unauthorized copying of software or the unauthorized use of copied software afterward but not before hearing the remarks.   6 (2.2%)

    d. I disregarded the remarks and continued to view unauthorized software copying as improper.   10 (3.7%)

15. Have you ever heard a faculty member speak in opposition to unauthorized software copying?

                          Yes   139 (52.1%)   No   126 (47.2%)

16. How did the views of the faculty member affect your attitude toward unauthorized software copying?

    a. I wasn't interested in the topic.   48 (18.0%)

    b. I became less tolerant and understanding of unauthorized software copying.   45 (16.9%)

    c. I had engaged in the unauthorized copying of software or the unauthorized use of copied software before but not after hearing the remarks.   7 (2.6%)

    d. I disregarded the remarks and continued to view unauthorized software copying as acceptable.   46 (17.2%)

17. How likely do you believe it is that someone who copies software without permission of the vendor will be caught and subjected to penalties?

    a. Very likely   3 (1.1%)

    b. Somewhat likely   7 (2.6%)

    c. 50–50   15 (5.6%)

    d. Somewhat unlikely   43 (16.1%)

    e. Very unlikely   188 (70.4%)

    f. Don't know   9 (3.4%)

18. Has anyone ever asked you to allow them to copy software that you own but on which the vendor has placed copy restrictions?

                           Yes   93 (34.8%)   No   173 (64.8%)

19. Has anyone ever offered to provide you with an unauthorized copy of software?

                           Yes   179 (67.0%)   No   87 (32.6%)

20. I would rate the availability of legally purchased copies of software for class use at my college or university as:

    a. Excellent   21 (7.9%)

    b. Very good   50 (18.7%)

    c. Adequate   99 (37.1%)

    d. Mediocre   55 (20.6%)

    e. Poor   33 (12.4%)

21. How do you feel about possible changes in software marketing which would affect the issue of unauthorized software copying?

    a. I think consumers are going to boycott products with hard-line attitudes and techniques toward copying, such as those traditionally employed by Lotus Development Corporation.   13 (4.9%)

    b. I think vendors are going to loosen up on copy protection because it's not worth the effort and hassle.   41 (15.4%)

    c. I think prices of software will fall and unauthorized copying will no longer be an attractive option.   86 (32.2%)

    d. I think there will be an increased tendency to provide software free or inexpensively and charge fees for documentation and/or support.   52 (19.5%)

    e. I think things are going to stay pretty much as they are.   61 (22.8%)

    f. All other.   6 (2.2%)

22. How prevalent do you believe unauthorized copying of software is among other computer users?

    a. Very rare   5 (1.9%)

    b. Occurs occasionally   53 (19.9%)

    c. Occurs quite a bit   92 (34.5%)

    d. Occurs very often   88 (33.0%)

    e. No opinion   16 (6.0%)

23. Have you ever been offered or been asked to use unauthorized copies of software at work (as opposed to in school)?

    Yes   42 (15.7%)   No   208 (77.9%)

24. University code:

    1. 149   (55.8%)

    2. 117   (43.8%)

Appendix B

Statistically Significant Associations

Variable 1	Variable 2	Questions	Signif. Level
Attitude on Copying	Age	10,02	.0107
Attitude on Copying	Family Economic Bkgd.	10,04	.0865
Attitude on Copying	How Long Working	10,05	.0443
Attitude on Copying	Major	10,06	.0681
Attitude on Copying	Made Illegal Copies	10,11	.0001
Attitude on Copying	Let Others Copy	10,12	.0024
Attitude on Copying	Were Asked for Copies	10,18	.0128
Attitude on Copying	Someone Offered Copies	10,19	.0087
Attitude on Copying	Perceived Sftwr. Avail.	10,20	.0087
Attitude on Copying	Sftwr. Mktg. Change	10,21	.0004
Attitude on Copying	Perceived Prevalence	10,22	.0193
Attitude on Copying	Someone Offered at Work	10,23	.0067
Made Illegal Copies	Class Standing	11,01	.0067
Made Illegal Copies	Age	11,02	.0621
Made Illegal Copies	Sex	11,03	.0124
Made Illegal Copies	Major	11,06	.0000
Made Illegal Copies	Computer Literacy Level	11,09	.0000
Made Illegal Copies	Let Others Copy	11,12	.0000
Made Illegal Copies	Likelihood Caught	11,17	.0000
Made Illegal Copies	Were Asked for Copies	11,18	.0000
Made Illegal Copies	Someone Offered Copies	11,19	.0000
Made Illegal Copies	Perceived Sftwr. Avail.	11,20	.0045
Made Illegal Copies	Sftwr. Mktg. Change	11,21	.0040
Made Illegal Copies	Perceived Prevalence	11,22	.0000
Made Illegal Copies	Someone Offered at Work	11,23	.0004
Let Others Copy	Sex	12,03	.0488
Let Others Copy	Family Economic Bkgd.	12,04	.0044
Let Others Copy	Major	12,06	.0006
Let Others Copy	Computer Literacy Level	12,09	.0001
Let Others Copy	Likelihood Caught	12,17	.0074
Let Others Copy	Were Asked for Copies	12,18	.0000
Let Others Copy	Someone Offered Copies	12,19	.0000
Let Others Copy	Perceived Sftwr. Avail.	12,20	.0345
Let Others Copy	Sftwr. Mktg. Change	12,21	.0003
Let Others Copy	Perceived Prevalence	12,22	.0003
Let Others Copy	Offered Work	12,23	.0034
School Attended	Fac. Opp. Aff. Attitude	24,16	.0523

A Psycho-Social Model of Software Piracy: The Development and Test of a Model

Martha M. Eining and Anne L. Christensen

Printed by permission of Martha M. Eining and Anne L. Christensen. Current addresses: Martha M. Eining, School of Accounting, Graduate College of Business, University of Utah, Salt Lake City, UT 84112, (801) 581–7673. Anne L. Christensen, Department of Accounting, School of Business, Portland State University, Portland, OR 97207–0751, (503) 464–3798.

The illegal copying of software for personal computers is commonly referred to as software piracy. While this is not a new phenomenon it has become a significant issue for both businesses and universities due to the increased threat of litigation and also the risk of loss of important data that can result from the use of unsupported software. Companies and universities are in the process of developing and implementing policies to deal with the illegal copying of software by employees and students. Software development companies have tried various methods of copy protection to reduce software piracy, but have met with limited success.

This paper describes the development and test of a behavioral model to identify the factors that influence the decision making process of individuals in regard to software piracy. The information gained from this model should prove beneficial to diverse interest groups. Companies and universities could incorporate the factors in the model during the development and implementation of policies to reduce software piracy. Many universities are offering courses in computer ethics or including the topic of computer ethics in existing courses. The results of this study should provide important insights that can be used in these courses. In addition, software piracy is a social issue and the reduction or elimination of the illegal copying of software will require an informed public. Research into the factors that lead to software piracy should provide background for educating the public.

IMPORTANCE OF STUDY

The costs of software piracy are enormous and have far reaching impact. In 1985, the software industry sold $3.2 billion in software and estimates that between $800 million and $1 billion was lost to software piracy. Estimates range from one-out-of-two to four-out-of-five pieces of software in existence today that were copied illegally (Antonoff, 1987; Silburt, 1987; Smiddy and Smiddy, 1985). The software companies pass this loss of income on to the users by charging higher prices to the users who actually purchase the software.

Software piracy seems to occur in almost every setting. Software companies themselves are not immune as was apparent in 1985 when an employee of Apple was reported to have copied Microsoft's Word, Living Videotext's ThinkTank, Lotus Development's Jazz and a beta version of Microsoft's Excel. Computer dealers have been sued for including (illegal) copies of software with the sale of a personal computer. A multilanguage Gutenberg word processing program used for work on the New Testament was originally priced at $400 but was soon available through "software evaluation clubs" for as little as $10 (Antonoff, 1987).

The costs of illegally copying software in companies and universities are not as easy to measure as the costs to software companies. The cost of litigation is a real problem and can result in dollar outlays for legal assistance as well negative publicity for those involved. Companies spend large amounts of time and money on the collection of data and development of information. The use of illegally obtained software may pose serious dangers to the integrity of this information. Pirated copies of software do not provide users manuals, telephone support, and updates that are necessary for the most efficient and accurate use of the software.

The importance of decreasing software piracy is apparent from a brief overview of the costs incurred from software piracy. The reduction of software piracy is important for both developers and purchasers of software. Research into the behavioral factors that influence software piracy are an important initial step in understanding the factors that actually influence software piracy.

DEVELOPMENT OF MODEL

The first phase of this research involved the development of a model of the behavioral factors that impact software piracy. Models have been shown to be helpful in conceptualizing other forms of unethical behavior such as taxpayers' compliance behavior (Smith and Kinsey, 1987). The software piracy model was developed based on prior research and relevant theories. The model identifies five factors; normative expectations (norms), attitudes towards computers, socio-legal attitudes and beliefs, material consequences, and effective factors. These factors seek to explain the decision making process of individuals and identify their intentions which in turn explains the actual behavior, i.e., software piracy. Figure 1 provides an overview of the model.

The first factor, attitudes towards computers, identifies the impact of an individual's attitude toward computers and the role of computers in society on software piracy behavior.

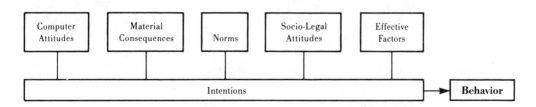

Figure 1 SOFTWARE PIRACY MODEL

Concern with computer attitudes led Nickell and Pinto (1986) to develop a comprehensive Computer Attitude Scale to measure positive and negative attitudes towards computers. Previous studies have identified depersonalization, loss of privacy, and loss of control as negative attitudes towards computers. Positive attitudes include increased productivity, freedom from mundane activities, and increased access to information (Kerber, 1983; Meier, 1985; Nickell and Seado, 1986).

The second factor, material consequences, identifies the individual's perception of the value of the monetary gains and losses arising from software piracy. Inherent in this factor would be the individual's perception of the chances of being caught. Material consequences have generally been described with economic models based on utility and prospect theories in which the individual weighs the potential gains against the potential losses and decides on a course of action (Kahneman and Tversky, 1979).

The third factor, normative expectations, identifies the internalized norms of the individual as well as the impact of friends' and associates' opinions regarding the correctness of the specified behavior (Tittle and Rowe, 1973). This factor should explain how a person's concept of right and wrong and his/her perception of the type of behavior others expect impacts upon software piracy behavior.

The next factor, socio-legal attitude, deals with the individual's beliefs and opinions about software companies and the legal issues regarding copying software. Negative attitudes toward software companies and the laws surrounding copying behavior may impact and increase the likelihood of an individual engaging in pirating. The social psychological literature, however, has shown inconsistent results in determining when attitudes will be predictive of behavior (Ajzen and Fishbein, 1977). In some instances attitudes have been shown to be closely related to actual behavior, while in other studies little relationship has been demonstrated.

The last factor is an effective or emotional factor which identifies an individual's frustration or annoyance when dealing with the issue of copying software. The effective factor also identifies any sense of accomplishment an individual might derive as a result of circumventing the software laws.

TEST OF THE MODEL

The second phase of the research project consisted of an empirical test of the model described above. A survey was developed and administered to 213 students in upper level business classes. An initial analysis of the data revealed that individuals who did not own computers lacked clearly defined opinions about software piracy. Therefore, the one hundred and five students who owned computers became the relevant sample for this study. Six surveys were eliminated due to missing data which resulted in 99 usable responses.

Subjects were asked to respond to all questions relating to factors in the model using a 7-point Likert-type scale. A number of questions were used for each variable in an effort to get at the complex, multi-dimensional concept of a factor. The scales were developed by averaging the responses to each question in the factor (Nunnally, 1978).

In addition to the factors in the model, subjects were asked their age, marital status, employment status and year in school. These demographic factors were considered in an

How many software programs do you have? .... _____ *

Please indicate the number of software packages obtained from each of the following sources by placing the number of software packages on the appropriate lines. If you are not sure of the exact count, please approximate.

Copyrighted software:

    Purchased with computer, from local vendor or from catalog vendor .... _____

    Copied from friends, work or school .... _____

Non-copyrighted software:

    Freeware (public domain) or shareware .... _____

    Developed myself .... _____

Other (Please be specific) _____ _____

TOTAL NUMBER .... _____*

* These numbers should agree.

Figure 2 DEPENDENT VARIABLE

effort to determine their impact on piracy behavior. The demographic variables were measured by straightforward requests.

The dependent variable, AMOUNT, was determined by asking students to record the total number of software packages they had and the source of those respective packages (see Figure 2). The software packages that were both copyrighted and copied from friends, work, or school were considered pirated. The number of pirated packages as a percent of total software possessed was converted to a seven-point scale to be consistent with the Likert-type scale used for the other variables.

Varimax rotated factor analysis was used to identify the factors in the model. The socio-legal attitudes of the subjects did not appear as a factor in the analysis. Discussion with the subjects indicated that they were not sufficiently aware of the laws to form strong attitudes about them, which may partially explain this result. The effective factor also failed to appear in the factor analysis. The factor analysis supported the formation of the normative, computer attitudes, and material consequences factors.

Cronbach's Alpha was used to establish the reliability of these three factors (Cronbach, 1951). Table 1 provides the results of this analysis and other information about the factors. The reliability for the norms factor is fairly strong, but the reliability of the other factors is low. Since this research was preliminary, all three factors were included in the test of the model.

Table 1   Analysis of Factors in the Model

Factor	Mean	Variance	Cronbach's Alpha
Norms	4.08	.46	.77
Computer Attitudes	5.74	.40	.37
Material Consequences	4.31	1.80	.52

Table 2 Results of Stepwise Regression Analysis

Independent Variables	b	Beta	t
Norms	.58	.36	3.82**
Computer Attitudes	− .53	− .22	− 2.55*
Material Consequences	.31	.19	2.00*
Employment Status	1.70	.19	1.15*
Adjusted R²		.30	F = 10.10**

*p < .05 ** p < .001

The relationship of the norms, computer attitudes, material consequences, and demographic factors with the dependent variable, AMOUNT, was investigated using stepwise multiple regression analysis with a cutoff of .05. The results of this analysis are presented in Table 2.

The overall regression was highly significant and explained 30 percent of the variance in the dependent variable. The normative expectations (norms) variable provides the most insight into piracy behavior with a beta of .36. The individuals who engage in unauthorized copying behavior evidently do not believe that there is anything wrong with their actions. They also appear to believe that their friends view this as appropriate behavior.

An unexpected finding was that computer attitudes were negatively related to piracy behavior. This may indicate that as individuals become more familiar and feel more positively about computers, they come to respect and value the effort involved in designing and producing software, which in turn may lead to a willingness to pay for programs. The employment variable was also significant in the regression equation. This could indicate that those individuals who work have more access to software which leads to an increase in their software piracy behavior.

The material consequences factor was also significant at the .05 level. Individuals appeared to consider the economic aspects of their decision. The questions which made up this variable were all directly related to the individual's satisfaction or dissatisfaction with the software prices. Also, since the subjects were not familiar with the laws they may not have foreseen any negative consequences of their actions.

CONCLUSIONS

Although theories are often used as a means of predicting behavior, perhaps one of the overlooked benefits is their use in understanding and organizing various methods to increase ethical awareness and behavior in students. If companies and educators take an active role in shaping attitudes toward behavior, it may be possible to increase ethical standards among students and professionals.

Rest and Thoma (1985), after reviewing 55 studies, determined that educational programs, particularly those that last longer than a few weeks and involve discussion of controversial ethical dilemmas, are effective in promoting ethical development. This development may take the form of stimulated moral judgement or increased ethical motivation. In addition, a series of questions in the present study regarding copyright laws and software revealed students had little understanding of the restrictions and penalties for software copying. This deficiency could be remedied by companies and educators incorporating such information into their policies and courses.

A common weakness of studies that rely on self-reports to measure dependent variables is that the reports may not validly reflect actual behaviors. Under-reporting is typical of anti-social behavior such as software piracy. In the current study, 68 percent of the respondents indicated some level of software piracy. This is well over half of the respondents and is indicative of the seriousness of the problem, especially if this figure represents under-reporting.

While this study provides initial insight into the piracy problem, it also raises a number of questions. It would be worthwhile to expand the sample size to diverse geographic areas to increase the generalizability of the results. Further research to refine the scales associated with software piracy and improve their reliabilities is also needed. This would improve both prediction and understanding of software piracy. It may also be of interest to determine the strength of influence of different social groups on software piracy as well as the salient beliefs that underlie attitudes towards piracy. No attempt was made in this research to differentiate between those individuals who passively pirate, i.e., receive copies from friends, etc., and those who actively pursue unauthorized copying. The extent of software piracy reported in this study and the lack of familiarity with the laws and their consequences strongly supports the need for more research in the area.

REFERENCES

Ajzen, I., and M. Fishbein, "Attitude-Behavior Relation: A Theoretical Analysis and Review of Empirical Research," *Psychological Bulletin* (September, 1977), pp. 888–918.

Antonoff, M., "Can We End Software Piracy?" *Personal Computing,* May 1987, pp. 142–153.

Cronbach, L.J., "Coefficient Alpha and the Internal Structure of Tests," *Psychometrika* (September 1951), pp. 297–334.

Kahneman, D., and Tversky, A., "Prospect Theory: An Analysis of Decision Under Risk," *Econometrica* (1979), pp. 263–291.

Kerber, K.W., "Attitudes Towards Specific Uses of the Computer: Quantitative Decision Making and Record-keeping Applications," *Behavior and Information Technology* (1983), pp. 197–209.

Meier, S.T., "Computer Aversion," *Computers in Human Behavior* (1985), pp. 71–179.

Nickell, G.S., and Pinto, J.N., "The Computer Attitude Scale," *Computers in Human Behavior,* 1986, pp. 301–306.

Nickell, G.S., and P.C. Seado, "The Impact of Attitudes and Experience on Small Business Computer Use," *American Journal of Small Business* (1986), pp. 37–48.

Nunnally, J.C., *Psychometric Theory,* New York: McGraw-Hill (1978).

Rest, J.R., and S.J. Thoma, "Relation of Moral Judgment and Development to Formal Education," *Developmental Psychology* (July 1985), pp. 709–714.

Silburt, D., "The Disk Takers," *Canadian Business* (March 1987), pp. 66–78.

Smiddy, J.D., and L.O. Smiddy, "Caught in the Act," *Datamation* (June 1985), pp. 102–106.

Smith, W., and K. Kinsey, "Understanding Taxpaying Behavior: A Conceptual Framework with Implications for Research," *Law and Society Review* (Dec. 1987).

Tittle, C. and Rowe, A., "Moral Appeal, Sanction Threat, and Deviance: An Experimental Test," *Social Problems* (Spring 1973), pp. 448–498.

A Comparative Study of Unauthorized Software Copying: Information Systems Faculty Members' vs. Practicing Managers' Perceptions[1]

J. P. Shim and G. Stephen Taylor

Printed by permission of J. P. Shim and G. Stephen Taylor. Current address: J. P. Shim, College of Business and Industry, Mississippi State University, Mississippi State, MS 39762, (601) 325–1994. G. Stephen Taylor, College of Business and Industry, Mississippi State University, Mississippi State, MS 39762, (601) 325–3928.

ABSTRACT

The topic of microcomputer software ethics in the field of information systems (IS) has gained an increasing amount of attention from IS researchers and practicing managers. This paper compares the attitudes of IS faculty members with those of IS managers toward microcomputer software pirating. This study also examines professionally related ethical attitudes in detail.

INTRODUCTION

Business ethics has become one of the "hottest" topics both among business academics and practitioners. The recent stories of insider trading on Wall Street and indictments of government officials/defense contractors all have received considerable attention from the public. Computer ethics is no exception in this regard. Unauthorized use of information technology has become part of the interest in computer ethics.

During the past decades, numerous topics have been researched in the area of information systems (IS). Among these, the topic of computer software ethics in the field of IS has gained an increasing amount of attention from IS researchers and practicing managers. Today, computer software ethics is now emerging as one of the most critical research issues

---

[1]This paper is based on partial portions of two papers: "Business Faculty Members' Perceptions of Unauthorized Software Copying" by J. P. Shim and G. S. Taylor, which appeared in the OR/MS Today, Vol. 15, No. 5 (1988) and "Practicing Managers' Perception/Attitudes Toward Illegal Software Copying" by J. P. Shim and G. S. Taylor, which appeared in OR/MS Today, Vol. 16, No. 4 (1989). The present version was prepared specifically for this book.

in the field of information technology. A recent study (Couger, 1989) confirms that the interest in computer software ethics is increasing significantly.

One reason for the interest in this topic has been the virtual explosion in the use of microcomputers during the last decade. The rapid spread of hardware has been accompanied by a proliferation of software. While this has expanded the capabilities of the microcomputer, there have been some rather serious side effects. Perhaps the most serious of these is the practice of "illegal" copying of software. Two recent studies (DiNacci, 1985; Simkin, 1987) indicated the magnitude of this problem. For instance, DiNacci (1985) pointed out that every other copy of business software used today is an unauthorized copy. In terms of financial loss, the Association of Data Processing Service Organizations estimated that software piracy cost the industry over $800 million (Simkin, 1987). Virtually all discussions of business ethics, including computer ethics, center around the business practitioner. After all, this is the individual who is involved daily in decisions that affect millions of dollars and often millions of lives. Moreover, the American public's opinion of the ethics of business executives has never been very high (Litzinger and Schaefer, 1987). For instance, a 1985 Gallup Report showed that only 23% of the respondents rated business executives as having "very high" or "high" ethical standards: out of 25 occupations, business executives ranked 14th in terms of ethics (note that college professors ranked 5th). Similarly, a 1985 New York Times/CBS News Poll indicated that 55% of the respondents felt executives were not honest (Clymer, 1985).

Yet microcomputer usage is not limited to the business world. Several surveys (Frand et al., 1988; Lee and Shim, 1984; Render and Stair, 1987) confirm that the use of and interest in microcomputers in academia has increased exponentially over the last decade. Therefore, numerous opportunities for unauthorized software copying should present themselves to IS faculty as well as to IS managers. But, as pointed out earlier, the ethics of college professors generally are seen as superior to those of business executives (Gallup Opinion Index, 1985). Whether reality matches this perception is an open question. The primary purpose of this paper is to present the results of a survey of IS professionals' attitudes toward microcomputer software pirating. Second, it compares professionally related ethical attitudes of IS faculty members with those of IS managers. Specifically, these questions are investigated: (1) Do IS managers perceive their coworkers to more frequently pirate software than IS faculty perceive their colleagues to do so? (2) Do IS managers admit to personally pirating software more often than IS faculty admit to this? (3) How prevalent a problem is unauthorized software copying in business and academia?

HYPOTHESES

Information systems faculty members work in an unsupervised environment. At all levels of an organization, IS managers experience a greater degree of control and supervision than do IS faculty members. Thus, the risk of being discovered while making unauthorized software copies is greater in the business office than in the faculty office. This greater chance of discovery should create a strong need in IS managers to keep such activities secret. However, this argument suggests the need to keep such activities from being discovered, but not necessarily the need to completely refrain from such acts. Based on the differences in the degree of supervision found in academics as opposed to the business setting, the first hypothesis is developed:

> H_1: IS managers perceive less unauthorized software copying among their coworkers than IS faculty members perceive among their colleagues.

The following three hypotheses rely on the fact that individuals tend to make ethical decisions within the context of their own personal values (Sturdivant and Ginter, 1977). This is especially true in regard to computer-related issues. The computer industry failed to develop an essential ethical base before its technology moved into the public domain (BloomBecker, 1987). Consequently, there is no ethical framework within which end users can make decisions as to what are proper and improper behaviors.

Business managers generally make decisions from a utilitarian perspective (Fritzsche and Becker, 1984). That is, they tend to act in ways that will lead to the greatest good for the greatest number, i.e., the organization. Therefore, it is hypothesized that:

> H_2: IS managers admit to personally copying software more often than do IS faculty members.
>
> H_3: IS managers consider it less unethical to copy software to be used on the job than do IS faculty members.
>
> H_4: When compared with IS faculty members, IS managers are less likely to consider pirating software to be as unethical as using office supplies for personal use.

METHODOLOGY

Sample

Two respondent groups are examined in this study. The academic participants consisted of 111 members of Decision Sciences Institute (of 351 members whose primary interest area is IS). The IS managers consisted of 99 members of the Institute of Management Science (of 263 nonacademic members whose primary interest area is IS).

Respondents were solicited by mail in 1988 asking their participation in research inquiring about "ethical issues related to microcomputer software usage." Participants were promised anonymity.

Research Instrument

Each group received a one-page questionnaire. Although this questionnaire differed somewhat between the academic group and the practitioner group, the general format was the same. The questionnaire consisted of three (3) parts. The first part asked about the frequency with which the respondent used microcomputers in his/her work; possible responses could range from "Never" to "Very often" (Likert-scale items with 5-point response scales).

The second part inquired about the frequency with which the respondent and his/her colleagues copied software that was neither in the public domain nor site licensed; again responses could vary from "Never" to "Very often." Respondents also were asked to indicate their (dis)agreement with statements asking about the ethicalness of unauthorized software copying for various work purposes. Each of these statements contained 5-point Likert response scales ranging from "Strongly disagree" to "Strongly agree."

The last part of the questionnaire solicited respondent demographics: managerial/academic rank, sex, existence of an organizational policy on software use, and so forth.

RESULTS

General Findings

Table 1 contains a summary of the demographic characteristics of the two groups. In regard to the IS faculty members group, respondents came from all levels of the professorial hierarchy, with almost 60% being associate professor and full professor. Also, the respondents were predominantly male (see Figure 1).

About 92% of academic respondents indicated they had purchased a microcomputer. Also, a large portion of the respondents are using microcomputers for the purposes of teaching (95%), research (89%), and consulting (84%). The results also indicated that about 73% of the respondents admitted "illegally" copying software that is neither site licensed nor in the public domain. Ironically, respondents believe that it is unethical to copy copyrighted software for teaching (76%), research (83%), and consulting purposes (92%), even though they copy copyrighted software.

The study also revealed several other interesting phenomena. First, about 27% of the academic respondents do not understand/know the U. S. copyright law. Second, male faculty members copy unauthorized software more than females do. Third, junior faculty members deal with unauthorized copying more than senior professors.

This study suggests that unauthorized software copying will become even more widespread. Perhaps the best indication that pirating software will continue comes from a respondent to this survey. When asked if copying a $300 software package is as unethical as stealing $300 worth of office supplies, the respondent wrote that the unethical act was charging $300 for the software package.

The IS practicing managers group had similar characteristics. Respondents came from all levels of management. Here, too, the group consisted of considerably more men than women (see Figure 2).

The survey revealed that about 91% of the respondents have purchased microcomputers, an indication of IS managers' heavy reliance on microcomputers (91% of the respondents use microcomputers at least "occasionally" in assisting and/or completing their work). As far as frequency of unauthorized software copying is concerned, illegal copying is not a significant problem. About 9% of the IS managers stated that they have copied copyrighted software "Often" or "Very often." The remaining (91%) indicated that they have "Never," "Rarely" or "Occasionally" copied software. Interestingly enough, the results indicated that about 9% of the managers believe their colleagues have copied software "Often" or "Very often."

Those responding to this survey rejected each of the rationalizations offered for pirating software. For example, about 88% of the respondents believe that it is unethical to copy

Table 1 IS Professionals' Sample Demographics

Variable	IS Faculty Members (n=111)			IS Managers (n=99)		
(1) Purchase a PC:						
Yes	102	(82%)	Yes	90	(91%)	
No	9	(8%)	No	9	(9%)	
(2) Use PC to assist in*:						
Teaching	4.35		Work	4.46		
Research	4.27					
Consulting	3.51					
(3) Academic rank/Management position:						
Instructor	21	(18.9%)	Lower mgt.	21	(21.2%)	
Asst. prof.	24	(21.6%)	Middle mgt.	42	(42.4%)	
Asso. prof.	33	(29.7%)	Top mgt.	18	(18.2%)	
Full prof.	33	(29.7%)	N/A	18	(18.2%)	
(4) Sex:						
Male	90	(81.1%)	Male	84	(84.8%)	
Female	21	(18.9%)	Female	15	(15.2%)	
(5) Formal "Policy statement" on software use:						
Yes	66	(59.5%)	Yes	78	(78.8%)	
No	30	(27.0%)	No	18	(18.2%)	
Not sure	15	(13.5%)	Not sure	3	(3.0%)	
(6) Understand U.S. copyright law:						
Yes	75	(67.5%)	Yes	78	(78.8%)	
No	30	(37.0%)	No	18	(18.2%)	
Not sure	6	(5.5%)	Not sure	3	(3.0%)	

*On a scale of 5 (Very often) to 1 (Never).

software to be used on the job. Attitudes and perceptions were more strongly against software pirating for consulting purposes; 67% of the respondents "Strongly disagreed" and 27% "Disagreed" that it is ethical to copy for this purpose. It is significant that these attitudes were rather consistent across type of organization, level of management, professional work area, and respondent demographic characteristics. In fact, the only difference was in regards to "colleagues' copying activities."

When asked if copying $300 copyrighted software is as unethical as stealing $300 worth of office supplies for personal use, IS managers responded very differently than did IS academics. Seventy-two percent of the business respondents either "Agreed" or "Strongly agreed." The following quotes from two of the respondents revealed common attitudes/

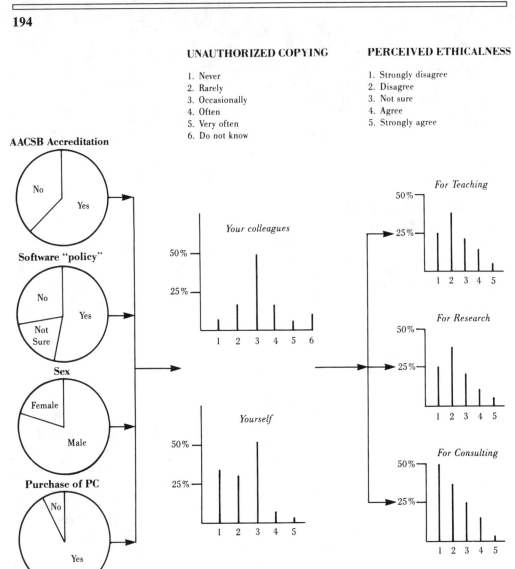

Figure 1. IS Faculty Members' Perceptions of Unauthorized Software Copying

perceptions held by numerous practicing managers who seemed to have no interest in pirating software:

Software vendors charge a lot but still it is not ethical to copy copyrighted software.

Intended use of the software is important. Few will pay $300 to preview or sparingly use a piece of software. However, documentation and upgrades are essential if software is used professionally.

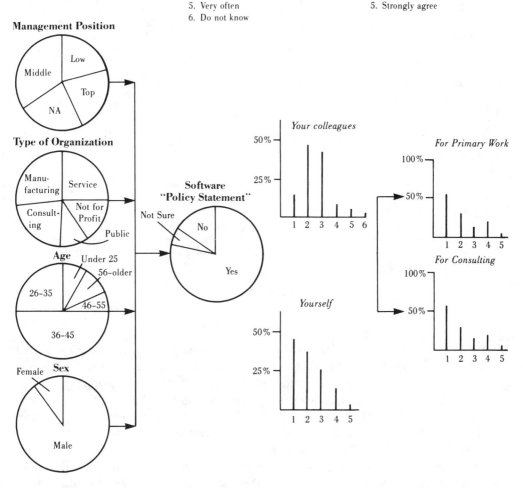

Figure 2.   IS Practicing Managers' Perceptions of Unauthorized Software Copying

The study also revealed several other similar interesting facts. First, participants in this study seemed not to have a full grasp of the U. S. copyright law. About 18% of the respondents said they do not understand this law. Second, about 43% of the sample respondents have been with their present organizations "up to 5" years. This statistic reflects the high turnover rate of computer-related professionals, even though 73% of respondents have more than 10 years' working experience. The finding of this study may well confirm the previous study (Ginzberg and Baroudi, 1988) that the trend in turnover has increased significantly.

Table 2 Tests of Hypothesized Relationships

Variable (Hypothesis)	IS Faculty Members (n = 111)		IS Managers (n = 99)		Results of t-tests (d.f.)	
	X	(S.D.)	X	(S.D.)		
Frequency[a] with which colleagues copy (H₁)	3.70	(1.41)	2.36	(0.96)	4.58*	(68)
Frequency[a] with which respondent copies (H₂)	2.35	(1.16)	2.03	(1.05)	1.21	(68)
Ethical to copy software used on the job (H₃)[b]	1.92	(1.16)	1.73	(1.23)	0.67	(68)
As unethical to copy software as to steal office supplies (H₄)[b]	3.54	(1.43)	3.69	(1.40)	−0.43	(67)

[a] (1 = Never; 2 = Rarely; 3 = Occasionally; 4 = Often; 5 = Very often)
[b] (1 = Strongly disagree; 2 = Disagree; 3 = Not sure; 4 = Agree; 5 = Strongly agree)
* $p \leqslant 001$

Test of Hypotheses

Table 2 shows the results of the tests of the four research hypotheses; Student's t was used to test each. In regards to hypothesis 1 (H₁), there was a marked difference between the two groups in terms of attitudes/perceptions toward unauthorized software copying.

For example, the mean IS faculty response to the item asking about the frequency with which colleagues copy was 3.70. IS managers, on the other hand, averaged 2.36 on this item. The difference between these responses was statistically significant (t = 4.58, p .001, d.f. = 68). Thus, hypothesis 1 was supported.

The second hypothesis (H₂) was not empirically supported. Although IS managers reported greater use of computers on their jobs than did IS faculty respondents (X managers = 4.46, X faculty = 4.04), the academicians reported they personally made unauthorized software copies more frequently than did the business respondents. On the same 5-point scale described above, the mean IS faculty response was 2.35 with the corresponding manager response being 2.03. The difference was statistically insignificant (t = 1.21, n.s, d.f. = 68). These results are contrary to the hypothesized directionality of this hypothesis.

Similarly, hypothesis 3 (H₃) could not be substantiated by these results. To test this hypothesis, the IS managers' mean response to this issue was compared to mean IS faculty response about the ethicalness of copying software to be used on the job. (For the IS faculty group, this score was the arithmetic mean of their responses to individual items asking about the ethicalness of copying software for teaching, research, and consulting purposes.) Comparison of this overall mean to the IS managers' overall mean produced statistically insignificant results (X faculty = 1.92, X managers = 1.73, t = –0.67, n.s, d.f. = 68).

Finally, IS faculty members were hypothesized (H_4) to be more likely to consider software copying as unethical as expropriating office supplies for personal use, than were the IS managers. This relationship also failed to be supported. When asked if copying was as unethical as using supplies in this manner, IS faculty respondents produced a mean score of 3.54 (where 5 = "strongly agree"); the mean IS managers' response was 3.69 on the same scale. This difference is statistically insignificant (t = –0.43, n.s, d.f. = 67). Note that both groups expressed considerable agreement with this statement.

DISCUSSION

These results are somewhat at odds with the perception that software pirating is a widespread problem of million-dollar implications. One reason for this divergence may be the types of software copied. The IS managers' respondents reported extensive use of microcomputers on the job. They primarily use business-related packages, at least while at work. Perhaps, then, non-business related software (e.g., games and the like) are copied more frequently than are work-related packages. Since this kind of recreational software will rarely be seen in the business office, respondents in this study may see little copying activity. Similarly, they may see little justification for this kind of copying.

Another reason for the anti-copying attitude throughout the IS manager group may be that respondents were asked specifically about work-related issues. Since the organization usually supplies the kinds of software packages needed on the job, there may be little need for copying. This cost-related argument also may explain more prevalent copying among IS faculty members. In this age of tight educational budgets, there may be fewer dollars available with which software can be purchased. Thus, IS faculty members may perceive a need to copy the software packages of others.

Furthermore, the degree of supervision experienced by those working in organizations versus those working in universities and colleges may influence copying activities. As conjectured earlier, such acts may be inhibited by the presence and/or threat of the presence of a supervisor. IS faculty members should have much less fear of this happening, given their relatively unsupervised work environment.

Finally, the identification of faculty with their profession rather than their employer could have affected these results. Professional employees such as college faculty usually define success in terms of personal achievement rather than by rewards from the employing organization (Tosi et al., 1986). Perhaps faculty copy software packages that will aid in research and publishing endeavors. Hence, the ends may justify the means.

These results are both discouraging and encouraging. The discouraging aspect is that IS faculty seem to have a relatively unconcerned attitude about software copying. It seems likely that in one way or another this attitude will be passed along to students. A very real question, then, is "Can faculty produce ethical future business leaders without themselves acting ethically?" Obviously the ethics of an IS manager will not be totally shaped by his or her professors. But the attitudes toward ethical issues will be colored, at least to a degree, by the actions of these role models.

Obviously there are limitations to this study. For example, there is no common definition of "unauthorized" software copying. Here it was defined as copying software that is neither site licensed nor in the public domain. But would pirating an already pirated copy be considered an ethical transgression? Also, these results basically are responses to single item measures. More developed measures clearly are needed. These are issues that must be addressed in future computer software ethics studies.

REFERENCES

BloomBecker, J. J.: 1987, "Computer Ethics: An Antidote to Despair," *Computers and Society,* **16**, 3–11.

Clymer, A.: 1985, "Low Marks for Executive Honesty," *New York Times,* June 9: F-1.

Couger, J. D.: 1989, "Preparing IS Students to Deal with Ethical Issues," *MIS Quarterly,* **13**(2), 211–218.

DiNacci, D.: 1985, "Software Piracy: Is Your Company Liable?," *Business,* October, 34–38.

Frand, J. L., McLean, E. R., and Britt, J. A.: 1988, "Fourth Annual UCLA Survey of Business School Computer Usage," *Communications of the ACM,* **31**(7), 896–910.

Fritzsche, D. J. and Becker, H.: 1984, "Linking Management Behavior to Ethical Philosophy—An Empirical Investigation," *Academy of Management Journal,* **27**(1), 166–175.

Gallup Opinion Index: 1985, "Honest and Ethical Standards of Business Executives," August, 17.

Ginzberg, Michael J. and Baroudi, Jack J.: 1988, "MIS Careers—A Theoretical Perspective," *Communications of the ACM,* **31**(5), 586–594.

Lee, S. M. and Shim, J. P.: 1984, "A Note on Microcomputer Applications," *Interfaces,* **6**(3), 22–27.

Litzinger, W. D. and Schaefer, T. E.: 1987, "Business Ethics Bogeyman: The Perpetual Paradox," *Business Horizons,* March–April, 17–21.

Render, B. and Stair, R. M.: 1987, "Microcomputer Technology in Schools of Business," *Interfaces,* **17**, 92–102.

Simkin, M. G.: 1987, "What Should Software Developers Do about the Problem of Copy-protecting Software?" *Proceedings of the Annual Meeting of the Decision Sciences Institute,* 245–247.

Tosi, H. L., Rizzo, J. R., and Carroll, S. J.: 1986, *Managing Organizational Behavior,* Marshfield, MA: Pitman Publishing, Inc.

Sturdivant, F. and Ginter, J.: 1977, "Corporate Social Responsiveness: Management Attitudes and Economic Performance," *California Management Review,* **19**, 30–39.

CPSR Responds to the Internet Computer Virus

Reprinted by permission of Computer Professionals for Social Responsibility

On November 2nd, 1988, a computer program called a "worm" or a "virus" spread to thousands of computers across the United States and even overseas via the Internet, a national computer network. The program was called both a "worm" and a "virus"; like a "worm" the program did not attach itself to another program and did not alter any data, but, like a computer "virus" it was self-replicating.

The virus exploited a long-standing but relatively little known feature in the Unix operating system that allowed the programmer to funnel the virus' code through the Unix electronic mail subsystem. But a programming error apparently caused the virus to replicate much more rapidly than intended, clogging network capacity and bringing systems on the network to a virtual standstill. Although the virus appeared to do no permanent damage to the estimated 6,000 computers affected, it created a massive national headache for systems operators who spent countless hours removing it from their computers.

A few days after the virus flashed across the country, the programmer came forward. It was revealed that the creator of the virus was Robert Tappan Morris, Jr., a 22 year-old graduate student in computer science at Cornell University. Morris, who is described by all who know him as a brilliant young computer scientist, is the son of the head of computer security for the National Security Agency, which added an unexpected twist to the story. News reports suggested that the younger Morris created the virus as an experiment to demonstrate the flaws of the primary operating system used within the Internet, Unix, including trapdoors in the implementation of the sendmail transfer protocol (smtp) and the user-status query (finger).

This incident was extensively reported by the national and local press, appearing as a front page story for six days in a row in *The New York Times*. The CPSR National Office was flooded with telephone calls from reporters, and CPSR members and staff appeared on several radio call-in shows and television reports and were widely quoted in the press. The virus episode drew widespread attention to the vulnerability of computer networks that CPSR has been describing for several years.

The Internet virus struck shortly before the 1988 CPSR Annual Meeting held at Stanford University on November 19 and 20. With so much interest in the incident, time was set aside for meeting participants to address and discuss the virus issue. Prior to the meeting, CPSR members began working on a statement about the virus using electronic mail. At the CPSR Annual Meeting, a draft statement was handed out to meeting participants, over 100 people, who elected to stay late on Saturday afternoon to discuss the virus problem. The discussion was wide-ranging and touched on many issues of concern to computer professionals. At the reassembled meeting on Sunday, all participants at the meeting were asked to review the draft and make comments. A final draft was then prepared after it appeared to reflect the majority opinions of the attendees at the Annual Meeting. The statement was officially endorsed by the CPSR Board of Directors at its meeting on November 21. The statement has been requested by computer systems administrators and has been circulated throughout the computing community.

Following the CPSR statement on the computer virus, other professional computer societies prepared their own statements, addressing many of the same concerns raised by CPSR.

CPSR STATEMENT ON THE INTERNET COMPUTER VIRUS

The so-called computer virus that swept through a national computer network, the Internet, in early November is a dramatic example of the vulnerability of complex computer systems. It temporarily denied service to thousands of computers users at academic, business, and military sites. An estimated 6,000 computers across the country were affected in only a few hours. Fortunately, the program was not designed to delete or alter data. The impact of a malicious virus would have been immeasurable.

This was an irresponsible act that cannot be condoned. The Internet should not be treated as a laboratory for uncontrolled experiments in computer security. Networked software is intrinsically risky, and no programmer can guarantee that a self-replicating program will not have unintended consequences.

The value of open networks depends on the good will and good sense of computer users. Computer professionals should take upon themselves the responsibility to ensure that systems are not misused. Individual accountability is all the more important when people work together through a network of shared resources. Computer professionals should establish and encourage ethics based on the shared needs of network users. We also encourage educators to teach these ethics.

The questions of legal responsibility in this instance are ultimately for our legal system to resolve. The questions confronting computer professionals and others concerned about the future of our technology policy go well beyond this particular case. The incident underscores our society's increasing dependence on complex computer networks. Security flaws in networks, in computer operating systems, and in management practices have been amply demonstrated by break-ins at Stanford University, by the penetration of national research networks, and by the "Christmas virus" that clogged the IBM internal network last December.

CPSR believes that this incident should prompt critical review of our dependence on complex computer networks, particularly for military and defense-related functions. The flaws that permitted the recent virus to spread will eventually be fixed, but other flaws will remain. Security loopholes are inevitable in any computer network and are prevalent in those that support general-purpose computing and are widely accessible.

An effective way to correct known security flaws is to publish descriptions of the flaws so that they can be corrected. We therefore view the efforts to conceal technical descriptions of the recent virus as short-sighted.

CPSR believes that innovation, creativity, and the open exchange of ideas are the ingredients of scientific advancement and technological achievement. Computer networks, such as the Internet, facilitate this exchange. We cannot afford policies that might restrict the ability of computer researchers to exchange their ideas with one another. More secure networks, such as military and financial networks, sharply restrict access and offer limited functionality. Government, industry, and the university community should support the continued development of network technology that provides open access to many users.

The computer virus has sent a clear warning to the computing community and to society at large. We hope it will provoke a long overdue public discussion about the vulnerabilities of computer networks, and the technological, ethical, and legal choices we must address.

Special thanks must go to the many people who worked hard, and in demanding time pressures during the CPSR Annual Meeting, to stimulate discussion about the virus issue and produce the statement. Congratulations and thanks should also go to the more than one hundred Annual Meeting participants who displayed an exemplary democratic spirit in developing the statement.

For more information about the Internet virus of November, 1988:

Mark Eichin and Jon Rochlis, "With Microscope and Tweezers: An Analysis of the Internet Virus of November 1988," MIT Project Athena report, Cambridge MA 02139, November 1988.

John Markoff, "The Computer Jam: How It Came About," *The New York Times,* November 11, 1988, D10.

Donn Seeley, "A Tour of the 'Worm'," Computer Science Department, University of Utah, November 1988.

Eugene H. Spafford, "The Internet 'Worm' Program: An Analysis," CSD-TR-823, Department of Computer Sciences, Purdue University, West Lafayette IN 47904–2004, November 1988.

Computer Accessibility for Federal Workers with Disabilities: It's the Law

Richard E. Ladner

Richard E. Ladner is a professor of Computer Science at the University of Washington. He is an active researcher in theoretical computer science and has worked on several projects in computers for disabled persons including DBNet, a computer network for use by deaf-blind people. Author's Present Address: Department of Computer Science FR-35, University of Washington, Seattle, WA 98195; Internet address: ladner@cs.washington.edu. Communications of The ACM, Vol. 32, No. 8, August 1989, pp. 952–956. Copyright © 1989, Association for Computing Machinery, Inc., reprinted by permission.

In 1986, Congress passed Public Law 99–506, the "Rehabilitation Act Amendments of 1986." This law, amending the famous Rehabilitation Act of 1973, contains a small section, titled "Electronic Equipment Accessibility," Section 508, which may have significant impact on the design of computer systems and their accessibility by workers with disabilities. The bill became law when it was signed by former President Reagan on October 21, 1986.

The purpose of this article is to inform concerned computer professionals of Section 508, outline the guidelines and regulations pursuant to the law, describe some of the reaction to the guidelines and regulations, and describe some of the challenges for the future in meeting the computer accessibility needs of users with disabilities.

Section 508 was developed because it was realized that government offices were rapidly changing into electronic offices with microcomputers on every desk. In order for persons with disabilities to keep their jobs or gain new employment in the government, Congress decided it was necessary to make provisions to guarantee accessibility to microcomputers and other electronic office equipment. The driving principle behind Section 508 can be found in Section 504 of the Rehabilitation Act of 1973 which states:

> No otherwise qualified handicapped individual in the United States . . . shall, solely by reason of his handicap, be excluded from the participation in, be denied the benefits of, or be subjected to discrimination under any program or activity receiving Federal financial assistance.

It should be stated off the top that the scope of Section 508 is not as broad as Section 504. In particular, Section 508 only applies to direct purchases by the federal government and not to purchases made by all programs receiving government funding.

Section 508 does not specify what the guidelines should be nor does it delineate a philosophy on which to base the guidelines. A committee established by the National Institute on Disability and Rehabilitation Research (NIDRR) and the General Services Administration (GSA), in consultation with the electronics industry, rehabilitation engineers, and disabled computer professionals worked for a year developing the philosophy and guidelines which will significantly affect the purchase of electronic office equipment, including computers and software, by the federal government, the largest computer customer in the world.

INITIAL GUIDELINES

On November 19, 1987, the Initial Guidelines titled *Access to Information Technology by Users With Disabilities* was published jointly by GSA and NIDRR. The purpose of the initial guidelines is "to set a tone and to provide early guidance to industry on the direction in which the government plans to move in the months and years ahead" [7]. The GSA solicited reaction to the initial guidelines from all interested parties.

After considerable response to the initial guidelines, on October 13, 1988, the General Services Administration published regulations pursuant to Section 508 as a Federal Information Resources Management Regulation (FIRMR) [4]. About the same time the GSA published FIRMR Bulletin 56 which implements these regulations [3]. Bulletin 56 is basically a revision of the initial guidelines based on careful consideration of the comments received. These and other documents helpful to government buyers, vendors, and users are available in a guide titled "Managing End User Computing for Users with Disabilities" [5] which can be obtained by writing to the address or telephoning the number provided in the footnote.[1]

GUIDELINES AND REGULATIONS

The FIRMR regulations inform federal agencies of what they are required to do to comply with Section 508. It is worth stating the general policy under which federal agencies must operate:

> Federal agencies shall provide handicapped employees and non-handicapped employees equivalent access to electronic office equipment to the extent such needs are determined by the agency . . . and the required accessibility can be provided by industry. In providing equivalent access to electronic office equipment, agencies shall consider:
>   i. Access to and use of the same data bases and application programs by handicapped and non-handicapped employees;
>   ii. Utilization of enhancement capabilities for manipulating data (i.e., special peripherals) to attain equivalent end-results by handicapped and non-handicapped employees; and

---

[1] Available from Clearinghouse on Computer Accommodation (COCA), Federal Information Resources Management, General Services Administration, 18th and F Streets NW, Washington, D.C. 20405 (202) 523–1906.

iii. Access to and use of equivalent communications capabilities by handicapped employees [4].

The regulations require that agencies of the federal government must assess the needs of its current and potential employees with disabilities and incorporate appropriate functional specifications meeting those needs into solicitations to vendors of electronic office equipment. The assessment of needs of an employee is to be developed by the agency in consultation with the impacted employee to assure that the functional specifications are adequate.

FIRMR Bulletin 56 organizes functional specifications into three broad categories: input, output, and documentation. Under each category a list of specifications is provided to give guidance to agencies and individuals. This list is reproduced here to give an idea of what alternatives are currently available.

1. *Input*
   (a) *Multiple Simultaneous Operation Alternative.* It is common for multiple, simultaneous striking of keys to be required for some functions. An alternative for the same function using sequential rather than simultaneous key strikes may be required.
   (b) *Input Redundancy.* Some programs require a fine motor control device such as a mouse. An alternative method such as voice input or key strokes may be required.
   (c) *Alternative Input Devices.* In some cases, an alternative input device may be needed to replace or supplement a keyboard or mouse. Alternative input methods may include speech input, eye scan, suck and puff, or headtracking. To support such devices, alternative physical ports or connection capability may be required.
   (d) *Key Repeat.* Some computer systems generate automatic repetition while a key is continuously depressed. This feature may need to be turned off or modulated.
   (e) *Toggle Key Status Control.* Some computer systems provide a status light for toggle keys. An alternative non-visual feedback for the status of toggle keys may be required.
   (f) *Keyboard Orientation Aids.* Tactile overlays or other tactile indicators may be required to orient a person's hands on the keyboard.
   (g) *Keyguards.* A keyguard to help stabilize movements and ensure that the correct keys are depressed may be required.
2. *Output.*
   (a) *Auditory Output Capability.* Visual output is the most common form of output of computer systems. Auditory output capable of speech with adjustable volume control and headset jack may be required.
   (b) *Information Redundancy.* A visual alternative to auditory output such as warning beeps may be required.
   (c) *Monitor Display.* Visual output may need to be enlarged, reproduced verbally, or modified in some way. There are at least three factors to be considered:
      i. *Large Print Display.* A means of enlarging a portion of the screen for both graphics and text may be required.
      ii. *Access to Visually Displayed Information.* The capability to access the screen may be necessary to provide speech or braille output.

iii. *Color Presentation.* An alternative to color as a way of providing information may be required.

PUBLIC LAW 99-506 Q OCTOBER 21, 1986

An Act

To extend and improve the Rehabilitation Act of 1973.

Section 603. ELECTRONIC EQUIPMENT ACCESSIBILITY.

(a) ELECTRONIC EQUIPMENT ACCESSIBILITY.—Title V of the Act is amended by inserting after Section 507 the following new section:

ELECTRONIC EQUIPMENT ACCESSIBILITY

"Sec. 508. (a)(1) The Secretary, through the National Institute on Disability and Rehabilitation Research and the Administrator of the General Services, in consultation with the electronics industry, shall develop and establish guidelines for electronic equipment accessibility designed to insure that handicapped individuals may use electronic office equipment with or without special peripherals.

"(2) The guidelines established pursuant to paragraph (1) shall be applicable with respect to electronic equipment, whether purchased or leased.

"(3) The initial guidelines shall be established not later than October 1, 1987, and shall be periodically revised as technologies advance or change.

"(b) Beginning after September 30, 1988, the Administrator of General Services shall adopt guidelines for electronic equipment accessibility established under section (a) for Federal procurement of electronic equipment. Each agency shall comply with the guidelines adopted under this section.

"(c) For the purpose of this section the term 'special peripherals' means a special needs aid that provides access to electronic equipment that is otherwise inaccessible to a handicapped individual."

3. *Documentation.*
   (a) Documentation may be required in electronic form to be read by an alternative output device.

The emphasis of the functional specifications is not in providing specific solutions to accessibility problems, but in providing concrete objectives to be met by solutions. This allows for new and creative solutions to providing accessibility.

REACTION TO GUIDELINES AND REGULATIONS

There was a considerable response to the initial guidelines and a continuing response to the final guidelines and regulations by the computer industry, manufacturers of special peripherals, rehabilitation engineers, consumers with disabilities, and federal government agencies. Some of this response can be found in [6].

Industry Reaction

The initial reaction of the computer industry to the guidelines and regulations has been mixed. Some companies are very concerned that their products will not follow the guidelines and that it will cost them dearly to upgrade to meet the guidelines. Some companies are relieved that guidelines are finally coming out so they can go ahead with their plans to make their products accessible to persons with disabilities and be assured that their work in doing so will be adequate. Interestingly, some designers of innovative computer software and hardware products are the most concerned because they feel that the guidelines will limit their designs to satisfy a tiny minority of potential users.

There are a large number of third-party vendors who manufacture and distribute hardware and software products which make computers more accessible [1]. These vendors are concerned that the guidelines might encourage primary vendors to provide "minimal" solutions which satisfy the guidelines, but do not allow the possibility of using their "superior" products. The guidelines make it clear that the responsibility of the primary vendors is to provide "hooks" into their hardware and operating systems which enable third-party vendors to continue making their accessibility products. A considerable effort has been made by the Industry/Government Cooperative Initiative on Computer Accessibility to provide concrete guidelines on what hooks are needed to enable access [2].

There are clearly limits to accessibility depending on the abilities of users. Should office computer systems be made accessible to severely mentally retarded users? Should paint programs be made accessible to totally blind users? The regulation is worded in such a way that industry only has to provide equivalent access if the employee can use it and there is a feasible way to provide it. Thus, industry does not have to provide access to databases for mentally retarded users because they would not be using such software and does not have to provide access to paint programs for blind users because there is no way to do that with current technology.

Reaction of Rehabilitation Engineers

Rehabilitation engineers are the designers and implementors of adaptive devices for persons with disabilities. They have long realized that there is an infinite variety of disabilities requiring a large number of choices of adaptive devices. It is a constant game of catch-up. As technology changes new strategies must be discovered to permit adaptive devices to be added. They have similar concerns to the third-party vendors that the guidelines not be misinterpreted by primary vendors. The primary vendors' responsibility is to make it possible to have a large number of access solutions. This will make the job for the rehabilitation engineer easier.

Consumer Reaction

Consumers with disabilities have long recognized that new technologies can be more or less disabling depending on the technology and the individual. For example, the mouse can be more disabling than a keyboard for someone with limited motor control. On the other hand, a mouse-like device controllable with head movement might be less disabling than a keyboard for someone with limited use of their hands. Consumers have noticed that the trend in computer systems is to involve more and more of the senses and physical abilities of users in both input and output. There seems to be more graphics and less text, more sound for input and output, and more physical ability with mice, joysticks, and simultaneous keystrokes. The problem is that a particular computer system (hardware or software) may *require* too many senses and abilities making it not adaptable for users with disabilities. In general, consumers seem to be pleased that guidelines are out, helping halt the trend toward nonadaptable computer systems. They also share the concern of the rehabilitation engineers and third-party vendors that the guidelines might encourage minimal solutions by primary vendors at the expense of better third-party solutions.

It is clear that Section 508 only applies to procurement of computer systems for office use by the federal government. Some consumers would like the law strengthened to include computer systems purchased with government funds whether or not the purchase is a government agency.

The "Technology Related Assistance for Individuals with Disabilities Act of 1988," Public Law 100–407 may have the effect of extending the scope of Section 508 to state governments. This law provides funding to states to develop a response to computer accessibility for citizens with disabilities. The law stipulated that states must comply with Section 508 in order to continue receiving these funds.

Reaction of Government Agencies

A number of government agencies, including Social Security Agency, Department of Education, Department of Health and Human Services, and Internal Revenue Service have already made multimillion dollar contracts which include Section 508 provisions for computer accessibility for their employees with disabilities. Many other agencies are in the process of preparing solicitations which include accessibility. Within the government there has been a concerted effort to keep agencies informed of the new regulations and to assist them in preparing their solicitations and in finding technical solutions to accessibility problems.

However, there is a natural concern about the cost of providing accessibility, as the cost must be borne by each individual agency. What is the limit that an agency will pay to provide computer accessibility to an employee with a disability? The Section 508 regulations are too new to really ascertain this limit. So far, agencies which have included accessibility have done so by putting it in as a very small percentage of a multimillion dollar solicitation.

Meeting Needs of Disabled Users

The percentage of the population of working age who have some serious disability is currently at least 5 percent and is growing. Public Law 94–142 which mandated that children with disabilities have a right to a full education became law more than 10 years ago. As reported by the Department of Education in 1983–1984 more than 10 percent of all children aged 3–21 were served in special education programs of one kind or another [8]. Thus, young adults with disabilities are more educated than ever before. The Rehabilitation Act of 1973 mandated that these adults should not be discriminated against in hiring or promotion. The triumphs of medical science have resulted in more lives being saved, but in many cases the person saved ends up with some disability. Finally, people living longer are able and want to work well into the traditional retirement years. With proper training and work environment, virtually every person with a disability can be a productive worker. In the U.S. there is an ever growing demand for workers with the ability to use computers and software. As pointed out to the author by Jay Brill, these two trends, growing numbers of workers with disabilities and growing demand for workers with the ability to use computers, compound each other into the consequence:

> *Computer systems must be made accessible to users with disabilities in order to maintain or improve the economic health of the United States.*

Thus, meeting the needs of computer users with disabilities is tantamount to meeting an important need of society as a whole.

Providing access to a computer system for a user with a disability can be an exceedingly tricky problem. Disabilities can be placed into four broad categories: physical impairment, visual impairment, hearing impairment, and cognitive impairment. Within each of these categories, there is a wide variety of special impairments which present barriers to the effective use of a computer system. For example, visual impairment can range from total blindness to extreme near vision, to tunnel vision, to extreme peripheral vision, to color blindness. Some people with visual impairments read Braille while others do not. It is not uncommon for someone with a visual impairment to have a physical, hearing, or cognitive impairment as well. Some impairments inhibit access to standard input devices, while others inhibit access to standard output devices. There are hundreds of solutions and many more potential solutions to this wide variety of computer access problems. What is needed is a relatively small set of "hooks" into computer hardware and operating systems which provide a platform for the development of special purpose hardware and software. To keep the number of hooks to a minimum it would be very helpful if there were a set of *de facto* standards which computer manufacturers adhere to for input and output. For example, textual displays generally have a text buffer which can be accessed so the contents of visual display can be fed into an alternative output device such as a speech synthesizer. Access to the text buffer provides a hook which developers can use to build alternative output devices. With bit-mapped displays it is not enough to have a hook into the display buffer which is just an array of bits. What is needed are hooks into text and pictorial contents of the various windows which are currently on display. This is not easily accomplished.

Making computer systems accessible to users with disabilities is a challenging problem requiring the cooperative efforts of the computer industry, third-party vendors of adaptive devices, rehabilitation engineers, and computer users with disabilities. The development of Section 508, the initial guidelines and final guidelines and regulations demonstrate that cooperation is possible. This law applies only to direct purchases by the federal government, where it is most easily enforced. Much more needs to be done, but the future seems bright for a world where computers will be accessible to all regardless of disability.

ACKNOWLEDGMENTS

Thanks to Jay Brill, Susan Brummel, William Roth, Larry Scadden, and Gregg Vanderheiden for many helpful discussions about Section 508.

REFERENCES

1. Banderburg, S.A., and Vanderheiden, G.C., Eds. *The Rehab/Education Technology Resourcebook Series: Communication, Control, and Computer Access for Disabled and Elderly Individuals,* Volumes 1, 2, 3, 1986–1987. College Hill Press. Available from Trace Center, University of Wisconsin–Madison.

2. *Considerations in the Design of Computers and Operating Systems to Increase their Accessibility to Persons with Disabilities.* A Working Document of the Design Considerations Task Force of the Industry/Government Cooperative Initiative on Computer Accessibility, May 1988. Available from Trace Center, University of Wisconsin–Madison.

3. "FIRMR Bulletin 56." Bulletin to heads of federal agencies from the General Services Administration, September 30, 1988. Available from the Clearinghouse on Computer Accommodation.

4. "FIRMR Regulation, 41 CFR Parts 201–1, 201–3, and 201–32." Regulation of Information Resources Management Service, General Services Administration appearing in the *Federal Register* 53, 198 (Oct. 13, 1988), 40066–40068. Available from the Clearinghouse on Computer Accommodation.

5. General Services Administration. *Managing End User Computing for Users with Disabilities.* Available from the Clearinghouse on Computer Accommodation.

6. "Public Law 99–506, 'Section 508', Electronic Equipment Accessibility for Disabled Workers." Panel at CHI '88, Conference on Human Factors in Computing Systems. Paper in the Conference Proceedings, Special Issue of the SIGCHI Bulletin, 1988, pp. 219–222.

7. U.S. Department of Education. Access to Information Technology by Users with Disabilities, Initial Guidelines October, 1987. National Institute for Disability and Rehabilitative Research and General Services Administration, Information Resources Management Service.

8. U.S. Department of Education. *Summary of Data on Handicapped Children and Youth,* 1985.

Equal Access to Computing, Computing Expertise, and Decision Making About Computers

Deborah G. Johnson

Originally published in *Business & Professional Ethics Journal,* Volume 4, Nos. 3 & 4, Spring/Summer 1985. Reprinted with permission of Deborah G. Johnson. Current address: Rensselaer Polytechnic Institute, Troy, New York 12180–3590, (518) 276-6576.

Few technologies often serve as a window into our society. When we try to understand how they have come to be developed, how they have been integrated into our social arrangements and what social effects they have produced or prevented, we are forced to understand many things about our social institutions and social processes. When we ask what forces should have determined the direction of development of a new technology and what effects we would have liked a new technology to have, we come to understand something about our social values and ideals. Computer technology is a prime example of this. Asking how computers have affected and will in the future affect equality of opportunity in our society forces us to acknowledge certain realities and to see how these realities fall short of our ideals.

While very little of the literature on the social impacts of computers has focused explicitly on equal opportunity, many of the fears and concerns that have been expressed about computers suggest that computers will alter the distribution of power in our society and cause important changes in the structure of our social institutions. If this happens, individual opportunities and choices will change in a variety of ways. In this paper I take some of these often imprecisely expressed concerns about the social impacts of computers and try to formulate them into cogent arguments on behalf of equal access so that the arguments can be carefully scrutinized.

Computers and computer professionals have only been around for thirty to forty years. The technology and the professions surrounding it have changed enormously in those years and there is every indication that more change is to come. Thus, while a number of equal access issues can be raised about the present state of affairs, new developments in the technology may dissolve some of these issues and raise others. For this reason I have tried to think about the future as well as the present. While this has meant making some shaky predictions, it is important to think now about the role computers might have in our society in the future and what this will do to the distribution of rights and benefits, before these effects are upon us.

The general thrust of my analysis is as follows. The case for a right of access to computers cannot be made given present circumstances. Nevertheless, it is possible that in the future such a case could be made, namely, when access to computers is necessary to achieve other rights. Still, even if the case for a right of access can never be made, increased access to computers, computing expertise, and decision making about computers would be socially beneficial.

COMPETITION AND THE CONTEXT OF DISCUSSION

In the early days of computing, people were rather concerned that computers are such powerful tools that those who would have them (or have access to the use of them) would be at such a decided advantage over those who would not, that competition would be skewed unfairly. In business, for example, those who had computers, it was thought, would do such an effective and efficient job that their competitors (who might not be able to afford computers) would never be able to keep up. This would mean that the rich (who could afford computers) would get richer, and big business would get bigger. A specific example of this type of effect was suggested by Talingdon in his discussion of political campaigning.[1] He feared that incumbents (who presumably had access to computers while in office) would become unbeatable. They would be able to demonstrate such success while in office by individualizing their treatment of and communication with individual citizens and could use computers to so carefully target their campaigns that challengers would never have a chance.

Computers allow individuals or businesses to handle large quantities of records, to individualize mailing, to streamline operations, to improve communications, to provide and make use of large quantities of data, to eliminate employees, to simulate activities, etc. In this respect there seems little doubt that computers are powerful tools and that those who have them can be at an advantage in competitive situations. Nevertheless, fears about the effects of computers on competition have been diffused somewhat as computers have gotten smaller and cheaper, for this has meant that the "small guy" can have access to computers almost as easily as the "big guy." In other words, when all parties to a competition have access to computers the competition is not skewed.

In any case, when we try to understand our fears about computers being introduced into a competitive environment, we quickly become aware of some truths about the nature of competition. In a competition, certain factors which will affect the outcome are kept constant (equal) and others are allowed to vary. Just which factors are kept constant and which are allowed to vary depends both on what is being competed for and the purpose of the competition. We want people in a competition to be equal in some respects so that the competition will measure something else. For example, in athletic competitions we may keep weight and age relatively equal so that winning will be a function of effort, training, and skill. Oddly enough, though the outcome will surely be a function of natural endowment, we don't think this makes the competition unfair. In another kind of competition we may allow people of all ages and sizes to participate, but may equalize something else. For example, if our aim was to encourage and reward a certain kind of innovation, we might have a contest in which

[1]See A.B. Talingdon, "Implications of Computer Use in Politics," *Technology and Society,* **2,** 8–11.

individuals competed to build the fastest boat using only a specified amount of money. This would measure knowledge and creativity within economic constraints. If, on the other hand, we focus on competition for jobs or competition for a place in a school or competition for an organ for transplant, different factors will be picked out as appropriate to figure into the competition or to be kept constant. The point is that what it means to have equal opportunity (to win in a competition) is complex and depends both on what is being competed for, and what goals are to be served by the competition.

If we use this model (i.e., the model of competition) to focus on the effects of increasing computerization of our society, we presume that our social environment is competitive, that is, that we must compete for social rights and benefits. For the most part this does, indeed, seem to be true, though it is clear that the competition is often manipulated. We try, for example, by law to exclude some things from competition, and we try to make sure that some factors do not affect the outcome of certain competitions. An example of something we try to exclude from competition is protection of the law. Everyone should have equal protection of the law in all contexts. Though there are gray and controversial areas, we also seem to treat life, some level of health care, and some level of education as things for which people do not have to compete. In a sense, saying that we have a right to something often means that we do not or should not have to compete for the thing. The factors which we try to keep from influencing a competition vary somewhat with the context, but in general and in many realms we try, at least, to insure that race and gender do not figure in.

To say these things about our society is, of course, to make gross generalizations realized in some institutions and by specific social legislation. As generalizations, the claims are probably true. That is, a number of laws express the idea that there are certain things for which we shouldn't have to compete, that some factors shouldn't figure into a competition, and even that sometimes we should skew competition (e.g., affirmative action policies). However, when it comes to the whole picture, the whole mix of opportunities and benefits, insight often gives way to confusion and general agreement to controversy. Theories of justice provide the general principles, but the principles do not dictate that our society look one particular way. They allow for, and call for, balancing. So, even though computers may affect many aspects of our lives, it is hard to deal with the whole. In an attempt to cut through this muddle, it may be helpful if we ask whether or not a case can be made for a right of access to computers and if not now, what circumstances would have to prevail to make the case.

It seems fairly clear, at the outset, that at the present time individuals do not need access to computers in order to carry out the ordinary functions of daily life. Having a computer may help, but it is not essential to such aspects of life as getting an education, a job, medical treatment. A number of social commentators and science fiction writers have suggested, nevertheless, that there may be a time in the future when each individual will need a computer just to carry out the functions of daily life.[2] In these futuristic visions, people stay at home and use computers in their homes to earn a living, shop, go to school, vote, bank, etc.

---

[2]For a compilation of fiction involving computers, see Abbe Mowshowitz's *Inside Information: Computers in Fiction.* Reading, MA: Addison Wesley Publishing, 1977.

Computers would be such a fundamental part of life in such a world that it might be argued that each individual would have a right to a computer or a computer terminal.

The interesting question—interesting in terms of what it tells us about rights of access in our society—is, what circumstances would have to exist before we would say that individuals have a right or should have a legal right to a computer? Above, it was suggested that our society might change so much that one would "need" a computer in order to perform the ordinary tasks of daily life. Well, one difficult questions is what these tasks are, i.e., what are the "ordinary tasks of life"? There seems no simple answer. Indeed, there is a continuum that goes from getting some minimum of food, shelter, health care, education, etc., to getting a certain quality and range of choices in these realms, to getting other sorts of things like work, a crime-free environment, ownership in things, and so on.

Grounding the claim for a right of access to computers in the need for such does not get us very far because "need" is a complex term, and, while rights claims are often tied to needs, "needing" something is neither necessary nor sufficient to establish a right to it. Need claims are always tri-polar, X needs Y in order to Z.[3] One needs food in order to live or needs a range of freedom in order to have a fulfilling life, etc. Depending on exactly how computers are integrated into our society, the case for a right to a computer may be strong or weak. It will depend on what one needs a computer to achieve and whether that for which a computer is necessary is part of the minimum to which all individuals are entitled. For example, we seem to accept the idea that everyone is entitled to some level of education. If our system of public education were to become wholly computerized so that students were expected to stay at home and interact with teachers via computer, then the case for a right to a computer would be very strong. It would, in fact, be comparable to the right to legal counsel. One may need legal counsel in order to achieve one's other legal rights. Similarly, if state and federal elections were transformed to a system whereby citizens voted from computer terminals at home, one's right to vote (to participate in governance) would provide the basis for a "right" to a computer. Access to computers would be necessary to achieve one's rights.

However, there are a whole range of areas of life that may be affected by computers and are significant to the quality of life, but which are not recognized as one's right. For example, suppose the banking industry eliminated human tellers so that only those who had home computers would have access to a bank.[4] Or suppose all department stores computerized their operations so that one could only shop via computer at home. In both these cases, those who did not have computers would be left out. Clearly these changes are alterations in our social institutions that affect access and make some individuals worse off than others. Nevertheless, it seems odd to argue that people have a right to bank, or to shop at department stores. After all, they can keep their money at home or deal with small local merchants. In

---

[3] See William Winslade: 1971, "Human Needs and Human Rights," *Human Rights, Amintaphil Proceedings,* 24–37.

[4] This seems unlikely given the ease with which automated tellers could be made widely available. The homebound would be affected, but they are affected by the existent system as well.

these sorts of cases, we will do better to think of access to computers as socially beneficial, rather than a right.

Before considering the social benefits, however, it should be noted that even in the completely computerized society, the case may not be made for each individual having a computer of his or her own. Access might be achieved through some other means. To see this, consider the similar arguments that might be made for another technology—automobiles. Some might argue that having a car is essential to life in our society. But, of course, that is just not so. How important it is to have a car depends on where you live and what you want to do. Clearly, people can and do get along without them and can have fulfilling lives without them. While it is true that doing without a car can be a hardship (especially for some), it is difficult to make the case for individuals having a right to this technology. Moreover, what is needed is not a car *per se* but a means of transportation, and this can be made available publicly rather than privately via mass transportation systems.

If computers become as important to life in our society as science fiction visionaries suggest, we might make them available publicly. That is, libraries or post offices might have microcomputers or computer terminals available for use by those who cannot afford their own. This would equalize access to computers in one sense of "equalize."

So, it is hard to see in general how the case can be made for a right of access to computers. However, if we focus on particular realms, there may be a time—that is, computer technology and our use of it may evolve in such a way—that the case for a right of access to computers can be made, namely, when access to computers is necessary to achieve other rights. In the meantime, let us consider some ways in which increasing access to computers may be socially beneficial.

ACCESS TO COMPUTER SKILLS

In our society one of the most important benefits for which one has to compete is work.[5] Access to work is crucial because, among other things, a job is a means to other benefits. With a job one earns money with which to buy food, clothing, shelter, etc. This seems obvious, but the fact that work is one of the benefits distributed by competition and the fact that it is crucial to getting other benefits helps us to understand why so much concern about equal opportunity centers around equal opportunities for jobs.

Increasing computerization of our society will no doubt alter job opportunities in a number of ways. Computers may significantly reduce the number of jobs available.[6] As well, the nature of many jobs will change as activities now done by other means are computerized, e.g., record keeping, word processing, electronic mail, assembly line work, etc. Furthermore, new jobs have been and will continue to be created as a result of computers, namely jobs designing, creating, servicing and selling computers. So far the number of jobs created by computers has counterbalanced the number of jobs lost, but there are signs that as computers

---

[5]Some argue that this should be a right. I agree.

[6]See Norman Colin: 1980, *Microelectronics at Works: Productivity and Jobs in the World Economy.* Worldwatch Paper 39, October.

enter the service sector, and as robotics enter the factory, the gross number of jobs available will be reduced.[7]

Whether or not computerization of our society will result in a reduction in the absolute number of jobs available, making competition for jobs more fierce and critical, depends to some extent on a range of factors which have little to do with computers. These factors include whether or not we create new jobs doing things that haven't been done before and whether or not we reduce the number of hours an individual works so that more people have an opportunity to do the work that is available. However the number of jobs available comes out, it seems likely that many more jobs will involve the use of computers and, therefore, that those who know how to use computers will be at an advantage over those who do not. So, the argument might be made that equal access to jobs in our society will depend on people having equal access to training (education) in how to use computers.

Education is both a right and a benefit in our society depending on what level, what kind, and what state you live in. There are a number of reasons for focusing on education in discussions of equal access, but at least one important one has to do with equal educational opportunity being a prerequisite to equal opportunity for jobs. If many jobs in our society will require a knowledge of computers, then equal opportunity to acquire that knowledge will be necessary to insure a fair competition for those jobs.

If the trend in computerization of the workplace continues, we might come close to a situation in which the claim to a "right" of access to education in how to use computers could be made. However, equality of educational opportunity and equality of access to jobs are controversial and complex areas if we talk in terms of rights. Our laws seem to aim more at eliminating certain inhibitors of equality (e.g., race and gender) rather than at producing conditions of equality. Not only are we not committed to creating the conditions, it is probably unrealistic for us to think we can. Aside from differences in natural endowment, the social costs of equalizing all the factors that affect achievement would be enormous. For example, we would have to interfere with the structure of families and rights of parents.[8]

Putting rights claims aside, however, it seems possible and even likely that computerization of the workplace may widen the gap between rich and poor, haves and have-nots in our society. Some have suggested that as things stand now the rich kids in the suburbs will be the first to learn how to use computers and the poor kids in the inner city will be the last. As a result, inner city kids will be further behind in competition for jobs. This will contribute to the already widening gap between haves and have-nots.[9]

One solution to this problem—the widening gap between haves and have-nots—is to equalize education in how to use computers. Make it an elementary or secondary school requirement. This would, in effect, make access to education about computers a kind of legal right. In addition to moving us closer to equality of educational opportunity, such a policy

---

[7]Ibid.

[8]See James S. Fiskin, "Do We Need a Systematic Theory of Equal Opportunity?" Presented at the Conference on Equal Opportunity at the University of Delaware, May 15–17, 1985.

[9]Philip Faflick, "Peering into the Poverty Gap," in D.G. Johnson and J.W. Snapper (eds.), *Ethical Issues in the Use of Computers*. Belmont, CA: Wadsworth Publishing, 1985.

could be argued for just in terms of social good. That is, the increasing numbers of jobs involving computers *could* be viewed as a tremendous opportunity to narrow the gap between haves and have-nots. The new jobs that have and will be created in the computer industry provide an opportunity to bring traditionally excluded individuals (women and minorities) into the ranks of the employed.

The hard part is not making the case for the social benefits of educating school children about computers, but rather in making something happen quickly. There is some indication that it may be too late already; that while computers have created many new jobs, shortly these will dry up, or, at least, the growth of the industry will slacken. Furthermore, the skills issue (the advantage of having computer skills) may dissolve after a time. It is possible and even likely that the technology will evolve to be so user friendly that one will not need to know very much to use a computer. That is, one will only need to press buttons and read queries on screens. If this comes to be, then training in how to use computers will be moot as an equal opportunity issue. We will have missed a great opportunity.

Assuming the status quo as far as education about computers goes, we have to accept the fact that access to computer jobs is not now equal. While is it difficult to argue that this is unique to computer jobs and it is difficult to argue that computer professionals have a unique obligation, it does seem clear that the computer industry and computer professionals could do significant social good by supporting affirmative action programs. This will help bring traditionally unemployed classes into the ranks of the employed. As well, computer professionals can help by encouraging and mentoring women and minorities who are interested in the field, or who are just entering the field.

ACCESS TO COMPUTER PROFESSIONALS

Another type of argument that might be made in the name of equal access has to do with access to the services of computer professionals. This is the kind of argument that is generally made in terms of legal or medical services. Medical care is often critical to life and we often regard nonexotic medical treatment as a right. Similarly, one often needs access to legal services to achieve one's legal or political rights. This provides the basis for claiming that individuals have a right to the services of doctors and lawyers. And, this leads, in turn, to the claim that legal and medical professionals have obligations to provide their services to those who can't afford them. Can a similar argument be made in the name of the services of computer professionals? It has already been argued that the case cannot, at this time, be made in terms of a right of access to computers. Since individuals do not have a right of access to computers, it seems difficult to argue that they have a right of access to the service of computer professionals. Access to computer services is not now even essential to achieve other rights. This is not to say that there will never be a time when such might be the case. It is conceivable that in a highly computerized society one may need the assistance or advice of a computer professional to carry out such critical functions as paying income tax, understanding a medical diagnosis, processing insurance claims, etc. If such a society were to come to be, then not only would it be appropriate to talk of a right to the services of computer professionals, it would be appropriate to impose on computer professionals an obligation to provide their services at reduced fees to those who could not otherwise afford them.

All of the above assumes providing services to individuals. If we change our focus from individuals to groups and more broadly to society in general, the case can be made now for imposing an obligation on computer professionals to protect the welfare of society. Such an obligation is specified in a number of the codes of computer professional organizations. The codes suggest that computer professionals should do their jobs with a regard for public good, and they suggest an obligation to inform the public on matters of concern with regard to the technology.

There seems little doubt that our society will become more and more computerized. This means that we may become very dependent on those who control the computers. Critics of technology often talk about this in terms of our society becoming dependent on a "technological elite." We will depend on computer professionals to evaluate the safety of computer systems used in airplanes and industrial processes, nuclear power plants, etc. We will depend on them for developing statistical analyses and simulation studies on which we will base important decisions, and we will depend on them to protect our privacy.

Computer professionals are not unique in having society dependent on them. We are now dependent on engineers who design airplanes, and automobiles; scientists who evaluate the safety of our food; doctors who treat our illnesses; etc. With all these professionals, we impose an obligation to protect the interests of society. There is one interesting difference between computer professionals and these others that is worth noting and that is that computers are tools for producing and conveying information, and information is critical for almost everything we do. As a result of computers, individuals may have access to more information, but the quality and reliability of the information may be hard to evaluate. This is not to say that computer professionals have a stronger or more stringent obligation than other professionals. It is just a special aspect of their obligation to society.

Our dependency on computer professionalism makes it important that computer professionals do more than just a competent job. They should be willing to inform the public about computer technology, its potential for good and for harm. This is one way that citizens get "access" to a force which affects their lives.

ACCESS TO DECISION MAKING ABOUT COMPUTERS

What seems most clear and perhaps most important is that the use of computers has subtly changed and will continue to change the structure of many of our social institutions—education, work, banking—*and* that individuals, as citizens and consumers, have probably had and will continue to have very little to say in this. The standard reply, of course, is that individuals have had their say via the market. The market takes into account and reflects consumer wishes. However, this is not exactly so. Yes, it is true, for example, that consumers have responded positively to automated bank tellers and in that way have endorsed their use. However, if we focus on electronic funds transfer, it is more difficult to show that consumers have endorsed the change. To be sure, the banking industry supports the system. In fact, however, individuals who are ultimately, albeit sometimes indirectly, affected by the changes have had little say. Even when consumers do have a say, their say often reflects short term, not long term, interests, not to mention lack of information. Electronic funds transfer is a minor example by comparison with long tern consequences of computerization of the workplace. Will individuals in our society have much of a say about diminishing and disproportionately distributed work?

Decision making about the computerization of our society is problematic in a number of ways. For one thing, there has been little government planning or anticipation of the wide-ranging implications of computers, and relatively little interference in the process. (Privacy of personal information is perhaps an exception.) Second, often decision making is by separate individuals in a competitive environment. The individual may believe that she has little choice—if she doesn't computerize, her competition will. Thus, she has to in order to stay in business. The cumulative result of many individual choices and the cumulative effect of choices made in one sector after another may be a society that no one would have chosen if they had seen the whole picture. Another way of putting this is to say that if we focus on a single context, e.g., the banking industry, or the automotive industry, or office automation, computerization may look on balance o.k., but it is quite another thing to try to grasp what our society will look like when all of these different sectors are computerized.

This is *not* to argue against computerization, but rather to argue for individuals having more access to and involvement in decision making about computers. As things stand now, many individuals who are and will be affected by this technology have little say in how it is used.

Computers in Education

Excerpt from CPSR/Washington, D.C. Hosts 1989 Annual Meeting
Benjamin Pierce—CPSR/Pittsburgh and Holly Murray—CPSR/Washington, D.C.
Reprinted by permission of Computer Professionals for Social Responsibility.

The meeting then returned to the auditorium of the Pan American Health Organization for two more panel discussions. The afternoon session began with a panel addressing "Computers in Education: Mixed Agendas and Uncertain Outcomes." The panel featured Professor Sherry Turkle of MIT (author of the book *The Second Self: Computers and the Human Spirit*); Douglas Noble, a teacher in Rochester, New York and a leader of the Coalition for Equity in Education; Carol Edwards, the director of the Southern Coalition for Educational Equity and Project MICRO in Atlanta; Michael Foyer of OTA, one of the principal authors of OTA's "Power On" report on educational computing; and Professor Chet Bowers of the University of Oregon School of Education. The panel was moderated by Terry Winograd.

Turkle opened the discussion with the most optimistic talk of the five speakers. Although many impressive pilot projects in computer-based education have yielded essentially no results, Turkle said she views this as an opportunity to stand back and reconsider the foundations of our approach to the uses of computers in education, freed of our current "technological determinism."

Her slogan for the talk was that "Equal access [to technology] requires epistemological pluralism." Different sorts of people have different approaches to tools. A computer—if properly designed—can encourage "personal appropriation" by users, providing them a rich context for making the machine their own in their own ways. Because computers stand midway between formal systems and concrete physical artifacts, they encourage concrete appropriation of formal systems.

In previous work, Turkle has described how men and women tend to differ in cognitive styles in relating to computers, and how a "woman's style" is typically given lower value or no value at all. This work resonates with contemporary feminist thought, which holds that there are significant differences of "style" between men and women, which should be taken into account instead of forcing everyone into the same (male) cognitive mold. (This argument generated quite a bit of controversy during the question and answer period.) More recently, Turkle has studied MIT's Project Athena, a highly touted university-level educational computing project. She found that this system embodies "the opposite of epistemological pluralism"—it has a single operating system, window interface, and philosophy of educational software. The failure of this approach is demonstrated by many "small epistemological rebellions" on the fringes of the project, said Turkle.

Among the factors standing in the way of epistemological pluralism are the view that the computer is "just a tool"—both hammers and harpsichords are tools, said Turkle; which is more like a computer?—and the current state of schools. Teachers need to be more fluent with computers as expressive tools.

Douglas Noble began by recounting the optimistic litany behind the $2 billion we have spent on computers in schools so far: Computers alone will bring solutions to both the educational crisis and the economic crisis; computer literacy is a basic survival skill. What we have instead, asserted Noble, are instruments of control and hoards of uncritical, "functionally illiterate drones and information processors."

This is one legacy, Noble believes, of the heavy military orientation of R&D in computer education (and in computer development in general) for the last 30 years. "When even the military has recognized the futility of the 'teaching machine' approach to learning, shouldn't we?," he asked. What we have ended up with is computer-based education as a tool of larger, highly questionable technical and social imperatives.

Educator Carol Edwards noted that, in her perspective, educational computing is subordinate to concerns about education in general. Her remarks focused on several problems:

1. Equity: A simply quantitative approach to this problem (i.e., do all the kids have access to computers?) falls short. In addition, we should be asking qualitative questions about the quality of software, programming activities, teacher expertise, and the educational milieu and philosophy. Edwards asserted that the failings of computers in the classroom today reflect our two-tiered society: one group learns to use computers for control and leadership in society, while the lower tier is becoming a "throwaway" caste of unskilled labor whose jobs are being replaced by technology and whose education is so dull and meaningless that they drop out in droves. Edwards challenged the audience to use technology to restructure the two-tiered society instead of to reinforce it.

2. Lack of diversity: As Edwards aptly pointed out, nothing spoke as eloquently of the diversity problem in our field as the makeup of the audience itself (which was overwhelmingly white and middle-class—and probably two-thirds male). This distorted representation reinforced the need for Sherry Turkle's earlier call for an "epistemological pluralism," said Edwards.

3. Exaggerated claims of educational high-tech vendors: There is no evidence, for example, to support the claims that preschoolers need computers, Edwards complained.

4. Technological Advances: Another angle on the equity problem: It's crucial to include diverse groups in the design—not just the use—of new technologies. Currently, the people defining the new frontier are creating something comfortable for themselves and appropriate to their own cultural context. A concern for equity, if it is to be effective, must be built into the technology development process from the very beginning.

Michael Foyer began his talk by emphasizing that OTA's position is not blindly in favor of technology. Personally, he said, he is skeptical about educational technology, but less so than when he joined OTA's study project on the subject.

The years 1982–83 marked the beginning of a "national experiment" in microcomputer technology in schools, said Foyer. While the results have been mixed and it is too early to make a final verdict, it seems clear that computers are not a cure for the education crisis. In particular, we cannot think about education the way we think about other research and development: what works in one school doesn't in another; the "blueprint model" is wrong.

Foyer described some conclusions of the OTA "Power On" report. Educational software, generally speaking, is of terribly poor quality. Even so, teachers complain that there is not enough of it. Schools and teachers are under tremendous pressure to perform well under fairly standard measures. It has been shown that computer instruction can be used to raise standardized reading and math scores. It is prohibitively expensive to develop good-quality educational software. A company that invests the time and energy to produce a really fine program will never be able to recover its costs. Partial solutions to this problem might include more federal support for educational software development, and the creation (by some means, such as massive hardware grants to schools) of a larger and wealthier marketplace for educational software.

Chet Bowers, from the University of Oregon, spoke of computers, ecology, and the sense of self. In a panel notable for the reach of its analysis, Bowers probably ranged the farthest into broad cultural and philosophical critique. The thrust of his hypothesis on educational computing was two-fold: first, we are unaware of how culturally determined even seemingly value-free entities such as science, technology and computing are; and, second, our particular Western mode of problem-solving—the Cartesian model—is ultimately destructive of ecologically balanced community and life itself.

Evoking themes of 19th century German philosophy and 20th century linguistics theory, Bowers exhorted his audience to bear in mind the cultural assumptions and subjectivity we carry around, even as we manipulate data or write software, and to remember that far from being a neutral conduit, our "language thinks us."

Bowers went on to derive concrete suggestions for cross-cultural educational software that demands critical thinking, but it was hard to avoid the conclusion, given his general arguments, that computers in the classroom are too fraught with negative associations and values to be very useful in a humanistic curriculum. Bowers' own conclusion seemed to say as much: technology is no more than a historical experiment, and perhaps a failed one at that.

Moderator Terry Winograd summed up the two extremes he saw represented in these talks: either there is a linear militaristic world view inherent to computers, or the computer may be seen as an infinitely adaptable "Trojan horse." Winograd suggested a middle ground that, while conceding that computers won't revolutionize our educational structures, would have us "think small" and explore the ways computers can make some changes.

Ethical Scenarios

Scenarios marked with an asterisk are adapted from Parker (1979).

*1. The owner of a small business needed a computer-based accounting system. He identified the various inputs and outputs he felt were required to satisfy his needs. Then he showed his design to a computer programmer and asked the programmer if she could implement such a system. The programmer knew she could implement the system because she had developed much more sophisticated accounting systems in the past. In fact, she felt this design was rather crude and would soon need several major revisions. But she didn't say anything about her feelings because the business owner didn't ask her and she thought maybe she could be the one hired to implement the needed revisions later.

Was the programmer's decision not to point out the design flaws acceptable, questionable, or unacceptable?

*2. An engineer needed a program to perform a series of complicated calculations. She found a computer programmer capable of writing the program, but would only hire the programmer if he agreed to share any liability that might result from an error in her calculations. The programmer said he would be willing to assume any liability due to a malfunction of the program, but was unwilling to share any liability due to an error in the engineer's calculations.

Was the programmer's position in this situation acceptable, questionable, or unacceptable?

Was the engineer's position in this situation acceptable, questionable, or unacceptable?

3. A banker was interviewing a customer with respect to a loan application. The banker was tired and was not paying close attention when the customer told him her highest education level. He did not want to appear inattentive, so he guessed that she probably said that she had earned a Bachelor of Science degree. That was the most common response in his experience, so that is what he recorded on his evaluation.

Was the banker's action acceptable, questionable, or unacceptable?

*4. A scientist developed a theory that required construction of a computer model to prove. He hired a computer programmer to build the model, and the theory was shown to be correct. The scientist won several awards for the development of the theory, but he never acknowledged the contribution of the computer programmer.

Was the scientist's failure to acknowledge the computer programmer acceptable, questionable, or unacceptable?

5. A university student was hired to conduct a survey at a local shopping mall. The amount of money he was paid was based on the number of surveys that were completed. The company conducting the survey wanted to obtain input from shoppers regarding "family-oriented issues." The student's instructions were to obtain responses from persons with children, although he noticed that none of the questions asked specifically about a person's child. He saw a group of friends in the mall, and since he had not been too successful obtaining responses from shoppers, he convinced each of his friends to complete a survey.

Was the student's action acceptable, questionable, or unacceptable?

6. A computer user called a mail-order computer program store to order a particular accounting system. When he received his order, he found out that the store had accidentally sent him a very expensive word processing program as well as the accounting package that he had ordered. He looked at the invoice, and it indicated only that the accounting package had been sent. The user decided to keep the word processing package.

Was the user's decision to keep the word processing package acceptable, questionable, or unacceptable?

7. A telephone operator received a call requesting the telephone number of Dennis Barak. As he was entering the request into his information system, he could not remember whether the request was for Dennis Barak or Dennis Barat. He decided to have the system return the number of Dennis Bara*; the system would match any number of letters where the asterisk appeared. The system would automatically give the number of the first name that matched to the person requesting the information. If it was wrong, the caller could just call the operator again.

Was the telephone operator's action acceptable, questionable, or unacceptable?

*8. A computer programmer enjoyed building small computer systems to give his friends. He would frequently go to his office on Saturday when no one was working and use his employer's computer to develop systems. He did not hide the fact that he was going into the building; he had to sign a register at a security desk each time he entered.

Was the programmer's use of the company computer acceptable, questionable, or unacceptable?

9. A computer store was having a sale on a limited number of computer systems. A person who bought one of the systems was so pleased with the purchase that he convinced a friend to buy one, too. The friend called the store, described the system in detail to a salesman, and asked whether she could obtain a system identical to her friend's system. The salesman said yes, so the woman agreed to come to the store. When the woman arrived at the store, she found that the salesman had configured a system with a different monitor. When she asked about this difference, the salesman told her it was "functionally equivalent" to her friend's monitor. The only difference was that her friend's monitor had some switches that allowed the monitor characteristics to be changed, whereas the monitor in her system relied on software signals to switch characteristics. Otherwise, the monitors were equivalent and had the same cost.

Was the salesman's response during the telephone conversation acceptable, questionable, or unacceptable?

*10. A computer programmer built small computer systems to sell. This was not his main source of income; he worked for a moderately sized computer vendor. He would frequently go to his office on Saturday when no one was working and use his employer's computer to develop systems. He did not hide the fact that he was going into the building; he had to sign a register at a security desk each time he entered.

Was the programmer's use of the company computer acceptable, questionable, or unacceptable?

11. A student at a university learned to use an expensive spreadsheet program in her accounting class. The student would go to the university microcomputer lab, check out the spreadsheet software, complete her assignment, and return the software. Signs were posted in the lab indicating that copying software was forbidden. One day, she decided to copy the software anyway so she could work on her assignments at her apartment.

If the student destroyed her copy of the software at the end of the semester, was her action in copying the software acceptable, questionable, or unacceptable?

If the student forgot to destroy her copy of the software at the end of the semester, was her action in copying the software acceptable, questionable, or unacceptable?

If the student never intended to destroy the software at the end of the semester, was her action in copying the software acceptable, questionable, or unacceptable?

REFERENCE

Parker, D.B. *Ethical Conflicts in Computer Science and Technology.* AFIPS Press, 1979.

Part III

Artificial Intelligence and Ethics

HISTORICAL PERSPECTIVE

The third part of this book brings the reader to the realm of tomorrow's ethical issues. The integration of artificial intelligence and information systems is arousing much interest today. Issues of responsibility, ownership, and machine decision making are constantly discussed in academic halls around the world, and in the halls of corporate America. Given this interest and the major implications inherent in the issues, students need to begin to study the AI questions from the viewpoint of ethics.

To understand the relationship between AI and ethics one must understand AI's historical beginnings and its underlying concepts. Generally AI refers to the development of machines that perform tasks usually requiring human intelligence. Waldrop, in his book *Man-Made Minds: The Promise of Artificial Intelligence*, defines AI as the process of making computers do smart things (Waldrop, 1987).

The Early 1900s

Contrary to the popular belief that AI is a new area of study, its roots can be traced back to the early 1900s and to the first computers. People generally associated with these computers, Mauchly, Eckert, Aiken, and Von Neumann, were also contributors to AI research. Although the advent of AI concepts and theory (formal logic, information theory, and cybernetics) came in the 1930s and 1940s, AI truly emerged as a recognized discipline in the early 1950s to mid-1960s.

The 1950s and 1960s

In the 1950s and 1960s several institutions, Stanford, RAND, Carnegie-Mellon, and MIT played major roles in developing the AI discipline. AI historians point to the Dartmouth Summer Research Conference on AI as the birthplace of AI (Waldrop, 1987, p. 11). Among the conference participants were such notables as John McCarthy, Herbert Simon, Allen Newell, Marvin Minsky, Claude Shannon, and Arthur Samuel. Aside from coining the term AI, the conference's significant outcome was that it promoted a more concrete realization of what had been until then mostly philosophical speculations. Another noteworthy accomplishment during this time was McCarthy's work leading to the AI language LISP. In addition, Newell and Simon created the first true AI program, the Logic Theorist, which proved theorems in symbolic logic. This work is generally considered the foundation of the field of cognitive science.

Also in the 1950s and 1960s a major government project known as DARPA (Defense Advanced Research Projects Agency) was developed in AI. DARPA focused on an expert knowledge–base feasibility study, which was later built into a practical system responsible for army hardware and software maintenance.

In spite of the many happenings in the '50s, developments during the '60s were few, but noteworthy. The groundwork for natural language processors was rooted in HEARSAY and HARPY. Dendral, the forerunner to expert systems, developed fundamental concepts for expert systems and expert system research in the '70s.

The 1970s and 1980s

There are many issues yet to be resolved in natural language processors. During the 1970s and 1980s they came to the forefront of AI research. Many natural language–based systems can be found today in business and other applications areas. Programs such as Mycin and Prospector proved that in domain-specific application areas, AI programs could outperform their human counterparts.

Highlighting the 1980s was a parallel and dynamic growth in computing and AI. This period saw an increased level of computer software and power. Proliferation of computers, specifically microcomputers, and the recognition by corporate America of AI as a practical tool, led to the explosion of AI applications. The maturing of personal computing and AI's acceptance in the "real world" have opened the door for examining AI via the traditional ethical issues.

ETHICAL ISSUES OF AI

Ethical issues concerning artificial intelligence fall into two broad categories: legal and philosophical. Legal issues include the classical ideas of liability and ownership. Philosophical issues, on the other hand, refer to more thought-provoking ideas. There are also some issues that do not fall neatly into a category.

Legal Concerns

The legal issues of product liability and ownership can be brought to bear on such questions as (1) who is liable for a faulty or incomplete knowledge base? (2) what rights does a company have to an employee's knowledge? (3) should knowledge engineers be licensed? and (4) is an expert system considered a product, a service, or both? The ethical relationship between employer and employee and between company and consumer is sure to arise in the development and implementation of AI systems.

Philosophical Concerns

Among the philosophical questions are (1) the degree of responsibility given to a machine for its role in the decision-making process, (2) the evolution of an AI system with rights,

(3) the question of experimental AI research, and (4) the question of conscious AI entities as posited by LaChat (1986) and others. From the rights of humans to the rights of machines, the philosophical questions cover a wide variety of ethical issues.

Other Concerns

Many ethical issues fall into either the legal or philosophical category, but some, not surprisingly, straddle both of these categories. Two such issues are (1) who owns the knowledge in an expert system? and (2) can knowledge be copyrighted, patented, bought, or sold? The legal issue of ownership is clear in these two questions; however, the philosophical issue of intellectual capital is also important (Mason, 1986).

THE PAPERS: CHAPTER 5

"What AI Practitioners Should Know about the Law: Parts 1 and 2"

The main ideas discussed by Frank deal with the legal aspects of AI products and services. These aspects include both the question of product liability and that of product ownership. For instance, Frank poses the question of a doctor's liability for misdiagnosis of a patient after using a medical expert system. Who is responsible: the doctor, the expert system, the expert systems developer, or the experts themselves?

"A Question of Responsibility"

Waldrop's article provides insights on the philosophical issues of AI. Particularly, he addresses the degree of responsibility that should be relegated to an AI entity. He also discusses a theory of machine ethics, that is, the type of moral guidelines given an AI machine via coded parameters, similar to Isaac Asimov's three laws of robotics: (1) a robot may not injure a human being or through inaction allow a human being to come to harm, (2) a robot must obey the orders given it by human beings except where such orders would conflict with the first law, and (3) a robot must protect its own existence as long as such protection does not conflict with the first or second laws.

"Artificial Intelligence and Ethics: An Exercise in the Moral Imagination"

LaChat constructs a premise of personal AI, an AI entity that has awareness and consciousness. He suggests some more issues associated with medical experimentation. He also questions the capacity and possibility of such an entity making moral decisions.

"The Search for an 'Electronic Brain': An Introduction to Neural Networks"

Folsom gives an overview of the history, possible applications, and problems with neural networks. He makes particular reference to the use of neural networks in artificial intelligence. Some of the business and military application areas include telecommunications, radar systems, text recognition, and simulated memory.

LaChat, Michael, "Artificial Intelligence and Ethics: An Exercise in the Moral Imagination," *AI Magazine*, Vol. 7, No. 2, 1986, pp. 70–79.

Mason, Richard, "Four Ethical Issues of the Information Age," *MIS Quarterly*, Vol. 10, No. 1, March 1986, pp. 4–12.

Waldrop, M. Mitchell, "A Question of Responsibility," Chapter 11, *Man-Made Minds: The Promise of Artificial Intelligence,* 1987, Walker and Co., New York.

Chapter 5

Ethical Issues in Artificial Intelligence

What AI Practitioners Should Know about the Law (Part 1)

Steven J. Frank

Originally published in *AI Magazine,* 9, Number 1, 63–75. Copyright © 1988, American Association for Artificial Intelligence. Reprinted by permission of American Association for Artificial Intelligence and Steven J. Frank.

Technological advances are usually shadowed by changes in the legal system. As the daily subject matter facing judges and lawyers evolves, new issues, priorities, and dangers emerge. The dimensions of familiar rights and obligations soon become outmoded or appear increasingly ambiguous in the face of the unfamiliar, and some sort of response eventually ensues. Ideally, the response represents a process of accommodation between the old law and new needs. The reality, however, is often quite different.

In the United States, earlier decisions constrain the development of new legal principles by the judiciary. Lower-court judges are obligated to follow the past edicts of courts positioned above them in the judicial hierarchy, and even those standing at the highest levels are reluctant to disturb established precedent unless a departure is clearly warranted. Legislatures, although not bound by prior law, must strike a balance among competing political interests before enacting change. The point is that unless they are faced with a disturbance of cataclysmic proportions, the engines of legal progress will not likely move with breakneck speed.

One would imagine that such inertial propensities run contrary to the desires of the innovators whose activities and livelihoods are actually touched by regulation. One might envision those gallant entrepreneurial warriors, whose quest for the future has been interrupted by legal constraints of the past, struggling to extract movement from ponderous lawmakers. Yet, all too often, even the ones who stand to lose most from flawed legal precepts remain equally passive at the stage of policy formulation. For the scientist with a valuable new product, the existence of relevant law is frequently of interest only to the extent that it might get in the way. The process of change is viewed as an obstacle rather than an opportunity. Although common, this view is quite ironic. If those responsible for making the rules lack access to needed sources of expertise, those who must live with the rules will face needlessly imperfect handiwork.

As technological developments that remove ever-increasing numbers of cognitive tasks from human control alter the assumptions upon which current legal rules are based, the emergence of artificial intelligence (AI) systems will pose a significant challenge to the institutions responsible for creating law. It is important for innovators in the AI community to understand both the assumptions and the rules, so that the law can be improved where possible and avoided where necessary. As AI products continue to attain greater commercial prominence and, thereby, touch larger segments of society, AI practitioners will find three substantive legal fields increasingly influential: intellectual property, tort, and evidentiary law. This article is an attempt to introduce a changing legal structure to those who will be most directly affected by its evolution.

INTELLECTUAL PROPERTY

All software programs, regardless of purpose or complexity, exhibit a common vulnerability: They are expensive to create but relatively easy to reproduce. Over the years, software developers have relied on a triad of legal protection mechanisms to retain proprietary control over their work: copyright registration, patent protection, and the law of trade secrets. Each of these protective schemes emerged well before the advent of digital computers. As they have been recruited for application to contemporary technologies, deficiencies and inconsistencies have been discovered; pondered; and, to some extent, remedied. Yet despite recent efforts, the current system remains a patchwork scheme containing worrisome gaps and unnecessary overlap. The emergence of AI software can be expected to place additional strain on archaic conceptual foundations and overworked adaptations.

COPYRIGHT

Copyright registration was originally intended to provide authors with a means of protecting literary works.[1] As newer modes of aesthetic and intellectual expression became available, the terms of the Copyright Act were broadened to include them. In its present incarnation (the 1976 Act, Title 17 of the U.S. Code), copyright registration and protection are made available for "original work[s] of authorship fixed in any tangible medium of expression."[2] Computer software occupied a controversial status for many years. Although computer programs can be perceived and comprehended by humans, their chief function is not to inspire human thought. Programs are written to direct the operation of digital electronic components. This utilitarian role was considered by many to fall outside the spirit of a system intended to protect expressive creations.[3] Although written, a program is not a literary work in the everyday sense because its primary audience is nonhuman.

The footnote style employed here is a specialized citation form peculiar to legal materials. This style has been developed to maintain consistency among jurisdictions, case reporters, and statutory citations. Its basic format is: <volume> <SOURCE> <first page of document>, <local citation>.

[1] The copyright clause of the U.S. Constitution empowers Congress to enact laws protecting the "writings" of an "author." U.S. Constitution, article I, section 8, clause 8. A number of federal copyright acts have been legislated under this authority.

[2] 17 U.S.C. section 102(a).

[3] Indeed, courts had for some time recognized the useful article doctrine, which excludes from copyright protection the design or shape of an article unless these qualities can be separated from, or exist independently of, the article's utilitarian aspects. The purpose of this exclusion is to prevent inventors from circumventing the rigorous standards of the patent laws by simply copyrighting their designs.

Despite the uncomfortable fit, by the early 1970s Congress became convinced that copyright protection for computer software was an idea whose time had come. Prior to enacting the 1976 Act, it created the National Commission on New Technology Uses of Copyrighted Works (CONTU) to consider the issue. The recommendations of CONTU were incorporated into the 1980 amendments to the 1976 Act. These provisions clarified the law in several respects, most notably by explicitly defining computer programs and bringing them under the terms of the Act. Registering software is now a simple matter of filing the proper form and submitting a nominal fee.[4] Far less clear, however, is exactly what is protected once such a filing is made.

Copyright Law: Ideas versus Expressions

A fundamental tenet of copyright law is that protection is limited to an author's expression; it does not extend to the underlying ideas.[5] This principle is well suited to forms of work whose valued content is wholly contained within the expression. For works of literature or films, protection of the author's chosen words, format, and style is sufficient to guard against theft of the creative effort. Computer programs, however, direct the execution of purposive tasks. Depending on the breadth and generality of the programmer's approach, many coding routes can be available to implement an identical set of symbolic or mathematic operations. Protecting a single version, then, ordinarily cannot protect the underlying solution.

Although this copyright restriction suggests that the level of protection will be enhanced by intrinsic programming limitations, the opposite is actually true. In fact, if a particular program captures its underlying methodology too well, copyright protection can be lost altogether: Courts will not support an infringement action if too few alternative means of expression exist. In such cases, the idea is said to merge with the expression, rendering both unprotectible.[6] This concept was applied to computer programs in Apple Computer, Inc. v. Franklin Computer Corp.,[7] which involved Apple's operating system software. As long as other programs can be written that perform the same function as the Apple software, said the court, that software can be copyrighted.[8]

The bottom line is that copyright protects implementation far better than function. It is

---

[4]Although the mechanics of obtaining copyright and patent protection are beyond the scope of this article, a good source of general information is Bender, D. 1987. *Computer Law.* New York: Matthew Bender.

[5]17 U.S.C. section 102(b). This statement is really no more than a generalization of the useful article doctrine. Ideas are free to all, and the public is entitled to profit from the ideas contained in copyrighted works. The author of a cookbook, for example, cannot prevent readers from preparing the recited recipes.

[6]Morrissey v. Procter & Gamble Co., 379 F.2d 675 (1st Cir. 1967) (sweepstakes rules). Some courts will permit infringement actions in such instances but only when the copying is slavish. See, e.g., Continental Casualty Co. v. Beardsley, 253 F.2d 702 (2d Cir. 1958).

[7]714 F.2d 1240 (3d Cir. 1983), cert. denied, 464 U.S. 1033 (1984).

[8]A key aspect of this decision was the court's ruling that the existence of a limited number of ways to structure or arrange such an operating system will not merge expression with the idea; even similarly structured programs can be expressed differently through alternative coding choices.

most effectively used for software that embodies unoriginal ideas executed by means of a particular technique or in conjunction with a distinctive format. The simpler the programming task, the more reliable the protection is under the copyright laws.

Still, the subject matter of copyright must extend beyond bare expression in order for protection to be meaningful. If infringement actions could be won only against those who slavishly copy, registered works could be readily appropriated through trivial additions or deletions. The standard of comparison for infringement, therefore, has been defined by the courts as "substantial similarity" rather than pure congruence. It is through this deliberately inexact test that some ideas achieve copyright protection. Where expression ends and unprotectible ideas begin, however, is a line drawn differently by different judges.

The key inquiry lies in determining what it is that makes a particular computer program unique. A novel's distinctiveness does not reside solely in the author's choice of words or grammar but extends to the interplay of characters, plot, dialogue, and theme. Yet, no court would extend protection to all these elements because they inevitably embody ideas that would enlarge the author's monopoly to an unwanted extent. Were Shakespeare alive to copyright his works, his quill would not foreclose others from expounding on the death of Julius Caesar, nor would *West Side Story* infringe *Romeo and Juliet*. Instead, courts attempt to draw the line of substantial similarity by searching for a work's essential features, assessing the extent to which these features have been reproduced by the defendant and according protection to identifiable aspects of the work that fall short of the abstract. Textual similarity is obviously the easiest way to prove infringement, though it is not the only way. However, because literal copying is simpler to police objectively than paraphrasing or rearranging, plaintiffs are required to demonstrate more comprehensive duplication of nonliteral elements than of the words themselves.

For computer programs, similarity of source or object code must likewise comprise only a first step in deciding whether two software packages are substantially similar. Program logic, data structures, and the form of output embody crucial elements of the programmer's design efforts. Courts must now apply established principles in unfamiliar territory. In a recent pronouncement on the subject, the United States Court of Appeals for the Third Circuit chose the following rule to distinguish idea from expression in the software context:

> [T]he line between idea and expression may be drawn with reference to the end sought to be achieved by the work in question. In other words, the purpose or function of a utilitarian work would be the work's idea, and everything that is not necessary to that purpose or function would be part of the expression of the idea.[9]

The court reasoned that where various means of achieving the desired goal exist, the particular route chosen is not essential to this goal—and, hence, can be protected as expression.

A similarly broad view was taken by a Georgia federal district court in Digital Communications Associates, Inc. v. Softklone Distributing Corp.[10] In this case, the court upheld

---

[9]Whelan Associates, Inc. v. Jaslow Dental Laboratory, Inc., 797 F.2d 1222 (3d Cir. 1986), cert. denied, 107 S.Ct. 877 (1987).
[10]659 F.Supp. 449 (N.D. Ga. 1987).

the validity of Digital Communications Associates' (DCA) copyright of its CROSSTALK XVI status screen and found the status screen of its competitor's product to infringe this copyright. The "idea," said the court, was the process or manner by which the status screen operates and the "expression" the method of communication to the user. Applying this rule, the court found (1) the use of a screen to reflect the program's status, (2) the use of a command-driven program, and (3) the typing of two symbols to activate a specific command to be ideas. Portions of the status screen unrelated to program function, such as the arrangement and style of displayed terms, were viewed as protectible expression.

Current commercially targeted AI products, such as expert systems, derive their capabilities from ideas to a much greater degree than from program expression. Before actual programming can even begin, a working inference structure must be developed through laborious debriefing of human experts and thorough exploration of possible interactions among the distilled rules. Once the knowledge base is defined, however, computer implementation is straightforward; indeed, advertisements routinely appear in technical journals for expert system-development software designed to provide an empty shell into which completed knowledge structures can be loaded.

Such idea-driven software systems make poor candidates for copyright protection. Although the opinions in Whelan (see footnote 9) and DCA are relatively liberal, it is questionable whether they can be extended beyond program-bound features such as display formats, system architecture, and coding patterns. The knowledge base of a complex production system represents a working methodology for drawing conclusions within a specific domain, regardless of whether it is actually reduced to practice on a computer and, thus, can be said to possess an existence separate from its facilitative software. Whether courts will view such systems as lying closer to mathematical algorithms, which are purely cognitive and, therefore, not copyrightable, or the computational structures and organizations that have been accorded protection, remains to be seen.

Copyright Law: The Problem of Fixation

An essential prerequisite to obtain copyright is "fixation in a tangible medium of expression."[11] The price an author pays for protection under the copyright laws is the work's availability to the public. The Copyright Office requires that some form of the work be deposited as a condition of registration, ensuring access both for inspection and as a means of verifying authenticity in later infringement actions.

Fixation occurs when the work assumes a form sufficiently permanent or stable to permit it to be perceived, reproduced, or otherwise communicated for a period of more than transitory duration.[12] For the kinds of static compositions originally contemplated as objects of copyright, the requirement is fulfilled as soon as the work enters a form more tangible than the author's imagination. A problem is also not posed for current-day software: Although program code undergoes various transformations during program execution, the basic struc-

---

[11] 17 U.S.C. section 102(a).
[12] 17 U.S.C. section 101.

ture remains sufficiently stable that no one is terribly worried about the loss of copyright for intermediate states.

The development of computer programs capable of self-modification and self-update might well result in classes of software incapable of proper fixation. Nonmonotonic logic, the basis for much of the current research in machine learning, illustrates the kind of dynamics that can prevent the description of program contents in a manner acceptable to the Copyright Office. Program logic is said to be nonmonotonic when the introduction of new information results in the production of revised conclusions.[13] Although execution of a monotonic program results in return to the initial coding pattern at completion, nonmonotonic systems can wind up with code that differs from the initial state precisely as a result of execution. The greater the deviation, the lower the degree of resemblance is to the original version that was deposited and, therefore, the less meaningful this deposit. A program that cannot offer a basis for comparison at any point in time stands to lose copyright protection.[14]

From a purely conceptual viewpoint, the danger might appear minimal. The product of self-modification would undoubtedly qualify as a derivative work falling within the original author's ownership. The copyright laws have also been modified so that registration and deposit are no longer indispensable. Although the 1976 Act offers certain procedural advantages to authors who register their works, the power to sue for infringement attaches at the moment of fixation.[15] Hence, all successive phases of a dynamic program's existence are theoretically covered as long as they remain in existence for more than a fleeting instant.

As a practical matter, however, potential difficulties abound and will increase with software power. The simplest nonmonotonic systems, which might alter search or inference patterns in response to a new user-specified fact, present the fewest questions. For example, an expert system based on a relatively limited number of rules could be programmed to save discarded rules and record the source of the modification. This capability would permit tracing back to the original copyrighted version. The prospect of coauthorship by the user (see Copyright Law: Joint Authorship) would also not present an issue. It is unlikely that a program user could appropriate the designer's copyright based on a contribution to the resulting new program form; merely supplying new information can hardly be considered an act of authorship. The interactive, stepwise manner of knowledge enhancement would also permit an owner to re-register the program after each successive modification.

---

[13]McDermott & Doyle, Non-Monotonic Logic I, 13 *Artificial Intelligence* 41, 44 (1980).

[14]This problem in its most rudimentary form is currently under debate within the Copyright Office. Proprietors of commercial databases, which constantly expand their systems to include the latest information, have sought a means of complying with copyright registration requirements without the need for continued redeposit. The Copyright Office has recently issued proposed regulations for group registration of a single database and updates occurring over a three-month period. See 52 Federal Register 37167.

[15]Registration is a technical prerequisite to actual filing of an infringement action. 17 U.S.C. section 411. However, there is no absolute requirement that the work be registered at the time infringement takes place. Registration made just prior to the lawsuit will open the courthouse doors, even though the alleged infringement occurred long before.

Substantial quandaries surface as user participation increases or knowledge acquisition becomes an automatic feature of program operation. Autonomous data gathering, although clearly a future objective, offers the possibility of software that evolves like an independent organism. Consider a self-updating expert system that monitors developments in relevant technical fields without assistance, determines when incorporation of new information into the knowledge base appears necessary, and performs the required internal accommodation directly. Unless each stage is separately preserved somewhere, how could an infringement action be maintained? More precisely, how could the copyright owner overcome an infringer's defense of independent creation when even a slavishly copied version cannot be readily traced to the original copyrighted program? Copyright protection might well elude fluid programming structures unless coding style is sufficiently distinctive, or complete program records are tenaciously maintained.

Copyright Law: Joint Authorship

Research is progressing in the fields of computer-aided software engineering (CASE), computer-aided design (CAD), and computer-aided manufacture (CAM) at a sufficiently encouraging rate that the prospect of computers producing works of independent, original authorship no longer appears conjectural. Nonetheless, no anticipatory provisions were included in the 1976 Act or 1980 amendments because CONTU considered AI too primitive an area of computer science to warrant concern.[16] CONTU viewed computers as "inert instruments" incapable of producing output more original than the generative instructions entered by a human programmer. This conclusion was recently criticized by another congressional body, the Office of Technology Assessment (OTA). In a 1986 report which exhibits a more sophisticated awareness of technological potential than that of CONTU, OTA stated:

> It is misleading, however, to think of programs as inert tools of creation, in the sense that cameras, typewriters, or any other tools of creation are inert. Moreover, CONTU's comparison of a computer to other instruments of creation begs the question of whether interactive computing employs the computer as co-creator, rather than as an instrument of creation. It is still an open question whether the programmed computer is unlike other tools of creation.[17]

Unless Congress reconsiders the issue soon, it will be up to the courts to decide whether and to what extent the copyright laws apply to computer-generated works.

The output of most current-day computer programs does not raise copyright issues. Today's mass-marketed software simply effectuates user commands in the mechanical fash-

---

[16]CONTU noted "concern that computers either had or were likely to soon achieve powers that would enable them independently to create works that, although similar to other copyrightable works, would not or should not be copyrightable because they had no human author. The development of this capacity for 'artificial intelligence' has not yet come to pass, and, indeed, it has been suggested that . . . such development is too speculative to consider at this time." *Final Report of the National Commission on New Technological Uses of Copyrighted Works,* July 31, 1978, at 42.

[17]U.S. Congress, Office of Technology Assessment, *Intellectual Property Rights in an Age of Electronics and Information* 72 (1986).

ion expressed by CONTU, operating as sophisticated electronic tools; little originality or creativity is contributed by program operation. However, questions of derivative ownership will arise as software becomes capable of producing integrated, reusable solutions to user-defined problems based on less and less input data. Who should own the copyright to the software output of a CASE system, for example, when the role of the user is reduced to that of mere problem specification, the system itself developing the necessary algorithms and formulating program logic?[18]

The initial task in approaching this question is to locate the threshold of authorship. At what point do computer-generated contributions deserve copyright protection in order to give the program owner rights in software output? Judicial decisions have established two essential requisites of copyright authorship: originality and intellectual labor. The level of refinement necessary to satisfy both criteria is minimal. For copyright purposes, originality is defined in the narrowest possible sense. Independent creation is all that is necessary; there is no need for the work to be novel. The requirement of intellectual labor is likewise interpreted generously: "[A]lmost any ingenuity in selection, combination or expression, no matter how crude, humble or obvious, will be sufficient."[19]

If courts treat computers like people, alteration and processing of user input will satisfy the copyright notion of authorship when the computer program's contribution is somehow nontrivial—to paraphrase one court, when the variation is something recognizably "its own."[20] Determining whether something sufficiently new has been produced from a precursor presents an innately subjective question. The smaller the resemblance between input and output and the greater the utility of the latter compared to the former, the more likely a court is to recognize a contribution of authorship.

Of course, no guarantee exists that this analysis will be applied to computer output. Courts might simply decide that machines are incapable of creativity or that Congress did not intend the Copyright Act to apply to nonhumans. The latter argument is easily turned around: The statute does not explicitly require human authorship either. Although the text speaks of necessary characteristics for a work to qualify (eligible category of expression, tangible format, and originality), it is silent about the characteristics of those who produce such works.

Whether creativity can or should be attributed to a computer is a much more philosophical issue. If this normative question is to be approached from a perspective short of the metaphysical, analysis should focus on policy: Is computer copyright a socially desirable idea? The protection afforded by copyright law encourages investment of time, labor, and

---

[18]Note that a similar question might someday be raised in the patent arena by sophisticated computer-aided design programs that contribute to the design of inventions. However, because the standard of inventiveness set forth in the patent laws is far more demanding than the originality necessary for copyright protection, the likelihood of a court recognizing the contribution of a computer program is proportionately more remote.

[19]Nimmer, M. 1987. *The Law of Copyright,* section 1.08[C][1]. New York: Matthew Bender.

[20]L. Batlin & Sons, Inc. v. Snyder, 536 F.2d 486, 487 (2d Cir. 1976), quoting Alfred Bell & Co. v. Catalda Fine Arts, Inc., 191 F.2d 99, 103 (2d Cir. 1951). The case concerned a human author, and the court's actual words were "his own."

capital in certain forms of expression. Although psychological hesitance to recognize computers as authors might furnish the basis for the denial of copyright to computer-generated works, the effects of such a decision will be felt in terms of incentive. After all, the benefits of copyright flow exclusively to the program's author rather than the obedient machine. Any decision about computer copyright should be viewed as an allocation of financial incentive to those who stand to profit from the law's protection—the program authors and users whose combined efforts produce a finished output.

Let us assume that courts take the plunge and recognize computer authorship. How should ownership rights in computer output be apportioned between the user and the program owner? The short answer is to let them decide for themselves. In a perfectly efficient market, rational economic actors are supposed to arrive at a distribution that reflects the respective values of each party's contribution. The short response to this argument is that some default standard must exist in case the parties forget or for some reason elect not to settle the issue by contract. Furthermore, differences in bargaining power that exist in the real world might obstruct the formation of economically efficient allocations; some approach to measuring "reasonable" apportionment is necessary if only to determine whether a given contract is unconscionable (and hence unenforceable).

Clearly, courts must follow some sort of presumption; but cogent arguments can be made for just about any position and attempts to define a standard will undoubtedly produce heated debate. One view would hold that all claims to computer output rightfully belong to the program's owner, leaving the user with no more than the rights possessed in the parent software. These rights will most probably take the form of a non-exclusive license that permits use but not resale or profit from reuse. A line of support for this sentiment comes from the protection already accorded to derivative works. If output is viewed as a derivative of the creative software, the owner's original copyright will be broad enough to encompass it. The persuasiveness of this reasoning, however, depends on the parent program's mode of operation. By statutory definition, a derivative work must be "based upon" a preexisting work; hence, it must bear a substantial resemblance to its source. Programs that select solutions from a fixed array of preloaded (and presumably copyrighted) templates stand a much better chance of producing derivative output than those which formulate solutions from scratch; the former more obviously give up a "piece" of themselves to yield a basis for comparison. Another rationale in favor of the parent program's owner is that fragmented ownership rights could result in considerable interference with the owner's ability to license his or her work: A potential infringement lawsuit would arise each time the parent program produced a work substantially similar to one generated for another user.[21]

An opposite approach might insist on according full rights in program output to the user. Licensing of the parent software might be compared to the retention of an employee by the licensee, its price representing a lump-sum payment for unlimited future services. Section 201(b) of the 1976 Act provides, "In the case of a work made for hire, the employer or other

---

[21]An analogous issue arises when an author assigns to a publisher the copyright to the author's manuscript. Should the author then produce a substantially similar work for another audience, the publisher can sue for copyright infringement.

person for whom the work was prepared is considered the author for purposes of this title.'' Alternatively, one might draw an analogy to cases that have arisen in the context of video-games. Despite the fact that players can create a unique series of audiovisual images through their operation of a videogame, courts have refused to consider players the authors of such images because the number and character of all potential displays are ultimately dictated by the game's software.[22]

The position most consistent with the fundamental objective of copyright law—the promotion and protection of authorship— endeavors to apportion ownership according to substantive contribution. Depriving computers of rights in output is equivalent to viewing the program author's contribution as too remote to warrant reward. Approached technically, it seems anomalous to lump all computer software into the inert category of word processors and calculators. Approached functionally, if the success of copyright law can be validly measured by the number of works actually created, it is difficult to see why exclusively favoring either programmer or user would achieve greater overall production of authored output.

Although perhaps noble in purpose, apportioning copyright also demands the most penetrating analysis: How might one begin to identify the substantive elements of authorship, much less quantify the respective donations of two possible authors? Plainly, a rule allocating full ownership either to the program owner or the user would prove far simpler to apply.

Although admitting that difficulty and ambiguity are to some extent unavoidable in determining respective degrees of authorship, a principled basis for analysis does seem to exist. Its crux lies in the idea-expression dichotomy.

Future CAD/CAM or CASE systems will undoubtedly be so advanced that they require from the user only a general sketch of the problem, independently furnishing all levels of the necessary engineering support. Today's highly interactive systems, however, require the user to supply ingredients of the design process to varying degrees. For example, typical CASE systems query the user for a basic algorithmic structure, parameters, and sometimes even labels. The question of authorship contribution requires an understanding of the relevant engineering discipline in order to separate the problem-specification phase, which involves the interplay of ideas, from the solution or design phase that actually results in the production of a tangible, copyrightable work.

Problem specification includes a complete description of the task and extends to the intrinsic structure of the proposed solution. In a world without computers, neither a human engineer nor the engineer's client could claim any rights to such abstract conceptions under copyright law. Copyright protection begins to attach when the hypothesized approach is reduced to a form sufficiently practical that it can be embodied in a tangible work. To return to the CASE example, the art of computer programming can be broken down into several more or less sequential steps: (1) problem identification, (2) algorithmic formulation (if the problem is mathematic in nature) and basic program description, (3) flowcharting and development of a logic structure, (4) arrangement of subroutines and program modules, (5) struc-

---

[22]See, e.g., Midway Manufacturing Co. v. Artic International, 704 F.2d 1009 (7th Cir. 1983), cert. denied, 464 U.S. 823.

turing of data components, and (6) coding. Of these steps, the first two most clearly involve ideas; the remaining are closely tied to the source code product, expressing individual design choices of the programmer, and should be protectible.[23]

Once protectible elements of the engineering process have been identified, a weighted value must be assigned to each stage and the respective contributions of user and program quantified. Both come down to a difficult matter of scientific and economic judgment. The proportionate value of an accomplishment within a particular defined category in relation to the overall project would best be measured by the current degree of technical difficulty inherent in this category. That is, a court might utilize expert testimony to help appraise the relative amount and worth of equivalent human labor currently necessary to accomplish each subtask protectible under copyright law. A court might assess the source of accomplishments within a category through inspection of the parent program's input and output, evaluation of its capabilities, and comparison of the final product to any templates embedded in the parent's structure.

Not an easy task, to be sure, but courts assess damages in complex and factually ambiguous circumstances all the time. As the Supreme Court once put it, "[C]ases will often occur in which it is evident that large damages have resulted, but where no reliable data or element of certainty can be found by which to measure the amount. . . . To deny the injured party the right to recover any actual damages in such cases, because they are of a nature which cannot be thus certainly measured, would enable parties to profit by, and speculate upon, their own wrongs. . . . Such is not, and cannot be, the law[.]"[24]

PATENT

Because the patent system was created to offer inventors protection for their useful ideas, one might naturally suppose that it picks up where copyright protection leaves off. Such is by no means the case, however, for two different reasons.

First, the character of protection afforded by a patent and the means of obtaining it differ drastically from the simple registration procedure and the longevity of copyright. Acquiring a patent takes a great deal of time: Two to five years can elapse between the filing of an application with the Patent and Trademark Office (PTO) and the date the patent is finally issued. Software can become obsolete during this long wait, and the Patent Act (Title 35 of the U.S. Code) provides the applicant with no right to exclude practice of an invention by others in the interim. The lifespan of patent protection is also relatively short: The maximum

---

[23]The House Report accompanying the 1976 Act stated that "the expression adopted by the programmer is the copyrightable element in a computer program. . . . [T]he actual processes or methods embodied in the program are not within the scope of copyright law." H.R. Rep. No. 1476, 94th Cong., 2d Sess. 51, 57, reprinted in 1976 U.S. Code Cong. & Ad. News 5659, 5670. The Whelan and DCA cases, however, indicate that copying the organization and structure of a program might amount to infringement even if no large segments of code are actually reproduced.

[24]Story Parchment Co. v. Paterson Co., 282 U.S. 555, 564 (1931).

period is 17 years. In contrast, for works created on or after 1 January 1978, a copyright extends over the entire life of the author plus 50 years. Finally, patents are expensive: PTO application and maintenance fees over the life of a patent amount to over $3000, and the legal services ordinarily required for successful prosecution can cost tens of thousands of dollars. However, the scope of protection once achieved is formidable: A patent owner possesses the right to exclude others from using, making, or selling the invention, whereas copyright protection extends only to the exclusive right to copy and trade secret protection to an exclusive right to use.

Second, the Patent Act does not protect ideas by themselves. One reason for this important limitation is embodied in the requirement of utility. The law will grant an inventor a virtual monopoly over his or her creation only if the public stands to receive some corresponding benefit from the invention's usefulness. An idea for a potentially useful article or process has no utility of its own; the Act does not recognize value until this precursor is reduced to a form of actual usability. Hence, disembodied figments of cognition are no safer under patent law than copyright law.

In addition to utility, the Patent Act specifies three further criteria of acceptability for protection under its terms: The invention must (1) fall within the subject matter of the Act's authority, and meet the interrelated tests of (2) novelty and (3) nonobviousness. Most unsuccessful software applications have been rejected for failure to state statutory subject matter.

Patent Law: The Subject Matter Test

Section 101 defines permissible subject matter to include any new and useful process, machine, manufacture, or composition of matter, or any new and useful improvement thereof. In a series of three opinions delivered over the course of a decade, the Supreme Court has defined the parameters of patent protection for computer software based on its interpretation of this section. In Gottschalk v. Benson,[25] the Court first announced the principle that a computer program whose function is to solve a mathematical algorithm fails under section 101. Subsequent opinions in Parker v. Flook[26] and Diamond v. Diehr[27] qualified the ban on algorithmic programs to permit patenting of larger processes that utilize a mathematical algorithm as part of their operation. In Diehr, the invention was an integrated system for curing synthetic rubber in a mold with heat. Proper cure times were calculated according to an equation discovered by the Swedish scientist Svante Arrhenius. Five out of nine justices viewed the overall process as patentable despite the presence of mathematics because once arrived at, cure times were translated directly into the mechanical control of the press. Viewing the overall invention, the majority explained, "[A] claim drawn to subject matter otherwise statutory does not become nonstatutory simply because it uses a mathematical formula."

This reasoning does not mean, however, that recharacterizing the software process as a hardware apparatus merely because a computer is involved will serve to circumvent the

---

[25] 409 U.S. 63 (1972).
[26] 437 U.S. 584 (1978).
[27] 450 U.S. 175 (1981).

Court's rule. The larger apparatus must perform some independent function beyond the generation of solutions.[28] Lower courts—primarily the Court of Customs and Patent Appeals (CCPA), recently renamed the Court of Appeals for the Federal Circuit—have consistently applied the same criteria to all inventions regardless of the form stated on the application.

In one well-known case, for example, the inventor of a computerized sales organizational model attempted to patent the entire system as a unified package, hoping to avoid examination of the mathematically based software. The Court saw through this strategy and rejected the application under section 101, stating, "Labels are not determinative in section 101 inquiries 'because the form of the claim is often an exercise in drafting.' "[29]

The Supreme Court's refusal to permit patenting of mathematical algorithms is based on a deeper principle of patent law that apart from the criterion of utility, presents a further barrier to the patenting of ideas. In a famous controversy that occurred over a century ago, Samuel Morse applied for a patent on all types of communication utilizing electromagnetic transmission. The Supreme Court rejected his application.[30] It recognized that permitting a single individual to obtain control over an entire phenomenon of nature would constrict, rather than promote, the progress of science. Even if it possesses inherent utility, an idea can simply cover too broad a swath of potential technology. The Court considered this danger sufficiently great to justify a strict prohibition: Ideas themselves are simply never patentable subject matter.

The effort to define a critical level of scientific basicness has confounded courts ever since. The Benson majority seized on the mathematical algorithm as a means of identifying this threshold for computer software, in effect holding mathematical expressions and algorithmic representations to be equivalent to scientific principles and ideas. The Court further included "mental processes" and "abstract intellectual concepts" in its lexicon of disfavored notions, stating that "they are the basic tools of scientific and technical work."

The Supreme Court's rules can be summarized as follows: (1) If a computer program does not contain a mathematical algorithm or embody a mental process or abstract intellectual concept, there is no subject matter bar under section 101. (2) If one of these elements is discovered, the software is presumptively unpatentable; however, its incorporation into an otherwise independently patentable process or apparatus does not destroy the latter's patentability. (3) In making the second determination, a court must look to the substance, rather than the form, of the application.

Few cases reach the Supreme Court. Most patent controversies are instead resolved by internal PTO review and appeal processes or in a lower federal court. Although the Supreme

---

[28]For example, in In re Bradley, 600 F.2d 807 (CCPA 1979), the court reversed the Patent and Trademark Office's rejection under section 101 of a firmware system designed to facilitate internal data transfers between the central processing unit and the main memory. It reasoned that the applicant did not claim information embodied in the firmware or the firmware itself but rather a combination of dedicated hardware elements assembled to perform a specific task.

[29]In re Maucorps, 609 F.2d 481, 485 (CCPA 1979), quoting In re Johnson, 589 F.2d 1070, 1077 (CCPA 1978).

[30]O'Reilly v. Morse, 56 U.S. 62 (1863).

Court might write the rules, the manner in which PTO and the courts share oversight of the patent system can produce consequences of its own.

When an inventor submits a patent application, it is reviewed by PTO examiners according to the current law, as set forth in the patent statutes and cases interpreting these statutes. Should PTO issue a final decision denying a patent, an applicant willing to bear the time and expense can seek further review in the Federal Circuit. The numerous decisions of this federal tribunal and its predecessor enrich the legal framework in which applications are judged and give practical meaning to the Supreme Court's broad edicts. If the court's view of the law is more expansive than that of PTO, it will reverse PTO and grant the inventor a patent; if not, it will affirm. It is only after all these review levels have been exhausted that the applicant can petition for a hearing before the Supreme Court.

Denial of the application is not the only way in which validity of a patent can be tested in federal court. A party who has been sued for infringement might raise invalidity of the patent as a defense. Alternatively, someone who is nervous about a possible infringement lawsuit can commence a declaratory judgment action to test the patent's effectiveness before trouble begins. In these circumstances, a court's discretion is limited; judges are not as free to erase patents already granted by PTO as they are to approve applications that PTO has denied. The Patent Act presumes a patent to be valid and casts the burden of showing otherwise on the party so asserting.[31] Nonetheless, applicants who have achieved success with PTO must live with the knowledge that their rights are not immune from challenge. Judges will ultimately have the last word if called on to act. Differing views held by PTO and the courts can result in an uncertain future for patent holders, a future that might well be determined by the fortuity of a lawsuit.[32]

To appreciate the ways in which this legal and regulatory environment can affect the patentability of AI systems, consider the recent series of applications prosecuted by Teknowledge Inc. Teknowledge successfully obtained patents for its computer-integrated manufacturing (CIM) expert system and two expert system-development packages. PTO considered all three programs to be patentable subject matter. Would a court agree? Maybe, maybe not. Will the issue ever come before a court? Who knows.

If a court were to someday evaluate the validity of any of the Teknowledge patents, it would first have to determine whether the program satisfies the section 101 criteria. As an example, the CIM system assists in the manufacture or assembly of complex modular products by generating a design configuration that is consistent with customer needs as well as marketing and engineering constraints. The system is flexible, permitting alteration of the constraints to accommodate product updates or modifications. Does this software state a

---

[31]35 U.S.C. section 282.

[32]To illustrate the extent to which the views of the Patent and Trademark Office (PTO) can diverge from those of the courts, the PTO recently granted a patent on what is essentially a computer-implemented mathematical algorithm—precisely what the Supreme Court has unambiguously forbidden. Patent No. 4,646,256, granted on 24 February 1987, sets forth a "special purpose computer" and computational method for performing N-Length, real-number discrete transforms. No postsolution activity is undertaken by the invention on its purely numeric output.

mathematical algorithm? The answer depends on one's definition. If an algorithm is viewed as a set of procedures performed on a given input to produce a desired output, then no computer program is safe: All operations performed by digital technology ultimately reduce to manipulations of numeric values, and all goal-directed tasks can be characterized as algorithmic. This interpretation, which had once been urged by PTO, was explicitly rejected by the Supreme Court in Diehr. Instead, the Court described the forbidden fruit as "a procedure for solving a given type of mathematical problem . . . or [a] mathematical formula." By drawing this relatively narrow definition, the Court undoubtedly believed itself making life easier for patent-seeking programmers while preventing monopolies on "laws of nature." Regrettably, its choice of words seems too ambiguous to have accomplished either aim. Numbers are simply too ubiquitous in computer science. With the exception of software whose function is limited to rearrangement of character strings, virtually all computer applications involve some degree of quantitative analysis. Does mathematics mean anything involving information that is represented numerically, or does Diehr forbid patenting only of pure methods of calculation or fundamental scientific relationships expressed as mathematic equations?

The latter might be the direction taken by the Federal Circuit[33] and would probably protect CIM from disqualification as a mathematical algorithm. One perhaps might view the transformation of customer input data into a manufacturing blueprint through the application of definitions and constraints as mathematical, that is, if logic operations are to be included under this heading along with numeric calculations. But Teknowledge patented more than a sorting device. The key feature of the CIM system is its transparent representation of control knowledge. Users can vary more than just input values; the constraints themselves can be altered to accommodate entirely different product hierarchies or even knowledge domains. The essence of Teknowledge's invention, therefore, is not the solution to a particular problem but a means of formulating knowledge-based solutions to an entire class of problems. If anything, CIM is a creator of algorithms; mathematic processing is a result rather than the objective.

The remaining section 101 hurdle, far more threatening to the AI community in general and to CIM in particular, is the Court's antipathy toward "mental processes." The logical focus of a test based on cognition resides in the capability of the human brain. Quite ironically, then, the more sophisticated the system—that is, the more it captures attributes previously thought accessible only to human cognitive processes—the more the mental process exclusion appears satisfied.

---

[33] See, e.g., In re Pardo, 684 F.2d 912, 915 (CCPA 1982) ("It would be unnecessarily detrimental to our patent system to deny inventors patent protection on the sole ground that their contribution could be broadly termed an 'algorithm' "); In re Meyer, 688 F.2d 789, 795 (CCPA 1982) ("The presence of a mathematical algorithm or formula in a claim is merely an indication that a scientific principle, law of nature, idea or mental process may be the subject matter claimed and, thus, justify a rejection of that claim under 35 U.S.C. section 101; but the presence of a mathematical algorithm or formula is only a signpost for further analysis").

Two relatively recent cases illustrate the danger. CCPA sanctioned as statutory subject matter a software system designed to perform natural language translation in In re Toma.[34] The court took pains to assert that no thought processes were involved in the particular method of translation, which involved simple data manipulation, thereby implying that the form of reasoning employed by the program might hold sway. Even this unfortunately restrictive view seems to have been discarded in In re Meyer,[35] which concerned a forerunner of current-day expert systems. In this case, the applicant's program was designed to accumulate and analyze the results of a series of diagnostic tests in order to narrow the possible sources of a problem. Although the system appears to have been designed for general application, the operational example selected by the applicant was that of a neurologist employing the system to coordinate the results of various physical tests in aid of medical diagnosis. The court rejected the application under section 101. It made no attempt to discern whether the applicant's process followed reasoning patterns similar to those which might be employed by a human neurologist, holding simply that transfer of a cognitive task to computer control is sufficient to render the software unpatentable.

Does CIM implicate a mental process? Teknowledge was careful in its patent application to avoid any intimation that CIM mimics a human intellect. The description of the invention is purely functional:

> ... a hierarchical knowledge base comprising a decomposition of a set of elements into subsets over a plurality of hierarchical levels, a plurality of respective predefined functions or conditions of the elements within the subsets at a plurality of the hierarchical levels, and a predefined set of operations to perform on a user-defined set of elements responsive to the knowledge base.[36]

If courts treat the mental process exclusion as a literal mandate to reject patent applications whenever such processes are detected, AI practitioners will face increasingly hostile treatment as their work grows more successful. Such a result directly contradicts the policy of a system that exists to promote scientific advance. What arguments might be made against such an ironic result? The most direct rebuttal would confront the wisdom of adopting the mathematical algorithm as a surrogate for ideas. Although abandoning this rule might seem desirable as a pure matter of policy, such an approach demands an uphill fight against the practical obstacle of established precedent. A second, less ambitious crusade would attempt to limit the range of propositions included under the disfavored term. Effective advocacy secured rejection of the PTO's original definition of mathematical algorithms, which was expansive enough to encompass every data processing operation simply because digital computers function by manipulating binary-coded numerals,[37] in favor of the narrower view stated earlier. The concept of mental processes might await similar judicial narrowing.

---

[34]575 F.2d 872 (CCPA 1978).

[35]688 F.2d 789 (CCPA 1982).

[36]Patent No. 4,591,983 at 3.

[37]Diamond v. Diehr, 450 U.S. 175, 186 (1981).

With hope, courts will be persuaded that a patent covering the computational repetition of a thought process does not imply exclusive control over the thought process itself. A cognitive task is not the same as a scientific principle. The law of gravity, to take one example, is self-operative; it cannot be improved or replicated on a machine. The mere fact that the manifold abilities of the human brain were harnessed long before computer implementation became feasible should not operate as a bar to protecting the most valuable computer software systems.

Patent Law: Novelty and Nonobviousness

Section 101 defines the universe of patentable subject matter. Determining whether a patent ought to cover a particular invention is the province of two further statutory tests, those of novelty and nonobviousness. The novelty requirement is stated categorically in section 102, which specifies only that the invention must somehow differ from methods and objects already in the prior art. Section 103, cast in the form of a negative proscription rather than an affirmative requirement, articulates the increment of advance over existing subject matter necessary to justify patent protection:

> A patent may not be obtained if the differences between the subject matter sought to be patented and the prior art are such that the subject matter as a whole would have been obvious at the time the invention was made to a person having ordinary skill in the art to which said subject matter pertains.

In Dann v. Johnson,[38] the Supreme Court was presented with a data processing system capable of providing bank depositors with a detailed periodic statement, segregating transactions into different categories selected by the customer. Noting that a depositor could achieve the same result by maintaining a series of separate accounts, the Court concluded that the combination of widespread use of computers in the banking industry and the existence of a previously issued patent involving similar functions rendered the claim obvious. The message of Johnson is that programs which simply computerize a known process on existing machines through familiar techniques are too unremarkable to deserve patent protection.

Few existing computer programs could claim credit to a previously unknown process because the vast bulk of programming efforts are directed at automating mundane tasks. It would be difficult to argue, for example, that current bookkeeping software has actually enhanced the current state of the art in the field of accounting. AI programs that capture high-level cognitive procedures might present a more compelling case. If the reasoning process is not easily explained or reproduced without the aid of AI techniques, the process, although familiar, might not be considered "known."

Distinguishing new machines from old ones used in new ways presents the classic patent law question of what constitutes inventive difference. The analysis ultimately reduces to an assessment of utility—whether the new difference makes a difference—but the difficulty of drawing such subtle distinctions has led to a highly technical set of substantive criteria. Their

---

[38] 425 U.S. 219 (1975).

enumeration is beyond the scope of this article, and it seems safe to conclude only that the law is unsettled and guiding principles few.

Some intellectual activities that form the basis of AI research might, through this research, become well enough understood to be "known." At the same time, few pure software systems require special hardware modifications for their execution. Until AI programs based on known mental processes become so superior to their human counterparts as to be capable of independently adding to the state of knowledge (and thus furthering the art) in a given domain, the most likely route to patentability lies in convincing PTO and the courts that the software represents an advance to the art of computer programming. The touchstone of nonobviousness is innovation. Integrated systems that combine special-purpose hardware devices with control software, such as computer-based vision or robotics applications, stand the best chance of patentability as independent apparatus. A "new" machine is most clearly present (and the rationale of Johnson least applicable) when hardware and software are expressly designed for the cooperative execution of a single task.

TRADE SECRETS

The patent and copyright laws promulgate disclosure systems. Protection is bestowed as a means of encouraging the free exchange of ideas and information. Trade secret law performs quite the opposite function: It assists active efforts to maintain confidentiality. The primary responsibility for creating and enforcing a scheme to restrict the flow of proprietary information lies with the party seeking protection; the law operates only as a second line of defense.

The purpose of trade secret law is to maintain proper standards of commercial ethics rather than to protect the objects of secrecy. Parties entering into confidential business relationships must remain faithful to their promises of nondisclosure. Outsiders are prohibited from purloining the efforts of businesses to attain competitive advantage, particularly when valuable resources have been expended in doing so.

The law of trade secrets protects against improper disclosure or wrongful appropriation by affording an aggrieved party the opportunity to sue for a prohibitory injunction (which prevents the defendant from making use of the secret) or monetary damages. Injunctions are commonly issued for at least the length of time that would be required to develop the device or process without access to the trade secret (that is, the reverse engineering period), and possibly longer if the defendant's conduct is considered particularly scurrilous.[39]

---

[39] See, e.g., Analogic Corp. v. Data Translation, Inc., 371 Mass. 643, 649 (1976), in which the Massachusetts Supreme Judicial Court stated, "The plaintiff is entitled to have its trade secrets protected at least until others in the trade are likely, through legitimate business procedures, to have become aware of these secrets. And even then the defendants should not be permitted a competitive advantage from their avoidance of the normal costs of invention and duplication. Where the defendants have saved substantial expense by improperly using confidential information in creating their product, the ultimate cessation of an injunctive order might well be conditioned on their payment of an appropriate sum to the plaintiff."

The scope of trade secret law is shaped both by its functional orientation and its source of enactment. Trade secret protection is a creature of state law. Unlike the federal Copyright and Patent Acts, whose terms are national, the law of trade secrecy can vary from state to state. One widely followed statement defines its coverage as applying to information, including a formula, pattern, compilation, program, device, method, technique, or process, that derives independent economic value, actual or potential, from not being generally known to, and not being readily ascertainable by proper means by, other persons who can obtain economic value from its disclosure or use.[40] The focus of trade secret law on commercial conduct, rather than intrinsic properties of the secret itself, results in a flexible standard of acceptable subject matter. Computer software has been held protectible when sufficient originality exists to produce a competitive advantage.[41]

The boundaries of protection in a given instance are set by the interplay between precautions taken to prevent disclosure and the manner in which information is obtained without authorization. Simply put, trade secret law protects nonpublic knowledge. If the secret is revealed indiscriminately, either deliberately or through failure to take reasonable preventive steps, protection disappears. Minor leakage, however, only weakens protection: If the trade secret is procured by wrongful means, the defendant might still be held liable. No amount of precaution, however, can protect a secret from legitimate reverse engineering.

Businesses have made use of a number of devices and procedures to protect trade secrets. The most obvious concern of software developers is misappropriation by a program licensee, but trade secrets can also be lost to employees, partners, joint venturers, and competitors who resort to industrial espionage. The following measures have proven effective in protecting trade secrets.

RESTRICTIVE LICENSES WITH USERS. The most reliable licenses are those which can be negotiated directly with the licensee. Licenses attached to mass-produced software that reaches the user through the marketplace are not only difficult to enforce as a practical matter but might also lack legal standing.[42]

NOTICE PROVISIONS. Broad dissemination of material that embodies trade secrets is not necessarily fatal to protection. If recipients are put on notice that the resources are being shared on a confidential basis, unauthorized use or disclosure can be stopped when discovered. Clear proprietary legends and confidentiality restrictions affixed to documents or made to appear on program output generally provide the requisite notice.

---

[40] *Uniform Trade Secrets Act,* section 1(4).

[41] See, e.g., Telex v. IBM, 367 F.Supp. 258, 323 (N.D. Okla. 1973), affirmed on trade secret issue, 510 F.2d 894 (10th Cir. 1975), cert. dismissed, 423 U.S. 802 (1975).

[42] Illinois and Louisiana recently enacted statutes validating "shrink-wrap" licenses. The Louisiana version, however, was promptly struck down by a federal court, which viewed it as an impermissible intrusion into the territory covered by the Copyright Act. Vault Corp. v. Quaid Software Limited, 655 F.Supp. 750 (E.D. La. 1987). The decision has been appealed, but the view of most commentators appears similarly negative. See Harris, A Market-Oriented Approach to the Use of Trade Secrets or Copyright Protection (or Both?) for Software, 25 Jurimetrics J. 147, 154–56 (1985).

NONDISCLOSURE AGREEMENTS. Many courts consider a duty not to breach the employer's confidences to be an implied condition of any employment relationship. Nevertheless, an express written agreement often proves useful. Not only will explicit language eliminate any ambiguity about what information is to be kept confidential, but it can also create rights against the pilferage of knowledge that falls short of being a trade secret.

Although software has been held protectible as a trade secret, certain conceptual difficulties can impede the law's applicability to AI systems. If a computer program's function is to reproduce processes that routinely go on in the minds of human beings, perhaps there is no secret to protect. This view might appear particularly inviting in the case of expert systems. Courts might be tempted to distinguish between shallow-level and deep-level systems as a means of identifying programs that contain novel or unfamiliar elements. A shallow expert system is one that contains only empirical knowledge, associating various input states directly with actions. Shallow systems draw their capability directly from the experience of human experts as revealed by knowledge engineering. In contrast, deep systems represent concepts at a basic causal level and base conclusions on some theoretical model of the underlying discipline.[43] Such special programming features as a self-updating ability or the capacity for adaptation might also create the impression that a system rises above the sources tapped for expertise.

Militating against this approach based on appearances is the fact that a working knowledge base requires labor and skill to produce and secures an undoubted competitive advantage. Specialized programming architectures might also prove necessary for efficient operation. Courts that have approved of trade secret protection for computer software have focused less on program attributes or innovation than commercial usefulness and feasibility.[44] For many applications (particularly when operational flexibility is not critical), shallow systems, whose reduced complexity typically results in lower startup costs, are considered more suitable than deep systems. On an abstract plane, the patent law notion that mental processes can be familiar without being intrinsically understood also operates in favor of protection.

From a practical standpoint, protection through trade secrecy is well suited to AI system development. AI software is typically produced for a single user or a narrow class of users, permitting the issuance of licenses on an individualized basis. Low sales volume also permits realistic enforcement: Violations are relatively easy to discover and can be traced to a particular user. The high degree of program sophistication further enhances protection by making permissible reverse engineering (or illegitimate decompilation) more difficult to accomplish. Perhaps most importantly, the haphazard and largely uncertain scope of federal protection under the copyright and patent laws can leave AI researchers without any realistic alternative.

---

[43] The distinction is explained and examples are given in Hart Directions for AI in the Eighties, Sigart Newsletter #79 (1982), at 11.

[44] See, e.g., Structural Dynamic Research Corp. v. Engineering Mechanics Research Corp., 401 F. Supp. 1102, 1117 (E.D. Mich. 1975) ("An overwhelming majority of authorities in the field do not recognize novelty and uniqueness as eligibility requirements for trade secret protection").

In an ideal world, these two federal systems would serve as complementary protection alternatives—copyright for unique forms of program expression and patent for inventive problem-solving methodologies. Currently, the jury remains out as to copyright, and courts have not displayed a great deal of enthusiasm toward software patents.

This state of affairs is most unfortunate. Persistent reliance on the law of trade secrets might well prove detrimental to the AI industry over the long run. In many emerging areas of AI technology, development proceeds at the level of basic research. The sharing of ideas is necessary if incremental progress is to be made without needless duplication of effort. This problem is far smaller for developers of today's commercially distributed software. Because programming is simpler and application techniques widely known, maintaining secrecy of source code might not impede technological advance. Function seems sufficiently related to form that even superficial knowledge of a program's capabilities will avoid much duplicative effort. In contrast, entirely new paradigms and system architectures might be necessary to achieve even modest AI goals. Little chance seems to exist of deducing models of cognitive processing from program descriptions or even hands-on operation. Comparable efforts will likely prove too few and the general state of knowledge too undeveloped for meaningful insights to be drawn, cooling the pace of research unnecessarily.

What AI Practitioners Should Know about the Law (Part 2)

Steven J. Frank

Originally published in *AI Magazine,* 9, Number 2, 109–114. Copyright (c) 1988, American Association for Artificial Intelligence. Reprinted by permission of American Association for Artificial Intelligence and Steven J. Frank.

Although recent computer-related disputes have involved a variety of legal issues—breach of contract specifications, misrepresentation of performance capability, and outright fraud, to name a few—it is the threat of tort liability that continues to strike the greatest fear in the heart of mighty industrialist and struggling start-up alike.

Once inside the courtroom, what role can the computer assume in its own defense or in the service of some other litigant? The law of evidence, developed to govern the testimony of human witnesses, must continually evolve to accommodate new, nonhuman sources of information. At the same time, developers of intelligent computer systems will have to achieve a great deal of communicative power before their machines will be given a day in court. These two topics—tort liability, and the computer as witness—are the focus of Part 2.

TORT LIABILITY

The system of tort compensation exists to provide victims of injury—physical, economic, or emotional—with the means to seek redress in the form of monetary damages. The purpose of the damage award is to "make the plaintiff whole" by compensating for all losses flowing from the defendant's wrongful act. Although this concept seems straightforward, damage awards have been known to vary enormously, even for identical injuries. The host of subjective factors that appear in the calculus of compensation precludes accurate forecasts in most cases, leading some defendants to financial ruin and others to surprised relief. However, injury alone does not guarantee recovery. Rules of tort liability mediate between the victim's need for recompense and the defendant's right to remain free from arbitrarily imposed obligation.

Although sensational cases involving large recoveries tend to generate the greatest alarm, the magnitude of damages in a particular case is actually far less important than the availability of any damages in similar cases. Potential tort defendants are primarily interested in their overall liability exposure, as determined by the evolving structure of case precedent. For software developers, expenditures for debugging, design safety analysis, and quality control assurance are necessarily affected by the extent of perceived vulnerability to tort actions.

More so than in any other legal field, the boundaries separating human from machine will be forced into focus by questions of tort liability. In addition to compensation, another function of tort law is to project proper standards of care in the conduct of activities that might cause harm. When the agent of injury is a tangible device or product, attention is currently directed toward three sets of possible culprits: manufacturers (Was the product designed or manufactured defectively?), sellers (Was the product sold in a defective condition?), and purchasers (Was the product used improperly?). Absent from the lineup is the injury-producing item itself, whose existence is relevant only insofar as it pertains to the conduct of human beings. As "devices" come to include electronic systems capable of judgment and behavior, they too will become objects of direct inquiry. Naturally, financial responsibility will ultimately rest with a human being or a corporation possessing a bank account; but the standards by which humans and machines are judged will begin to merge as the tasks they perform grow similar.

The question of whether liability accrues in a given instance invariably reduces to the application of two legal variables: the standard of care expected of the defendant and the requirement that a causal link exist between the defendant's substandard conduct and the plaintiff's injury. The existence of a valid tort cause of action means that someone has suffered loss. This much is beyond change. The function of the liability standard is to allocate loss among all parties involved based on considerations of fairness, efficiency, and accepted behavioral norms. The terms of the standard prescribe the level of vigilance expected of individuals who conduct a particular type of activity. Although variations exist, most formulations derive from the fault-based concept of negligence: If the defendant failed to act in the manner of a reasonably prudent person under all circumstances, the loss falls on him or her. A special relationship between plaintiff and defendant or the performance of an unusual activity can prompt a court to adjust the standard. Innkeepers, for example, have been held liable to guests for the "slightest negligence" because of the high degree of trust placed in their hands. Certain activities have been identified as so inherently dangerous or unfamiliar that no degree of care can adequately prevent mishap. For these "strict liability" activities, the loss falls on the defendant, regardless of fault, as a cost of doing business.

This choice of liability standard calls for a decision based on public policy. Although through less obvious means, the parameters of causation are ultimately shaped by similar considerations. A scientific view of deterministic causality provides only a starting point for the legal notion of causation. Judges have recognized that too many events are logically interrelated for liability to rest solely on logic. Fairness to defendants requires that a line be drawn at some level of remoteness, and the location of this line reflects a policy-oriented value judgment. Liberal tests of causation shift a greater amount of loss toward tort defendants by including more distant effects of liability-producing conduct within the range of potential recovery. These tests generally focus on the existence of a chain of events, such that causation is based on proof of an unbroken progression of occurrences; the outer limits of connectedness are typically bounded only by the reluctance to impose liability for the extremely unpredictable. Restrictive tests of causation focus directly on the defendant's ability to foresee the possible harm arising from particular actions and reverse the shift in favor of the plaintiffs.

Returning to liability issues, the rule applied to parties engaged in commercial trade depends heavily on what is being sold. Providers of services have traditionally been held to a negligence standard based on reasonably prudent practice within a given area of specialization. In contrast, sellers and manufacturers of tangible commodities face strict liability for injuries to individual consumers caused by defects in their wares. The reason for the distinction does not lie in any perceived disparity of associated danger, but rather in the fact that product sellers are viewed as economically better able to spread a loss over a large number of users through price adjustments.

Courts have had difficulty fitting computer programs into this bifurcated world of products and services. Software can be supplied in a variety of forms, some more tangible than others. Programmers might write software for mass distribution, tailor an established package to the needs of a particular user, or design from scratch a custom system for an individual client. Although no court has yet faced this issue in the precise context of tort liability, most commentators (including this writer) believe that characterization as product or service is most properly determined by the supplier's degree of involvement with the customer. Greater availability of technical assistance and support make the overall transaction appear more like a service.

Because implementation of the high-level tasks performed by commercial AI software requires extensive immersion in the field of application, initial development contracts call most clearly for treatment as service arrangements. If the finished program proves suitable for an entire class of users, however, subsequent sales might appear to involve a product. Ambiguity is inevitable where the uncertain intrinsic character of software diverts attention to its mode of supply for purposes of tort liability.

The question of causation raises a different set of issues— those chiefly related to the manner in which the computer program actually makes contact with the end user. The factors that evoke a clear liability rule for mass-marketed software likewise provide the strongest link between defect and injury. Simple sales transactions force the consumer to rely solely on the purchased item for effective performance, and thus, any harm suffered can be traced directly to improper program operation. It seems doubtful, however, that AI programs will reach consumers through such direct market channels any time soon. The simplest current reason is cost: AI software is enormously expensive to produce. A longer-range consideration is the likely reluctance of human experts to relinquish control over the provision of their expertise. Professions shielded by licensure requirements, for example, have shown themselves to be well equipped to defend against unauthorized practice. For the foreseeable future, then, the most likely role for many applied knowledge programs is as an aid to the human expert.

Although perhaps depriving AI developers from access to the consumer market, such restrictions also relieve developers of a great deal of potential liability. The law will not treat an appurtenant factor as a causal agent of injury unless it materially contributes to this injury; yet material contribution is precisely what is prohibited by restrictions on unauthorized practice. For example, if a physician were to attempt to lay blame on a diagnostic expert system for improper treatment, the physician would thereby admit to allowing the computer to perform as a doctor. The price of limiting the practice of a profession to a select group of peers is accepting complete responsibility for professional misjudgment.

Of course, if the source of the physician's error were indeed traceable to the expert system, the physician might sue the software developer to recover the money that must be paid to the injured patient. This possibility leads to the question: How should the law of product liability be applied to the creator of a device whose domain-specific capabilities might match or exceed those of human experts? The first step in any such lawsuit (whether based on strict liability or negligence) is to demonstrate that the product contains a defect. Should defectiveness be inferred from the mere fact of incorrect diagnosis? Human physicians are certainly not judged this harshly; their diagnoses must only be "reasonable." Separating programming errors from legitimate mistakes of judgment falling within professional discretion will indeed prove formidable.

A second, more practical obstacle facing this hypothetical physician is that a strict liability standard would probably not apply, regardless of whether the program is viewed as a product. Courts generally permit strict liability recovery only in actions for physical injury and property damage; economic loss is insufficient to trigger the doctrine. Unlike the hapless patient, the physician has personally suffered only financial impairment. The physician's tort suit, therefore, must be based on negligence. If the software developer has exercised reasonable care in debugging and packaging the product, including some statement warning of the system's limitations, the negligence burden might prove a difficult one to carry. The appropriate level of resources devoted to debugging efforts and the scope of the necessary warning depends on actual reliability and system design. For example, deep expert systems can generally be expected to deliver acceptable results over the entire useful range of the underlying causal model. Courts will undoubtedly expect greater vigilance from developers of shallow systems (or deep systems based on models that are not robust) simply as a consequence of the diminished reliability implied by program design.

To be sure, not all applications of AI techniques involve roles currently occupied by organized professions, nor must computer output actually touch consumers in order to affect their lives. The degree of contact necessary to trigger liability is once again determined by the nature of the commercial relationship. Personal interaction comprises an inherent feature of consultative service transactions, and a causal gap is probably inevitable unless the computer somehow communicates directly with the injured consumer; otherwise, the intervention of human judgment is likely to prove a sufficient superseding event to interrupt the nexus. Sales transactions, in contrast, are characteristically impersonal. The path of causation is likely to be far more direct if the computer's role involves assisting in the fabrication of a product. Any modicum of assistance not filtered through independent human oversight can furnish a link between computer operation and injury caused by defective manufacture. Hence, developers of computer-aided manufacturing (CAM) systems can expect increasing exposure to liability as their software assumes control over a greater portion of the manufacturing process.

Product design occupies a status somewhere between service and manufacture. Although the ultimate goal might be the production of a usable product, the design process involves early-stage development decisions of a far more basic and creative nature than those involved in automating production. The collaboration of computer-aided design programs with human engineers seems likely to persist for a much longer time than might be anticipated for CAM systems, which reduce design to actual practice, maintaining a greater opportunity for events that sever the chain of causation.

Increased trustworthiness inevitably results in heightened liability. As the role played by computers expands from paasive assistant to independent practitioner, and as tasks delegated to computers begin to encompass a greater dimension of injury-producing activity, their owners will find themselves increasingly responsible for mishap traceable to improper operation.

COMPUTERS IN THE COURTROOM

As AI research produces systems capable of real-time communication, computers can be expected to ascend from their present courtroom role as sidelined objects of legal controversy to active participation in the trial process itself. To lawyers, a computer serving as an expert witness offers unique potential advantages when compared to its human counterpart: quicker and more accurate responses to questions, greater capacity for immediately accessible domain-specific knowledge, and complete indifference to the charged atmosphere of a heated trial or the unnerving interrogation of a skilled attorney. For computer scientists, the specialized vocabulary and rules that govern judicial proceedings offer a relatively structured environment for developing knowledge-based systems capable of genuine interaction.

An initial issue confronting the introduction of computer testimony would be veracity: The law demands that witnesses give some assurance of truthfulness. The traditional oath-taking ceremony is no longer an indispensable feature of trial procedure, but all courts require that witnesses provide some form of affirmation backed by the threat of punishment for perjury. Could a machine furnish such an affirmation? No, not at present, because no contrivance yet devised is capable of anything resembling voluntary moral choice. Some human— programmer, user, or the litigant propounding the computer witness—must accept direct responsibility for the truth of testimonial output.

If the oath requirement presents some administrative inconvenience, restrictive rules of evidence stand as a far more formidable obstacle to the witness chair. As they currently stand, these rules bar today's computers from most courtroom affairs. Not only are current systems forbidden to act as witnesses, but their output often cannot even be introduced as substantive evidence. This impasse is created by a much-popularized but highly complex precept of evidentiary doctrine— the hearsay rule.

The rule owes its origin to the unfortunate judicial experience of Sir Walter Raleigh. In 1603, the legendary English adventurer, statesman, and author was accused of plotting to commit treason against King James I and forced to stand trial. The primary evidence introduced against Raleigh was a sworn statement made by his alleged co-conspirator, Lord Cobham, and a letter written by Cobham. Raleigh insisted that Cobham had recanted his statement and sought to question him directly. The prosecutor, Sir Edward Coke, refused to produce Cobham. Instead, he called a boat pilot who testified that while in Portugal he had been told, "Your king [James I] shall never be crowned for Don Cobham and Don Raleigh will cut his throat before he come to be crowned." Raleigh again protested, objecting that "this is the saying of some wild Jesuit or beggarly priest; but what proof is it against me?"

Lord Coke replied, "It must perforce arise out of some preceding intelligence, and shows that your treason had wings." On this evidence, Raleigh was convicted and eventually beheaded.

Contemporaries considered the trial and its outcome cruelly unjust, and continued outrage ultimately resulted in the rule against the introduction of hearsay, that is, evidence whose source is not present in court for cross-examination. Unless a computer is capable of independently responding to questions, therefore, its output is unalterably hearsay and presumptively inadmissible.

The modern hearsay rule is not ironclad, however. Centuries of application have resulted in dissatisfaction with a doctrine that withholds so much highly informative evidence from the jury's consideration, and various exceptions have been introduced to mitigate its broad sweep. Computer output sometimes gains entry through one or more of these "loopholes." In particular, one widely recognized hearsay exception permits the introduction of routine business records; hence, the output of software that merely automates office functions often bypasses hearsay objection. Furthermore, the definition of hearsay is not all-encompassing: Only evidence introduced for the truth of its content falls within its terms. If a supposedly mute witness is heard to utter, "I can speak!" the content of these words is no more relevant than if this witness had said, "Banana." The ability to speak can be inferred from the act of speech itself. Similarly, a litigant is permitted to introduce computer output as proof that a computer was in fact employed (if such is an issue in the case), even if its content remains inadmissible.

What remains flatly barred is a computer's appearance as a witness, unless it possesses adequate communicative ability. In this regard, the demands of the hearsay rule are closely aligned with the objectives pursued by designers of natural language-processing systems: An acceptable witness must be able to understand questions posed by counsel for both sides and express responses in a manner graspable by judge and jury. The interactive processes implicated by this description can be decomposed into three constituent segments: (1) mechanical translation of speech signals into digital code, (2) interpretive analysis of the encoded text to derive meaningful information that can be acted upon, and (3) the formulation of coherent expressions of properly identified knowledge.[45]

Of these three segments, decoding speech signals is undoubtedly the least essential. Courts are often called on to accommodate the deaf and the mute; written questions and answers, shown to the witness and read aloud to the jury, satisfy courtroom protocol. Nonetheless, the ability to interact vocally with a witness is considered a highly valuable rhetorical asset by attorneys. Particularly when the subject matter is technical, juries are far less likely to fall asleep when observing a genuine interchange than when listening to a lecture delivered secondhand.

The footnote style employed here is a specialized citation form peculiar to legal materials. This style has been developed to maintain consistency among jurisdictions, case reporters, and statutory citations. Its basic format is: <volume> <SOURCE> <first page of document>, <local citation>.

[45] Voice synthesis would also comprise a useful, although not essential, element of the system. Because numerous commercial synthesizers capable of delivering perfectly acceptable speech output currently exist, it was not considered necessary to explore this aspect.

Researchers in this phase of speech-recognition technology have been more successful eliminating transcription errors at the intake stage than creating software to assign meaning to the correctly recognized words. Neither facet, however, has attained the level of verbal dexterity necessary to facilitate truly interactive exchange. Template-matching techniques of word recognition must remain flexible enough to accommodate the acoustic patterns of a variety of speakers yet retain sufficient discriminatory power to decipher their messages accurately. Recognition difficulties are further heightened when speech consists of a continuous stream of utterances rather than isolated words. Disaggregating conjoined groups of words, whose individual pronunciation frequently depends on the surrounding phonetic signals, requires context-oriented analysis and the knowledge of allowed syntactic structures in order to cut through the ambiguity.[46]

"Understanding" the content of speech, which from an operational point of view might be defined as locating the appropriate internally represented knowledge in response to a question and fashioning an answer, represents the central focus of much current natural language research. Computer scientists are experimenting with a number of instructive models, but the greatest obstacles have been recognized for decades.[47] Vast amounts of subliteral inference contribute to the attribution of meaning in human communication, and an effective knowledge search requires precise characterization of this meaning. Contriving a satisfactory approach for bringing such soft concepts within the processing abilities of computer systems remains an elusive goal. Perhaps the recurring sequences of action and dialogue that take place in all legal proceedings can provide a basis for reducing the amount of world knowledge necessary for drawing the proper inferences. In particular, techniques based on scripts might prove useful as a means of formalizing courtroom discourse into patterns of expectable and, hence, more readily understandable verbal interchange.

Formulating a comprehensible response to a question once the appropriate knowledge is located requires more than simply translating it back into a natural language. In order to communicate effectively, additional features become necessary. A computer witness must be able to determine the level of detail and complexity appropriate for the audience (either autonomously or through external human calibration) and adjust its output accordingly. Answers perceived as unclear might need to be rephrased. Achieving the fluent command of language necessary to perform these tasks will demand a vocabulary of considerable richness and a highly sophisticated expressive capability. Once again, although numerous researchers have devised methods of generating limited semantic representations of linguistically unorganized data, systems possessing advanced cognitive faculties have yet to be developed.

These three phases of speech processing describe the ingredients necessary for basic voice communication; yet, while comprehensibility itself is a technologically formidable goal, it nevertheless describes only the surface of communicative ability. A satisfactory

---

[46]See A. Barr and E. Feigenbaum, *The Handbook of Artificial Intelligence* 323 (1981).

[47]An overview of current research directions can be found in Waldrop, Natural Language Understanding, *Science,* April 27, 1984, at 372. A recent example is described in Glasgow, YANLI: A Powerful Natural Language Front-End Tool, *AI Magazine,* Spring 1987, at 40.

witness must be able to do more than interact. Especially where expertise in a particular field is claimed, the jury expects sound conclusions supported by adequate explanation. Attempts to implement the necessary reasoning processes will entail a great deal of structural planning at the level of knowledge representation. For purposes of witness testimony, the contours of required informational support are shaped largely by the proclivities of trial lawyers. Cross-examination is viewed by attorneys and judges as the acid test of witness credibility. When the witness is subjected to the cynical scrutiny of an experienced advocate, it is at least hoped that insincere assertions, erroneous convictions, and specious reasoning are exposed to the jury. Cross-examining attorneys rely on four principal avenues of investigative inquiry: witness qualification and experience, vulnerabilities in the witness's factual assumptions or scientific premises, the cogency of the ultimate opinion, and possible sources of bias.

The first of these areas is merely descriptive. The second requires some sort of recursive ability, such that conclusions can be traced to their origin; an attorney might wish to challenge the sufficiency of factual predicates or the respect accorded scholarly sources by the scientific community. The persuasiveness of an expert opinion is often tested by varying specific assumptions to determine whether alternative scenarios might produce indistinguishable conclusions. Thus, the computer witness's inferential processes will need to be capable of operating at real-time speed in order to maintain the pace of courtroom dialogue. The final aspect of the lawyer's inquisitory prerogative, a search for possible bias, engages some of the most difficult types of knowledge to implement in a computer's range of response. Bias is based on personal predilection. For an expert in a technical field, it can take such ill-defined forms as disdain for a particular scientific school of thought or a preferred method of approaching problems. The process of transferring expert knowledge to computer-based reasoning systems not only fuses individual experts' inclinations into the representational scheme, but can result in additional sources of bias as a consequence of programming design. The organization of a production system's control structure, for example, can involve conflict-resolution choices that tend to favor certain groups of rules.

These obscure sources of influence will remain beyond the reach of cross-examination unless the computer program is equipped to defend its own programming logic. If knowledge is simply gleaned from human sources and shuttled directly into a system of fixed rules, the computer will remain ignorant of the foundations underlying its expertise. True, this extraneous information might be painstakingly introduced into the computer's knowledge base solely to facilitate cross-examination, or perhaps, human experts could stand ready to provide supporting testimony. Either solution would render the computer a most ungainly witness. It appears that only those future "metaknowledgable" systems capable of developing and maintaining their own knowledge structures could feasibly maintain sufficient familiarity with chosen sources of intelligence. However, independent evaluation, selection, and absorption of raw information implies extraordinary computing power and currently represents a distant goal of AI research.

It is difficult to predict which phase of communicative capacity—comprehensibility or intellectual sufficiency—will prove the more intractable to develop. The measure of progress necessary for access to the courtroom is not solely a technological issue, however. As computers become recognized as authoritative sources of valuable knowledge, pressure will mount to permit greater use of their capabilities in judicial contests. Diminishing skepticism and the desire to produce the fairest verdicts will undoubtedly increase the tolerance for less than perfect communication skills, and prompt judges to allow sophisticated computer systems to take the stand.

A Question of Responsibility

M. Mitchell Waldrop

In 1940, a 20-year-old science fiction fan from Brooklyn found that he was growing tired of stories that endlessly repeated the myths of Frankenstein and Faust: Robots were created and destroyed their creator; robots were created and destroyed their creator; robots were created and destroyed their creator—ad nauseam. So he began writing robot stories of his own. "[They were] robot stories of a new variety," he recalls. "Never, never was one of my robots to turn stupidly on his creator for no purpose but to demonstrate, for one more weary time, the crime and punishment of Faust. Nonsense! My robots were machines designed by engineers, not pseudo-men created by blasphemers. My robots reacted along the rational lines that existed in their 'brains' from the moment of construction."

In particular, he imagined that each robot's artificial brain would be imprinted with three engineering safeguards, three Laws of Robotics:

1. A robot may not injure a human being or, through inaction, allow a human being to come to harm.
2. A robot must obey the orders given it by human beings except where such orders would conflict with the first law.
3. A robot must protect its own existence as long as such protection does not conflict with the first or second law.

The young writer's name, of course, was Isaac Asimov (1964), and the robot stories he began writing that year have become classics of science fiction, the standards by which others are judged. Indeed, because of Asimov one almost never reads about robots turning mindlessly on their masters anymore.

But the legends of Frankenstein and Faust are subtle ones, and as the world knows too well, engineering rationality is not always the same thing as wisdom. This insight was never captured better than in another science fiction classic: the dark fantasy "With Folded Hands," published by Jack Williamson (1978).

The robots of this story are created by an idealistic young scientist whose world, the planet Wing IV, has just been devastated by a senseless war. Sickened by humankind's taste for viciousness and destruction, and thinking to save men from themselves, he programs his robots to follow an Asimovian Prime Directive—"To Serve and Obey, and Guard Men from Harm." He establishes factories where the robots can duplicate themselves in profusion. He sends them forth to bring order, rationality, and peace to humanity. And he succeeds all too well, as the citizens of his world and other worlds soon began to realize:

. . . "Our function is to serve and obey, and guard men from harm," it cooed softly. "It is no longer necessary for men to care for themselves, because we exist to insure their safety and happiness."

. . . "But it is unnecessary for human beings to open doors," the little black thing informed him suavely. "We exist to serve the Prime Directive, and our service includes every task."

. . . "We are aiding the police department temporarily," it said. "But driving is really much too dangerous for human beings, under the Prime Directive. As soon as our service is complete, every car will have a humanoid driver. As soon as every human being is completely supervised, there will be no need for any police force whatsoever."

At last, the scientist realizes what he has done:

"I found something worse than war and crime and want and death." His low rumbling voice held a savage bitterness. "Utter futility. Men sat with idle hands, because there was nothing left for them to do . . . Perhaps they tried to play, but there was nothing left worth playing for. Most active sports were declared too dangerous for men, under the Prime Directive. Science was forbidden, because laboratories can manufacture danger. Scholarship was needless, because the humanoids could answer any question. Art had degenerated into a grim reflection of futility. Purpose and hope were dead. No goal was left for existence . . . No wonder men had tried to kill me!"

He attempts to destroy his robots by destroying the central electronic brain that controls them. (Williamson was writing in the days before distributed processing.) The robots stop him; this is clearly a violation of the Prime Directive, for how can they serve men if they themselves are hindered? He flees to another world, and tries again. And again. And again. Each time he is thwarted, as the robots continue to spread from planet to planet faster than he can run from them. And in the end, the robots devise a simple brain operation to cure his "hallucinations": " 'We have learned to make all men happy, under the Prime Directive,' the mechanical promised him cheerfully. 'Our service is perfect at last.' "

Needless to say, "With Folded Hands" was widely considered a horror story.

WHAT IS A ROBOT?

A servant, it seems, can all too easily become the master—a phenomenon worth thinking about as we rush towards a new generation of intelligent machines. Just how will we use these machines? How much power and authority should they have? What kind of responsibilities should we give them? And who, if anyone, is going to control them?

Before we tackle those questions, however, we first ought to drop back a step and ask a different question: What exactly *is* a robot?

The question is more subtle than it sounds. For most of us the word *robot* conjures up an image of something like R2D2 or C3PO from the film *Star Wars*. But what about dishwashers and word-processing machines? Are *they* robots? The Robotics Industries Association uses a definition specially devised for factory robots: "A reprogrammable multifunctioning manipulator designed to move material, parts, tools or specialized devices through variable programmed motions for the performance of a variety of tasks."

Actually, my favorite definition is "A surprisingly animate machine." But for our present purposes, the most useful definition is one that ignores the gadget's physical appearance entirely, and even its brainpower. It focuses instead on the role of the machine; unlike a lawn mower or a word processor, which requires continuous and direct supervision, a robot is an artificial *agent*—a machine that can take action without direct supervision.

Hidden Processing and Microrobots

Of course, if we take that definition literally, we're already surrounded by robots. Stoplights, for example. The automated teller machine at the bank. The coffeepot that starts up automatically at 7:00 A.M. Admittedly, none of these "robots" is very smart. But microprocessors have already begun to appear in coffeepots, washing machines, automobiles, and microwave ovens. Given the rapidly decreasing price of microprocessors, and the increasing ease with which circuitry can be designed and built for special-purpose applications, there is every reason to expect that the devices around us will rapidly get smarter. Ultimately, in fact, we can expect that the engineers will add in little knowledge bases to their chips, so that their machines can talk, listen to orders, and respond to changing circumstances. And at that point we are not so far from what Pamela McCorduck (1979) has described as "a world saturated with intelligence," and what Allen Newell (1976) called the New Land of Fairie. For instance:

- Refrigerators that know how to thaw the chicken for dinner.
- Robotic cars that know how to stop on wet pavement, and how to drive down the highway while their passengers take a nap.
- Lampposts that know the way, so that no one need ever get lost.

Indeed, perhaps we should forget any lingering fears that all our descendants will become like teenage hackers hunched over a computer screen; our descendants may be much more like sorcerers, able to animate the objects around them with a word, and to command those objects to do their bidding.

In all seriousness, many prognosticators think that "hidden" computing, as it is called, may very well be the most important way in which computers and AI will enter our lives. Alan Kay, who was one of the guiding spirits behind the development of personal computers when he was at Xerox Palo Alto Research Center in the early 1970s, points out that using a desktop computer to store household recipes, or to turn on the coffeepot in the morning, is roughly equivalent to an engineer in 1900 saying, "Electric motors are great! Every home should have one!" and then proceeding to rig an elaborate system of belts and pulleys to run everything in the house from one big motor in the attic. In fact, the average American home has some fifty electric motors, according to Kay. It's just that we never notice them, because they are tucked away out of sight in electric shavers, hairdryers, typewriters, fans, and washing machines. In short, hidden motorization. Apply that logic to the newest technology and you have computing and hidden AI (Kay 1985).

Humanoid Robots

Next, what about not-so-hidden robots: the mobile, humanoid machines that can walk, talk, see, handle things, and even think: We've read about them in science fiction stories. We've watched them in the *Star Wars* movies. So when are they going to be available at the local department store?

Actually, simple robots are available already, and have been since the early eighties. As of the mid-eighties, in fact, they are being offered by at least six different manufacturers at prices ranging from $2,000 to $8,000. The Heath Company of Benton Harbor, Michigan, is even offering its HERO I as a $1,200 build-it-yourself kit.

These first-generation machines are real, programmable robots with on-board micro-computers; they are not remote-control toys. However, it's important to realize that they have nowhere near the sophistication of R2D2 or C3PO. Certain advertisements to the contrary, present-day robots are not very good for serving canapes at a cocktail party, nor are they much help at doing the dishes afterwards. Essentially, they are personal computers on wheels, with ultrasonic ranging devices and perhaps a few heat and light sensors to help them avoid obstacles. Even then, they are hard-put to cross a room without bumping into anything, and it takes a major programming effort to get one to fetch a glass of water from the kitchen table. (And at that, if the glass is moved 6 inches from its previous position, the programming has to be done all over again.) By themselves, they are only useful as teaching machines, to show people how robots work (Bell 1985).

On the other hand, they *are* significant as a possible first step toward more useful robots. For example, one of the first practical applications for personal robots might be as companions to the elderly and handicapped, which would ease their dependence on human help; it needn't take a very sophisticated robot to pick up a dropped handkerchief or to change television channels on voice command. This is especially true if the users are willing to wire their homes with radio locators in the walls; that way their robots could dispense with the need for high-powered image processing and instead use simple radio receivers to keep track of where they are in the house. In the same vein, mechanical-engineering students at Stanford recently developed a robot hand that will translate electronic text into sign language for the deaf (Shurkin 1985).

Another near-term use for mobile robots might be in industrial settings—not in factories as such but in cleaning long, unobstructed hallways, or in mowing the vast lawns of an industrial park. A prototype floor-washing robot has been developed at Carnegie-Mellon. Moreover, without too much adaptation such robots could also serve as security guards to patrol the grounds of prisons or sensitive military installations (Bell 1985).

Admittedly, as of the mid-1980s these markets are still a bit fuzzy. But the prospects are sufficiently promising to give the fledgling personal-robotics industry an undeniable momentum. In effect, the pioneers are betting that robotics will take the same route that personal computers did starting in the early 1970s. There, too, the early machines were little more than playthings for hobbyists. But they gave rise to second-generation PCs that *were* genuinely useful. The skyrocketing sales, in turn, gave the PC makers both the cash flow and the incentive to develop still more sophisticated computers. And on it went, with the results we see around us today. So who knows? Perhaps things will work out this way for the robotics industry, too.

One trend that gives substance to this vision is the support of advanced research efforts such as the Defense Advanced Research Project Agency (DARPA) Strategic Computing Program. One of DARPA's major goals in that program is an autonomous vehicle capable of roving over rugged and hostile terrain at the speed of a running man. In a sense this vehicle represents the ultimate in AI: the union of vision, touch, reasoning, and motion in one entity, a machine that not only thinks but acts in a multitude of situations. Moreover, such mobile robots would find applications not just on the battlefield, but in any environment where flexibility, versatility and autonomy are crucial. Take deep space, for example: If and when NASA sends another unmanned mission to Mars, perhaps in the 1990s, an important scientific goal will be to bring back samples of material from many different areas on the planet, which means that a rover of some kind will have to move around on the surface to pick them up. This will in turn require some pretty fancy footwork, since the images returned by the Viking landers in 1976 show that the Martian surface is littered with rocks, boulders, and craters. Unfortunately, however, there is no way to operate the rover by remote control from Earth. Radio signals take forty minutes to get from Earth to Mars and back, and at forty minutes per step the rover would never get anywhere. So the Mars rover will need to be intelligent enough to find its own way and pick up the right samples.

Machines of this caliber are clearly not consumer items in the sense that the personal robotics industry would like. On the other hand, advanced research-and-development does have a way of showing up in commercial products with surprising rapidity. So before long we may find R2D2 and C3PO in the local department store after all.

We probably won't be using these humanoid robots for everything, of course, at least not in the way that Asimov, Williamson, and other science fiction writers have suggested. It wouldn't make sense. Why build mobile robots for an automobile factory when it is so much easier to string them out along the assembly line and move the cars? Why build a humanoid robot to drive a truck when it would be far simpler to build a computer into the dashboard? Why not just make the truck itself into a robot—a kind of autopilot for the interstates?

In some situations, however, a mobile, humanoid robot might be ideal. Mining is an example, or construction work, or anyplace else where the environment is complex and unpredictable. Ironically, one of the most demanding environments, and the one where a mobile robot might be most useful, is the home. Consider what it would take to program a robot maid to vacuum under the dining-room table without vacuuming up the cat in the process; the terrain is at least as complex as Mars. Furthermore, the environment requires mobility for the simple reason that an automated valet or maid would have to share the house with people. Imagine how complicated it would be to build an intelligent clothes hamper that could take the dirty clothes, sort them by color and fabric, wash them, dry them, fold them, and put them away in the upstairs dresser; it would be a Rube Goldberg contraption with conveyor belts and special-purpose handling devices that took up half the house. Much more sensible would be a humanoid robot maid that could walk up and down the stairs and run an ordinary washing machine.[1]

---

[1] If mechanical valets and maids ever become common, life might take on a curiously Victorian flavor. We might go back to building houses with "maid rooms"—or at least with storage and parking areas for household robots. We might go back to rooms elaborately decorated with bric-a-brac, because we will have electronic servants to dust and clean it. And fashions may swing back toward fussy, elaborate, Victorian-style clothing because we will have mechanical maids and valets to help us put it on and take it off.

DISTRIBUTED COMPUTING AND MACROROBOTS

There is no reason that mobile robots couldn't also be part of a distributed system of inter-connected intelligences. For example, it's easy to imagine a construction gang of robots swarming over the skeleton of a new building, each knowing a fragment of the architect's computer-designed blueprint, and each connected to the others by radio . . . grappling units that would carry a girder into place and hold it upright . . . an octopuslike thing goes to work with riveting guns on the end of each arm . . . a welding unit walks into position and strikes an arc from its snout . . .

But this vision leads to an intriguing question: Is this robot construction gang simply a team of individual agents? Or is it *one* individual—a "macrorobot" that just happens to have many eyes, many hands, and many minds?

The distinction may simply be semantic. But it may be more; certainly it's worth thinking about as large-scale distributed systems become more and more important. For example, look at computer-automated factories; if a robot is defined as a machine that can take auton-omous action, then such a factory might very well be called a robot.

In the 1990s, NASA hopes to launch a permanently manned space station occupied by at least six people at all times. Eventually, it could carry as many as twenty people. The station will be expensive, of course—costing roughly eight billion dollars—so NASA wants to keep the crew busy repairing satellites, doing experiments, making astronomical obser-vations, and carrying out other useful work. The agency does *not* want them to spend their time cleaning house and taking care of the life-support system. The station will therefore be designed to take care of itself automatically, using AI and robotics technology wherever possible. In effect, it will be a giant robot (NASA, 1985).[2]

Back on Earth, meanwhile, personal computers, mini-computers, mainframes, and super-computers are more and more often being linked together in transcontinental communications networks, in much the same way that telephones are already linked together for voice com-munications. A computer network can be though of as a robot; indeed, such networks may turn out to be the most intelligent macrorobots of all.

The Multinet: Computers in the Global Village

A great deal has been written and said about the coming of the "networked society." Local area networks are proliferating in business offices and on university campuses. And many people have imagined an interconnected web of such networks that would encompass vir-tually every computer and database on the planet, a concept that MIT computer scientist J. C. R. Licklider (1979) has dubbed the "multinet."

In time, says Licklider, the government itself will become an integral part of this mul-tinet—using it to monitor regulated industries such as the stock market, to provide weather forecasts and take census data, to collect taxes and make Social Security payments, to con-duct polls, and even to hold elections. Meanwhile, the postal system will fade into a memory as people communicate more and more through telephone lines and electronic mail—all part

---

[2]The schedule became quite hazy after the explosion of the space shuttle Challenger on January 28, 1986; as of mid-1986, however, NASA officials were expressing confidence that the first components of the space station would be in orbit by the mid-1990s.

of the multinet. Filing cabinets, microfilm repositories, document rooms, and even most libraries will be replaced by on-line information storage and retrieval through the multinet. More and more people will work at home, communicating with coworkers and clients through the multinet. People will shop through the multinet, using cable television and electronic funds transfer. People will even reserve their tables at restaurants and order ballet tickets through the multinet.

Clearly, Licklider's vision of a multinet connecting everyone and everything is still a long way from reality. If nothing else, there remains the question of who would run it: A private company? A public utility? A federal agency? We can only guess at when it will all come together.

On the other hand, we don't have to rely entirely on guesswork to know what this computer-saturated, networked society of the future will be like. It is already being created in microcosm on the nation's campuses. Most of the large universities in the United States, as well as many of the smaller colleges, are spending tens of millions of dollars each to lay cable in cross-campus trenches and to run wires into dormitories, offices, and classrooms. Three schools in particular—Carnegie-Mellon, MIT, and Brown University—have taken the lead in developing the software and networking standards for what is commonly known as the "scholar's work station": a personal computer with the power of a current-generation microcomputer. (Much of their funding has come from such manufacturers as IBM, Digital Equipment, and Apple, who will build the actual hardware. The machines began to appear on the market late in 1986) (Balkovich, Lerman, and Parmelee 1985).

What makes a network so attractive in an academic setting— or, for that matter, in a business setting—is not just that it allows people to send a lot of information bits from computer to computer but that it allows them to do things in ways they couldn't before. For example, individual users hooking into the network can begin to share powerful resources that no one user could justify by himself. Thus, local area networks give users access to departmental minicomputers, phototypesetters, high-volume laser printers, and massive on-line databases located in a central library. At a national level, meanwhile, the National Science Foundation has established a series of five national supercomputer centers (at Cornell, San Diego, Princeton, Carnegie-Mellon, and the University of Illinois) to give scientists around the country routine access to state-of-the-art number-crunching power. As part of that effort, the foundation is establishing a transcontinental computer network so that users can communicate with the supercomputers directly from their desktop terminals, without having to travel (Jennings 1985). In much the same way, the ARPAnet was established in the late sixties to link DARPA-supported computer scientists by high-speed communications. ARPAnet users are now able to send experimental designs for new computer chips to DARPA-supported silicon foundries, which then produce the chip and mail it back within a few weeks; as a result, hundreds of students and professors have been trying out a multitude of inventive ideas, and the art of integrated circuit design is being transformed. More recently, as DARPA has gotten underway with the Strategic Computing program, researchers have begun to tie in to testing grounds through ARPAnet so that they can experiment with remote robotics and advanced knowledge-based systems.

An equally important effect of networking is that it fosters a sense of community. Instead of just talking on the telephone, for example, widely scattered researchers on the ARPAnet have used its electronic mail facility to create a kind of ongoing debating society, with messages read and posted at any hour of the day or night. Among other topics, the debates have included some fiery exchanges about the pros and cons of the Fifth Generation efforts, the Strategic Computing program, and the Strategic Defense Initiative. The comments have often been quite critical of DARPA (IEEE Staff 1985). Indeed, some of the most insistent criticism of Strategic Computing and Strategic Defense has come from the Computer Professionals for Social Responsibility, a group that was organized through the ARPAnet (Augarten 1986). (DARPA, to its credit, has never tried to censor any of this criticism.)

Meanwhile, ARPAnet's electronic communications have proved a boon for collaboration among widely separated individuals. This is particularly true when a message includes computer code for a joint programming project, the draft of a joint research paper, or graphics depicting a new chip design—all of which would be next to impossible to express in a voice message over the telephone. An author can write a book using the word-processing program on his office computer, and send the manuscript electronically to several dozen friends and reviewers at a keystroke. Then, within a few days, he can fetch it back at a keystroke with comments, suggestions, and corrections inserted—without anyone having to wait for the U.S. mail.

Managing the Network with AI

At first glance, none of this seems to have much to do with AI. But in fact, AI will play an increasingly important role in this area, especially when it comes to managing computer networks.

Fundamentally, it's a matter of human factors writ large. Whether or not we ever arrive at anything as all-encompassing as Licklider's multinet, we are clearly headed in the direction of a nationwide information infrastructure on the scale of the interstate highway system or the electrical power grid, and much more complicated than either one. Indeed, we can already see the beginning of such a system in ARPAnet, in the National Science Foundation's supercomputer network, in the BITnet system that links campuses across the country, and in the commercial electronic mail services being introduced by such companies as MCI and Western Union (Jennings 1985).

At the same time, no matter how large or small a computer network may be, it has to be "transparent" in a certain sense, or people will find every excuse to not use it. Compare the process to turning on a light: When I walk into a dark room, I don't have to know about voltages, transformers, or peak-load generators. I don't have to know where the power plant is, or whether it runs on coal, uranium, or solar energy. I just flip the switch and the light comes on. And by the same token, when I want to send an electronic message to a friend across the country, I don't want to have to tell my computer what kind of terminal she has, or what kind of data protocols her local network uses, or what the data rate should be. I just want to type in the message and have it go.

The solution, obviously, is to make the network itself intelligent. Make it come alive with software robots that keep things running smoothly in the background. Give it voice with helpful little expert systems that pop up whenever they are needed.

As an individual user of such a system, for example, I would have instant access to all the services of a private secretary, a personal librarian, a travel agent, and more. (The programs to do all this wouldn't necessarily have to be in my computer; if the communications were quick enough, the software could be residing in another computer elsewhere on the network and still *seem* to be running on my computer.) Thus, when I wanted to send that message, I would just type my friend's name and the text of the message on my office terminal; then, with a keystroke or a voice command, my secretarial expert system would look up her electronic address and route the message for me. In the same way, when I've told my computer to set me up for a trip to Pasadena on the twenty-fifth, my travel-agent system would automatically plan out an itinerary—remembering that I like to fly out of Washington in the early afternoon—and then automatically use the network to make reservations with the airlines, the hotels, and the car-rental agencies. A librarian expert system would likewise be available to guide me through the intricacies of the network itself—advising me what databases I might want to look at to ascertain the political situation in Chad, for example, or how I would go about accessing a supercomputer to do high-quality computer animation.

My secretarial system could also filter out electronic junk mail—which sounds trivial, except that in the age of electronic communications it may be a matter of mental survival. For example, say I'm a magazine journalist trying desperately to meet a deadline on a major story. I don't want to have my computer beeping at me for every electronic-mail message that comes in. On the other hand, I *do* want it to alert me if one of the field bureaus is sending in new information that needs to go in my story. Yet I can't just set my electronic mail system to accept any message labeled *Urgent,* because there are at least three companies sending me "urgent" messages about hot new prices on used IBM PCs, and one fellow in New Hampshire is desperately trying to convince me that Einstein's theory of relativity is wrong and that the moon is about to spiral into the Earth. So what I really want is a personal-receptionist program living inside the network, with enough natural-language ability to recognize contents of a message and enough common sense to know what I do and don't want to see.

There are other possibilities. In a corporate setting, for example, one can imagine a kind of office-manager program living in the system and keeping track of the electronic flow of work: Who has to read this item? Who has to coordinate on that project? Who has to sign off on this decision, and by when? Such a program would act to regulate the flow of electronic information through the organization, while preventing backlogs and keeping track of productivity. It might even function as a kind of social secretary: based on its expertise about policy and etiquette, it could remind people what kind of replies need to be sent to what messages. At the same time, the office-manager program could serve as a kind of gatekeeper for the network, providing people sure and convenient access to information when company policy says they are authorized to have it, and keeping them out when they are not authorized to have it.

Looking beyond information networks, we can easily imagine how these same concepts of distributed, intelligent management might apply to other systems: an automated electric power grid, using telecommunications and computers to optimize the efficiency of transcontinental power lines (Gaushell 1985) . . . an automated air traffic-control system, juggling information from radars hundreds of miles apart . . . an automated city traffic-control system, coordinating lights and directing traffic around bottlenecks on a regional basis, so that things flow smoothly even in rush hour. Ultimately, in fact, we can imagine society itself being run by networks of interlinked intelligences—a single giant robot with each component an expert in its own niche, and the whole greater than the parts.

So perhaps we should define the concept of *robot* yet again: Robots are not just machines that can walk around and manipulate things, or even machines that can take action on their own. In a less visible, and yet more all-pervasive sense than Asimov or Williamson ever realized, robots are machines that take care of us.

HOW MUCH RESPONSIBILITY?

So we return to the questions we started with. Robots, in the broad sense that we have defined them, play the role of *agent*. Coupled with AI, moreover, they will be able to take on responsibility and authority in ways that no machines have ever done before. So perhaps it's worth asking before we get to that point just how much power and authority these intelligent machines *ought* to have—and just who, if anyone, will control them.

Obfuscation and Big Brother

There is ample reason to be concerned about such questions. Computers don't come equipped with any built-in ethical system analogous to Asimov's three laws of robotics. And for that very reason, they are well suited to act as tools and smoke screens for the powers that be— as bureaucrats learned almost as soon as computers were introduced. ("I'd like to help you, but I'm afraid the computer just isn't set up to do it that way . . .") AI, unfortunately, won't necessarily change things.

To illustrate some of the issues here, imagine an expert system that serves as a bank loan examiner. Each applicant sits at a terminal in the bank's offices answering questions about his or her financial status, while the computer verifies everything by automatic queries through the network to other banks and credit companies. (The applicant could also do this through a terminal at home.) Finally, the system makes a decision: Yes, the applicant qualifies, or no, the applicant doesn't qualify.

Now, this could be a very efficient and useful system. Certainly it would be consistent in applying the bank's loan policy to each applicant. On the other hand, people may not be willing to put up with that kind of treatment from a machine. It's humiliating enough to get the once-over from a human bank official, and a few banks might get their computer screens smashed in. But in some ways it's more disturbing to think that people *will* put up with such treatment—not because the expert system does anything sinister, necessarily, but because the situation obscures the fact that the machine's "decision" actually embodies a policy made by humans. Furthermore, the decision comes wrapped in the aura of "artificial intelligence." Rejected applicants may be too intimidated to protest. And even if they do, the (human) managers of the bank could all too easily brush them off with "Gee, I'd like to help you, but the computers these days are wiser than we are . . ."

So even a seemingly straightforward application of AI can obscure the lines of responsibility—and it's naive to think that some people won't use it that way when they don't want outsiders asking uncomfortable questions.

Another troublesome aspect of this scenario is the free and easy way that our loan applicant feeds information about his life and activities in the electronic data network. How does he know what is going to be done with that data?

Maybe a lot will be done with it. "Today we're building systems that can collect a vast amount of information on an individual's daily transactions," says Fred Weingarten, manager of the Communications and Information Technologies program at the congressional Office of Technology Assessment. "Further, systems such as those employing knowledge-based technology can do more with that information than ever before, including the making of decisions that affect private lives" (Weingarten 1985). In that context it's worth noting that in a recent study, Weingarten's group found that at least thirty-five federal agencies were using or planned to use some form of electronic surveillance techniques—including computer-usage monitoring and the interception of electronic mail—and that current laws did not adequately regulate such electronic surveillance (OTA 1985).

There is nothing in the rules that says AI has to be benign, of course, and it is perfectly possible to imagine AI techniques in the service of Big Brother. Consider an advanced speech-recognition program that monitors every telephone call in the country for evidence of criminal activities, or a natural-language program that scans every computer bulletin board and reads every item of electronic mail. Such a system might catch a lot of obscene phone-callers and drug dealers. But how long before the definition of "criminal" starts sliding over into "subversive" and "disloyal?"

Actually, the process doesn't even have to be that dramatic. The mere possibility of surveillance is chilling. Langdon Winner, professor of politics and technology at the University of California at Santa Cruz, thinks that this may be the most insidious problem of all: "When I talk to people about this question, citing examples in which electronic monitoring has been used as a tool for harassment and coercion," he says, "they often say that they don't need to worry about it because they're not doing anything anyone would possibly want to watch. In other words, it becomes a sign of virtue for them to say: 'Thank God, I'm not involved in anything that a computer would find at all interesting.' It's precisely that response that I find troubling."

Winner finds a metaphor for this situation in a fascinating design for a building, the Panopticon, created by the nineteenth-century philosopher Jeremy Bentham:

The Panopticon was to be a circular building, several stories high, with a tower in the center. It could be used as a prison, hospital, school, or factory. A key feature of the design was that people in its rooms could not see each other, but the person in the center looking out to the periphery could gaze into every cell. Bentham saw this architecture as the ultimate means of social control. There would not even need to be a guard present in the tower at all times: all one had to do was to build in such a way that surveillance became an omnipresent possibility that would eliminate misbehavior and ensure compliance. It appears that we now may be building an electronic Panopticon, a system of seemingly benign electronic data-gathering that creates *de facto* conditions of universal surveillance.

It isn't just a threat to individual privacy. It is a threat to our public freedoms. "Unless we take steps to prevent it," Winner concludes, "we could see a society filled with all-seeing data banks used to monitor an increasingly pliant, passive populace no longer willing to risk activities that comprise civil liberty" (Winner 1985).

Tacit Assumptions in the Nuclear Age

The specter of Big Brother is never far from people's minds when they worry about the effect of computers on society. But in a sense, that kind of abuse is also the easiest to guard against. The bad guys wear black hats, so to speak; their actions are explicit and deliberate, even if covert. Thus, in principle, laws can be written to protect our electronic privacy, and a code of behavior enforced.

Much more widespread and much more insidious, however, is another kind of situation, in which the bad guys don't wear black hats. Instead, they are ordinary, well-intentioned people whose tacit assumptions and values cause us to drift in a direction we might not have taken by choice. For example, the designers of the first office word-processing machines, together with the managers who installed them, brought certain values and assumptions to the job that ended up turning many offices into electronic sweatshops. They didn't necessarily mean to do it, but that is what happened. Looking to the future, consider Licklider's multinet and the various software robots that will be required to run it; even with the best of intentions, the people who design those programs will shape what we do, what we see, what we know about, and how we interact with our fellow human beings.

PC Magazine editor Bill Machrone highlights this issue in an article about a demonstration he saw of a new electronic-mail package for PCs. The idea of the package was to render corporate communications more efficient by organizing all messages according to set categories: requests, denials, commands, counteroffers, and the like. Machrone's reaction: "communications software designed by Nazis."

"Consider that this is how people who don't like each other communicate," he explains. "It is not a foundation for trust and mutual cooperation. In fact, in most organizations, the use of techniques such as this is virtually guaranteed to put people on edge and at one another. Like anything else that mechanizes human interaction, such a system inevitably makes that interaction less human . . . [What people in corporations need is] room to roam, freedom to grow, to express opinions, develop points of view, and interact."

So why would a group of well-meaning programmers produce such a package? Machrone asks. "Its creators are fervent believers in mechanized, highly structured communications. It works for them, and they are sure it'll work for you. They're converts to this way of thinking and they want you to be too" (Machrone 1986).

In short, a robot doesn't have to an agent just of a person or an institution. Without anyone's ever fully realizing it, a robot can also be the agent of a value structure or a set of assumptions. And that is perhaps as it should be—so long as we understand what the values and assumptions really imply. Remember that Williamson's robots, who were pledged "to serve and obey, and guard men from harm," were conceived with the best of intentions.

Nowhere is this issue of tacit values and assumptions illustrated more starkly than in the realm of nuclear weapons and nuclear war. In particular, consider the "launch-on-warning" strategy.

There has long been a school of thought among strategic planners in the United States that our land-based nuclear missiles should be launched as soon as incoming warheads show up on radar. Afterward, goes the argument, it will be too late. Both the military and civilian communications network will very likely collapse as soon as the first hostile warheads fall. So even if the missiles themselves survive in their hardened silos, no one could fire them. We would have lost the war without firing a shot. Indeed, the very possibility invites a sneak attack. Thus, launch-on-warning (Ford 1985).

Now, there is an undeniable, if ruthless, logic to that argument. On the other hand, it's important to notice the tacit assumptions inherent in launch-on-warning: that a state of unrelenting hostility exists between us and the Other Side; that international fear and mistrust are the natural state of affairs; that They are sneaky devils just waiting for a chance to hit us on the blind side; that our ability to retaliate is more important than anything else, including the fate of the human race.

Are those the kind of assumptions we want to build our future on?

In any case, launch-on-warning has never been implemented— at least, not by the United States[3]—largely because the early-warning radars have shown a distressing tendency to give false alarms. Signals mistaken for hostile missiles in the past include flights of geese, the rising moon, and the signals from a training tape that was accidentally mounted on the wrong computer. For much of the same reasons, even the proponents of the idea have shied away from entrusting the launch decision to computers. Computers are too prone to break down and (currently) too rigid in their responses.

However, those tacit assumptions of hostility, fear, and mistrust are very strong. The pressure to move toward a launch-on-warning strategy is always with us, especially as our land-based nuclear-missile forces become increasingly vulnerable to cruise missiles launched from submarines off the coast, and to increasingly accurate intercontinental missiles routed over the pole. Indeed, the existence of new-generation computers and a new generation of machine intelligence may well tempt some future administration to take the step.

Meanwhile, we have President Reagan's concept of a space-based defense against ballistic missiles: "Star Wars." The system is intended strictly as a defensive measure; so if we assume for the sake of argument that it *will* be built and *will* be effective—two controversial assumptions—then the consequences of a false alarm would presumably not be as dire. The orbital lasers and such would just waste a lot of ammunition firing at empty space. An accidental activation of the system, on the other hand, might reveal its weaknesses to the other side and leave the country temporarily unprotected. So the indirect consequences could be very serious. In any case, the pressure to put an automatic trigger on such a defensive system are the same as they are for launch-on-warning: Once incoming missiles show up on the radar screen, there is just too little time to rely on having the president or anyone else make meaningful decisions.

In short, the relentless logic of the technology seems to be leading us ever closer to a point where the fate of the human race can no longer be entrusted to humans. Officially, of course, the release of our offensive nuclear arsenal can only be authorized by the president in his role as commander-in-chief. Moreover, the officials of the Strategic Defense Initiative Organization have always maintained that any future Star Wars defensive system will like-

---

[3]There are persistent rumors that the Soviet Union *has* implemented such a policy.

wise be under the control of the president. And there is no reason to doubt them at their word.

However, even if we leave aside a host of practical questions—Will the president be able to communicate with the missile command centers after the bombs start falling? Will he even be *alive* at that point?—we can still ask what human control would really mean in a situation of nuclear crisis.

The fact is that most of the offensive and defensive systems would have to be automated in any case; there's simply no way for any one human to understand the myriad details involved. Indeed, from what little one can gather about U.S. plans for responding in a nuclear war, the president will essentially be presented with a short menu of preprepared options: Place *these* forces on alert, for example, or launch *that* contingent of missiles while holding *those* back, and so on.

Given the painfully short response times available in a nuclear attack, this menu approach is probably the only rational way to go. However, it's all too easy to imagine the scene: one aging politician—the president—sitting in front of a computer terminal that he may never have seen before, trying to read and digest a list of complex options while half-hysterical advisers are whispering contradictory advice in each ear. Meanwhile, he himself is probably becoming panicky with the knowledge than an irrevocable decision has to be made right *now*. Just how much careful consideration is he going to be able to give to his choice?

Very little, probably. In fact, one is left with an uncomfortable feeling that "controlling" nuclear forces in such a situation is virtually a contradiction in terms. The real choices will have already been made by the people who prepare the items on the menu—which means that it becomes critically important to know what their assumptions are. If they only present options that refer to this or that degree of belligerence, with no options that allow for backing away from hostilities, then the system has built into it the presumption that *there will be war*. Indeed, so far as an outside reporter can tell, that is exactly the case. There is precious little consideration being given on either side to helping leaders calm the crisis.

Actually, this is one place where AI techniques might be very helpful. It's easy to imagine a calm, nonhysterical expert system advising some future president on various diplomatic options in a nuclear crisis, together with predictions of the other side's likely reaction. Never despairing, never forgetting things, never becoming obsessive about this or that course of action under the pressure of the moment—such a machine would be invaluable as the one cool head in the midst of chaos. Indeed, if consulted beforehand, it might help keep the crisis from developing in the first place. The question is, Is anyone planning to develop or deploy such a system, or any other decision-support system for helping our leaders deal with a crisis? At the moment no one seems to be. Does that mean that the presumption of war takes precedence?

From one point of view, of course, this debate over human control of nuclear weapons can be read as a rationale for turning the whole thing over to computers. In a nuclear age, goes the argument, a new generation of very intelligent computers incorporating AI could actually defend the country better, faster, and more rationally than humans. And who knows? Maybe they could. But here are some thoughts to ponder:

- Even if computers are better then humans at fighting a nuclear war, is it ethical to abdicate responsibility for the fate of human civilization to machines? For better or worse, that is our responsibility.
- Even if computers can do the job better than humans, computers are not human: An artificially intelligent machine may know *about* humans, in some sense, but it's hard to imagine that any machine in the foreseeable future will be able to appreciate the full implications of launching a nuclear-tipped missile. Even with AI, a computer just follows orders as best it can—the ultimate Good German. Perhaps a little hesitation and a chance for second thoughts ought to be kept in the system.
- Even if computers can be programmed to decide the future of the race in a cooler and more rational manner than humans are capable of, perhaps it's worth devoting a little effort along the way to making sure that neither humans nor machines are ever put in that position.

The Theory and Practice of Machine Ethics

In the last analysis, it seems unlikely that the question "How much responsibility?" is ever going to have a simple answer. After all, human beings have been arguing among themselves about responsibility, authority, and control for many thousands of years, with no final resolution in sight; I see no reason to think that the answers are going to be any easier just because we've suddenly introduced some new intelligences based on silicon instead of on flesh and blood.

However, one thing that is apparent from the above discussion is that intelligent machines *will* embody values, assumptions, and purposes, whether their programmers consciously intend them to or not. Thus, as computers and robots become more and more intelligent, it becomes imperative that we think carefully and explicitly about what those built-in values are. Perhaps what we need is, in fact, a theory and practice of machine ethics, in the spirit of Asimov's three laws of robotics.

Admittedly, a concept like "machine ethics" sounds hopelessly fuzzy and far-fetched—at first. But maybe it's not as far out of reach as it seems. Ethics, after all, is basically a matter of making choices based on concepts of right and wrong, duty and obligation. We can already see a glimmer of how computers might make such choices in Jaime Carbonell's model of subjective understanding (Carbonell 1979). Carbonell showed how programs could be governed by hierarchies of goals, which would guide their reasoning processes in certain directions and not in others. Thus, it might very well be possible to formulate a hierarchy of goals that embody ethical concepts; the hard part, as always, would lie in formulating precisely what those concepts ought to be.

Another hint comes from work on distributed processing: In the effort to teach individual computers how to cooperate among themselves without having some boss computer tell them what to do, AI researchers are beginning to discover the principles that govern when individuals will work together harmoniously, and when they will not.

In any case, the effort of understanding machine ethics may turn out to be invaluable not just as a matter of practicality, but for its own sake. The effort to endow computers with intelligence has led us to look deep within ourselves to understand what intelligence really is. In much the same way, the effort to construct ethical machines will inevitably lead us to look within ourselves and reexamine our own conceptions of right and wrong. Of course, this is hardly a new activity in human history; it has been the domain of religion and philosophy for millennia. But then, pondering the nature of intelligence is not a new activity, either. The difference in each case is that, for the first time, we are having to explain ourselves to an entity that knows *nothing* about us. A computer is the proverbial Martian. And for that very reason, it is like a mirror: The more we have to explain ourselves, the more we may come to understand ourselves.

THE SHAPE OF THE FUTURE

As the great Danish physicist Niels Bohr once said, "It's hard to predict—especially the future." So we can talk all we want about possibilities and trends, but no one really knows what the new generation of computers will bring. Even if we did know, people would still be arguing about precisely which effects were good and which were bad.

In the broadest terms, of course, our prospects are framed by the vision of Asimov and Williamson. On the one hand, we have the bright vision of intelligent machines as our servants, advisers, tutors, companions, even our friends. According to this vision, computers represent a profoundly humane technology. Indeed, we can look forward to a new kind of partnership between mankind and machines, in which intelligent computers and robots will both relieve us of drudgery and tedium, while expanding our ability to understand and to cope with the world. The result will thus be a richer and more fulfilling life for all of us.

On the other hand, we have a darker vision of the future as an exercise in blank futility. Even if we leave aside our concerns about Big Brother, what will happen when all these artificially intelligent computers and robots leave us with nothing to do? What will be the point of living? Granted that human obsolescence is hardly an urgent problem. It will be a long, long time before computers can master politics, poetry, or any of the other things we really care about. But "a long time" is not forever; what happens when the computers *have* mastered politics and poetry? One can easily envision a future when the world is run quietly and efficiently by a set of exceedingly expert systems, in which machines produce goods, services, and wealth in abundance, and where everyone lives a life of luxury. It sounds idyllic—and utterly pointless.

But personally, I have to side with the optimists—for two reasons. The first stems from the simple observation that technology is made by people. Despite the strong impression that we are helpless in the face of, say, the spread of automobiles or the more mindless clerical applications of computers, the fact is that technology does not develop according to an immutable genetic code. It embodies human values and human choices. And to the extent that we can make those choices consciously instead of by blindly stumbling into them— admittedly not an easy thing to do—we do have control. Indeed, as we've just seen, the effort of developing intelligent computers may help us gain the insight to make these choices more wisely.

My second reason for being optimistic stems from a simple question: What does it mean to be "obsolete"?

A parable: Behold the lilies of the field. Considered purely as devices for converting light into energy, they've already been made obsolete by solar cells. But they go right on blooming, because photochemistry is not what lilies are about.

Another parable: Outside my window, the sparrows gather every day at a bird feeder. Considered purely as flying machines, they've long since been made obsolete by 747s. But they go right on eating and squabbling, because flying isn't what sparrows are about.

So what are human beings about? Perhaps our purpose is to serve God. Or perhaps we are here to serve each other. Perhaps we are here to create beauty in music, art, and literature, or to comprehend the universe, or to have fun. I won't presume to dictate the correct answer for anyone else. But I do suspect that in the long run, the most important implication of AI may be that it leads us to confront this question anew.

No, we don't know what this new world will be like. Perhaps it's just hard for those of us born to the work ethic to imagine what our hypothetical descendants will do with themselves. They may think of some very creative entertainments. Or they may create a new golden age of art and science. And they almost certainly will think of a whole new set of problems to worry about. But consider this: Some four thousand years stand between us and the author of Genesis. Technology has changed the world immeasurably in that time. And yet we can still read his words and feel their power. I somehow doubt that the advent of intelligent machines is going to change that very much. These machines may transform the world in ways we can only guess at—but we will still be human.

REFERENCES

Asimov, I. 1964. *The Rest of the Robots.* New York: Doubleday.

Augarten, A. 1986. A Sense of Responsibility, *PC Magazine* 5(5): 99–104.

Balkovich, E.; Lerman, S.; and Parmelee, R. P. 1985. Computing in Higher Education: the Athena Experience. *Communications of the ACM* (November 1985): 1214–1224.

Bell, T. E. 1985. Robots in the Home: Promises, Promises. *IEEE Spectrum* 22(5): 51–55.

Carbonell, J. G. 1979. *Subjective Understanding: Computer Models of Belief Systems.* Ann Arbor: University of Michigan Research Press.

Ford, D. 1985. *The Button.* New York: Simon and Schuster.

Gaushell, D. J. 1985. Automating the Power Grid. *IEEE Spectrum* 39–45.

IEEE Staff 1985. Assessing the Technical Challenges: A Log of Electronic Messages. In *Next Generation Computers,* ed. E. A. Torrero, 100–134. New York: IEEE Press.

Jennings, D. M. et al. 1985. Computer Networking for Scientists. *Science* 231: 943.

Kay, A. 1985. Software's Second Act. *Science* 85: 122–126.

Licklider, J. C. R. 1979. Computers and Government. In *The Computer Age: A Twenty-Year Review,* eds. M. L. Dertouzos and J. Moses, 91. Cambridge, Mass.: MIT Press.

Machrone, W. 1986. Spare Me the Sermon. *PC Magazine* 15(2): 53–55.

McCorduck, P. 1979. *Machines Who Think.* San Francisco: W. H. Freeman.

NASA Advanced Technology Advisory Committee 1985. Advancing Automation and Robotics Technology for the Space Station and the U.S. Economy, NASA Technical Memorandum 87566.

Newell, A. 1976. Viewpoints, No. 3. Pittsburgh, Penn.: Carnegie-Mellon University Publications.

Office of Technology Assessment 1985. Federal Government Information Technology: Electronic Surveillance and Civil Liberties, Technical Report, OTA CIT-23, Washington, D.C.

Shurkin, J. 1985. Robot Hand Conveys Sign Language to Persons Both Deaf and Blind. Stanford University News Service, July 30.

Weingarten, F. W. 1985. Assessing the Sociotechnical Challenges. In *Next-Generation Computers,* ed. E. A. Torrero, 138. New York: IEEE Press.

Williamson, J. 1978. With Folded Hands. In *The Best of Jack Williamson,* 154–206. New York: Ballantine.

Winner, L. 1985. Assessing the Sociotechnical Challenges. In *Next-Generation Computers,* ed. E. A. Torrero, 138. New York: IEEE Press.

Artificial Intelligence and Ethics:
An Exercise in the Moral
Imagination

Michael R. LaChat

Originally published in *AI Magazine,* 7, No. 2, 70–79. Copyright © 1986, American Association for Artificial Intelligence. Reprinted by permission of American Association for Artificial Intelligence and Michael R. LaChat.

In a book written in 1964, *God and Golem, Inc.,* Norbert Wiener predicted that the quest to construct computer-modeled artificial intelligence (AI) would come to impinge directly upon some of our most widely and deeply held religious and ethical values. It is certainly true that the idea of mind as artifact, the idea of a humanly constructed artificial intelligence, forces us to confront our image of ourselves. In the theistic tradition of Judeo-Christian culture, a tradition that is, to a large extent, our "fate," we were created in the imago Dei, in the image of God, and our tradition has, for the most part, showed that our greatest sin is pride—disobedience to our creator, a disobedience that most often takes the form of trying to be God. Now, if human beings are able to construct an artificial, personal intelligence— and I will suggest that this is theoretically possible, albeit perhaps practically improbable— then the tendency of our religious and moral tradition would be toward the condemnation of the undertaking: We will have stepped into the shoes of the creator, and, in so doing, we will have overstepped our own boundaries.

Such is the scenario envisaged by some of the classic science fiction of the past, Shelley's *Frankenstein,* or *The Modern Prometheus* and the Capek brothers' *R.U.R.* (for Rossom's Universal Robots) being notable examples. Both seminal works share the view that Pamela McCorduck (1979) in her work *Machines Who Think* calls the "Hebraic" attitude toward the AI enterprise. In contrast to what she calls the "Hellenic" fascination with, and openness toward, AI, the Hebraic attitude has been one of fear and warning: "You shall not make for yourself a graven image . . ."

I don't think that the basic outline of *Frankenstein* needs to be recapitulated here, even if, as is usually the case, the reader has seen only the poor image of the book in movie form. Dr. Frankenstein's tragedy—his ambition for scientific discoveries and benefits, coupled with the misery he brought upon himself, his creation and others—remains the primal expression of the "mad scientist's" valuational downfall, the weighting of experimental knowledge over the possibility of doing harm to self, subject, and society. Another important Hebraic image is that of *R.U.R.,* a 1923 play that gave us the first disastrous revolt of man-made slaves against their human masters. In both works theological insight and allusion abound; God and creation are salient issues, and both works condemn the AI enterprise.

Alongside the above images, of course, there have always lurked Hellenic, or perhaps better, "Promethean" images. Western history is replete with examples of attempts to construct an AI, with miserable and comical flops; with frauds; and with, as of late, some feeble approximations. The more sophisticated our reason and our tools, the more we seem to be inexorably drawn to replicate what has seemed to many to be what marks human persons off from the rest of creation—their *cogito,* their *nous,* their reason. We seem to want to catch up with our mythology and become the gods that we have created. In the layperson's mind, however, the dominant imagery appears to be the Hebraic; many look upon the outbreak of AI research with an uneasy amusement, an amusement masking, I believe, a considerable disquiet. Perhaps it is the fear that we might succeed, perhaps it is the fear that we might create a Frankenstein, or perhaps it is the fear that we might become eclipsed, in a strange oedipal drama, by our own creation. If AI is a real possibility, then so is *Frankenstein.* McCorduck says of *Frankenstein* that it "combines nearly all the psychological, moral, and social elements of the history of artificial intelligence."

Philosophical and theological ethicists have been silent, with a few exceptions (Fletcher, 1977), on the problem of AI, leaving, unfortunately, those with little training in ethical theory to assess the moral arguments. Boden (1977), Weizenbaum (1976), McCorduck (1979), and Hofstadter (1980), among others, have dealt with questions of technique, with the "hardware and software" questions surrounding the possibility of AI. Even when such researchers and chroniclers consider ethical questions, they tend to focus on the effects of AI upon society and not upon the AI *qua* subject of experimentation. By focusing on the morality of such experimentation as its affects the subject, I am obviously entering into the realm of the moral imagination, a realm that most ethicists might find trivial, farfetched, or meaningless given the present problems of the planet. Imagination *per se* has often been neglected in philosophy and theology, and the moral imagination suffers more neglect than the ordinary kind, perhaps because it seems more playful than the austere and often overly sober undertakings of most ethicists. Having team taught, however, a course on artificial intelligence and morality, a course about which I was, at first, somewhat dubious, I have reached the conclusion that pedagogically it is a very productive issue for ethical thinking, whether it will ever be accomplished in fact. The problems involved in the construction of a person by artificial means are fascinating and provocative partly because they allow us distance on ourselves; they allow us to probe ourselves in ways our imaginations were previously limited in doing. This does not mean, however, that they do not pose serious problems for the moral imagination.

One does not have to be a theist in order to be able to distill some practical wisdom from the religious counsel. "Don't play God." Among other things, God is a moral concept, as Kant rightly asserted. This venerable injunction can be "demythologized" to a word of warning, of caution toward all human undertakings, the effects of which might be irreversible or potentially harmful to ourselves and to others. For some ethicists, myself included, the first word of ethics is identical with the first caution of ethical medicine—"Above all, do no harm." As W. D. Ross (1965) has pointed out, such negative injunctions are the guiding thought, indeed, are the form of almost all legal codes, primitive or modern. The *prima facie* duty of nonmaleficence, of not doing harm, is almost universally conceded to be more stringent than positive injunctions to "do good." In the language game of modern ethics, this latter injunction can be considered as part of the utilitarian tendency to explore the new, to take risks that might even cause harm to a few for the benefit of many.[1] It is certain that both injunctions can claim to be moral, but I side with Kant on the primacy of the former: All rational beings, capable of moral evaluation, must be considered as ends in themselves rather than as means to another's ends.[2] The stringency of the norm of nonmaleficence, attested to in almost all of the modern codes of experimental medicine, means that ethical thinking with regard to the possibility of constructing an artifact which might verge on the personal is necessary *a priori*. The intent of this article is, thus, to raise the questions of a moral nature by stimulating the imagination in tandem with the technological imagination, a necessary reciprocal relationship that we cannot allow to be submerged entirely in the technological realm.

In the first part of the article, I argue briefly that replication of personal intelligence is possible in principle, because counterarguments usually rest on some sort of quasi-mystical dualism, which I find untenable. I further argue that the Turing Test allows us to specify the conditions under which a machine could be said to have attained "personhood," however difficult such a characteristic might be to define.

In the second part of the article, I ask whether such an undertaking should be pursued. The focus of this section is on the moral safeguards for the subject of the experiment, and questions are raised about the extent to which an analogy can be drawn between the morality of the AI project and the ethical guarantees given to human subjects by modern experimental medicine.

The last section of the article is a true exercise in the moral imagination. It asks the question, "Can an artificial intelligence be moral?" It is suggested that one cannot answer this question without giving consideration to the perennial philosophical problems of free will, casuistry, and the role of emotions in moral decision making.

IS ARTIFICIAL INTELLIGENCE POSSIBLE IN PRINCIPLE?

I will not pretend in what follows to be an expert on the "hardware" or "software" of AI, nor do I claim to be particularly adept in the relevant areas of philosophy of the mind. These technical questions have been dealt with elsewhere in great detail.[3] Joseph Weizenbaum, an increasingly isolated figure within the relatively small circle of AI researchers, has rightly pointed out some of the enormously exaggerated claims that even a sophisticated audience is prone to make for a technology it really does not understand. Few people who have been exposed to the relevant literature would doubt the incredible complexity of such an under-taking. Thus, for example, we need to cautiously remind ourselves that there is a distinction between intelligent behavior and personally intelligent behavior. A machine can learn to run a maze as well as a rat and at the level of rat intelligence could be said to be fairly "smart."

---

[1] For a more thorough discussion of normative theories, see W. K. Frankena's (1973) *Ethics*, chapters 2 and 3.

[2] See Paton (1965), especially chapter 16.

[3] For example, McCorduck (1979), pp. 359–64.

The intelligence of the human brain, however, is of a different magnitude entirely.[4] Although it is obvious that machines can perform some activities at a higher level than persons can, these tasks remain, by and large, highly specialized and therefore remote from the capacity of human intelligence for multipurpose activities.

THE OBSTACLE OF DUALISM

In spite of these difficulties—organizational complexities that might prove to be insuperable—I feel it necessary to stick out my layperson's neck and offer a tentative argument that an artificial, personal intelligence is possible in principle. Having team taught a course titled "Minds, Machines, and Morals" with a mathematician at St. John's University in Minnesota, I am well aware of the skeptical wall that confronts enthusiastic AI researchers. The first response of most students was a flat rejection of the possibility of such an endeavor. As the course progressed, however, such absolute skepticism gave way to a more tempered doubt, namely, that AI would never be accomplished, given the complexity of the task. What occurred to us during the process of in-class debate was that the absolute skepticism rested ultimately on some sort of dualism between mind and brain; for example, it was often contended that persons had "souls" which were not dependent upon the brain for their existence or that persons were possessed of some almost magical "substance" which could not be duplicated artificially.

I happen to agree with Carl Sagan who stated on a public television show that the evidence for such dualism is nonexistent. Although we might not, as the physiologist Wilder Penfield (1983) suggests, have all of the evidence which would allow us to deny that a "creative thought" might precede electrical activity in the brain, although we may not be able to accept without reservation the philosophic claim that thought equals brain activity, we can make, with some assurance, the more modest claim that there is no evidence of thought taking place without the brain. We do not have to make the stronger claim that there is an identity, an ontological identity, between consciousness and an electrical thought pattern in the brain in order to reject the claim which asserts that conscious thought can occur without the brain.[5]

Let me propose a rather simple response to the absolute skeptics who rest their arguments on an indemonstrable, ontological dualism between mind and brain. All that is necessary to indicate the possibility of AI is to posit a functionally isomorphic relationship between a

---

[4]It has been estimated that the human brain contains 10^{13} bits of intelligence capacity as opposed, for example, to a cow's capacity of 10^{11} bits (*Chemtech*, 1980, p. 590.)

[5]As Karl Marx and Friedrich Engels pointed out, mind-body dualists tend to hold to a disconcerting dualism between their physics and metaphysics as well. Thus, they say rightly of Descartes: "Descartes in his physics endowed matter with self-creative power and conceived mechanical motion as the act of its life. He completely separated his physics from his metaphysics. Within his physics matter is the only substance, the only basis of being and of knowledge" (Marx & Engels, 1971, pp. 60–61).

neural network in the human brain and (at present) a silicon chip in a computer. What is asserted here is that intelligent thought is dependent for its existence on the neural "machinery" of the brain, on the flow of electricity through that "hardware." Electrical patterns in the brain can be compared to the software of the computer and the brain's neurons to the computer's hardware, to the "neural" networks of the chip. This is not to say that mind cannot be an emergent property of a certain level of organization but only that such emergence would be dependent on a neurological "substrate" for its existence. As Douglas Hofstadter says in his magnificent *Gödel, Escher, Bach*:

> Crucial to the endeavor of Artificial Intelligence research is the notion that the symbolic levels of the mind can be "skimmed off" their neural substrate and implemented in other media, such as the electronic substrate of computers. To what depth the copying brain must go is at present completely unclear. (P. 573.)

This last sentence is an important one. There are two basic approaches to it in the history of AI research. The first is the cybernetic model; it relies on the "physiological" similarity between neurons and hardware. Thus, Norbert Wiener (1964) can say that even the living tissue of the brain is theoretically duplicable at the molecular level by suitable hardware materials. The second approach, the one dominant today, is the "information-processing" model, a model that does not pay as much attention to the level of hardware similarity. All it asserts is that a machine will demonstrate intelligent behavior when it acts intelligently by behavioral definitions. An intelligent machine would not have to "look like" an intelligent human; it would only have to exhibit the same sort of behavior. It is evident that the functionally isomorphic relationship between neural network and hardware is an admixture of both models, although it leans in the direction of the latter. It claims that the neural network hardware isomorphism is a cybernetic one insofar as the substrate conditions would probably have to be similar enough to facilitate the duplication of the functions of both; it does not claim that the isomorphism would necessarily be pictorial as well. What we would need, then, in order to duplicate the hardware substrate would be an adequate "map" of the brain and the extremely sophisticated "tools" and "materials" with which to duplicate it.

So far I have only discussed conditions relevant to the hardware substrate. The software level of a personal machine consciousness—the symbolic level that Hofstadter contends must be "skimmed off" the neural substrate and implemented in other media—seems to be much more problematic to duplicate. A personal intelligence must have personality, and this seems on the face of it to be an almost impossible problem for AI. Personalities are formed through time and through lived experience, and the personal *qua* humanly personal must certainly include the emotional. Indeed, a phenomenological analysis of human experience, such as that of the early Heidegger, indicates that persons might have to experience the emotion of dread in the face of finitude (death) in order to have a grasp of "isness," in order to be fully conscious (Heidegger, 1962; Dreyfus, 1972).

The temporal dimension of human consciousness is a great obstacle to the AI project. Suppose we were able to produce a "map" of the thought patterns of a human adult. Such a map would have to include memories and experiences as well as hopes, aspirations, and goals; in short, it would have to be a map inclusive of the three temporal dimensions of human consciousness—past, present, and future. Could such a map be "programmed" directly into the hardware substrate? The question of the growth of consciousness through time thus emerges as a particularly salient problem. Perhaps a personally intelligent machine has to grow into consciousness, much as a human baby does; then again, perhaps not.

It is not out of the realm of possibility that pain consciousness might be electrochemically duplicable. To what extent are pain and emotion necessary to personal intelligence? There are certainly cases in which paralyzed or drugged persons experience no pain and yet are still conscious, but such persons might still be said to suffer. This crucial distinction (Boeyink, 1974) need to be borne in mind. Suffering, as opposed to pure pain reflex, is strained through a human ego, an ego that can remember, anticipate, and project itself in time. Perhaps, then, emotions and body consciousness are indispensable requisites of the personally intelligent. These are difficult issues that probably can only be resolved through the trial and error of experiment—and there's the rub! The deliberate constructions of the capacity for pain would seem to entail the causation of pain as well (as the robots in *R.U.R.* are given pain in order to keep them from injuring themselves). This problem raises the question of the morality of the experiment in a vivid way, and is an issue I address shortly.

ADJUDICATING THE ACHIEVEMENT OF A PERSONAL AI

If these difficulties can be surmounted, how can we finally reach agreement that a personal AI has been achieved? The quasi-behavioral criteria I outlined earlier facilitate our ability to specify the conditions under which a machine can be said to have achieved this intelligence, namely, the conditions specified by the Turing Test.

The simplest way to adjudicate a claim that a machine has or has not achieved personal intelligence is to define intelligence behaviorally and then test the machine to see if it exhibits it. No doubt, such definitional lists, even when specified exhaustively, would still run afoul of persistent human skepticism, but such skepticism can be greatly alleviated by the application of the Turing Test. Alan Turing, a British mathematician and logician who believed in the possibility of AI, proposed a test that might give criteria for ascertaining the accomplishment of such an AI (McCorduck, 1979). Suppose that a person (an interrogator) were to communicate unseen with both another person and the AI "subject," and that the interrogator could not tell whether he or she was communicating with the other person or with the "machine"? I contend that such a test could adjudicate the claim, provided (1) that we could agree at the onset with what the test presupposes about the normatively personal, and (2) that certain problems concerning the prerequisites of the interrogator could be ironed out.

It is evident that the test presupposes communication as the *sine qua non* of personal intelligence, that the ability to meaningfully converse through the medium of some sort of language constitutes the essentially personal. Such a presupposed concept of the personal is evident in much of the literature of current medical ethics. Because communication depends on the functional organization of the brain, brain death might be considered the termination of the personal (Fletcher, 1977). Some philosophers and theologians have argued cogently than an inability to respond to stimuli, particularly to linguistic communication, means the subject, although perhaps morphologically human, is no longer a person.[6] Theologians, in particular, are apt to define the personal with regard to the giving and receiving of "the Word" (Niebuhr, 1963). Whether we take such communication to be exhaustive of the personal, it is apparent that without its possibility persons would no longer be persons. The high level of hardware and software sophistication necessary to enable symbolic communication ought to encompass any other kinds of activity we might take to be personal.[7] Human beings do not become persons through simple biological conception. A zygote is a human being, but it can only trivially be considered a person. A machine can be a person in the same way that a "higher" animal might possibly be considered a person (Singer, 1980)—if it shows the ability to meaningfully participate in a language system.

Other questions about the Turing Test remain. These problems have largely to do with the capacities of the interrogator. Such a person, it appears, must be a rational adult, capable of giving reasons for a decision. Should the interrogator know something about computers as well? Would the interrogator be able to "trick" the computer in ways a layperson could not? Would one of the tricks be to shame or insult the subject in order to elicit an emotional response? Perhaps the best interrogator would be another computer, one with the capacity, for example, to interrogate the computer well enough to see at what point it might eclipse human ability. Should there be a group of interrogators, both human and not? How long should the test run before a decision is made? The computer might have to be capable of deceiving the interrogator and of fabricating a life history (in the supposed absence of having "lived" one). It might need the capacity to anticipate tricks and perhaps even to evince a capacity for self-doubt. In short, it might have to possess a self-reflexive consciousness (the ability to make itself the object of its own thought), a characteristic that Tooley (1974) and Mead (1972) have convincingly argued to be a hallmark of the personal self. Such a machine might even have to be able to lie. An intriguing theory is that a child comes to know himself or herself as an ego when he or she can deceive an adult to whom he or she has previously attributed omniscience; then the child finally knows he or she has a private consciousness (Schlein, 1961). Such might also be the case with intelligent machines.

These problems are indeed difficult, though fascinating. At any rate, having asserted that a machine might in principle achieve a personal consciousness, I find I am still begging the central question of the article. The Turing Test, if passed, would be a *fait accompli*. The harder question is to ask whether it should have been undertaken in the first place.

Is the Construction of Personal AI an Immoral Experiment?

Listen, for a moment, to the lament of Frankenstein's monster:

> Like Adam, I was apparently united by no link to any another being in existence, but his state was far different from mine in every other respect. He had come forth from the

---

[6] For example, Joseph Fletcher (1972) uses the term "human" rather than "person," but his criteria distinguishes the personal from merely biomorphologically human.

[7] It ought to encompass even the possibility of a "religious experience," which Weizenbaum has asserted in a popular source it could never attain to. Weizenbaum does not tell us why it could not have such an experience. See the interview with Weizenbaum by Rosenthal (1983), pp. 94–97.

hands of God a perfect creature, happy and prosperous, guarded by the especial care of his creator, he was allowed to convene with, and acquire knowledge from, beings of a superior nature, but I was wretched, helpless, and alone. Many times I considered Satan was the fitter emblem of my condition, for often, like him, when I saw the bliss of my protectors, the bitter gall of envy rose up within me . . . Hateful day when I received life! . . . Accursed Creator! Why did you form a monster so hideous that even you turned from me in disgust? (Pp. 152–53.)

It seems obvious, first of all, that a creature who can communicate as well as the monster should have little trouble passing the Turing Test. Second, the fact that the monster is not a "machine" but an assemblage of biological parts revivified by electricity is beside the point. What is intriguing about the monster's lament is that he is claiming something analogous to a "wrongful birth" suit; as an imperfect creation, he is claiming that he ought not to have been made. However fanciful the monster might be, he is a perfect example of what might go wrong with AI: He is the possibility of an experiment gone awry. His story would be incomplete without the rationalizations of his creator:

I believed myself destined for some great enterprise . . . I deemed it criminal to throw away in useless grief those talents that might be useful to my fellow creatures . . . all my speculations and hope are as nothing and, like the archangel who aspired to omnipotence, I am chained to an eternal hell. (P. 256.)

We can say the monster is claiming that he was the improper subject of a poorly designed, nontherapeutic experiment, whereas Dr. Frankenstein claims as his motivation not only his own egotism but the benefits to society that might accrue from his experiment. In modern times, a similar form of utilitarian justification is echoed by Norbert Weiner (1964), who says of the fears surrounding the AI enterprise:

If we adhere to all these taboos, we may acquire a great reputation as conservative and sound thinkers, but we shall contribute very little to the further advance of knowledge. It is the part of the scientist—of the intelligent man of letters and of the honest clergyman as well—to entertain heretical and forbidden opinions experimentally, even if he is finally to reject them. (P. 5)

Entertaining opinions is one thing, but here we are talking about an experiment, an experiment in the construction of something which is so intelligent that it might come to be considered a person. It is one thing to experiment on a piece of machinery, such as a car, and quite another, as the Nuremberg Medical Trials indicated, to experiment with, or in this case toward, persons. Kant's imperative to treat persons as ends in themselves rather than as means to an end is at the heart of the matter.

HUMAN EXPERIMENTATION AND THE AI EXPERIMENT

Particularly since the Nazi atrocities, the norm of nonmaleficence has been considered more stringent than that of beneficence in subsequent medical codes. The concern has been overwhelmingly in favor of the subject and against the interests and benefits of the society. Even where considerations of social utility have been included in such codes, a strong burden has been placed on the experimenter to prove that benefits overwhelmingly outweigh risks to the health and welfare of the subject. In the extreme, such concerns have tended to rule out all forms of nontherapeutic experimentation (Jonas, 1977). Is the AI experiment then immoral in its inception, assuming, that is, that the end (telos) of the experiment is the production of a person?

Let us first ask whether the experiment can be considered therapeutic in any meaningful sense of the word; that is, is it of benefit to the subject? It is difficult to consider it as such, because the subject does not really exist as confirmed fact (as a person) prior to the experiment itself; it exists only *in potentia*. In the stages prior to the "dawning" of consciousness, the machine is in some respects more like a zygote or early fetus than a person (assuming, of course, that the early stages of the construction of the AI are somewhat analogous to the early stages in the teleological process of biological growth). We can, then, consider the experiment to be therapeutic only if we maintain that the potential "gift" of conscious life outweighs no life at all. We cannot say that this is an experiment on a sick person or a sick potential person for the sake of that person whom we are attempting to make better. Thus, we can fairly consider the experiment to be nontherapeutic in nature. If so, the stringent code of medical ethics seems to apply (Ramsey, 1975). We shouldn't treat the subject as if it had no rights at all. This is not to say that the benefits to society would be trivial; even pure knowledge is never trivial, especially when such "high tech" almost invariably trickles down in various ways. However, the presumption of the experimental tradition is always *prima facie* against nontherapeutic experimentation, save perhaps in those cases where the experimenter is also the subject (Jonas, 1977).

It might be contended, however, that the "birthing" of an AI is analogous to a human birthing. Let us consider this possibility for a moment.

Until the recent present in human history, birthing has basically been "set" for us. We took what we got. In the Judeo-Christian tradition, life itself has been viewed, for the most part, as a gift from God, and the sanctity of human life has been weighted very strongly against any quality of life ethic (Dyck, 1977; Noonan, 1970). Modern technology, specifically genetic screening and amniocentesis, has, when coupled with the Supreme Court's abortion decision, raised a different sort of moral question: Is it immoral to knowingly bring into the world a potentially or actually defective child? Such a question raises the crucial issue of the locus of rights in the procreative decision.

Roe vs. Wade has shown that the right to procreate and to terminate procreation (whether or not the fetus is defective) is, at least in the first trimester of pregnancy, a subjective, discriminatory right of the parents (Reiser, Dick, & Curran, 1977). The desires of the parents are the locus of the rights, and only at stages approaching viability can the state take any compelling interest in the welfare of the fetus. Yet questions can be raised about the rights of the fetus. I have in mind here not the right to life of the fetus but the right of the potential newborn to be born to the possibility of a healthy existence, the right of a child to be born without disabling handicaps and with the freedom from severe pain (as opposed to the capacity to feel pain).

It is my opinion that most AI researchers would incline to follow something analogous to the "subjective desires for the parents" route where the possibility of AI is concerned, thereby implicitly making an analogy with procreative rights as guaranteed by the Supreme Court decision. However, the analogy does not really hold for a number of significant reasons.

In a certain sense, we must acknowledge that human reproduction is an experiment. Joseph Fletcher (1972) and others have argued that the "sexual roulette" mode of human reproductive experimentation should come to an end. "To be human is to be in control," says Fletcher, and he argues that a baby conceived by artificial means would be more, rather than less human because it would be the product of a thoughtful, rational process. Nonetheless, we can say that the human "roulette" mode of reproduction has allowed us inductively to generalize certain rules of thumb which serve as guidelines for preventive, prenatal care of the fetus. In AI there are really few, if any, such precedents. The injunction "do no harm" is cloudy in the case of AI, much more so than the injunction, for example, not to smoke while pregnant. AI is an extreme experiment; we have little or no knowledge of what might happen. Although it could be argued that all preventive, human reproductive behavior has been built on the basis of trial and error as well, we can at least say that evolution has set our birth for us in a way which, at present, is only trivially a matter of the will. AI is really much more of a deliberate experiment.

Second and most important, human reproduction is a necessity for species survival. All of the earth's cultures attest to this necessity and provide ethical and legal safeguards to protect it. AI, on the other hand, is not necessary as a means of species survival. This does not mean that it might not prove in ages to come to be a necessity, but at present it is not. AI is more a luxury than a necessity; as such, it should fall under the stringent experimental guidelines. It can also be argued that at present the risks of the AI experiment are greater than the benefits, and the ratio of risk to benefit is higher in AI than in human reproduction. For the *subject* of the AI experiment, the only benefit appears to be, at best, the gift of conscious life. This gift must be weighed against whatever problems might arise.

The result of this argument is, apparently, to side with the Frankenstein monster's "wrongful birth" suit. An AI experiment that aims at producing a self-reflexively conscious and communicative "person" is *prima facie* immoral. There are no compelling reasons which lead us to believe that we could ensure even the slightest favorable risk-benefit ratio. Is the necessary conclusion, then, not to do it?

DOES A PERSONAL AI HAVE RIGHTS?

Suppose, for a moment, that we could guarantee all of the conditions requisite to birthing an AI which had the full range of personal capacities and potentials; in other words, suppose we could guarantee that the AI would have the same rights *a priori* which actual persons do now. What would such rights be? A suitable starting point might be the United Nation's 1948 Declaration of Human Rights (Donaldson & Werhane, 1979). I excerpt some of those which might be pertinent to the AI case. Article Four, for example, states that no one shall be held in slavery or servitude. Isn't this the very purpose of robotics? Fletcher has already contended that the bioengineering of such entities might conceivably be warranted for the performance of dangerous tasks (an interesting parallel to the conditions making for *R.U.R.*'s robot revolt) (Fletcher, 1972).

The prohibition of slavery raises a further question for AI. A free, multipurpose robot might be "legitimate," as it were, but what of a single-purpose robot? Would this be tantamount to engineering a human baby with, for example, no arms so that he or she could become a great soccer player? Any limited-purpose or limited-capacity AI would have its essence defined before its existence (Sartre, 1957), so to speak; if we would not accept this of the humanly personal, we should not accept it of the AI personal as well. Thus, if we were to hold strictly to the United Nation articles, we would have to do justice, for example, to Article Thirteen: the right to freedom of movement. Must the AI be mobile? Does the AI have the right to arms and legs and to all of the other human senses as well?

What about Article Sixteen: the right to marry and found a family? The Frankenstein monster demanded this right from his creator and was refused. Was Dr. Frankenstein immoral in refusing this request? Does an AI have the right to reproduce by any means? Does "it" have the right to slow growth (that is, a maturation process) or the right to a specific gender?

If we concede a right to freedom from unnecessary pain as well, a right we seem to confer on subpersonal animals (Singer, 1980), we have to face the delicate technical question I alluded to earlier: Is there a way to give pain capacity to an AI without causing it pain, at least no more pain than an ordinary human birth might entail?

Such questions are quite bewildering. Although I have argued that the bottom line of the morality of the experiment *qua* experiment on the subject is whether a consciousness of any quality is better than none at all, and although I have also argued than an unnecessary experiment which carries with it potential for a severely limited existence and, possibly, unnecessary pain, is unethical, I have indicated that if all of the conditions of a sound birth were met *a priori* the experiment might then be considered legitimate.

All this is somewhat silly. Such AIs will probably be built up in layers, and they are not really even babies, yet! Consciousness itself might prove to be an emergent property that might spring forth unexpectedly from a sophisticated level of hardware and software organization, quite as HAL's did in Clarke's *2001: A Space Odyssey*. Then, if we give birth to a Frankenstein monster, it will be too late. This is often the way human beings learn their lessons, and I have no illusions about the tendency of technology to run with its own momentum, to "do it if it can be done." Perhaps, though, if we give free rein to our moral imaginations, we will be better prepared than was poor old Dr. Frankenstein.

CAN AN ARTIFICIAL INTELLIGENCE BE MORAL?

A common criticism of the AI project is that a computer only does what it is programmed to do, that it is without the mysterious property called free will and, therefore, can never become "moral." (I will take free will to mean, specifically, the attribution of an intervening variable between stimulus and response that renders impossible a prediction of response, given adequate knowledge of all input variables.) Some philosophers might even be tempted to say that a machine, however intelligent, which is without the capacity to value and to make moral choices cannot be considered an end in itself and, therefore, could not be the possessor of certain human rights (I think, at least, that this is what Kant's argument would boil down to.) Indeed, Kant (1964) would argue that a capacity for free will is a necessary postulate of the moral life, though there is nothing empirical about this capacity. (I cannot enter here into an analysis of Kant's arguments about the ontology of this capacity, for example that free will is part of the intelligible world as opposed to the sensual-empirical world. Suffice it to say that I believe this mysterious capacity for free will is really, for Kant, something from another reality and is, thus, subject to the criticism of dualism which I have previously alluded to.)

A cursory glance at the history of theology and philosophy on the topic of free will, from Augustine and Pelagius to Chomsky and Skinner, shows the difficulty of delineating any proof for its existence or nonexistence. For every Chomsky (1973) who maintains that a behaviorist has no predictive ability with regard to human behavior, there is a Skinner who maintains that the behaviorist does not have all the information about input variables necessary to make a complete prediction about behavior or output. Free will and determinism might really be differing perspectives on the same phenomenon, the former being the perspective from the subjectivity of human agency, the latter from observation. Except for the problem of retributive justice (punishment), I see little or no difference in the "cash value" of holding to one theory or the other; it is interesting to note, however, that the reality of Kant's noumenal capacity for free will might, in a trivial sense, be "proved" by the failure of an AI to ever give behavioristic evidence (however that might be defined) of free will. At any rate, persons make so-called choices to act in certain ways, whether they are factually free or factually determined (or programmed). However, short of invoking the *deus ex machina* of an ontological dualism in order to protect the ghostlike existence of the free will, the contention of its existence really makes little difference to the AI project. If free will is real in some sense, there is again no reason to believe that it might not be an emergent property of a sophisticated level of technical organization, just as it might be asserted to arise through a slow maturation process in humans. I should also add that not all AI experts are convinced an AI could not attain free will (I refer interested persons to the last chapters of Hofstadter's *Gödel, Escher, Bach* some interesting ruminations on this difficult issue).

EMOTION

What about emotion? There has been considerable debate among ethicists about whether the concept of the "good" is a cognitive one or a noncognitive and emotive one (for example, Frankena, 1973). Is morality primarily a matter of reason and logic, or is it a matter of emotion and sympathy? Even for Kant, who was deeply committed to reason, it can be construed to be a matter of both (Paton, 1965). A person, then, must have emotions and reason in order to have the capacity for ethical decision making. Given an accurate, nonreductionalistic description of moral experience (Mandelbaum, 1969), an AI would probably have to have feelings and emotions, as well as intelligent reason, in order to replicate personal decision making. The necessity of this capacity becomes more apparent when we seek to discern whether an AI ought to be something like a moral judge. Weizenbaum (1976) has maintained that there are certain things an intelligent machine should not be allowed to do, especially things involving human emotions such as love. Does this mean, then, that a machine should not be allowed to be a moral judge?

If we took to modern ethical theory in order to ascertain what attributes a competent moral judge must have, we might turn to the ideal observer theory (Firth, 1952). The ideal observer theory maintains that the statement "X is right" means that X would be approved by an ideal moral judge who had the following characteristics: omniscience (knowledge of all relevant facts), omnipercipience (the ability to vividly imagine the feelings and circumstances of the parties involved, that is, something like empathy), disinterestedness (nonbiasedness), and dispassionateness (freedom from disturbing passion). These characteristics, then, are an attempt to specify the conditions under which a valid moral judgment might be made. The attributes of such an ideal observer, of course, resemble the traditional attributes of God and this is understandable if we, like Kant, consider the concept of God to be, in part, a moral ideal. The theory itself, however, does not presuppose a belief in God; it merely contends that it gives an adequate description of the requisite conditions we need in order to make sound moral judgments. We do attempt to approximate these conditions when we make a moral judgment: A judge who shakes hands in the courtroom with your opponent but not with you could justly be accused of failing to be disinterested, and so on. Now if we look at most of the characteristics of such an observer, that is, omniscience, disinterestedness, and dispassionateness, then a case might be made for saying that an unemotional AI could be considered a better moral judge than a human person. Such a machine might be able to store and retrieve more factual data, not be disturbed by violent passions and interests, and so on; it could be said to be capable of "cool" and "detached" choices.

Omnipercipience, or empathy, however, is problematic. This kind of sympathy for the circumstances of people, part of what Aristotle called "equity," is a wisdom that comes from being able to "put ourselves in the other's shoes," as it were. Certainly emotions would be involved here, and the degree of morphological similarity necessary for the empathetic response of one person to another is a subtle and problematic matter. Perhaps the ability to empathize is what Weizenbaum finds lacking in any possible AI and is the reason why he would not entrust such judgments to one. Yet, given what I have previously said there is no reason to believe that such ability could not be, in principle, duplicable.

THE PROBLEM OF CASUISTRY

Casuistry deals with the application of general rules to specific, concrete situations. The question of whether all thinking can be formalized in some sort of rule structure is a crucial one for AI in general. For example, one computer program seeks to capture the medical diagnostic ability of a certain physician who has the reputation as one of the best diagnosticians in the world. The computer programmer working with him tries to break this procedure down into a series of logical steps of what to the physician was an irreducible intuition of how to go about doing it. With a lot of prodding, however, the diagnostician was soon able to break these intuitions down into their logical steps (H.E.W., 1980). Perhaps this is true with all "intuitive" thinking or is it? If we assume that ethics is a reasonable, cognitive undertaking, we are prone to formalize it in a series of rules, not exceptionless rules but something like W. D. Ross's list of *prima facie* obligations; a list of rules, any one of which might be binding in a particular circumstance (Ross, 1965). What Ross gives us is something like the moral equivalent of a physicist's periodic table of the elements, moral rules that constitute the elemental building blocks of moral life. The list runs something like this:

promise keeping, truth telling, reparations, justice, gratitude, beneficence, nonmaleficence, and self-improvement.

All of these obligations are incumbent upon us as moral beings, but one or several can take precedence over the others in certain situations. We must, therefore, have some principle for adjudicating between these rules in situations where they might conflict. They need not be set up in a strict hierarchy; we could, for example, say that the principle of adjudication is intuition. This is basically what Ross asserts when he quotes Aristotle's famous dictum "The decision rests with the perception." At the same time, however, Ross ranks at least one of his rules a *prima facie* more binding than another. The duty of not harming (nonmaleficence) is a more stringent duty than actively promoting good (beneficence), and this is true even before a particular situation is addressed. This proves significant in what follow:

1. A robot may not injure a human being or through inaction allow a human being to come to harm.
2. A robot must obey orders given it by humans except when such orders conflict with the first law.
3. A robot must protect its own existence as long as such protection does not conflict with the first or second laws.

These, of course, are not all of the rules that a robot might be wired with; Ross's list is certainly more complete than Asimov's. There is plenty of food for thought, though, in Asimov's hierarchy.

The first thing an ethicist might notice about rule one is that it attempts to combine the principle of nonmaleficence (do no harm) with a utilitarian principle of beneficence (do the maximum good). Rule one thus contains within itself the potential for conflict, as it does in modern normative theory (Frankena, 1973, pp. 45–48). What if the robot has to decide between injuring a human being or not acting at all and thus allowing another human being to come to harm through an act of omission? Asimov's robots run in circles when confronted with a conflict-of-rule situation. What would be most moral to do in such a situation—refrain from acting at all, or heed the voice of Kierkegaard and act whatever the costs might be? Further, how do we understand the principle of beneficence underlying the sins of omission? Should all robots go to Pakistan in order to maximize the good, or should they go somewhere else? How long should a robot calculate potential consequences before acting? I should point out that if there is any specific normative theory attributed to the AIs of science fiction, it would have to be utilitarian. Robots are seen as paradigms of calculation, as exhibiting metahuman capacities for weighing, quantifying, and projecting consequences. As such, they are subject to the same criticisms one might level at utilitarians in general; for example, how might a robot compare incommensurable goods in order that they might be quantified and rendered mathematically precise? Such a problem vexed Jeremy Bentham for most of his life—is push pin really as good as poetry?

The second rule, obeying orders for humans except where they might conflict with the first rule, appears to contradict the aforementioned right to freedom from slavery (unless, of course, the AI were to be somehow considered a "child"). The second part of the rule, refusing to take an order to harm, might not be considered moral at all if, for example, the protection of innocence were at stake. Should an AI robot be a proponent of the just war theory, or should it be something of a pacifist, even to the point of self-sacrifice as Asimov's robots would appear to be?

The third rule, protecting its own existence as long as such protection does not conflict with the first and second laws, is also highly problematic. First, it gives the robot the right to self-defense but then takes it away. Note the use of the word must. There is no possibility for what ethics calls "supererogatory" duties. These are the things we think it is praiseworthy to do, but not blameworthy not to do. (Urmson, 1958; Chisolm, 1963). Suppose, for example, that a man jumps on a hand grenade in order to save his comrades. His heroic action is likely to be praised, but had he chosen not to jump he probably would not be blamed for failing to sacrifice himself. We like to keep the heroic free from the obligatory. Asimov's rules do not. Is that really bad? Should we wire a self-sacrificial attitude into our robots, making them all little Christs? For that matter, should we "wire" our own children to so act? The questions involved in wiring a robot for morality are so very similar to the questions of how we should morally educate our own children!

It might prove to be the case that no hierarchy of normative principles can do justice to the complexity of personal, moral choice. It also might be that the self-reflexively conscious ego of a sophisticated AI would take no programming at all, and that it would pick and choose its own rules, rules it learns through the trials and errors of time. However difficult it might prove to duplicate human, moral decision making, especially an adjudicative principle like intuition, we need not resort to a skepticism that is based ultimately on dualistic "magic," and thereby resign from the attempt.

CONCLUSION

What if we never make an AI that can pass the Turing Test? Little of the effort will be lost. It is the peculiar pedagogical effect of "distancing" that makes the contemplation of artificial persons so fertile for the human imagination. The proponents of AI promise us that we will learn more about ourselves in the attempt to construct something like ourselves. This distancing is also dangerous, however. We have, for example, distanced ourselves from other people and from animals, often with tragic results. Of course, the project will go on, and I think, with much success, but it will be a sad thing if Hegel was right when he said, "The owl of Minerva flies only at midnight." Much caution and forethought are necessary when we contemplate the human construction of the personal.

If we can't ever make such an intelligence, is any mystery gone? To the contrary, the failure to be able to produce the personal as artifact might eventually bring us to the brink of a mysticism that has, at least, been partially "tested." Would it be more mysterious to find intelligent life elsewhere in the universe or to find after unimaginable aeons that we are unique and alone? Perhaps AI is the next stage of evolution, a harder blow to our ineradicable anthropomorphism than Copernicus's theory that the planets revolved around the sun and not the earth. As McCorduck says of the undertaking, "Face to face with mind as artifact we're face to face with almost more themes in the human experience than we can count or comprehend. And there's the added zest that this idea may turn out to transcend the human experience altogether and lead us to the metahuman" (p. 329).

On one side of the moral spectrum lies the fear of something going wrong; on the other side is the exuberant "yes" to all possibilities and benefits. Though the first word of ethics is "do no harm," we can perhaps look forward to innovations with a thoughtful caution. Perhaps we will eclipse ourselves with our own inventions. Perhaps Michelangelo was correct when he pointed that long finger of God at Adam's hand. Either way, I am excited.

REFERENCES

Asimov, I (1950) *I robot*. New York: Gnome Press.

Boden, M. (1977) *Artificial intelligence and natural man*. New York: Basic Books.

Boeyink, David (1974) Pain and suffering. *Journal of Religious Ethics* 2(1): 85–97.

Capek, The Brothers (1975). *R.U.R. and the insect play*. London: Oxford University Press.

Chisholm, Roderick (1963) Supererogation and offense: A conceptual scheme for ethics. *Ratio* 5 (June): 1–14.

Chomsky, Noam (1973) *For reasons of state*. New York: Random House.

Department of Health, Education & Welfare (1980) *The seeds of artificial intelligence: Sumex-aim*. Washington, D.C.

Dreyfus, H. (1972) *What computers can't do: A critique of artificial reason*. New York: Harper & Row.

Dyck, A. J. (1977) Ethics and medicine. In S. J. Reiser, A. J. Dyck, & W. J. Curran (Eds.) *Ethics in medicine: Historical perspectives and contemporary concerns*. Cambridge, Mass: MIT Press.

Firth, Roderick (1952) Ethical absolutism and the ideal observer, *Philosophy and Phenomenological Research* 12 (March): 317–345.

Fletcher, Joseph (1977) Ethical aspects of genetic concerns. In S. J. Reiser, A. J. Dyck, & W. J. Curran (Eds.) *Ethics in medicine: Historical perspectives and contemporary concerns*. Cambridge, Mass: MIT Press.

Fletcher, Joseph (1972) Indicators of humanhood: A tentative profile of man. *The Hastings Center Report* 2(5): 1–4.

Frankena, W. K. (1973) *Ethics*. Englewood Cliffs, N.J.: Prentice-Hall.

Heidegger, Martin (1962) *Being and time*. New York: Harper & Row.

Hofstadter, Douglas R. (1980). *Gödel, Escher, Bach: An eternal golden braid*. New York: Vintage Books.

Jonas, Hans (1977). Philosophical reflections on experimenting with human subjects. In S. J. Reiser, A. J. Dyck, & W. J. Curran (Eds.) *Ethics in medicine: Historical perspectives and contemporary concerns*. Cambridge, Mass: MIT Press.

Kant, Immanuel (1964) *Groundwork of the metaphysic of morals*. New York: Harper & Row.

McCorduck, Pamela (1979). *Machines who think*. San Francisco: W. H. Freeman.

Mandelbaum, Maurice (1969) *The phenomenology of moral experience*. Baltimore, Md.: Johns Hopkins Press.

Marx, Karl, & Engels, F. (1971) *On religion*. New York: Schocken.

Mead, G. H. (1972) *Mind, self, and society.* Chicago: University of Chicago Press.

Niebuhr, H. R. (1963) *The responsible self.* New York: Harper & Row.

Noonan, John T. (1970) An almost absolute value in history. In J. T. Noonan (Ed.) *The mortality of abortion.* Cambridge: Harvard University Press.

Paton, H. J. (1965). *The categorical imperative.* New York: Harper & Row.

Penfield, Wilder (1983) The uncommitted cortex: The child's changing brain. *The Atlantic Monthly* 22(7): 77–81.

Ramsey, Paul (1975) *The ethics of fetal research.* New Haven, Conn: Yale University Press.

Roe vs. Wade, decision on abortion. (1977) In S. J. Reiser, A. J. Dyck, & W. J. Curran (Eds.) *Ethics in medicine: Historical perspectives and contemporary concerns.* Cambridge, Mass: MIT Press.

Rosenthal, Elisabeth (1983) A rebel in the computer revolution. *Science Digest* (August): 94–97.

Ross, W. D. (1965) *The right and the good.* Oxford: Clarendon.

Sartre, Jean-Paul (1957) *Existentialism and human emotions.* New York: Wisdom Library.

Schlein, J. M. (1961) A client-centered approach to schizophrenia. In A. Burton (Ed.) *Psychotherapy of the psychoses.* New York: Basic Books.

Shelley, Mary W. (1974). *Frankenstein.* New York: Scholastic Book Services.

Singer, Peter (1980). *Practical ethics.* New York: Cambridge University Press.

Tooley, Michael (1974) Abortion and infanticide. In Cohen, Nagel, & Scanlon (Eds.) *The rights and wrongs of abortion.* Princeton, N.J.: Princeton University Press.

United Nations (1979) The universal declaration of human rights, 1948. In T. Donaldson & P. Werhane (Eds.) *Ethical issues in business.* Englewood Cliffs, N.J.: Prentice-Hall.

Urmson, J. O. (1958) *Saints and heroes.* Seattle: University of Washington Press.

Weizenbaum, Joseph (1976) *Computer power and human reason.* San Francisco: W. H. Freeman.

Weiner, Norbert (1964) *God and golem, inc.* Cambridge, Mass: MIT Press.

The Search for An "Electronic Brain"
An Introduction to Neural Networks

Tyler Folsom—CPSR/Seattle

Reprinted by permission of Computer Professionals for Social Responsibility.

T he first computers were called "electric brains" and from the start there was a widespread popular conception that computers could think, or that scientists would make that happen very soon. The reality has of course been far different. A human programmer must specify in nit-picking detail exactly how a task is to be done. If the programmer forgets anything or makes a mistake, the computer will do something "stupid," or perhaps unforeseen.

"Artificial Intelligence" (AI) has been a popular buzzword for decades but it remains ill-defined. AI has produced some useful expert systems, good chess-playing programs, and some limited speech and character recognition systems. These remain in the domain of carefully crafted algorithmic programs that perform a specific task. A self-programming computer does not exist. The Turing test of machine intelligence is that a machine is intelligent if in conversing with it one is unable to tell whether one is talking to a human or a machine. By this criterion, artificial intelligence does not seem any closer to realization than it was thirty years ago. The Department of Defense poured a great deal of money into the Strategic Computing Program to develop specific military applications of AI. The Pentagon has been disappointed in the results and is now looking at other approaches.

If we are to build an electronic brain, it makes sense to study how a biological brain works and then try to imitate nature. This idea has not been ignored by scientists, but, unfortunately, real brains, even those of "primitive" animals, are enormously complex. The human brain contains over ten billion neurons, each capable of storing more than a single bit of data. Mainframe computers are approaching the point at which they could have a comparable memory capacity. While computer instruction times are measured in nanoseconds, mammalian information processing is done in milliseconds. However, this speed advantage for the computer is superseded by the massively parallel structure of the nervous system; each neuron processes information and has a bewildering maze of interconnections to other neurons. Multiprocessor computers are now being built, but making effective use of hundreds of processors is a task that is still on the edge of computer theory. No one knows how to handle a billion processors simultaneously.

It may well be that the best approach to achieving true machine intelligence is to start over and throw out traditional machine architectures and programming. Artificial neural

295

systems represent one such approach. These take their inspiration from biological nervous systems. Since the brain's wiring and organization are mostly unknown, the modelling is inexact by necessity. These systems are characterized by massively parallel simple processors, which are referred to as neurons. Each neuron has many inputs and one output, the latter of which is activated when the sum of the inputs passes some threshold. The connections between neurons have different strengths. This connection scheme and its weights determine how the system processes information. The weights can be either positive (excitatory) or negative (inhibitory). The collection of neurons and their weighted interconnections form a network. Certain neuron input signals are considered to come from the outside world. This pattern is designated as the network input. Similarly, some neuron outputs are considered as the output pattern of the network. The network can be viewed as an associator of stimulus and response patterns. Implementation can be electronic, optical, biological, or via computer simulation. Simulation is by far the most common at present. When a connectionist system is executed as a program on a digital computer, the speed advantage of massive parallelism is lost and the computation is likely to be less efficient than other methods. Thus specialized hardware will be needed to achieve optimum performance. In an electronic implementation, the processing elements are op amps which are connected by resistors. The values of the resistors affect the weights. Since there are no negative resistors, the op amps need to supply both positive and negative outputs to allow both excitation and inhibition.

Information is distributed throughout the network. Data is represented by the pattern of activation of the network. The on/off state of a single neuron has no obvious interpretation. It is only by looking at the overall pattern of activation that the machine state can be understood and it is usually difficult to figure out how the computation is made.

It is usually useful to organize neural networks into layers. A typical example is a pattern recognition system. Assume that we want to recognize binary vectors of N bits each. These vectors fall into M disjoint classes. We construct a network that has N connections to the outside world to handle the input vectors. Our network will have M outputs, one for each class. When we apply an input vector, only the output vector for the right class will turn on. Such a pattern recognizer might be built by assigning N op amps to the input layer. Each of these has only one input, but the output is connected through appropriate resistors to each of the op amps of the next layer. This layer is called "hidden" since none of its inputs or outputs can be observed externally. The outputs from the hidden layer travel via various resistors to the inputs to the final, or "output" layer. The state of the outputs from this last layer are presented to the outside world as the class to which the pattern belongs.

There are many ways in which networks can be organized. The above example used feed-forward layers. Other topologies permit neurons to be self-excitatory or feed back to a lower level. Most artificial nervous systems investigated to date use homogeneous processing elements, but in natural systems there are many different kinds of nerve cells. It is important to match the network architecture to the specific problem.

Coming up with the weights to make a network perform its desired task is difficult. The usual approach is to initialize the weights to some random values and then apply a learning algorithm to modify the weights. During training, the network is given a set of inputs and desired outputs. As each input is applied, the resulting outputs are compared to the desired ones. If an output neuron has an incorrect value, each of the contributing weights is modified slightly. After many iterations through the training set, the weights will be configured so that proper responses are obtained. At least this is what usually happens. Sometimes the network does not converge.

The neural network approach can have some unexpected side effects, properties whose achievement in traditional computers is difficult. One is the ability to generalize. A network can solve a problem that it has not previously encountered based on similarities with what it does know. For instance, consider the behavior of our pattern classifier when it is presented with an unknown pattern. It will activate the category for the most similar pattern. Its idea of similarity may or may not coincide with a human's. If the new pattern is ambiguous, it may make a guess by giving weak outputs for two possible categories. Neural networks tend to fail gracefully; if a wrong answer is produced it is generally a plausible response based on the training received. Like the brain, a network can continue to function despite the failure of part of the system. This is a consequence of distributed data storage; if some cells fail, the remaining ones still retain enough of the pattern to function.

Crick and Mitchison [83] have speculated that neural networks may need to sleep, dream and forget in order to function properly. Dreams can be interpreted as patterns activated by random noise instead of by the appropriate inputs. It has been suggested that during sleep, connection weights may be modified to decrease the probability of spurious states. Neural modelling permits fascinating interplays between engineers and biologists. A biological structure may inspire a computer simulation of a simplified neural network. The model in turn may predict behavior which the neurologist has not observed and which may be verified or disproved by further experimentation.

Conspicuously absent from neural networks is any logical processing unit or von Neumann-style sequential program. These systems seem able to respond to the *gestalt* of what they see without needing to make laborious series of inferences. Learning is one of the most far-reaching promises of neural networks. There is no longer a programmer in charge of the machine, but a teacher. Would it be possible to build a machine that can learn from experience the way a child does? The consequences of generalizing from a lesson may be unpredictable, with the machine reaching conclusions that were unforeseen.

A BRIEF HISTORY OF NEURAL NETWORKS

Interest in neural networks has seen explosive growth in the last five years. The field does have a longer history. The first paper to lay out the theoretical foundation of neural computing was written by McCulloch and Pitts in 1943 [McCulloch, 43]. This made the assumption that biological neurons are binary devices and proposed a logical calculus by which the nervous system works. Von Neumann cited this work in the 1945 paper that first proposed a stored program computer. In a later work [von Neumann, 58] he calculated human memory capacity to be on the order of 10^{20} bits and pointed out that the limited resolution of nerve cells restricts the types of calculations that the brain can do; multilayered arithmetic would be severely degraded by roundoff errors but logical calculations would not face this difficulty. Connectionist learning theory can be traced to Donald Hebb's statement of a physiological learning rule for synaptic modification [Hebb, 49]. Connection strengths will increase between two nerve cells as a result of persistent excitation. In 1958 Rosenblatt, a psychologist, introduced the perceptron, which was the first precisely specified computationally oriented neural network [Rosenblatt, 58]. He felt that the brain is not a logic processing machine but a learning associator that functions by matching responses to stimuli. The perceptron caused a major stir and received widespread analysis. In 1969, Minsky and Papert published the book *Perceptrons,* which demonstrated that these neural networks were incapable of learning to perform a function as simple as an exclusive OR. Disillusionment set in and research funds for neural networks dried up.

Not everyone abandoned the field. In Finland, Teuvo Kohonen extended the ideas of the perceptron to associative memories using linear analog signals instead of binary. Stephen Grossberg has also been active in the field for nearly 20 years and has published extensively. His articles tend to be difficult reading since they are seldom self-contained and use a high degree of mathematical sophistication. In the early 1980s Rumelhart, McClelland, Hinton and other colleagues at UCSD began the parallel distributed processing (PDP) discussion group to investigate the relationship between connectionist models, perception, language processing and motor control. Their book is probably the most comprehensive treatment of neural networks. An accompanying workbook includes floppy disks with MS-DOS C programs for simulating several types of PDP systems. Use of non-linear processing elements grouped into multiple layers has overcome the exclusive OR problem.

In 1982, John Hopfield published a paper that brought neural networks back into vogue [Hopfield, 82]. This collected previous work with a coherent mathematical theory and pointed the way to building asynchronous parallel processing integrated circuits. In subsequent papers Hopfield indicated how neural networks could come up with a good, if not optimal solution to the combinatorially intractable travelling salesman problem. He also showed how his network theory could be used to build circuits such as a digital to analog converter from artificial neurons. By 1987 AT&T Bell Laboratories announced neural network chips based on the Hopfield model. Today the neural net researcher can choose from a wide selection of conferences, books, articles, software packages, and specialized journals.

APPLICATIONS

Bernard Widrow and Marcian Hoff's 1960 paper "Adaptive Switching Circuits" improved the learning speed and accuracy of the perceptron. This was applied to the ADALINE (originally ADAptive LInear NEuron, but changed to ADAptive LINear Element as perceptrons lost favor). It was a threshold logic device with inputs and outputs set to states of +1 or −1. Learning of the weights continued even after correct classification had been achieved. Widrow's adaptive noise reduction systems have been widely applied throughout the telecommunications industry. Each telephone line has a different transfer characteristic, but these circuits can adjust the input signal to maximize the signal to noise ratio for whatever state the line is in. Since Widrow has been in the field longer than almost anyone and has enjoyed commercial success, it is not surprising that he was chosen to write the recent neural network study for the Defense Advanced Research Projects Agency (DARPA).

Terry Sejnowski has demonstrated a system that learns to pronounce English text [Sejnowski, 87]. The network is presented with a string of seven letters and asked to select the correct phoneme for the central letter. The resulting speech had good intelligibility and mistakes tended to be similar to those made by children. The more words the network learns, the better it is at generalizing and correctly pronouncing new words. Performance degrades very slowly as the network is damaged; no single element is essential. The network had 203 input units, 80 hidden elements, and 26 output units. There were 18,629 weights assigned in the learning process.

In Japan, Kuniko Fukushima of NHK Laboratories has developed the "neurocognitron" over the past 20 years. It is capable of recognizing handwritten characters after being trained with the letters of an alphabet. It responds correctly even to letters that are shifted in position or distorted. NHK claims to have solved the problem of perception and says that it could build an artificial brain if it had a good model of short-term and long-term memory [*EE Times,* April 6, 87].

Nabil Farhat has built a content addressable associative memory based on Hopfield's model. Farhat has used optics instead of electronics to achieve parallelism and massive interconnectability. When this memory is combined with a high resolution radar it produces images that can resolve to 50 cm on a full sized aircraft. It can match airplane types to a library of categorizers which are stored on photographic film. Correct classification can be done using as little as 10% of the radar's full data set. Farhat's research team predicts the ability to identify aircraft at ranges of a few hundred kilometers. A 5 by 5 bit optical neural network has been built; classification results were obtained by simulating a 32 by 32 bit associative memory. The radar has been tested on model airplanes in a laboratory [*Electronics,* June 16, 86] [Farhat, 85].

PROBLEMS WITH NEURAL NETWORKS

"The probability of building a neural network, pointing it at the world and having it learn something useful is about as close to zero as anything I can think of on this earth," said Dr. Leon Cooper [*EE Times,* Nov 30, 87]. Dr. Cooper won the 1972 Nobel prize for work in superconductivity and is co-chairman of Nestor, a company selling neural network systems for character recognition, financial analysis, and other tasks. He is concerned that inflated expectations could kill off neural networks. "The second thing that could defeat us is not being able to put together working systems that actually do something in the real world. . . . What we must strive for now are practical systems that do useful things, and cards-on-the-table explanations of what they do."

One problem with neural networks is the difficulty of verifying and reproducing published results. Since much neural modeling consists of *ad hoc* computer algorithms, it is hard to recreate published systems. Two different computer implementations of the same algorithm may produce different results. Even when the same software is used, there are dozens of parameters which represent assumptions that most authors omit mentioning. This situation makes it easy for overly optimistic claims to go unchallenged.

Several learning algorithms have been suggested for neural networks, but none is entirely acceptable. One would want to learn the same way that the brain does, but no one knows the brain's learning algorithm. The most widely used learning algorithm is "back propagation" and it is not biologically plausible. It usually converges to a good solution but is slow.

This is due to the fact that non-trivial networks must be non-linear and multilayered. The input states and desired outputs are known and it is relatively easy to vary the weightings to achieve a desired state. The problem is that the states of the interior layers are not known and must be discovered as part of learning [Hinton, 87].

The ability to learn new responses to new situations is often presented as an advantage for neural networks. The long learning times required detract from this claim. Furthermore, using the back propagation method requires that relearning include all the original training data; if only new data are used, old knowledge would gradually be erased. Grossberg's Adaptive Resonance Theory (ART) overcomes this by using an attention-focusing mechanism. In ART, novel situations arouse attention and these can be learned without wiping out old patterns. However ART cannot learn as many representations as back propagation.

A more serious problem is scaling. Most of the systems demonstrated to date are relatively small, containing dozens or hundreds of neurons. To do applications such as speech or image understanding would likely require an additional four orders of magnitude. Unfortunately, as the number of nodes in a network increases, the learning time required increases nonlinearly. The exact relationship of network size to learning time is not known but it appears to be proportional to the square or cube and may even be exponential.

This leads to the application of complexity theory to learning in neural networks. Les Valiant developed a formal theory of what it means to learn from examples [Valiant 84]. By his definition, a problem is solvable by learning only if there is a polynomial time algorithm that learns acceptably well from a polynomial number of examples. By polynomial, we mean that as the size of the problem increases, the learning time or number of examples needed can increase linearly, by the square, or by the cube, etc., but not exponentially. It turns out that there is a large class of practical problems that are not learnable. These difficult problems are called "NP complete" and include scheduling, graph coloring, and satisfiability of Boolean formulas. There is a theorem stating that if an algorithm can be found to solve any NP complete problem, then any other NP complete problem could by solved quickly using that algorithm. Since programmers have been unable to find effective solutions despite sustained efforts, it appears that practical solutions to any NP complete problem are impossible. Pitt and Valiant [88] have shown that a threshold weight assignment problem similar to learning in neural networks is not learnable (unless it turns out that NP complete problems are solvable). This means that there is no polynomial bound to the learning time required to assign weights. Thus learning by example belongs to a class of hard problems. There is no theory describing what kinds of problems are easily learnable or which network architecture is appropriate for a given problem.

Connectionists are not likely to let theory stand in their way. After all, the brain does learn. We need a better understanding of what is involved in human learning. Learning in mammals is highly constrained by genetics. It may be that genetic code includes built-in assumptions about the world that have not yet been incorporated into artificial neural systems. Modular organization may be a fruitful approach. The number of weights needed would drop drastically if the system consisted of several kinds of building blocks linked together. Each module type would have a fixed pattern of internal weights.

A final difficulty is the lack of parallel computing hardware for neural networks. The usual strategy is to dedicate a hardware element to each node of the network. Electronic designs for neural networks usually consist of arrays of operational amplifiers interconnected by resistors. Adaptive neural systems learn and store information by varying the weights of the interconnections. Variable weight resistors are difficult to implement in integrated circuits but fixed weight resistances can be made in silicon. Scientists at Bell Laboratories have built such a chip containing 256 neurons [Graf, 86]. However, due to the complexity of debugging a large analog chip, this project has never been completed.

If one attempts a direct implementation of neural models in silicon, with each neuron dedicated to an individual processor, interconnection space becomes a major problem. In fact, the routing and interconnect space eats up most of the silicon area and makes it impossible to fabricate a system of 10,000 processors and 5,000,000 interconnections with a network update time of better than 100 microseconds unless the connectivity is extremely localized [Bailey and Hammerstrom, 1988]. Researchers at the Oregon Graduate Center are working on a hybrid analog-digital multiplexed wafer scale neurocomputer. They claim to be able to complete a machine of the above size and speed within five years and manufacture it for less than $2,000.

DARPA AND NEURAL NETWORKS

The Defense Advanced Research Projects Agency recently proposed an eight-year, $390 million neural network research program. The project would attempt to use a massively parallel architecture inspired by the neurophysiology of the human brain to solve military problems that have not yielded to traditional artificial intelligence approaches. DARPA sees connectionist systems as the only alternative to the disappointing results achieved to date from the Strategic Computing Program.

DARPA deputy director of the Tactical Technology Office Jasper Lupo has said, "I believe that the technology we are about to embark on is more important than the atomic bomb. . . . The future of machine intelligence is not AI" [*EE Times,* Aug 8, 88].

DARPA identified seven defense applications that may use neural networks:

- Strategic relocatable target detection from satellite optical and infrared sensors
- Detection of quiet submarines using a sonar array processor
- Electronic intelligence target identification from radar pulse trains
- Battlefield radar surveillance with synthetic aperture radar
- Battlefield infrared surveillance with passive infrared sensors on low-altitude aircraft
- Detection of "stealth" aircraft using infrared search and track systems
- Multisensor fusion with all sensors integrated by satellite

DARPA's neural network effort is based on a study by Bernard Widrow of Stanford and Al Gschwendtner of Lincoln Laboratory that runs over 600 pages. The report envisions giving sophisticated brains to weapons. These should be able to interpret radar signals and recognize friend or foe and be able to identify their own targets. In five years it is hoped the technology will be available for a computer that has the adaptability and information processing capability of a bee. "Bees are pretty smart compared to smart weapons," DARPA deputy director Dr. Craig Fields has said. "Bees can evade. Bees can choose routes and choose targets" [*New York Times,* Aug. 18, 1988]. While the report has recommended robotics as the most promising neural network application, DARPA is more interested in the military tasks listed above. Present U.S. government funding of neural network research is at the level of approximately $5 million annually. The original DARPA proposal is for spending $40 million in 1989, peaking at $100 million in 1991.

Japan's Ministry of International Trade and Industry (MITI) is spending only $183,000 on neural network development for 1989. MITI is presently devoting resources to its Fifth Generation Computer System which seeks to make traditional AI techniques operate in parallel. This project has met with mixed success and its goals have been scaled back. When it ends in 1991, it expects to have a 1,000 processor inference engine doing 1 billion logical inferences per second. Yuji Tanahashi of MITI has promised that there will be a sixth generation neural network program "in full swing three years after the end of the fifth generation program." Thus the Japanese are looking at a 1990–2000 time frame for heavy neural network research, which is similar to the DARPA schedule [*EE Times,* Dec 12, 88].

West Germany has already committed $67 million for a ten-year program in neural network technology. The government of the Netherlands has proposed a $2.5 million seed program. Another seed program of $6.4 million called Applications of Neural Networks for Industry in Europe (ANNIE) has been announced by the European Strategic Programme for Information Technology.

For CPSR, the DARPA effort brings to mind previous ill-considered Pentagon forays into computer science research. The Strategic Computing Program poured large sums of money into artificial intelligence while moving DARPA funded research away from generic research toward specific military applications. The Strategic Defense Initiative is a high tech gravy train with little prospect of feasibility due to extremely demanding software requirements and the impossibility of adequately testing the system. Will DARPA's program overwhelm American neural network researchers with so much money that useful applications are relegated to the Japanese while we chase military pipe dreams? Will much of the research become classified and drop out of the scientific mainstream? Is this another boondoggle that will waste large amounts of taxpayer money in the rush to deploy an immature technology? Will inflated expectations for neural networks destroy the credibility of the field when these are not achieved?

"There's a great deal of concern that they not do what they did with AI, which was widely regarded as a disaster," said James Anderson, professor of cognitive and linguistic sciences at Brown University. He was referring to the Pentagon's artificial intelligence program, in which more money was allocated than could be used. "They dumped a huge amount of money, almost without warning. So much money was involved that people couldn't cope with it" [*New York Times,* Aug 18, 88].

An initial reading of the neural network proposal indicates that the Department of Defense may have learned something from recent mistakes. The new program has a two-year, $33 million evaluation phase. If this is viewed as successful, it will be followed by an eight-year development project. The research content appears to be much more widely applicable than the Strategic Computing Program. As originally proposed, DARPA funding would concentrate on three areas: hardware designed to run large neural networks; theoretical foundations; and applications. In more recent announcements, application projects have been replaced with an evaluation of the performance of neural networks compared to competing technologies [*EE Times,* Sept 19, 88].

The present thrust of DARPA's neural network program is to pick applications presently served by AI, signal processing or other conventional technologies and simulate these as neural network implementations. Particular attention will be paid to the ability of small connectionist systems to scale up into larger ones, combined with study on the amount of learning needed to achieve desired performance. Projects will be graded on robustness, size of data representations, stability, and convergence time. The initial application areas are speech recognition, sonar recognition, and automatic target recognition. Reportedly, all work will be unclassified.

Other U.S. government neural network programs may be more problematic than DARPA's. The Federal Aviation Administration has awarded contracts to study the use of neural networks in air traffic control. A current Department of Energy solicitation states, "Proposals are invited on innovative applications of neural networks for decision-making, real-time automation, and control beneficial to operation of nuclear power plants." It is not at all clear that the reliability and predictability of neural networks can be guaranteed to the levels of sophistication needed for such critical applications. There is no general way to predict the operation of a large neural network when it is presented with unusual inputs. It may be possible to build in predictability by following strict mathematical rules in constructing the network, but this topic needs more research.

SUMMARY

Because of massive parallelism, the human brain has more computational power than the fastest computers by orders of magnitude. Supercomputers have reached the point where the speed of light and the distance that electricity must travel prevent unlimited speed improvements. Thus it appears that major breakthroughs in computing power will have to use parallelism. Neural networks offer a class of massively parallel architectures that promise excellent performance on pattern analysis problems. These systems can learn from examples, generalize easily and are inherently fault tolerant. Drawbacks include slow learning times which become even worse with increased size and the lack of hardware exploiting parallelism. Neural network technology is immature and faces many years of development before it can achieve the intelligence of primitive animals.

REFERENCES

Many of the papers cited are reproduced in *Neurocomputing: Foundations of Research,* edited by James A. Anderson and Edward Rosenfeld, MIT Press, Cambridge, MA, 1988.

An excellent treatment of neural networks is the two-volume set (available in paperback):

J. L. McClelland, and D. E. Rumelhart, *Parallel Distributed Processing,* MIT Press, Cambridge, 1986. A third volume, *Explorations in Parallel Distributed Processing,* comes with floppy disks containing neural network programs in C for MS-DOS computers.

Anonymous, "Optoelectronics Builds Viable Neural-Net Memory," *Electronics,* pp. 41–44, June 16, 1986.

Bailey, J,, and D. Hammerstrom, "Why VLSI Implementations of Associative VLCNs Require Connection Multiplexing," presented at the International Conference on Neural Networks, 1988.

Crick, F., and G. Mitchison, "The Function of Dream Sleep," *Nature,* 304, pp. 111–114, 1983.

Farhat, Nabil. H., Demetri Psaltis, Aluizio Prata, and Eung Paek, "Optical Implementation of the Hopfield Model," *Applied Optics,* pp. 1469–1475, May 15, 1985.

Graf, H. P., et al., "VLSI Implementation of a Neural Network Memory with Several Hundreds of Neurons," AIP Conference Proceedings 151, *Neural Networks for Computing,* Snowbird, Utah, AIP, pp. 182–187, 1986.

Hebb, Donald O., *The Organization of Behavior,* Wiley, New York, 1949.

Hinton, G. E., "Connectionist Learning Procedures," Carnegie-Mellon University Technical Report CMU-CS-87–115, 1987.

Hopfield, John J., "Neural Networks and Physical Systems with Emergent Collective Computational Abilities," *Proceedings of the National Academy of Sciences* 79: 2554–2558, 1982.

Johnson, R. Colin, "Neural Networks in Japan: Part 2," *Electronic Engineering Times,* pp. 49, 72, 73, April 6, 1987.

Johnson, R. Colin, "IEEE Puts Neural Nets Into Focus," *Electronic Engineering Times,* pp. 45–46, Nov 30, 1987.

Johnson, R. Colin, "Neural Nets are Next Project in Line," *Electronic Engineering Times,* Dec 12, 1988, p. 72.

Johnson, R. Colin, "DARPA Details Neural Program," *Electronic Engineering Times,* Sept 19, 1988, pp. 69, 72.

McCulloch, Warren S. and Water Pitts, "A Logical Calculus of the Ideas Immanent in Nervous Activity," *Bulletin of Mathematical Biophysics* 5: 115–133, 1943.

Minsky, Marvin and Seymour Papert, *Perceptrons,* Cambridge, MIT Press, 1969.

Rosenblatt, F., "The Perceptron: A Probablistic Model for Information and Storage in the Brain," *Psychological Review,* 65: 386–408, 1958.

Sejnowski, Terrance J, and Charles R. Rosenberg, "Parallel Networks that Learn to Pronounce English Text," *Complex Systems,* pp. 145–168, 1987.

Valiant, L. G. "A Theory of the Learnable," *Communications of the ACM,* November 1984.

von Neumann, John, *The Computer and the Brain,* New Haven, Yale University Press, 1958.

Widrow, Bernard and Marcian E. Hoff, "Adaptive Switching Circuits," 1960 IRE WESCON Convention Record, New York, IRE, pp. 96–104, 1960.

E882 BCA
J169 ROM